TRUE
TRACKS

TERRI JANKE is an Indigenous lawyer of Meriam and Wuthathi heritage. In 2000 she set up a law firm, Terri Janke and Company, focusing on Indigenous Cultural and Intellectual Property (ICIP) law and commercial law. She has acted for Indigenous and non-Indigenous clients, artists, community-controlled organisations, government and corporates.

'With the global information landscape shifting almost daily, Janke is here to help us all navigate not only the law, but the social norms, protocols and preferred language codes of the ever-expanding frontiers of Indigenous knowledge. Whether you're a black CEO making an encrypted ledger for an art co-op, or a white soccer mum making a multicultural Halloween costume, this book might spare you a lot of heartache down the track. The kind of book that stays on the dinner table for months, getting tea and curry stains across its pages during a lot of heated yarns.' *Tyson Yunkaporta*

'*True Tracks* provides an authoritative guide that simplifies complex laws and cultural protocols, providing examples for those working in many sectors to enact key principles for Indigenous engagement, including respect and self-determination. If you are principled in your daily life, then the principles outlined here will not be a challenge to you, rather, they will serve to enrich your work by and with Indigenous peoples.' *Anita Heiss*

'Terri Janke's book is the answer to the grand cultural theft perpetrated on Aboriginal and Torres Strait Islander peoples over more than two centuries. Terri is an expert in intellectual property laws and as she rightly points out they 'do not protect oral-based cultures, but in fact allow the taking of them'. Throughout, Janke provides the answers to this dilemma for all Indigenous cultural producers in Australia, coherently and acutely addressed in a series of historical cases. Protocols, ethics and institutional responses are the key. While the denial of their intellectual and cultural property rights remains legally sanctioned, there is much that can be done to protect them. It begins with respect.' *Marcia Langton*

'Dr Terri Janke's *True Tracks* is a fantastic resource for understanding and engaging with Indigenous art, culture and traditional knowledge.' *Turia Pitt*

TRUE TRACKS

TERRI JANKE

Respecting Indigenous
knowledge and culture

UNSW PRESS

A UNSW Press book

Published by
NewSouth Publishing
University of New South Wales Press Ltd
University of New South Wales
Sydney NSW 2052
AUSTRALIA
newsouthpublishing.com

© Terri Janke 2021
First published 2021

10 9 8 7 6 5 4 3 2 1

This book is copyright. Apart from any fair dealing for the purpose of private study, research, criticism or review, as permitted under the Copyright Act, no part of this book may be reproduced by any process without written permission. Inquiries should be addressed to the publisher.

 A catalogue record for this book is available from the National Library of Australia

ISBN   9781742236810 (paperback)
        9781742245270 (ebook)
        9781742249834 (epDF)

Cover design Debra Billson
Cover artwork Terri – Butterfly Flowers Dreaming, 2020, by Bibi Barba.
    © Bibi Barba/Copyright Agency, 2021

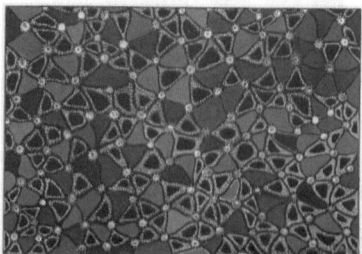

Internal design Josephine Pajor-Markus

All reasonable efforts were taken to obtain permission to use copyright material reproduced in this book, but in some cases copyright could not be traced. The author welcomes information in this regard.

CONTENTS

Cultural information	xi
1 Introduction	**1**
Finding a path through the law	2
Understanding and protecting Indigenous cultures	7
Indigenous Cultural and Intellectual Property (ICIP)	8
The *Our Culture: Our Future* report	10
Setting up Terri Janke and Company	12
Developing True Tracks	13
True Tracks: A best practice framework for ethical Indigenous engagement	15
Unpacking the True Tracks principles	16
Making protocols the norm	27
Notes	29
2 Who owns Indigenous languages?	**30**
The impact of publishing language without Indigenous consent	31
Our languages, our future	33
Awakening Indigenous languages in Australia	34
Protocols and ethical guidelines	37
Protocols in action	40
Caring for our language collections	45
The curse of copyright for Indigenous languages	48
Using language in a resource or project	50
The challenge of speaking up	53
Resources	55
Notes	55
3 Drawing a line in the sand: Stopping Indigenous arts appropriation	**58**
Art centres and the burgeoning of art	59
Advocates for art	61

Stamping out fake arts	63
Buying ethical Indigenous art	70
Copyright in artworks	73
Aboriginal art cases	74
Exploitation of Australian Indigenous art	83
Protocols and licensing in the visual arts	85
Labelling and certification	87
A vision for a National Indigenous Cultural Authority	88
Resources	90
Notes	90

4 Restructuring Indigenous architecture and industrial design — 93

The Australian Indigenous Art Commission at the Musée du quai Branly	93
Barangaroo's *Shell Wall*	96
Indigenous-led architecture and design	98
Protocols in architecture and design	100
Patents, inventions and Indigenous knowledge	101
Traditional designs	104
Indigenous traditional design case studies	105
Aboriginal and Torres Strait Islander flags	107
Indigenous designs beyond country	109
Resources	110
Notes	111

5 Fine-tuning: Indigenous music, copyright and protocols — 114

Old music, respect for ritual	116
Growing national presence: Contemporary songs	121
Protocols for better engagement	124
Resources	134
Notes	134

6 Cross-cultural lens: Shifting the focus in Australian film and television — 136

Protocols in the film and television industries	139
Legacy films: Films made before protocols	152

	Celebrating David Gulpilil	156
	Resources	157
	Notes	158
7	**How the story got its black voice back: Amplifying Indigenous voices in writing**	**161**
	The rise of Indigenous writing	162
	Indigenous authorship and identity	164
	Don't turn sacred culture into fantasy!	165
	Copyright favours the person with the pen	167
	International appropriations of story	169
	Non-Indigenous writers and protocols	170
	Indigenous writers and protocols	175
	Respecting Indigenous stories	180
	Resources	183
	Notes	183
8	**Dancing country and acting up**	**185**
	Dance companies: Connecting with culture	185
	Performance, dance and the law	189
	Drama and theatre	195
	Performing for Indigenous excellence	200
	Resources	201
	Notes	202
9	**The rainforest is our supermarket: Bush foods and traditional medicine**	**203**
	Biopiracy: What is it and how can we prevent it?	205
	The problem of patents	207
	The trouble with trade marks	212
	Reforms to the IP system in Australia	213
	Bush foods and products	214
	Indigenous leadership in the bush foods industry	224
	Resources	226
	Notes	227

10 Cultural cognisance: Bringing ancient knowledge and science together — **230**

- Integrating Indigenous and Western science: Legal considerations — 233
- Caring for country: Applying Indigenous knowledge in environmental management — 236
- Holistic healing: Indigenous medical doctors in Australia — 243
- Gazing at the sky: Indigenous astronomy — 244
- Indigenous science in the classroom — 246
- A vision for a First Nations Science Centre — 247
- Indigenous science meets Western science head on — 248
- Resources — 249
- Notes — 250

11 Rethinking Indigenous research — **253**

- A difficult history — 254
- The problems encountered during Indigenous research — 255
- University policies — 261
- Research partnerships: Positive potential — 262
- Indigenous-led research — 264
- Indigenous genomics — 267
- Indigenous data sovereignty — 270
- The research approach: Working together — 271
- Resources — 274
- Notes — 274

12 Enabling Indigenous voices in education — **277**

- Indigenous trailblazers in education — 280
- ICIP protocols in education — 284
- Bringing culture and people into the classroom — 288
- Resources — 290
- Notes — 290

13 Indigenous excellence in digital and technology — **291**

- Artificial intelligence: Who owns the rights? — 296
- Indigenous data sovereignty — 297

Indigenising new technologies	300
Indigenous digital futures	302
Resources	304
Notes	304

14 Creating harmony in galleries, libraries, archives and museums (GLAM) — 306

Who owns Indigenous collections?	309
Protocols in GLAM institutions	312
Repatriation: Returning cultural materials to country and community	315
Ancestral remains	317
Truth-telling: Indigenous-led exhibitions	319
The Ten-Year Indigenous Roadmap	323
The way ahead	326
Resources	327
Notes	327

15 Reimagining Indigenous tourism — 330

Supporting Indigenous-led tourism	332
Respecting cultural sites and traditional knowledge	333
Using Indigenous knowledge in tourism	339
Knowing country: The future direction of Indigenous tourism	342
Resources	345
Notes	345

16 Taking care of business – the ICIP way — 347

What all businesses can do	349
Indigenous businesses and ICIP	356
Indigenous language words in business names	358
Big business and Indigenous cultural heritage	361
Business is an opportunity	363
Resources	366
Notes	366

17 Appreciate, don't appropriate: It's fashionable to be culturally respectful   **368**

   The rise of Indigenous fashion designers   369

   Inspiration or stealing? Cultural appropriation in the fashion industry   371

   Intellectual property and Indigenous fashion design   373

   Ethical collaborations in fashion   377

   Reviving clothing traditions: Possum skin cloaks   379

   Flags and fashion   379

   Setting a trend of respect   381

   Resources   382

   Notes   383

List of acronyms   **385**

Glossary   **386**

   Notes   389

Acknowledgments   **391**

Index   **395**

CULTURAL INFORMATION

I acknowledge the traditional owners of the lands and seas of Australia and thank them for the knowledge and cultural expressions. I acknowledge elders, past and present. I acknowledge the youth coming through who will keep our cultures strong.

In this book, I have referred to Indigenous Cultural and Intellectual Property (ICIP), and we have spoken to the people and groups about this representation. Any further use of this information by readers should only be done with consent.

I am grateful to my ancestors, Meriam and Wuthathi.

I also acknowledge the Bidjigal and Gadigal people, on whose lands I live and work, and where most of this book was written.

Language
The terms 'Indigenous', 'Indigenous Australians' and 'Aboriginal and Torres Strait Islander' are used throughout this book to refer to the First Nations peoples of Australia.

Cultural notice on the use of spelling of Indigenous community names
This book contains Aboriginal and Torres Strait Islander language words. I acknowledge that there are alternative spellings of names of Indigenous groups. Respectfully, I have used the spelling preferred by the people who I refer to in the book to enable them to describe themselves. Where the names are generally used, I have taken the most commonly used spelling, and in some cases noted a common alternative.

Warning

This book contains references to deceased Aboriginal and Torres Strait Islander people.

Some of the case studies describe content that is culturally sensitive and offensive. These are included to illustrate the behaviour that this book seeks to change. We have consulted with Aboriginal and Torres Strait Islander groups, who have given their consent for the inclusion of this material. However, Indigenous people should exercise care when reading the case studies.

Traditional Custodian notices

This book contains references to Indigenous Cultural and Intellectual Property. All rights to ICIP remain with the relevant Indigenous owners of the knowledge and cultural expression, and should you wish to use or publish any ICIP, you will need their permission.

Legal notice

The laws and policies cited in this book are current as at April 2021.

This book is not intended to be legal advice. If you require legal advice for a specific matter, seek professional legal advice from a qualified legal practitioner.

© True Tracks® ICIP Principles

The True Tracks model is protected by copyright and trade mark. If you wish to use this model, please contact Terri Janke and Company.

1
INTRODUCTION

In the early 2000s, I was invited to present a workshop in Cairns, Queensland, to speak about protecting Indigenous art and knowledge. I was returning to the town I was born, the place I had left as a child of eight. Growing up there, I had felt invisible – a young black kid with few prospects. Now here I was, returning as a lawyer. In the audience were artists, lawyers, gallery owners and people from the local community. I had just started up my law firm in Sydney and was still finding my feet. I didn't have many clients at the time, and I was unsure if I was on the right track. There were ways law could help protect Indigenous knowledge, but there were still so many gaps.

After the workshop, the local newspaper and TV station interviewed me about protecting Indigenous culture. The next day, I got up early to catch a flight to the Torres Strait. To my surprise, when I opened my hotel door and looked down at the floor, I was on the front cover of the paper, branded a 'cultural crusader'. I was shocked. *What are people going to think?* I wondered. *'She's a big noter. She thinks she's smart.'*

I was pleased I was leaving so I could escape. I headed to the airport. Sitting back in my seat on the plane, just as I was about to sigh with relief, the flight attendant handed out newspapers to everyone on board. The Torres Strait Islander woman sitting next to me turned her head towards me, smiling. She swung the newspaper in the air between us. 'Hey! That's you, isn't it?'

I saw my picture on the front cover. My stomach dropped.

'You're the deadly cultural crusader. Well done, girl, setting up your law firm. You can stop this theft of our knowledge.'

'No, Aunty, I'm just starting out,' I told her. 'I haven't solved all the problems. There's still a lot to do.' My voice was bumpy. I was uneasy with that label. Secretly, I felt like an impostor.

She gave me a big smile. 'Don't worry about that. You be strong. You've just got to stay on track and, if you listen with your heart, they will be true tracks. People will follow.'

Her words let my skin breathe. I didn't have to do it alone. I just had to lay the tracks and people would follow.

Finding a path through the law

My desire to seek social justice for Indigenous peoples arises from my own cultural heritage. I have heritage that is both Aboriginal and Torres Strait Islander. My father's mother, Agnes, was born in 1921 on Mer (Murray Island), in the Peibre clan. She was the daughter of Azzie Leyah, a Meriam woman, and Victor Blanco; Victor's mother Annie – my great-great-grandmother – was from Old Mapoon in Cape York and married Juan Blanco from the Philippines. My maternal grandmother, Modesta (Maudie) Mayor, was born on Thursday Island, and her Torres Strait Islander heritage can be traced back to Gebar Island. Maudie married Kitchell Anno, of Wuthathi and Malay descent, who was also born on Thursday Island. They moved to Cairns in the 1940s, where both my parents were born. I, too, was born in Cairns. I pay my respects to my ancestors.

My interest in culture started early, as I became conscious of my Aboriginality and the attempted eradication of it by the dominant culture. It was not taught in schools, or spoken about in social circles when I was growing up. The history of dispossession that we were taught ignored the details. I was made to feel ashamed of my culture; it was not valued. But from the 1960s, First Nations people were growing in strength. The 1967 referendum, the Tent Embassy, land rights, human rights, self-determination and rights to education enabled Indigenous people to assert and raise their voices. So I became passionate about social justice.

I was inspired to study law by my sister Toni, who was a strong role model in my life. I didn't do as well in those early years, and struggled to find my pathway in the law. I first became inspired to focus on Indigenous arts and intellectual property issues when I went to work at the Australia Council for the Arts for its Aboriginal Arts Board. I'd dropped out of law school temporarily. While I had done well in my first year, receiving great marks as a new and eager student, in my second year I'd had too much fun, working as a waitress, going out to nightclubs and missing classes. I managed to pass, but by my third year I was working almost every night at an Italian restaurant in Woollahra and hardly making it to university at all.

There were other factors besides my lifestyle that had led me to drop out. I had not yet found my path in the law. Most Indigenous graduates were expected to work in criminal, land or human rights law. But when I went to the courts I found them too oppressive for Aboriginal people. Criminal laws were punitive. Australia's first laws had been about controlling and limiting people, not empowering them, and the legal system was a revolving door. I'd also had an experience during a summer clerkship where the judge had mistaken me for the defendant in the courtroom because I was black. That had really crushed me, and I lost interest in my studies.

But at the Australia Council I learned about copyright law. Indigenous artists were starting to have international exhibitions, and I saw that these laws and this knowledge could be very important to Indigenous people. The law could be a positive tool for Indigenous people, I realised, not a punitive one. That realisation came just after the Mabo case, and that really opened my eyes too. When the Mabo decision overturned *terra nullius* in Australia – the idea that the land belonged to no one – it put in my head the possibilities of the law for advancing people's rights.

THE MABO DECISION: A TURNING POINT

The Mabo case of 1992 confirmed that *terra nullius* – the idea of Australia being 'nobody's land' – was a legal fiction.[1] In confirming the continuing connections of the Meriam people to their land on Mer (Murray Island) in the Torres Strait, it also recognised that

Indigenous Australians held certain rights to land that existed before invasion – rights that can continue to exist. These rights include the right to live and camp in an area, hunt and fish, and visit places of cultural importance.

It's important to note that the Mabo decision did not *create* native title. It recognised that native title as a right had existed before, during and after European colonisation. It just had never been acknowledged. Native title rights continued where Indigenous people were able to show that the land and seas continued to be traditionally owned, in accordance with law and customs.

The Keating Government's agenda for rights recognition included the *Native Title Act 1993* (Cth), the establishment of an Indigenous land fund (now the Indigenous Land and Sea Corporation) to assist Aboriginal and Torres Strait Islander people to acquire and manage land, and a third component – the Social Justice Package, designed to redress the longstanding disadvantage suffered by Indigenous Australians as a result of dispossession of land and dispersal of Indigenous people. The Social Justice Package would address health, economic and social disadvantage. It would also include Indigenous Cultural and Intellectual Property (ICIP) rights – that is, Aboriginal and Torres Strait Islander peoples' rights to their heritage, including the land and seas and everything connected to them, such as knowledge, stories, song and dance. The Social Justice Package remains unfinished business.

A key issue yet to be clarified in the Native Title Act is whether native title rights include rights to cultural knowledge. The foundation principles of the Mabo case could allow for the protection of Indigenous knowledge, and cultural and intellectual property rights. However, the courts have steered away from recognising Indigenous cultural knowledge as a right within native title. In 2002, in the Miriuwung Gajerrong case (*Western Australia v Ward*),[2] the High Court majority did not acknowledge that the right to protect and prevent the misuse of cultural knowledge was part of native title rights. The majority of the High Court justices noted that such a right

Introduction

would extend beyond the rights to deny or control access to land held under native title.³

Indigenous knowledge and cultural material such as art, songs, recorded oral histories and films of ceremonies are used in native title claims as evidence. The claimants have the burden of proving a continuous connection to establish the existence of native title. To do this, they must show how they have rights and interests in relation to land or waters under traditional laws that are acknowledged by them, and according to customs they observe, and that by those laws and customs they have a connection with the land and waters claimed. The stories, songs, art, dances and cultural knowledge form the proof of the connection to land and seas for native title. The Federal Court rules have developed to allow Aboriginal people to give evidence by way of singing, dancing and storytelling. An example is the *Ngurrara Canvas II* created in 1997 by around 50 artists for the Walmajarri, Wangkajunga, Mangala and Juwaliny groups to illustrate their customary law and connections to their lands in the Kimberley region.

But having to give evidence of the deeper spiritual connection to country can also be a problem if it is sacred or secret information. Aboriginal cultural knowledge is orally given by Indigenous people, recorded and entered into evidence to demonstrate a continuing connection, then ultimately stored. There are cultural law considerations for Indigenous people when giving evidence of their sacred stories, as once they are on the court record there are risks of disclosure and use beyond the court. Indigenous people need to disclose their stories as evidence to get native title rights, but they may lose control of the captured notes, affidavits, recordings and evidence. Copyright may arise in respect of connection reports and other evidence in accordance with copyright law, but not under Indigenous law. In a paper I wrote with Eamon Ritchie, we advocated for lawyers, practitioners and organisations to follow or develop ICIP frameworks, including protocols, to recognise the continuation of cultures to the next generations.⁴

Eddie Mabo's fight for justice blazed a new trail for Indigenous people. Great people have a way of inspiring us beyond our own perceived limitations. The case gave me hope, and a belief that the Australian legal system could shift to accommodate Indigenous rights and needs. It was as much about culture and knowledge as it was about land. It wrote Indigenous stories into the legal textbooks. It overturned the lie of *terra nullius*. It was saying, 'You don't have to be invisible anymore.'

There were links emerging within me, too: links between culture, country, knowledge and destiny; links between the past and the future. These were growing stronger in my mind. I began to see a place for myself in keeping and strengthening these connections for ancestors. It was no longer just about me. I also began to understand that the only person who could turn things in my life from negatives into positives was me.

So, when the Mabo case was beamed around the world in the news, I saw how the law could be used by Indigenous people. The case called me back to law school. Returning to university, I had a newfound focus and drive that came from a deeper place. I made sure that the subjects I chose supported my vision. I looked back on the so-called bad incidents in my life and turned them into fuel for my motivation, and that really helped get me through law school. I then received the Law Council of Australia's first John Koowarta Reconciliation Law Scholarship during my final year of study.

When I completed my studies in the mid-1990s, I began working at the National Indigenous Arts Advocacy Association (NIAAA) while a groundbreaking Aboriginal art copyright case was unfolding. The 'carpets case', which I'll talk about later in the book, concerned a group of eight Aboriginal Australian artists whose artworks had been reproduced on carpets without their permission. They took copyright action against the company that made the carpets and were successful.[5]

I assisted the legal advisers who were working on the case, and was inspired by barrister Colin Golvan, now a Queen's Counsel, to consider the application of copyright law to protect Aboriginal and Torres Strait Islander cultures. The case broke new ground because it showed how the law can be flexible, to a certain extent, to protect Indigenous cultural expressions. Colin was able to apply his knowledge of copyright to Aboriginal art and influence the courts, which set precedent in the carpets case and in the *Bulun Bulun v R & T Textiles* case that followed in 1998. Colin encouraged me to focus on IP and Aboriginal art, and has continued to support me throughout my career.

Understanding and protecting Indigenous cultures

For non-Indigenous people, the word 'culture' has a narrow meaning that pertains to the arts of the social elite, such as the opera or theatre. Culture for Indigenous people has a much wider meaning. For Indigenous people, culture equals life. Culture means Indigenous ways of seeing and being connected to the world, to the plants, animals and all things on the land, in the sky and in the sea. It is about people, their relationships to each other, and the way they interact with their world – to sustain themselves through food, to find shelter, to enlighten themselves. Culture is the story of survival and interconnection since time immemorial.

For generations, cultural practices and knowledge have been passed down by each generation to the next. The elder ones taught the younger ones. They spent time in ceremony. They drew and painted information. They sang, danced and told stories about the past, about the future, and about how to live and survive in the world. All of this still happens today.

But in 1788, the colonisation of Australia was like a tidal wave crashing into Indigenous peoples' ways of life. The taking over of Indigenous land for settlement, agriculture and extraction took people away from their land. The forced removal of Indigenous people to missions and reserves branded Indigenous people as outcasts. Their languages and cultural practices were banned. The assimilation policies and the removal of children disrupted the transmission of Indigenous cultures.

Today, Indigenous people are asserting their rights to their cultural inheritances, and are reclaiming their cultures. They have continued to practise culture, and the fact that they have had their land stolen makes it even more of a treasure – a gift, a legacy, a heritage that is precious and passed on to the next generations.

Indigenous cultures in Australia are diverse. There is no single 'Indigenous culture' that exists in Australia but many different cultures, each with different cultural practices, knowledges and identities. The many different clans or language groups each have their own culture, languages, stories and experiences. Indigenous people may have heritage from one part of the country and live in another. People identify as Indigenous – not partly, but wholly – even if they have other heritage. Using the terms 'part-Indigenous' or 'half-Indigenous' is offensive because it demeans that cultural connection and inheritance.

The Australian Institute of Aboriginal and Torres Strait Islander Studies (AIATSIS) has produced a colourful map that attempts to represent the languages and nations of Aboriginal and Torres Strait Islander Australia.[6] The many different territories are marked in green, blue, pink, orange and yellow and do not adhere to the usual Australian state and territory borders. Some areas are bigger than others: those of the desert nations cover great stretches of arid country, and smaller nation areas are found in the north-east, where there are rainforests, wide rivers and rain. When I look at that map, I think of 65,000 years of continuous cultures being nurtured as people cared for country. The 200+ years since colonisation are but a flash in time, yet they have had considerable impact on culture and country. Indigenous landscapes continue to be destroyed. Indigenous cultures are exploited in offensive and harmful ways for economic gain that is not shared with the custodians. This not only distorts and debases culture but ignores Indigenous ownership over culture and the right to control its use.

Indigenous Cultural and Intellectual Property (ICIP)

Indigenous cultures are like Indigenous lands – they are not free to be taken. In Australia, Indigenous peoples have been calling for stronger ways to protect their cultural heritage under the law. They seek their place as the rightful owners of their cultural assets – to negotiate use, to be recognised as the cultural source, to receive payment where benefits accrue, to protect culture from harm and destruction, and to ensure that culture remains intact so it can be handed on to future generations.

Today, Indigenous culture and knowledge are sought after in so many different sectors, all around the world – in the arts, science, research, education, tourism, environmental management and many more areas. The protection of Indigenous Cultural and Intellectual Property (ICIP) rights is a critical issue of our time.

WHAT IS ICIP?

ICIP refers to Indigenous peoples' rights to their cultural heritage. This cultural heritage includes:

- artistic works
- literature
- performance
- languages
- knowledge
- cultural property (including objects held in museums)
- human remains
- immovable cultural property such as sites and places
- documentation of Indigenous people and culture.

ICIP rights are the rights to control who can use and adapt this ICIP; the right of attribution; the right of integrity; and the right to benefit sharing.

Collectively owned, this cultural heritage connects Indigenous people to each other, and to the lands and seas they have interacted with for more than 65,000 years. Culture grows, changes and adapts as people and their relationships to the world change, so it is a living and changing body of material that is continuously nurtured.

The term 'Indigenous Cultural and Intellectual Property' originates from the 1992 United Nations Draft Declaration on the Rights of Indigenous Peoples. That draft referred to both the tangible and intangible heritage passed on through the generations that enables indigenous peoples to express their culture. A UN Human Rights Commission study in 1994 by Erica-Irene Daes, the founding chair of the UN's Working Group on Indigenous Populations, also used the term 'Indigenous Cultural and Intellectual Property'. This study influenced the terms I used in the research project that culminated in the report *Our Culture: Our Future* (see below). I was also influenced by Indigenous lawyers who used this language, particularly James (Sa'ke'j) Youngblood Henderson, a member of the Chickasaw Nation, who visited Australia in the 1990s.

The *Our Culture: Our Future* report

Not long after finishing law school, I joined Michael Frankel and Company, a boutique law firm that focused on the arts and film industries, as a solicitor. The firm won a tender to prepare a report on Australian ICIP rights, which was commissioned by the Aboriginal and Torres Strait Islander Commission (ATSIC) and AIATSIS. Michael rang to tell me we had won the tender a week after I had given birth to my daughter, Tamina. Writing *Our Culture: Our Future – Report on Australian Indigenous Cultural and Intellectual Property Rights* (1998) took three years, and I had another child, Jaiki, by the time it was launched.[7]

I was thrilled to have the opportunity to work on this report so early in my career. It was my first big project, and some of the best lessons of my professional life came during this time – especially the lessons about how Indigenous people viewed protocols, and what they needed to manifest a strong and healthy culture.

Russ Taylor, then principal of AIATSIS, led the project, with Dr Mary Edmunds; the steering committee was made up of ATSIC representatives. Russ Taylor was inspiring to me, as an Indigenous man who ran AIATSIS and who had the ability to steer through the complexities. He understood bureaucracy and management but was also encouraging and guiding. The team at Michael Frankel was very supportive, and I was also informed by a national Indigenous reference group, which was chaired by Ian Delaney, then a commissioner with ATSIC.

I travelled around Australia talking about ICIP. I wrote a discussion paper and managed the creation of a website to gather feedback and encourage discussion nationally. There were more than 80 submissions to the report. I wrote it while pregnant with Jaiki; he was four weeks old when the report was finally launched in 1999. I still remember that launch, at the Museum of Contemporary Art in Sydney: the view of the Harbour Bridge and the Sydney Opera House, and the shining water; my mother, who was there to mind Jaiki; Gatjil Djerrkura, now deceased, then chair of ATSIC; and Mick Dodson, who was at the time the Aboriginal and Torres Strait Islander Social Justice Commissioner. I remember the steady beat of clapsticks, the didgeridoo and a performance by Aboriginal and Torres Strait Islander dancers. The report was launched to a packed room that included Indigenous community members, members of the government, industry leaders and media. I was overwhelmed by the turnout but also very relieved that the long process of putting together the report was over. I also felt anxious about how the report might be received, afraid that Indigenous people might think it did not reflect their rights adequately, and nervous that government and industry would not respond favourably. I knew there was a still a lot of ground to cover, but the report was a chance to get the topic out there.

Our Culture: Our Future was the first time a report had set out the issues with ICIP in Australia, and their effects on Indigenous Australians – what they felt was being exploited, how it made them feel, and what rights they needed to prevent appropriation and allow them to control the dynamic of their own cultures. A substantial part in the middle of the report analysed the law – copyright, intellectual property and heritage laws, and the newer native title laws. The most ambitious part of the report was the final section, which called for changes to laws, practices and policies, and the establishment of a National Indigenous Cultural Authority. *Our Culture: Our Future* put together a comprehensive strategy in both legal and non-legal areas. It outlined things that government, industry, artists, writers and individuals could do for Indigenous empowerment.

But the biggest recommendation of the report was a standalone law to provide protection for all ICIP. This was not seen as a priority by government. ATSIC established implementation plans, but when it was forced to close its doors in 2003, the recommendations lost any coordinated approach.

Setting up Terri Janke and Company

In 2000, I decided to set up my own legal firm, Terri Janke and Company, because I saw the need to provide Indigenous people with specialised legal advice to protect and share their culture. I wanted to help people make informed decisions and make the most of opportunities, whether in business or in their creative practices. I wanted to empower them to create new things and to grow their cultural and economic prosperity. The firm specialises in intellectual property and commercial law, with a focus on ICIP. (I talk a little more about setting up the firm in chapter 16.)

We focused on the things that we could do, like raising awareness of rights, negotiating agreements, developing protocols and using notices. It was all about asserting rights as best as we could within the existing legal framework. We worked on a range of matters, including acting for artists such as Rene Kulitja (chapter 3) and Jonathan Jones (chapter 4) in negotiating uses of their artworks. We have developed many protocols for the arts, for film and for the sale of art. We worked on the Bibi Barba art case (see chapter 3). We have helped publishing companies with contracts, and negotiated agreements and licensing arrangements for use of ICIP in recording projects. We aim to be strategic and innovative in our approach to ICIP.

In 2007, the United Nations Declaration on the Rights of Indigenous Peoples (UNDRIP) was officially adopted by almost all of the countries that make up the UN General Assembly. Australia was one of the four countries that initially voted against it, a position that changed in 2009 after a change of government. The UNDRIP recognises ICIP or cultural heritage rights, particularly in Article 31. Here, ICIP is referred to as 'cultural heritage, traditional knowledge and traditional cultural expressions':

> Indigenous peoples have the right to maintain, control, protect and develop their **cultural heritage, traditional knowledge and traditional cultural expressions**, as well as the manifestations of their sciences, technologies and cultures, including human and genetic resources, seeds, medicines, knowledge of the properties of fauna and flora, oral traditions, literatures, designs, sports and traditional games and visual and performing arts. They also have the right to maintain, control, protect and develop their intellectual property over such cultural heritage, traditional knowledge, and traditional cultural expressions.[8]

The passing of the UNDRIP was a great occasion for the many indigenous peoples who had contributed to it over the years. The Draft Declaration of 1994 had informed so much of the *Our Culture: Our Future* report I worked on, and to see it finally become a signed-off declaration was a big achievement. However, declarations occupy a low rung on the ladder of international law. Their impact is to influence policy and decision making. The UNDRIP does not transfer into domestic law in the same way that an international convention like the Berne Convention for the Protection of Literary and Artistic Works in 1886 brought us to the Copyright Act. Canada, however, has been considering a law based on UNDRIP; Australia has not. As we discuss treaties and constitutional changes, ICIP rights may be raised as an important part of any rights framework.

Developing True Tracks

While working in my firm, I was still very interested in writing and thinking more about the theoretical concepts and underpinnings of the Western legal system, and how Indigenous Cultural and Intellectual Property rights slip between its cracks. Indigenous people have called for new laws at least since the *Copyright Act 1968* (Cth) came into force. So, I embarked on a PhD on the topic, which took about eight years to finish. It allowed me to think deeply about the many attempts in the past 50 years to create legal frameworks to protect Indigenous knowledge, and the models developed for self-determination. (By 'self-determination', I mean solutions that are in the control of Indigenous people.)

By that time I had developed a model for advising clients on ICIP protocols and called it the 'True Tracks' framework. I chose the name because, after that meeting with Aunty on the plane from Cairns, I understood that it was impossible to work and fix every rip-off or issue. It would be better, I realised, if I could set a track or a pathway that people could follow. In this way it was proactive, not reactive. Taking action in courts after knowledge or culture has been stolen is a much harder thing to do. In the absence of Western law to protect ICIP, this principles-based framework could be used voluntarily for ethical practice, and would be effective for making agreements. All that was needed was the goodwill and understanding of the party engaging and using the Indigenous knowledge or cultural expression. In recent years, we have been able to use the framework for a range of clients including artists, universities, museums, galleries, IT companies, construction companies, archives, research organisations and education institutions. It is adaptable to different kinds of projects and collaborations. Education and awareness is key; we still hold workshops to teach people about the concepts.

Using the self-determination lens as I worked on my PhD thesis, I was able to review the True Tracks framework, and I hypothesised that these principles could be used to inform new law. This, however, requires the will of governments – and this has been a problem for the past 50 years, along with the perceived complexity of the issues. But the True Tracks principles are perhaps most useful in supporting successful collaborations. They address the deeper relationship that exists between Indigenous and non-Indigenous people and the value they place on each other's knowledge and value systems.

Introduction

True Tracks: A best practice framework for ethical Indigenous engagement

True Tracks involves ten principles. Although they may appear sequential and separate, they are deeply interconnected. Their power lies in how they work in combination. Ultimately, True Tracks is about creating meaningful relationships and connections. It is about enabling Indigenous peoples to actively practise, manage and strengthen their cultural lives, keeping tracks into the future to empower the next generation.

THE TEN TRUE TRACKS PRINCIPLES

1 Respect
Indigenous peoples have the right to protect, maintain, own, control and benefit from their cultural heritage.

2 Self-determination
Indigenous peoples have the right to self-determination and should be empowered in decision-making processes within projects that affect their cultural heritage.

3 Consent and Consultation
Free, prior and informed consent for use of ICIP should be sought from Indigenous people. This involves ongoing consultation and informing custodians about the implications of consent.

4 Interpretation
Indigenous peoples have the right to be the primary interpreters of their cultural heritage.

5 Integrity
Maintaining the integrity of cultural heritage information and knowledge is important to Indigenous people.

6 Secrecy and Privacy
Indigenous people have the right to keep secret their sacred and ritual knowledge in accordance with their customary laws. Privacy and confidentiality concerning aspects of Indigenous peoples' personal and cultural affairs should be respected.

7 Attribution
It is respectful to acknowledge Indigenous people as custodians of Indigenous cultural knowledge by giving them attribution.

8 Benefit Sharing
Indigenous people have the right to share in the benefits from the use of their culture, especially if it is being commercially applied. The economic benefits from use of their cultural heritage should also flow back to the source communities.

9 Maintaining Indigenous Cultures
In maintaining Indigenous cultures, it is important to consider how a proposed use might affect future use by others who are entitled to inherit the cultural heritage. Indigenous cultural practices such as dealing with deceased people and sensitive information should be recognised as important and be respected.

10 Recognition and Protection
Australian policy and law should be used to recognise and protect ICIP rights. Copyright law, for example, as well as new laws and policies should be used to protect these rights. These issues can be covered in contracts, protocols and policies for better recognition.

....

Unpacking the True Tracks principles

I'm going to take you through some of the key issues explored in this book, all of which are underpinned by the ten principles in the True

Introduction

Tracks framework. These principles do overlap and intertwine. They are designed to help you think through the issues that might arise for projects that include ICIP.

1 Respect

Respect is about recognising Aboriginal and Torres Strait Islander people as the first peoples of Australia, and recognising that their cultures, laws and traditions are based on a strong connection to the lands and seas of this great country. The land and the seas are our mother, and form a strong foundation for identity. This is why, in an acknowledgment of country, people say, 'I'd like to pay my respects to the traditional owners of country.' The people from the country that you are on must be respected. This ancient tradition acknowledges that the country you walk through belongs to clans who have lived on and nurtured this land for thousands of years. It shows how Indigenous people respect others, and it demonstrates their connection to place and to people.

After the Mabo case, acknowledgement of country and welcome to country became established practices at conferences and events where Indigenous people gathered. Now these practices occur at gatherings all over Australia – at the football, at the opening of Parliament, in boardrooms and even in my yoga classes. There are signs in banks and shops, and in New South Wales, as we drive on the highways, there are NRMA billboards that remind us when we are moving into Dharawal, Wonnarua and Wiradjuri country. As I attend Zoom events and meetings, people acknowledge the country they are beaming in from, and all the countries of the people they are connecting with.

Showing respect for Indigenous people and their cultures picks up two key messages. First, in the past, Indigenous peoples' rights to the land were blatantly disregarded through invasion. We, as people, became invisible, while our names, languages and cultural practices slept in the land, in the archives and in ourselves. Indigenous peoples' knowledge and connection to country were considered primitive folklore. We were studied and probed and collected, all under the banner of ethnography.

Our cultural objects and artworks were hung in galleries, labelled 'artist unknown' or 'unknown author', and our ancestors' bodies were collected for science – the sacred on display. Sound and film recordings of us, and field notes and books about us, fill the walls and shelves of libraries and galleries throughout the world. Someone else was always the expert on us, and someone else made the decisions. Lies were told about colonisation. Now is the time for truth telling and reconnection so that all Australians can know our history, and we can build a strong future. Respect is the necessary shift.

Second, showing respect enables culture to continue by giving the cultural custodians the space to have power over their cultures, over the laws and protocols that Indigenous people have had throughout the generations, to ensure that the cultural dynamic continues. This is where the healing can begin. Each community is rebuilding their cultural governance, so that the things we hold special stay in our families or clans. It's like that old family brooch a white person might hold as a family heirloom that gets passed down through the generations – multiplied by 100 000. Indigenous people want to be able to continue to practise knowledge and cultural practices that have been passed on through the generations. You see this in the weaving and fibre arts of Arnhem Land in the Northern Territory,[9] or in the sacred Wandjina spirit figures of the Worrorra, Ngarinyin and Wunambal Gaambera people from the Kimberley region in Western Australia.

2 *Self-determination*

The power to exercise choice is the basic meaning of self-determination. This right is recognised for all people in many international human rights doctrines that refer to economic, social and cultural development.[10] However, put simply, self-determination for Indigenous people flows on from the first principle of respect – respect for the first peoples and their connection to the land. The lives of Aboriginal and Torres Strait Islander peoples during the 200+ years of European contact have been managed by the laws and policies of the colonial powers. What Indigenous people want is the power to have a say in how their cultural future is determined.

Think about all those things Indigenous people need to express and pass on for their cultural identity: languages, art and stories connected to country; the management practices in caring for land, sea and the things on and in them; land and sea rights; native title; caring for heritage in sites; the bodies of our ancestors; belonging; and powerful culture, living languages, good health, no poverty, positive youth, revered elders, strong identity and connected communities. Is this what a strong Indigenous cultural future might look like?

There are benefits in empowering Indigenous people to be in decision-making roles in caring for country, and in the use of their traditional knowledge and cultural expressions. It will take a shift from the paternalistic practices of the last two centuries. It will also require people to stand back and enable Indigenous voices to tell their own stories; to make way for Indigenous peoples to be key creatives, curators and project designers; and to let them write the stories and be celebrated in the textbooks and reports. 'Nothing about us without us' was the catchcry from the consultations I did for the Australian Museums and Galleries Association Indigenous Roadmap in 2017–19. This means that Indigenous people should be the primary curators and interpreters of their cultural objects and associated knowledge. So often in the past, this has been a different story, and Indigenous objects have been viewed as relics. Projects and programs involving Indigenous peoples and their cultures should only be done with their consent, leadership and engagement. Their voices should be the ones telling the stories. The old ethnographic gaze was challenged by the people I spoke to, and this critical change is happening now in the galleries, libraries, archives and museums (GLAM) sector.

Self-determination is about thinking about the long term, and the opportunities that can be created for Indigenous people to exercise choice. When non-Indigenous people want to use ICIP, one of the questions they should ask is: How can I enable the Indigenous people whose heritage this is? For instance, instead of recording and owning Indigenous stories, you can shift the focus onto how you can enable Indigenous voices in your projects. Terms like 'Indigenous co-design', 'Indigenous-led' and 'Indigenous-controlled' are often used for these projects.

Megan Davis, professor of law at the University of New South Wales and a member of the United Nations' Expert Mechanism on the Rights of Indigenous Peoples, has written extensively on self-determination. The call for changes to the Australian Constitution to recognise Indigenous Australians, and the Uluru Statement from the Heart, make clear the importance of this right.[11]

3 Consent and Consultation

Consent and consultation are inseparable from respect and self-determination. They involve the right of Indigenous peoples to engage in free, prior and informed consent (FPIC), a process in which accurate information is provided to Indigenous people on all the proposed uses of their cultural heritage, and on the future implications of consent.[12] Indigenous people must be informed about projects that affect their cultural heritage well in advance of their commencement and be given enough time to make decisions.

Proper consent and consultation involves open, ongoing communication and creating relationships – well beyond the rubber-stamping that has occurred in the past. Consent and consultation must be meaningful, give relevant information, and give sufficient time for Indigenous people to talk to the group and consider the issues. It cannot be a process of 'Let's tick the box'. There must be scope for negotiation, and a recognition that Indigenous people have the right to say no.

There are other complexities that arise for people here. If I tell companies and government departments to consult and get consent, they say, 'Who with? How do we identify Indigenous people in authority? What if everyone does not agree?' There are complexities, yes, but as Indigenous people are increasingly recognised by non-Indigenous people to hold these positions of respected authority, infrastructure and systems are developing, and protocols are evolving to support FPIC systems.

Consent may also require thinking about what form the consent should take. A person can give their oral consent, but it might not be clear what they are agreeing to, and it certainly might not be known by their family after they pass on. Consent processes are becoming more formal through memorandums of understanding (MoUs) with communities, licence agreements, research agreements and clear communications processes set out in writing.

Consent procedures will differ from group to group. Some communities have formal procedures, like permit processes, while others are less formal: meeting with people in authority and asking who is the right person to approach. Communities are complex, and you will have to talk to factions and groups to ensure the wider discussion is had. Consultation must take time and there should be information given to how the knowledge and cultural expression will be used.

It is important to ask whether you need to talk to other people. People will have different views. What if there is disagreement? You should consider if you can make changes that accommodate the concerns raised. But if the relevant people don't want their knowledge or cultural expression used at all, you should consider whether you should go ahead. If the material is something that has never been published before, or if it is of high cultural significance, you might have to stop. Obviously, the wider the use and the bigger the impact on cultural futures, the greater the consultation you will need to undertake.

A key first step is to ask: Am I the person to tell this, or do this? You might have a cultural connection yourself, but it is a good idea to consider your own reasons. The approach should be: Am I the one to tell this story, or make this product? Am I empowering Indigenous people or is it appropriation? If your motives are clear, then it is about ethics. The AIATSIS Code of Ethics is a good first reference point, as well as the Australia Council's Protocols for using First Nations Cultural and Intellectual Property.[13] You should do your research and involve Indigenous people. It is about building relationships. Aboriginal and Torres Strait Islander people might share culture during tourism or in educational contexts, or during art and community events such as markets and festivals. But their knowledge and stories cannot just be taken. Stories, expressions, dances and arts come from *place*. They are people's insignia. As the Meriam people say, 'Tag Mauki Mauki, Teter Mauki Mauki' – 'Your hand can't take something that does not belong to you unless you have permission. Your feet cannot walk in or through someone else's land unless there is permission.'[14]

Ongoing consent requires you to constantly reconnect with communities about future uses of their ICIP, and to remember that things can change. Many non-Indigenous people want certainty of use; they want to negotiate all rights. It's not uncommon in written agreements for the licensing of knowledge to see licences for the use of materials in perpetuity, in all forms of media now known and those yet to be devised. This seems over-the-top in terms of the legal situation; you might not even need all these rights. It is an example of the Western legal premise of taking everything you can, rather than taking what you need. Instead, the best approach is to seek informed consent for what you know at the time, and speculate about the future, but in the end come back and consult again if things change. It's all about building trusting and long-term relationships.

4 Interpretation

Interpretation refers to how content and material is discussed, referenced, presented and thereby understood. Interpretation is powerful. It shapes perceptions about how people and ideas are understood and valued.

In Australia, almost 200+ years of settler colonialism has led to the interpretation of cultural practices, artefacts and knowledge by non-Indigenous people such as anthropologists, historians, writers and the media. These interpretations (in the form of things like historical manuscripts, books, articles and documentary films) were often created without any input from the Indigenous people whose cultures they concerned, and they then made their way into institutions such as libraries, museums, galleries and archives.

Non-Indigenous interpretations are often Eurocentric: they privilege Western ideas and value systems, reinforcing ideas about the inferiority of Indigenous cultures. In the past, these interpretations determined the way exhibitions about Indigenous art and culture were designed and set out. Cultural objects were presented to audiences as relics of a bygone era, with no connection to the country they come from. If you look further into these outdated interpretations of Indigenous cultural heritage, you will discover that many of them are ethnographic and preservationist. They treat cultural objects as relics rather than treasures connected to living peoples.

Indigenous cultures and knowledges are not static and locked in the past but are dynamic and ever changing, and nurtured through the generations – like cultures anywhere in the world. And as the societies, characteristics and needs of Indigenous groups change, so too does their cultural heritage and the interpretations of it. In this way, Indigenous people have the right to be the primary interpreters. Interpretations may include new media and digital technologies. This does not mean it is no longer a cultural expression; it may simply involve a new transmission method.

It is important that Indigenous cultural heritage is interpreted through Indigenous perspectives and voices, and not just treated as subject matter. This is also about seeing Indigenous people as researchers, scientists, writers, educators and lecturers; having Indigenous faculties in universities being led by Indigenous people; and enabling where possible the perspectives of Indigenous people to be told from an Indigenous standpoint.

Interpretation is deeply connected to cultural integrity – the next principle.

5 *Cultural Integrity*

Maintaining the cultural integrity of ICIP is important to Indigenous peoples so that the cultural significance and meaning of the material remains vital and intact. Indigenous peoples value integrity so that they can maintain their practices and also their diversity.

Cultural integrity is about recognising that ICIP comes from country and place, and from people. In the old days, story and patterns in the sand depicted knowledge or encoded information in detail that was understood by the people with the right to be given the knowledge. It was through reaching a certain level in the group that a person was able to understand, and then have the rights to retell that knowledge. The form and context in which it was shared was paramount, especially in the oral or performance transmission of knowledge.

This is cultural integrity: staying true, keeping culture strong. It means recognising and addressing the fact that cultures are complex systems and that cultural heritage is embedded in, and emerges out of, the ongoing relationship between people and country.

Cultural integrity rights for Indigenous people are about stopping the derogatory and demeaning treatment of their culture by others. It is a bit like the moral right of integrity, recognised in copyright law, that gives artists the right to stop others from altering their works where the alteration is harmful to their reputation. The principle of cultural integrity becomes important when culture is used in a new context, or is being altered and adapted for a new work – including via technological and digital means.

Indigenous art and stories are cultural markers and identifiers. Maintaining cultural integrity keeps the connection with the past, and decisions about changes are made with protocols through respect for tradition. This is why Indigenous people get so offended when people copy and alter things, or use knowledge, without recognising the origin of that knowledge or the process of seeking consent for its use and for changes in its use. A leap into a new context can be startling, and it takes time for people to consider the reinterpretation of cultural material.

6 Secrecy and Privacy

Indigenous peoples have the right to keep secret their sacred and ritual knowledge in accordance with their customary laws. Privacy and confidentiality concerning aspects of Indigenous peoples' personal and cultural affairs, particularly where they seek to maintain the secrecy of certain areas of Indigenous knowledge, should be respected.

Within Indigenous groups, ICIP is structured according to robust laws and restrictions as to who can access, use and transmit it. Secrecy laws in traditional cultural practices uphold and protect the ceremonial nature of much ICIP. The inability of Indigenous people to control the secrecy of their beliefs, practices and ceremonial objects can weaken the society, and undermine its social fabric and systems of authority.

7 Attribution

It is respectful to acknowledge Indigenous peoples as traditional owners and custodians of their ICIP through proper attribution. Relevant Indigenous language groups or communities should be recognised and named when their cultural heritage material is being used in new works or projects.

Attribution means acknowledging Indigenous people as the custodians of Indigenous cultural knowledge. There is a strong history of Indigenous people being the informants for research, evaluations and theses but not being credited for their contribution. Today, Indigenous people are seeking the right to be acknowledged as the owners of this knowledge and information.

Where possible, the source of Indigenous music, songs and traditional knowledge should be noted by stating the name of the performer, if applicable, and the relevant Indigenous group or community. In this way, the music and knowledge can be traced back to the person, family or clan.

Along with copyright notices, Traditional Custodian notices should be included in any published works. These can acknowledge an individual custodian, community and/or language group, as well as any co-owners of the material. The appropriate wording should be decided on in consultation with the people being acknowledged. Here is an example of a Traditional Custodians notice used on the website of Yinarr Maramali, a Gomeroi weaving arts business:

> The weavings, paintings and images in this website embody traditional ritual knowledge of the Gomeroi community. It was

created by and with the consent of the custodians of the community. Dealing with any part of this website for any purpose that has not been authorised by the weavers and custodians is a serious breach of the customary law of the Gomeroi community, and may also breach the Copyright Act 1968.[15]

8 Benefit Sharing

Indigenous peoples have the right to share in the benefits from the use of their culture, especially if it is being commercially applied or used in culture-based businesses. The economic benefits from the use of ICIP should flow back to the source communities and groups. These benefits could be monetary or non-monetary.

Benefit sharing requires users of ICIP to negotiate terms of use and commercial arrangements with the Indigenous peoples concerned, particularly regarding the sharing of fees and the involvement of Indigenous people in the work's creation and promotion.

9 Maintaining Indigenous Cultures

Indigenous cultural heritage is maintained and reproduced across generations and has always adapted and evolved in response to changing circumstances. The maintenance and ongoing transmission of ICIP needs to be in the hands of Indigenous peoples to align with their own self-determined choices. So, it is important to consider how a proposed use of ICIP might affect its future use by others who are entitled to inherit the cultural heritage.

This principle involves all the others too. It also recognises that respect should be given to Indigenous cultural practices dealing with initiation rites, deceased people and sensitive information, and that the importance of these practices should be understood.

Introduction

10 Recognition and Protection

Australian policy and law should be used to recognise and protect ICIP rights. For example, copyright laws, protocols and contracts can be used to help ensure ICIP recognition and protection.

This principle advocates for the strategic use of Australian law, policy and program guidelines to recognise and protect ICIP rights. This includes the reform of existing intellectual property laws but also the adoption of new laws and policies that recognise the unique nature of ICIP rights. Gaps in the law can be covered by using contracts, protocols and other tools, which may also be valuable supplements to any new laws that are adopted.

Making protocols the norm

To help our clients protect ICIP rights in collaborative projects, we use the existing IP laws to their full extent, and we base our contracts and protocols on True Tracks. Protocols encourage ethical conduct and promote interaction based on good faith and mutual respect, especially where the law doesn't offer enough protection.

Protocols have also gained recognition as a major way of protecting Indigenous knowledge in Australia, offering an appropriate way of working with Indigenous cultural material, and interacting with Indigenous people and their communities. They are widely used to reflect Indigenous cultural values and customary laws.

The True Tracks principles have been used to develop protocols for a variety of organisations and projects over the years, including the Australia Council for the Arts, Screen Australia, the City of Sydney and Lendlease. For example, the Australia Council's *Protocols for using First Nations Cultural and Intellectual Property in the Arts* is an organisation-wide set of protocols, first published in 2002, that all grant applicants must adhere to in order to receive funding from the organisation. City of Sydney protocols also implement the True Tracks principles to govern the interactions of their employees and volunteers with Aboriginal and Torres Strait Islander peoples and communities. Lendlease's *Place and Protocols: Indigenous Art, Languages and Cultures* is a set of protocols for everyday use by Lendlease employees. Informed by the True Tracks principles, these protocols are used as a reference for respecting and protecting the rights of Indigenous Australians. Non-government organisations such as Oxfam Australia have also used the framework to set standards, specifically ensuring that they respect cultural beliefs and practices in their work. Collecting institutions such as the National Museum of Australia and Museum of Applied Arts and Sciences (MAAS) have led best practice in protocols so that they become the foundation of all museum policies.

So, how do we design a robust protocol system that is workable and enforceable over time among a diverse range of parties? To be legally enforceable, protocols must be put into legal contracts to cover the issues that the law doesn't embrace. They must be viewed as more than just loose guides and become mandatory practices. When protocols and contracts are used together with intellectual property laws, such as copyright and trade mark law, the protection of Indigenous cultural heritage is enhanced, despite the gaps in these laws.

This book explores stories that impress and inspire, with Indigenous excellence shining through and leading the way in positive collaborations. Many of these collaborations applied ICIP protocols to protect Indigenous knowledge and cultural expressions. But this book also looks at troubling stories of Indigenous culture and knowledge being exploited, stolen and disrespected – the stealing of Indigenous art and designs for cheap rip-off 'Aboriginal-style' products, for example, or the unauthorised use of Indigenous knowledge and resources for research commercial gain.

More work needs to be done so that protocols to protect ICIP become the norm. The more widespread they become, the more empowered Indigenous knowledge holders will be, and the more they will call the shots on how their cultural heritage assets are managed and used. There is still a need for new law and specific laws, and the protocols can set a pathway towards this. There is much that can be gained by the Voice to

Parliament supported by the Uluru Statement, and it is also interesting to see the treaty-making process in Victoria, which can also be useful to advance ICIP rights and to empower Indigenous Australians.

Notes

1. *Mabo v Queensland* (No 2) [1992] HCA 23.
2. *Western Australia v Ward* [2002] HCA 28.
3. *Western Australia v Ward* [2002] HCA 28 at 58–60.
4. Eamon Ritchie and Terri Janke, 'Who owns copyright in native title connection reports?', *Indigenous Law Bulletin*, vol. 8, no. 20, 2015, pp. 8–11.
5. *Milpurrurru and Others v Indofurn Pty Ltd and Others* (1994) 54 FCR 240; 130 ALR 659.
6. David R Horton and AIATSIS, *Map of Indigenous Australia*, AIATSIS, 1996, <https://aiatsis.gov.au/explore/map-indigenous-australia>.
7. Terri Janke, *Our Culture: Our Future – Report on Australian Indigenous Cultural and Intellectual Property Rights*, report commissioned by the Australian Institute of Aboriginal and Torres Strait Islander Studies (AIATSIS) and Aboriginal and Torres Strait Islander Commission (ATSIC), Michael Frankel & Company, 1998, <www.terrijanke.com.au/our-culture-our-future>.
8. United Nations, United Nations Declaration on the Rights of Indigenous Peoples, Resolution 61/295, 13 September 2007, Article 31, <www.un.org/development/desa/indigenouspeoples/declaration-on-the-rights-of-indigenous-peoples.html>.
9. Bawinanga Aboriginal Corporation, *About Weaving*, Maningrida Arts & Culture, 2021, <https://maningrida.com/artworks/weavings/about-weaving/>.
10. Australian Human Rights Commission (AHRC), *Right to Self Determination*, AHRC, 30 April 2013, <https://humanrights.gov.au/our-work/rights-and-freedoms/right-self-determination>.
11. Megan Davis, 'Self-determination and the right to be heard', in Shireen Morris (ed.), *A Rightful Place: A Road Map to Recognition*, Black Inc, Melbourne, 2017, pp. 119–146; The Uluru Statement from the Heart, <https://ulurustatement.org/the-statement>.
12. Food and Agriculture Organization of the United Nations (FAO), *Free Prior and Informed Consent*: An indigenous peoples' right and a good practice for local communities, FAO, 2016, <www.un.org/development/desa/indigenouspeoples/publications/2016/10/>.
13. AIATSIS, *AIATSIS Code of Ethics for Aboriginal and Torres Strait Islander Research*, AIATSIS, 2020, <https://aiatsis.gov.au/research/ethical-research/code-ethics>; Australia Council for the Arts, *Protocols for Using First Nations Cultural and Intellectual Property in the Arts*, Australia Council, 2019, <www.australiacouncil.gov.au/programs-and-resources/Protocols-for-using-First-Nations-Cultural-and-Intellectual-Property-in-the-Arts/>.
14. See Terri Janke, *2011 Mabo Oration: Terri Janke*, 2011, p. 5, <www.qhrc.qld.gov.au/__data/assets/pdf_file/0003/2289/2011-Mabo-Oration.pdf>.
15. Yinarr Maramali, <www.yinarrmaramali.com>.

2

WHO OWNS INDIGENOUS LANGUAGES?

In 2019, I attended the PULiiMA Indigenous Languages & Technology Conference in Darwin. PULiiMA means 'making voice' in the Awabakal language, the traditional language of Newcastle, Lake Macquarie and the Lower Hunter region of New South Wales.[1] Held since 2007, the conference has blossomed into a huge event with talks, workshops and networking for people working on the ground in communities to revitalise and strengthen Indigenous languages. I caught up with Theresa Sainty, a Pakana (Tasmanian Aboriginal) woman who has been part of a team working tirelessly over the last two decades to retrieve and revive Aboriginal language in Lutruwita (Tasmania).

Due to the destructive effects that European colonisation has had on Pakana people and culture, only remnants of the original Tasmanian Aboriginal languages have survived. Materials such as colonial manuscripts, audio recordings, oral stories and family memories reveal evidence of between 8 and 16 languages that together serve as the source of a revived Tasmanian Aboriginal language called palawa kani, which combines both vocabulary and grammatical usages from as many of the original languages as possible. This work is carried out by the palawa kani Language Program of the Tasmanian Aboriginal Centre, a community organisation operating across the state since the early 1970s, with a key focus on important cultural heritage initiatives, such as negotiating the return of Aboriginal land and ancestral remains.

Theresa proudly showed me a copy of the palawa kani dictionary, titled *mina tunapri nina kani* ('I understand what you say'). It includes a large word list, and information about the methods and research that the community has employed to reconnect with the sleeping languages of their ancestors. Theresa's eyes lit up with pride as she explained the linguistic rigour of the process, and the cultural consultations. Flicking through the book, she showed me notes from old diaries of the colonial elite and explained the historical and cultural background to particular words.

Despite the bloody terror of the frontier wars, some Tasmanian Aboriginal people did survive, on islands in Bass Strait north of Tasmania and at Cygnet in the south of the state. Members of families in both areas still remembered some language into the 20th century. Reviving palawa kani is an empowering act of reclaiming and reconnecting with culture. Today, the language is taught to members of the Tasmanian Aboriginal community of all ages by Aboriginal community language workers through resources such as books, games, songs and digital apps.

Theresa closed the dictionary and placed it in my hand. 'This book honours our old people and their languages, strengthening culture for the future generations of Pakana,' she said.

The impact of publishing language without Indigenous consent

Back in 2007, a Wikipedia contributor called Akerbeltz created and published a Wikipedia page on palawa kani that listed the translations of pronouns, verbs, numerals, place names, other words and phrases. In 2012, the Tasmanian Aboriginal Centre (TAC) asked Wikipedia to take down the page on the grounds that it had infringed their copyright and contained incorrect and inauthentic language. The request was rejected by the Wikimedia Foundation, which stated:

> We refused to remove the article because copyright law simply cannot be used to stop people from using an entire language or to prevent general discussion about the language. Such a broad claim would have chilled free speech and negatively impacted research,

education, and public discourse – activities that Wikimedia serves to promote.²

TAC says that the key issue was that cultural materials, only intended for the use of Aboriginal people, were made globally public without the knowledge or consent of the Aboriginal community.³ This conflict highlights the tension between legal conventions such as copyright law and the cultural heritage rights of Indigenous peoples. Wikimedia refused to remove the article because languages cannot be owned under Australian or international copyright law. But this Western view of ownership doesn't reflect the involvement of Indigenous people who have nurtured their languages over the years.

For the Tasmanian Aboriginal community, developing palawa kani has been a means of moving forward after the devastating effects of colonisation. And so they wish to protect the language from manipulation by others.

Article 31 of the United Nations Declaration on the Rights of Indigenous Peoples (UNDRIP) asserts the rights of indigenous peoples around the world to maintain and control their cultural knowledge and expressions.⁴ Indigenous languages are a form of cultural heritage, traditional knowledge and traditional cultural expression. By failing to seek consent from the Tasmanian Aboriginal Centre before publishing palawa kani language online, Wikipedia clearly breached the UNDRIP. Their actions completely disregarded Indigenous peoples' rights to self-determination and compromised the cultural integrity of the language.

The problem is that there is no pathway in the law to prevent Wikipedia's actions: the UNDRIP isn't enforceable as international law but rather functions as a framework for countries to use in their own legal systems. So, unfortunately, the Wikipedia palawa kani webpage has remained online.

Our languages, our future

Indigenous cultures, including languages, are living, dynamic and evolving. Aboriginal and Torres Strait Islander languages are incredibly diverse, with over 250 different language groups and 800 dialectal varieties. The Cape York Peninsula in Far North Queensland, for example, is home to around 149 language varieties belonging to 55 language groups, including Gudang, Wik-Ngathan, Atampaya and Wuthathi.[5] Languages are core to the cultural heritage and identity of Indigenous peoples and are intertwined with cultural practices, cultural expressions and knowledge. They not only transmit information but embody it – carrying knowledge and world views developed over thousands of years in relation to specific environments, social interactions and customary laws.

Given that languages are integral to Indigenous culture, revitalisation is a key pathway for cultural revival. This includes developing languages and the rights to control their cultural practice. Indigenous groups have their own cultural obligations and rules of ownership for maintaining and protecting languages, as they do with all the other aspects of their cultural heritage. For some, language is considered sacred and interrelated with the land, ancestral connections, ceremony, kinship and laws. A language may be collectively owned by a community or be considered to belong to country – to the land and the sea – with the community as the custodian.

How can people wishing to engage with Indigenous languages make sure they respect these rules? Language workers, linguists, museums, libraries, archives, websites like Wikipedia, artists, authors and songwriters should be asking this question if their work involves languages. This chapter looks at an approach involving protocols, ethical guidelines and written agreements that go beyond the limitations of Western laws. This approach can be used to avoid situations like the Wikipedia webpage conflict and to respect Indigenous cultural heritage rights.

Awakening Indigenous languages in Australia

Indigenous languages are under threat in Australia. Invasion, dispossession and the forced removal of Indigenous children from their families (the stolen generations) meant that many Indigenous people were moved away from their cultural groups. Living on missions and reserves, many Aboriginal and Torres Strait Islander people were forbidden from speaking their native tongue and practising their culture.

Many languages are sleeping or in a state of recovery and reawakening, with only around 120 still spoken.[6] Of these, approximately 90 per cent are endangered, with some having only a handful of living speakers.

Melissa Kirby is a Wayilwan Ngiyambaa, Yuwaalaraay and Paakantyi Maraura woman who has done work to restore her languages from the western region of New South Wales. Melissa says, 'We are all obligated and accountable to maintain our language. Being interested, talking a few words in the language and sharing it with the family is the beginning of reclaiming our mother tongue.'[7]

Like the languages of western New South Wales, the Noongar language of the south-west corner of Western Australia is also considered endangered, with around 475 speakers according to the 2016 census.[8] Luckily, this number is on the rise, says Noongar woman Kylie Bracknell (Kaarljilba Kaardn), an accomplished actress, television presenter, voice-over artist, writer, producer and director. Kylie, who is conversant in the language, says, 'My grandmothers taught me our Noongar language. Being with them, sitting with them and listening to them was one of the most important lessons in my life. It sparked my love of the Noongar language, a connection to them and the old ways that is forever in my heart and informs the way I share our language with others.'[9]

Kylie is at the forefront of the Noongar language revitalisation movement, with a vision to use the arts to strengthen language and culture in her community, but also raise broader awareness within Australia and internationally. She worked with her cousin Kyle J Morrison, who she calls a 'modern theatre visionary', to develop a full Shakespeare work in the Noongar language. 'It took us over six years, and many workshops but the result was empowering for the Noongar actors. The ensemble of nine Noongar actors reclaimed their ancestral language through the process of performing *Hecate*, a 90-minute adaptation of Shakespeare's *Macbeth*,' says Kylie.[10] The production was a big success, but Kylie says that the real achievement was supporting more than nine Noongar people to speak the language now and into the future.[11]

In her 2014 TEDx talk, Kylie asked the Australian audience if anyone knew how to say 'hello' in an Indigenous Australian dialect. No one did. Yet, she pointed out, most Australians are quick to recite the greetings of overseas languages such as French, Greek, Italian or Japanese.[12] A confronting thought – and one to reflect on if you live on indigenous land anywhere in the world.

Do you know how to greet someone in any of the 250 language groups of Indigenous Australia? Across languages, there are many ways to address or acknowledge someone, and not all of them translate to 'hello'. The word or phrase may also be a polyseme (having multiple meanings). Kylie Bracknell says 'kaya', a Noongar word for 'hello' and 'yes'. In Awabakal, a language from the mid-north coast of New South Wales, 'kaayi' is a word for getting someone's attention. In palawa kani, the language of Tasmanian Aborigines, hello is 'ya'.[13] Jack Buckskin, a trailblazer for the reclamation and revitalisation of the Kaurna language (Adelaide Plains), says 'niina marni', a Kaurna greeting that means 'are you good'. Magdalen Kelantumama from Bathurst Island says 'awungana', Tiwi for 'hello'.

The First Languages, Law & Governance Guide

There is a vast network of community-led Indigenous language centres across Australia. In 2019, the then Department of Communications and the Arts (now merged into the Department of Infrastructure, Transport, Regional Development and Communications) asked my firm to write a guidebook to help these centres manage the legal and cultural issues they face. The *First Languages, Law & Governance Guide* took many months of work and consulting with people who very generously gave us their time and feedback. I worked on the project with Laura Curtis, a solicitor at Terri Janke and Company who had studied conservation and heritage before becoming a lawyer.

Our goal was to empower language centres to manage the copyright in their recordings and documents. In the past, the issue of copyright ownership had not been discussed. The copyright in important language resources was owned by the researchers and linguists who had worked with mostly elderly Indigenous speakers – those who still had living memory of language when it was more widely spoken. We talked to centres, including the Victorian Aboriginal Corporation for Languages (VACL) in Melbourne; the Far West Languages Centre (FWLC) in Ceduna, South Australia; Wangka Maya Pilbara Aboriginal Language Centre in north-west Western Australia; and Miromaa Aboriginal Language and Technology Centre in Hamilton, New South Wales. Each centre focuses on a language or languages specific to their region. Lynette Ackland is a Gugada and Mirning woman who manages the FWLC. She says, 'We work to revive and restore the Gugada/Kokatha, Mirning and Wirangu languages of the local surrounding areas, concentrating on community engagement and developing fluent speakers.'[14]

As we wrote the guidebook, we also worked with the team at First Languages Australia (FLA), the peak organisation for Aboriginal and Torres Strait Islander languages. We spoke with their manager, Faith Baisden, whose country is Yugambeh in south-east Queensland; Annalee Pope, a Wakka Wakka woman from central Queensland; and Carolyn Barker, Project Manager at FLA. Faith Baisden said, 'First Languages Australia has been advocating for many years for the rights of communities to exercise control over the use of their languages. We are frustrated by the absence of a legal pathway to restrict use of language and so we concentrate our efforts on education around the cultural heritage rights of Australia's first language speakers.'[15] Here, Faith is talking about the lack of legal protections for Indigenous people to control their language dynamic. As Indigenous languages are developed and strengthened, Indigenous people want to have control over them, and they want the respect of others who might use the words so that these people will come back to the language centre or group and discuss the use of language words – and attribute the source. Language centres do so much hard work in bringing the community together, talking to living speakers, developing word lists and turning those lists into dictionaries. Therefore, FLA has focused on educating people.

Working with such an enthusiastic, experienced and knowledgeable team brought a great energy to the *First Languages, Law & Governance Guide* project. They really got us to see how this important work lifts communities and strengthens identity. So many languages are sleeping, devastated by the impact of invasion and the movement of Aboriginal and Torres Strait Islander people away from their communities and families, and the result is that many Indigenous people today do not speak their language. Language revival is needed because so much has been taken.

People all over the world are working to revive and strengthen indigenous languages. The United Nations shone a spotlight on this by declaring 2019 the International Year of Indigenous Languages. They have now designated 2022–32 as the International Decade of Indigenous Languages, calling upon the world to take urgent steps at national and international levels.[16] This is raising awareness of the work that indigenous language-speakers and organisations across the world are doing to revitalise and strengthen their languages. It is also highlighting that the complex knowledges and cultures they foster are strategic resources for good governance, peace building and sustainable development.[17]

Protocols and ethical guidelines

The challenge for anyone working with Indigenous languages or planning to develop Indigenous language resources such as apps, websites, dictionaries, books, broadcasts and databases is to be aware of the cultural and legal issues. This can be achieved by developing a protocol for working with the Indigenous knowledge in the project. Using the ten True Tracks principles, you can establish a pathway based on mutual respect and good faith. These principles have been used and accepted by many Indigenous and non-Indigenous creators when dealing with Indigenous people and their cultures, and offer a framework for best practice.

An example of this is the ethics protocols, language approvals and copyright agreements that the Far West Languages Centre has integrated into their operations as they ethically engage Aboriginal language speakers, collect and document language, and protect it for future generations. The FWLC has a three-step process that acknowledges and promotes the rights of Indigenous peoples, and incorporates the True Tracks principles at its core. This process, and the subsequent protocols, are utilised by the FWLC in every interaction and engagement with Aboriginal language speakers in the area.

The Indigenous company Indigital, founded by its CEO Mikaela Jade, is another example of how the True Tracks principles are accepted when engaging with Indigenous peoples. As part of their (now completed) Digital Custodians Project, a collaboration with Microsoft and the Shared Path Aboriginal and Torres Strait Islander Corporation, Indigital utilised the ten True Tracks principles to create a participation form for Indigenous participants. This form not only covers Indigital's process of ethical and respectful engagement, but also ensures that all participants are credited for their participation and retain their ownership of the cultural property, and that their free, prior and informed consent is given before they participate. (See chapter 13 for more about Mikaela Jade.)

All projects that use Indigenous culture and knowledge, including language, should be driven by respect for Indigenous control of that culture and knowledge. This involves ensuring that Indigenous people are involved in all stages of the project and that the nature of the use of knowledge is properly understood by community. Partnerships may be formed to build trusting relationships. Language resources should only be created if the relevant language group or community provides consent after they have understood everything that is involved. It is best to record consent using written agreements and clearance forms.

Contributors have the right to proper attribution, such as a Traditional Custodians notice (see chapter 1, page 25), and the form of attribution should be decided in consultation with the custodians of that knowledge. Contributors should also benefit from the use of their culture. This could be monetary (e.g. royalty payments, a project fund) and/or non-monetary (e.g. employment, skills development, copies of the published work, facilitating community events). Like attribution, the appropriate kind of benefit sharing should be negotiated with those involved. An example is the process established by Kaurna Warra Pintyanthi (KWP), a body of Kaurna people, teachers, linguists and language enthusiasts who are passionate about the revitalisation of the Kaurna language of the Adelaide Plains.[18] KWP developed a process for individuals and organisations seeking to request to use Kaurna language words and this process has now been adopted by its incorporated sister organisation, Kaurna Warra Karrpanthi (KWK). There is a fee paid for the use, and attribution must be given. This is an example of how benefits for commercial use of language can flow back to the communities to fund more language work. As explained by KWP, 'We expect that when people use words or phrases from the language, they will do so with respect. In taking something from the language, and in taking up our valuable time and effort in research and translation, it would be good if people would reciprocate and give something back to the language, to help it grow. In some cases, commercial concerns have made substantial donations, which have allowed us to run workshops and develop materials, and with this reciprocal process the language will continue to grow strong.'[19]

It is also important to consider long-term use and future access to the work that is created. How will the work be backed up and archived? Who can access the online storage and archive facilities? How will the knowledge be preserved as technology changes? These questions are crucial to the preservation of languages, especially with the rise of digitisation and new technologies.

Protocols in action

Queensland Indigenous Languages Project

Archival collections hold vast amounts of material related to Indigenous peoples, cultures and family histories. Libraries hold manuscripts, recordings, diaries and books on Indigenous culture, and often these are relevant to the revitalisation of languages. As colonial institutions, they have a history of managing this material in ways that have neglected Indigenous cultural heritage rights. But things are changing, and libraries and archives are now seeking to build stronger relationships with communities, and to manage their collections through Indigenous consultation and cultural protocols.

In response to the rapid decline of traditional language and threat of language loss in Queensland, the State Library of Queensland (SLQ) introduced the Queensland Indigenous Languages Project. The main factor driving the project was Indigenous control, as it was acknowledged that non-Indigenous academics generally had a monopoly over Indigenous language documentation and recordings.

The project brought together library staff with Indigenous language consultants. Their discussions acknowledged the past practice of outsiders visiting communities and recording, writing and leaving with the outcomes of their research. This research has ended up in archives, in the form of books and historical documentation, without any credit given to community members as the custodians of the knowledge they have shared. The connection was lost or forgotten in the process. In many cases, Indigenous people have been left with the challenge of gaining access to materials relevant to their families and cultural heritage,[20] or even discovering that such material exists.

To move beyond this kind of approach, SLQ formed partnerships with community representatives and listened to the needs of the community groups regarding ownership and storage of resources. They held training workshops to empower Indigenous people to record and create their own language resources. SLQ also formed partnerships with the North Queensland Regional Aboriginal Corporation Language Centre (NQRACLC) and local Indigenous radio stations, who provided facilities, equipment and broadcasting opportunities. NQRACLC taught language groups how to use audio and video equipment to record languages and export them into a useable format.[21]

As well as being the manager of First Languages Australia, Faith Baisden is also part of the Queensland Indigenous Languages Advisory Committee. Faith was excited about the SLQ project. She writes that it is 'inspiring to see the commitment of the SLQ to support Aboriginal people and Torres Strait Islanders in creating their own records of history and culture in this state; the message and the hope to tell your own story, and be heard in your own voice.'[22] By following appropriate protocols and ethical guidelines, the project sets a benchmark for institutions wishing to support Indigenous people in accessing their collections and revitalising their languages.

Wiradjuri language in The Yield by Tara June Winch

The traditional lands of the Wiradjuri people are in central New South Wales. Tara June Winch is a Wiradjuri author whose novel *The Yield* (2019) won the Miles Franklin Award and the Christina Stead Prize for Fiction at the NSW Premier's Literary Awards. The novel looks at the effects of dispossession on Indigenous culture, land and familial connections. She includes the story of fictional character Albert 'Poppy' Gondiwindi, a grandfather who is working to pass on the Wiradjuri language and stories of his people as he approaches his death. He is writing a dictionary, which appears at the end of the novel. Many language words and phrases also appear throughout the narrative. Tara says, 'We must have open truth telling of our history in order to change the status quo, which for a significant portion of the population has been one of pervasive apathy toward Aboriginal and Torres Strait Islander culture, connection to land, politics, and language.'[23]

When she decided to include Wiradjuri language in her novel, Tara wanted to make sure she consulted with the broader community.

Tara says, 'I spoke with Wiradjuri elder Dr Uncle Stan Grant Snr, who has been a strong leader in language revitalisation, putting together the Wiradjuri dictionary. He was enthusiastic and gave me his support.'[24] Tara also consulted with language practitioners Aaron Ellis, Wiradjuri man and educator, and Geoff Anderson, a Wiradjuri man and member of the Wiradjuri Council of Elders, and the Wiradjuri Dictionary app developed by the Wiradjuri Study Centre at the Wiradjuri Condobolin Corporation. Connecting with language custodians and knowledge holders ensured that her use of Wiradjuri aligned with the broader interests of the community. As Tara says:

> I think as a nation there is an opportunity for all of us, as Australians, new and old, to embrace the mother tongue of where we live – whether it be by supporting local language centres and linguists or lobbying for First Nation language programs to be taught in our local schools and early childhood curriculums – feeling proud of our cultural history as a nation, acknowledging the horrors openly and giving all of us a real fighting chance to be so proud of our country's future and the resilience of our first people.[25]

TRUE TRACKS PRINCIPLES IN *THE YIELD*

- **Respect** – Wiradjuri custodianship and ownership of language is embedded into the narrative and themes of *The Yield*. Tara's engagement with the Wiradjuri language is connected to her own cultural identity as a Wiradjuri person. This connection is the platform for her to respectfully explore the ICIP in consultation with custodian and elder Dr Uncle Stan Grant Snr.
- **Self-determination** – Tara is reclaiming the use and relevance of the Wiradjuri language as part of her heritage.
- **Consent and Consultation** – The writing process involved consultation with Wiradjuri knowledge holder and elder Dr Uncle Stan Grant Snr. It also involved the input of linguist

Dr John Rudder, who has worked with Uncle Stan for many years on Wiradjuri language revitalisation. Both figures have played highly significant roles in its reconstruction and revival.

- **Interpretation** – Consultation with Uncle Stan, John Rudder and other language practitioners was a key way to ensure the language was represented appropriately in *The Yield*, and to enable interpretation of local historical records dating back to the 1880s.
- **Cultural Integrity** – *The Yield* relates to the bigger picture of Wiradjuri culture and history, despite it being a fictional work. Tara brought her own experience as a Wiradjuri woman and wrote with an awareness of the multilayered nature of intercultural experiences.
- **Secrecy and Privacy** – Tara ensured that no secret or confidential content relating to Wiradjuri language and culture was contained in the book.
- **Attribution** – The book recognises Wiradjuri custodianship of languages, including acknowledging past language work by custodians. The author's note in the book acknowledges Uncle Stan and the *New Wiradjuri Dictionary*.
- **Benefit Sharing** – *The Yield* promotes the Wiradjuri language more widely, and a percentage of royalties from the sale of the first 1000 books went to the Parkes Wiradjuri Language Group through the Parkes Aboriginal Education Consultative Group. Free copies of the books were given to Uncle Stan and the Wiradjuri community.
- **Maintaining Indigenous Cultures** – *The Yield* contributes to the language revitalisation movement and raises public awareness of Wiradjuri culture with respect to the ongoing connections of this heritage to people living today. This sense of cultural value and reclamation reaches both Indigenous and non-Indigenous readers.
- **Recognition and Protection** – Tara is recognised as the copyright owner, and has clearly acknowledged her Wiradjuri heritage, and the role of Uncle Stan and the community.

Songwriting with Indigenous language: 'Yanada' by The Preatures

The Preatures are an Australian indie rock band whose song 'Yanada' (2017) features the Darug language, a key language of Sydney to the Blue Mountains. The word yanada is Darug for 'moon'. In the early stages, vocalist Isabella Manfredi saw the need to engage an Indigenous voice as the song was about connecting with the land around Sydney where she lives. She was introduced to Jacinta Tobin, a Darug elder and songwoman, and they worked together to write the parts that featured traditional language.

In collaborating with Jacinta, the band wished to use their music to reach new audiences and highlight the continuum of Indigenous languages in the contemporary era. The Preatures incorporated Darug language into their song production by following cultural protocols, and respecting the self-determination and cultural authority of its Indigenous collaborators. Isabella Manfredi and Jacinta Tobin wanted to ensure that the Darug community was consulted about the use of language in the song, and letters of support were provided by key representatives of this community. Jacinta says:

> I believe that when we are singing in language, we are massaging the country and my ancestors are happy. The band did walk with me into some harsh meetings as well as talking to my people for their blessings … which was given. Due to the sensitive nature of the subject, I did put the call out to Eagle to show itself for confirmation, that the ancestors were ok with this decision. Many may laugh at that way, but I had to be sure and nature has always been my guide in cultural matters. After three days of anticipation, two Eagles showed themselves in Richmond which is my Grandfather's Yarramundi Country. Job done [and] blessing was given in more ways than one.[26]

The Preatures also fundraised for the re-publication and updating of *The Sydney Language*, a dictionary put together by Jakelin Troy. This will assist the Sydney language groups to develop and strengthen their languages.

Caring for our language collections

In 2019, I visited the State Library of NSW to see the big exhibition on Aboriginal languages called *Living Language: Country, Culture, Community*. At the entrance of the exhibition, visitors were greeted by life-sized projections of language custodians, standing on country and speaking. These people, such as Tyronne Bell, a Ngunawal man from Canberra, were on the language reference group for the exhibition. Others on the reference group include Rhonda Ashby (Gamilaraay/Yuwaalaraay), Caroline Bradshaw (Dhanggati), Callum Clayton-Dixon (Anaiwan), Raymond Ingrey (Dharawal), Michael Jarrett (Gumbaynggirr), Diane McNaboe (Wiradjuri), Brad Steadman (Wahwangiya/Gangarahmakay/Barrinahtji) and Maureen Sulter (Gamilaraay).

Walking through the show was a deeply immersive experience, with beautiful images of country, interviews with language custodians, original historical documents and intimate sound recordings of stories told in traditional language. The space was alive with language and story. Behind the scenes, the exhibition involved extensive consultation with Indigenous language custodians like Tyronne, who enhanced how the Aboriginal language materials in the library's collection were understood.[27]

Importantly, the notebooks of William Dawes were on display. Dawes was a young British officer who arrived in Sydney in 1788, and who was informed of the Sydney coastal languages by a young Gamaraigal woman named Patyegarang. Dawes' notebooks show that he and Patyegarang likely spent time together at the observatory at Point Maskelyne in Sydney Harbour, now known as Dawes Point, where she shared the Sydney language as chief teacher and, in effect, the first Aboriginal linguist.[28] The pair bonded, and shared details of their daily lives – including emotions and humour – with mutual respect while in each other's company.[29] The work that Patyegarang did with Dawes in turn led to the first field notes of an Aboriginal language that provides sufficient information for reconstruction.³⁰ This material is vital for the revival of the Sydney Aboriginal language and was on international loan for the show. There were also other significant notebooks on display, including one by American linguist Horatio Hale, who documented the Awabakal language in Newcastle between 1839 and 1840.

'It is possible to decentre the colonial perspective without undermining the integrity of the institution. What we are understanding now is that we need to support Indigenous people to explicate the knowledge from these resources,' says Palawa man Damien Webb, who manages Indigenous Engagement at the State Library of NSW and was one of the curators of the exhibition. 'It is hard work, but these records don't make sense on paper, they make sense on country and in the mouths of elders. Returning that content becomes so important.'³¹ This way, agency and authority are returned, whereas previously the outsiders owned the copyright and were given credit for collecting words, but the people who spoke them barely existed.

The collections of the State Library of NSW include an extensive array of material related to Indigenous peoples. As well as the language records and word lists, there are photos, drawings and manuscripts reflecting Aboriginal life and culture by non-Indigenous people such as government officers, missionaries and ethnographers. There are also unique works by prominent Indigenous people, including author Ruby Langford Ginibi, inventor David Unaipon, now passed, and Mickey of Ulladulla, an artist who lived during the 19th century, and the talented artists Penny Evans and Bronwyn Bancroft, based in the Northern Rivers region of NSW.³²

Many of these items are now being digitised to help reconnect them with communities. The library has adopted an open-source digital platform called Mukurtu. (Mukurtu means 'dilly bag' or a safe keeping place in Warumungu language from the Northern Territory; the Warumungu community was involved in the creation of the software, and elder Michael Jampin Jones chose the name.) The Mukurtu CMS (content management system) allows communities to access their digital heritage and apply their own cultural protocols and labels to control access, use and attribution. Kirsten Thorpe, Worimi woman, who previously worked with the State Library of NSW and continues to work with the library as a researcher through the University of Technology Sydney (UTS) Jumbunna Institute for Indigenous Education and Research, says of the NSW Australian Mukurtu Hub project: 'It's very much about community being in the driver's seat of their cultural heritage materials ... At the core of all of this is that digital stewardship engagement, so that we take community members with us so that they're in control.'[33] Tranby Indigenous College in Sydney will be one of the first pilot spokes for the NSW Australian Mukurtu Hub utilising the open source Mukurtu software.

Another important collection involves the Centre for Australian Languages and Linguistics (CALL), a language centre at the Batchelor Institute in the Northern Territory. Batchelor Institute provides tertiary education for Aboriginal and Torres Strait Islander people. The CALL Collection is managed by Batchelor Institute Library in partnership with CALL. It includes a large amount of Indigenous language materials that are now being digitised. I worked closely with Karen Manton, the project officer for the collection, to develop protocols for the Collection and its website, as well as a suite of consent forms, end user licences and website terms that enable some materials to be accessible online (with consent). ICIP protocols underpin the approach to make sure people whose work is included are respected and acknowledged. Karen said, 'We take the responsibility for caring for materials really seriously and use protocols to protect the creators and users of the collection.'[34]

These protocols and terms were informed by CALL's community-based language activities in the Northern Territory as part of the Australian Government's Indigenous Language and Arts programs. Early development of the protocols and licences were part of two True Tracks workshop series we delivered at the Institute, including sessions focused on the Collection and Batchelor Institute Press.

The curse of copyright for Indigenous languages

Under Australian copyright law, Indigenous languages aren't recognised as being owned by the people of the language group – not in the way that Indigenous people traditionally see their role as custodians in safeguarding the stories and culture. This is an issue when Indigenous languages are recorded by outsiders, which creates copyright in the books and documents that result. The general laws of copyright provide that the person who writes the text, story or narrative becomes the owner of the copyright in that expression. This means that the linguists, researchers or their employer universities are the copyright owners of the field notes, sound and film recordings. For example, Indigenous groups must seek permission from the copyright owners to access recordings of their ancestors speaking their language, or dictionaries and word lists. When the Indigenous speakers and the linguists they worked with are deceased, it is the children of the linguists who then own copyright – because it lasts for 70 years after the death of the author. However, the descendants of the Indigenous speakers are not given the right to access the words of their culture.

If Indigenous people are to control and manage their languages, copyright must be used to their advantage and frameworks developed for managing who owns copyright in the resources where languages are stored. As well as considering copyright, people can follow protocols and ethical guidelines that ensure Indigenous people continue to own and control their own languages and culture.

In 2017, the NSW Government introduced a special law for Aboriginal Languages called the *Aboriginal Languages Act 2017*, the first legislation in Australia that acknowledges the significance of Indigenous languages. This established an Aboriginal Languages Trust in New South Wales, with a Board of Indigenous members to manage it, to develop a strategic plan for the growth and nurturing of Aboriginal languages at local, regional and state levels. While it does acknowledge Aboriginal custodianship of Aboriginal languages, there is nothing in the legislation about how intellectual property should be dealt with. So, although this law is a step in the right direction, it is limited in protecting Indigenous ownership of languages.

Authorship belongs to the writer

In Australia, copyright is set by the *Copyright Act 1968* (Cth), which protects original literary, dramatic, musical and artistic works that are reduced to a material form.[35] The general rule is that the identifiable creator of a work owns the copyright in that work for their lifetime plus 70 years after their death.

As copyright only applies to things that have been put into a material form, Indigenous languages can only be protected by copyright if they are in a material form, such as into a dictionary or word list. This has led to situations where the person who writes down the language, such as a non-Indigenous linguist, becomes the copyright owner rather than the Indigenous language speaker who provided the knowledge. For example, non-Aboriginal researcher Dr John Rudder was invited to work with Wiradjuri language speaker Dr Uncle Stan Grant Snr AM to create *A New Wiradjuri Dictionary* together. To publish the work, Rudder established Restoration House Press and, by virtue of the rules of copyright law, became the copyright owner of his contributions to the dictionary, without any formal contract being entered into. In 2020, Rudder and his family, understanding the role of language revitalisation in renewing the lives of Wiradjuri people, commendably reassigned Rudder's copyright to Grant as a senior custodian.

Another requirement for copyright is that works must be considered original. A work is original if the author has invested a certain level of intellectual effort into producing it. As such, it is very difficult to prove that copyright subsists in a single word. This is problematic because it means people can freely publish dictionaries and lists of Indigenous words. Furthermore, copyright doesn't consider communal ownership, which is at odds with how Indigenous languages are the collective responsibility of the relevant language group and do not belong to a single individual.

Who owns copyright?

Copyright only protects the expression of language in material forms. The table below shows the different components of language projects and how Australian copyright law does or does not apply to the materials.

Language material	Copyright work/material
Oral words	No copyright protection
Words in songs handed down through the generations, not attributed to a songwriter and not recorded	No copyright protection
Composed song/music in Aboriginal language	Musical work
Language dictionary	Literary work – compilation
Printed dictionary	Published edition has copyright
Language website	Compilation of literary work, artistic works
Language software	Literary work
Language video resources	Film
Oral tapes/recordings taken of Aboriginal speaker	Sound recording
Mobile phone apps and podcasts	Literary works, artistic works – compilation

Using language in a resource or project

With more and more Indigenous language resources such as apps, websites and online databases appearing, it is important to understand the underlying copyright and cultural heritage rights issues. Digital language applications are particularly popular, with the accessibility of smartphones and tablets being used for teaching and learning purposes. These apps often provide English-language translations of words and phrases from Indigenous language groups, as well as background information on the relevant language, pronunciation guides, voice recordings, images, film clips, culture, art and Dreaming stories. They are presented in a colourful, fun and user-friendly format. There are dictionary apps for Wiradjuri, Mutti Mutti, Barngarla, Miriwoong and many more Indigenous Australian languages. In multimedia resources such as these, a different person could own the copyright in the individual elements such as music, sound recordings, photos, videos, illustrations and graphics. This is important to be aware of when creating resources.

Many Indigenous language resources are publicly available. For instance, AIATSIS has compiled the AUSTLANG database, which assembles information about Aboriginal and Torres Strait Islander languages (including variant spellings, number of speakers, geography, resources and programs). The Living Archive of Aboriginal Languages has made available online picture books and endangered texts in Aboriginal languages of the Northern Territory. Accessing the online Murdi Paaki Languages Hub in New South Wales requires a login, which has to be requested from the project coordinator. The National Indigenous Television (NITV) channel often broadcasts programs that feature Indigenous languages.

Since 2014 there have been efforts by the Noongar community in Western Australia to set up an Aboriginal language site through Wikimedia called NoongarPedia.[36] The difference between this and the Wikipedia page on palawa kani is that here, Indigenous people are in full control of what content is shared and how.

Naming a project, room, building or public place

What if you wanted to use an Indigenous language word or phrase to name your project, event or program? Or if you were a company looking to name a meeting room in your office building, or a business wanting to trade mark Indigenous words? This is where you need to think first about whether the use of the language is respectful and appropriate. There is a need for a genuine connection to the Indigenous people and history of the place. If the connection is genuine, then the second step is to enable genuine consultation and collaboration with Indigenous people for use of their language. This means connecting and having conversations with the relevant Aboriginal land council, organisations and community members. From here, written agreements and benefit sharing arrangements can be made to keep the relationship respectful and sustainable in the long term. The bottom line is that the language choice should be culturally informed and approved by community, with benefits going back to them.

Terri Janke and Company was engaged by global professional services firm KPMG, who wanted to demonstrate their commitment to and respect for Indigenous Australia by naming some of the meeting rooms in their offices around Australia after Indigenous words, places and people. We helped them with the protocols that involved consulting with the relevant community groups and families, and following the process of obtaining free, prior and informed consent. It took time to allow the groups and families to discuss and make decisions, ensuring that the final chosen names were respectful and appropriate.

It is also interesting to see the rules around geographic naming of places, and how this is now moving towards dual naming or reverting to the Indigenous names for places. The NSW Geographical Names Board has a policy that states a preference for use of Aboriginal names for geographic features. Where a feature currently has a non-Aboriginal name, it may be considered for a dual name provided that documentary or oral evidence of the Aboriginal name is provided.[37] Other states have also developed policies, such as Western Australia's Aboriginal and Dual Naming Guidelines.[38]

Controlling copyright ownership

To ensure that the rights to language materials remain with custodians and communities (e.g. language groups, families and clans), written agreements can be drawn up at the outset of a project stating who will own the copyright in the resulting resource. This approach allows Indigenous language centres to engage linguists and resource developers while ensuring that their ICIP rights are protected.

While copyright law favours the author or the writer of language resources, written agreements can change this and provide clauses that allow control of written materials by Indigenous language custodians. Therefore, when conducting Indigenous language projects, it is important to have a written framework that sets out who owns the intellectual property, and who has rights to the ICIP. For example, the broader language community could have ICIP rights to language, traditional knowledge and traditional cultural expression, while an Indigenous individual who is the language expert may be assigned the copyright in the recording. Or a non-Indigenous linguist may own the copyright for their contributions (such as notes) but could assign the rights to the custodians and community so they can freely adapt and use the material in future language resources. Copyright clearances should also be obtained from the copyright owners of pre-existing works and archival materials.

There are cultural clearance forms available from the Arts Law Centre. Working in collaboration with First Languages Australia, the Arts Law Centre has developed template contracts and explanatory notes for Indigenous language centres.

The challenge of speaking up

When working with Indigenous languages, the focus should be on empowering language groups and their future descendants to maintain and strengthen their connections to language and culture.

WHAT YOU CAN DO ...

- For Indigenous communities, research and plan for Aboriginal community language projects. (See *Junyirri: A Framework for Planning Community Language Projects*, listed in the Resources below.)
- When recording languages and engaging outside professionals to assist, Indigenous communities should ensure that they maintain the rights to the materials that are created. This can be done in writing, by using agreements that assign copyright to community organisations. See the *First Languages, Law & Governance Guide* listed below.
- Get advice and use written agreements to ensure that the materials can be used by the Indigenous language organisation and the future generations of Indigenous language speakers.
- Follow ICIP protocols that uphold Indigenous self-determination and respect for Indigenous custodianship.
- Companies should not commercialise Indigenous words without consulting with Indigenous people to understand the meaning of the words, and to consider if the use is appropriate and not offensive. Consent and benefit sharing should also be considered. First points of contact are the language centres and elders working on language revitalisation. Do not apply for a trade mark using Indigenous words without consultation and consent. Respect this practice of consultation and consent for naming rooms and programs using Indigenous words, places and important historical figures.
- Be conscious of how you use and refer to Aboriginal languages in media. Do not refer to languages as 'dying' or 'extinct' but rather as 'sleeping'. See the *Note to Assist Reporting ...* document listed below.
- If in doubt, seek legal advice on the publication of language resources and the development of language projects and programs. (See the Arts Law Info Hub listed below for sample agreements.)

Resources

First Languages Australia (FLA): www.firstlanguages.org.au
Junyirri: A Framework for Planning Community Language Projects (First Languages Australia, 2015): www.firstlanguages.org.au/resources/junyirri
Note to Assist Reporting on Aboriginal and Torres Strait Islander Languages (First Languages Australia, 2019): www.firstlanguages.org.au/images/Reporting_on_languages_8_LR.pdf
Living Languages (AIATSIS): https://aiatsis.gov.au/explore/living-languages
50 Words Project (Research Unit for Indigenous Language, University of Melbourne): https://50words.online/
First Languages, Law & Governance Guide (Terri Janke and Company, 2019): www.terrijanke.com.au/first-languages-law-governance-guid
National Indigenous Languages Report (Australian Government, 2020): www.arts.gov.au/documents/national-indigenous-languages-report-document
'Why written agreements are important for First Languages projects' (Terri Janke and Company, 2020): www.terrijanke.com.au/post/why-written-agreements-are-important-for-first-languages-projects
Arts Law Centre of Australia Info Hub (search for 'Sample Agreements'): www.artslaw.com.au/info-hub/
CALL Collection, Batchelor Institute: https://callcollection.batchelor.edu.au
Mobile Language Team, South Australia: www.mobilelanguageteam.com.au

Notes

1. PULiiMA, *What is PULiiMA?*, PULiiMA, n.d., <https://puliima.com/home/about>.
2. Wikimedia Foundation, *Wikimedia Foundation Transparency Report/2014/Requests for Content Alteration & Takedown*, Wikimedia, 2014, <https://meta.wikimedia.org/wiki/Wikimedia_Foundation_Transparency_Report/2014/Requests_for_Content_Alteration_%26_Takedown>.
3. Tasmanian Aboriginal Centre, personal communication, 17 February 2021.
4. United Nations, United Nations Declaration on the Rights of Indigenous Peoples, Resolution 61/295, 13 September 2007, Article 31, <https://www.un.org/development/desa/indigenouspeoples/declaration-on-the-rights-of-indigenous-peoples.html>.
5. Pama Language Centre, *Paman Languages of Cape York*, Pama Language Centre, n.d., <www.pamacentre.org.au/new-languages-map-and-resources/>.
6. Doug Marmion, Kazuko Obata and Jakelin Troy, *Community, Identity, Wellbeing: The Report of the Second National Indigenous Languages Survey*, AIATSIS, Canberra, 2014, <https://aiatsis.gov.au/sites/default/files/research_pub/2014-report-of-the-2nd-national-indigenous-languages-survey_2.pdf>.
7. Melissa Kirby, personal communication, March 2020.
8. Clint Bracknell, 'Rebuilding as research: Noongar song, language and ways of knowing', *Journal of Australian Studies*, vol. 44, no. 2, 2020, pp. 210–23.
9. Kylie Bracknell, personal communication, March 2021.
10. Kylie Bracknell, personal communication, March 2021.
11. Kylie Bracknell, 'Noongar words and philosophy are the true hero in our *Macbeth* adaptation *Hecate*', *The Guardian*, 14 February 2020, <www.theguardian.com/commentisfree/2020/feb/14/noongar-words-and-philosophy-are-the-true-hero-in-our-macbeth-adaptation-hecate>.

12 Kylie Farmer (Bracknell), *Keep our Languages Alive: Kylie Farmer at TEDxManly*, TEDx Talks, YouTube, 10 March 2014, <https://youtu.be/SAxhh6DguUo>.
13 Palawa kani is the language of Tasmanian Aborigines, included here with thanks to the Tasmanian Aboriginal Centre (TAC).
14 Lynette Ackland, personal communication, March 2020.
15 Faith Baisden, personal communication, 19 June 2020.
16 Australian Government, *International Decade of Indigenous Languages*, indigenous.gov.au, 5 February 2020, <www.indigenous.gov.au/news-and-media/announcements/international-decade-indigenous-languages>.
17 United Nations Department of Economic and Social Affairs, *2019 International Year of Indigenous Languages*, United Nations, 12 January 2019, <www.un.org/development/desa/dspd/2019/01/2019-international-year-of-indigenous-languages/>.
18 Kaurna Warra Pintyanthi, <www.adelaide.edu.au/kwp/>.
19 Kaurna Warra Karrpanthi, *Re: Kaurna Translations and Requests for Names etc.*, information sheet, n.d., <www.adelaide.edu.au/kwp/requests/>.
20 Faith Baisden, 'Libraries, languages and linking up', in John Hobson, Kevin Lowe, Susan Poetsch et al. (eds), *Re-Awakening Languages: Theory and Practice in the Revitalisation of Australia's Indigenous Languages*, Sydney University Press, Sydney, 2010, p. 357.
21 Faith Baisden, 'Libraries, languages and linking up', pp. 357–59.
22 Faith Baisden, 'Libraries, languages and linking up', p. 360.
23 Tara June Winch, personal communication, 2 July 2020.
24 Tara June Winch, personal communication, 25 May 2019; Stan Grant and John Rudder (compilers), *A New Wiradjuri Dictionary*, Restoration House, Canberra, 2010.
25 Tara June Winch, in Prudence Clark, 'Tara June Winch yields to Byron Writers Festival', *Blank*, 27 June 2016, <https://blankgc.com.au/tara-june-winch-yields-to-byron-writers-festival/>.
26 Jacinta Tobin, personal communication, 17 February 2021.
27 State Library of NSW (SLNSW), *Living Language: Country, Culture, Community*, SLNSW, 2019, <www.sl.nsw.gov.au/exhibitions/living-language-country-culture-community>.
28 Alexis Moran and Jai McAllister, 'Patyegarang was Australia's first teacher of Aboriginal language, colonisation-era notebooks show', *ABC News*, 11 March 2020, <www.abc.net.au/news/2020-03-11/patyegarang-and-how-she-preserved-the-gadigal-language/12022646>.
29 Alexis Moran and Jai McAllister, 'Patyegarang was Australia's first teacher of Aboriginal language'.
30 Alexis Moran and Jai McAllister, 'Patyegarang was Australia's first teacher of Aboriginal language'.
31 Damien Webb, personal communication, 3 November 2020.
32 SLNSW, *Why Collect Indigenous Voices*, SLNSW, 2016, <www.sl.nsw.gov.au/about-library/services/indigenous-services/why-collect-indigenous-voices>.
33 Kirsten Thorpe, *ICIP in Practice – Kirsten Thorpe, Jumbunna Institute for Indigenous Education & Research*, presentation at Blurring Lines – the Australian Digital Alliance Copyright Forum 2020, Australian Digital Alliance, YouTube, 6 March 2020, <www.youtube.com/watch?v=Z1r6TtK1YWA>.
34 Karen Manton, personal communication, 23 February 2021.
35 *Copyright Act 1968* (Cth), subsection 22(1).
36 Monica Tan, 'Aboriginal language Wikipedia faces cultural hurdles, say researchers', *The Guardian*, 26 May 2015, <www.theguardian.com/australia-news/2015/may/26/aboriginal-language-wikipedia-faces-cultural-hurdles-say-researchers>.

37 Geographical Names Board (NSW), *Geographical Names Board of NSW Policy: Place Naming*, Geographical Names Board, 2019, <www.gnb.nsw.gov.au/__data/assets/pdf_file/0017/220148/GNB_Place_Naming_Policy.pdf>.
38 Landgate, *Aboriginal and Dual Naming: A Guideline for Naming Western Australian Geographic Features and Places*, Western Australian Government, 2020, <https://www.landgate.wa.gov.au/maps-and-imagery/wa-geographic-names/aboriginal-and-dual-naming>.

3
DRAWING A LINE IN THE SAND: STOPPING INDIGENOUS ARTS APPROPRIATION

While taking a break from law school in the 1990s, I went to look at the job ads in the old CES, the Commonwealth Employment Service, at Bondi Junction – where people went to look for jobs before the internet. Ads were pinned to boards all around the room. One caught my eye – it said, 'Aboriginal Arts'.

It was a secretarial position at the then Aboriginal Arts Board of the Australia Council for the Arts. Created in 1967, the Australia Council supports the arts through policy, programs and grants for Australian artists and creative organisations. The Aboriginal Arts Board was set up in 1973. This was a time when the policy of self-determination had been adopted by the Whitlam government, supporting the right of Indigenous people to be involved in decision making that affected them.

The aim of the Board was to promote 'a renaissance of Aboriginal culture and to stimulate Aboriginal artistic endeavour in all forms of the arts, both traditional and non-traditional.' It was made up of Indigenous artists, authors, performers, activists and cultural leaders.[1] A lot of prominent people have contributed to its success since it was established. Dick Roughsey, Mornington Islander, was the first appointed chair of the Board. The second chair was Wandjuk Marika, a Yolngu man, painter and activist who was awarded an OBE in 1979. Professor Gary Foley, a Gumbainggir man, was the first Aboriginal director of the Board. Other influential people on the Board have included activist Ruby Hammond, the first Indigenous South Australian to seek election into federal parliament;

Charles 'Chicka' Dixon, who co-founded the Aboriginal Tent Embassy in 1972 and was the inaugural 'Aboriginal of the Year' in 1983; Eddie Mabo, perhaps most known for his role in the landmark High Court case that overturned the doctrine of terra nullius; and artist Lin Onus, recipient of an Order of Australia in 1993 for his work promoting Aboriginal artists and their work. The Board set out to support Indigenous artists show their work in international exhibitions in places like the US, Italy, Canada and across Asia.

Art centres and the burgeoning of art

During this time, the vast network of Aboriginal and Torres Strait Islander art centres that exists across Australia today was beginning to develop. Papunya, 250 kilometres north-west of Mparntwe (Alice Springs), is home to the Papunya Tula art movement that formed in 1972. The Papunya settlement was established in the late 1950s and includes five main groups of people – Pintupi, Luritja, Warlpiri, Arrernte and Anmatyerre. It was the birthplace of the Western Desert art movement, characterised by the dot-painting style derived from traditional sand and body painting. Some of Australia's most famous painters came out of this movement, such as Clifford Possum Tjapaltjarri and Billy Stockman Tjapaltjarri. Today, the Papunya Tula Artists' studios are based in Kintore and Kiwirrkurra communities, with the retail gallery in Alice Springs, and represent around 80 artists from the Western Desert region. There is also Papunya Tjupi Arts, a more recent centre established in 2007 and based in Papunya itself.

There are many different styles and traditions of Aboriginal and Torres Strait Islander art. If you visit the big museums and galleries, like Brisbane's Gallery of Modern Art or the National Gallery of Australia in Canberra, you can become familiar with the different styles of each region. Like the Papunya dot paintings, the barks of Arnhem Land are world famous. John Mawurndjul is an acclaimed senior artist whose long and successful career is connected to the Maningrida Arts & Culture centre in the heart of Arnhem Land. The art centre began as a craft shop in the 1960s. Mawurndjul's magnificent bark paintings and sculptures toured nationally in 2019 and 2020 in the exhibition *John Mawurndjul: I Am the Old and the New*. His works have had such reach that for the exhibition they had to be extracted from 63 private and public collections all over the world.[2]

I saw the exhibition when it was showing at the Museum of Contemporary Art Australia in Sydney. Mawurndjul's bark paintings are mesmerising. He is an expert in rarrk (crosshatching) painting; the white, ochre, brown, black and red lines are extremely fine and detailed. Animals, landscape, people and plants – and the stories of Kuninjku culture – that surround Mawurndjul's home in western Arnhem Land are all illustrated on the dark wood. Mawurndjul is a master; his lore, his language and his craft keep the connection to his stories and culture strong.

Art centres assist Aboriginal and Torres Strait Islander artists to create their art and to find markets, enabling them to pursue national and international careers from their homelands. Governed by boards of Aboriginal and Torres Strait Islander directors, art centres have also become important for protecting artists' copyright and ICIP. Today, there are many Aboriginal and Torres Strait Islander art centres that support artists to cultivate their cultural expressions that are so intimately linked with country and knowledge. These are mostly through the north and centre of Australia, with some in the west and in Queensland, and in the Torres Strait Islands. Alliance organisations such as Arnhem, Northern and Kimberley Artists (ANKA), Desart, Ku Arts, Aboriginal Art Centre Hub Western Australia (AACHWA), APY Art Centre Collective and the Indigenous Art Centre Alliance (IACA) help support the practice of Aboriginal and Torres Strait Islander arts and culture.

Some thriving art centres include Maruku Arts at Uluru; Artists of Ampilatwatja in the Northern Territory; Mangkaja Arts in Fitzroy Crossing, Western Australia; and Warmun Art Centre in the Kimberley region, and there are many more.

Let's not forget the Torres Strait Islands. Erub Arts is an art centre on Erub (Darnley) Island in the Torres Strait where the surrounding sea is the lifeblood of culture on the island. Living so close to the sea, the community has seen the devastating effects of ghost nets (abandoned fishing nets) that pollute the water and harm marine life. The artists at Erub Arts are internationally recognised for their ghost net artworks, using weaving techniques to make sculptures of turtles, fish, rays, jellyfish and even a big hammerhead shark. Lavinia Ketchell, a young Erub artist, says, 'I love how I can turn something so harmful to our reefs into a beautiful artwork.'[3] Their sculptures are collected by museums and galleries in Australia and in the United Kingdom, Switzerland and Canada. Other Torres Strait Islander art centres include Badu Art Centre on Badu Island, Moa Arts on Mua Island and the Gab Titui Cultural Centre on Thursday Island.

What about in urban places? Boomalli Aboriginal Artists Co-operative was established in 1987 by a group of ten Aboriginal artists working in Sydney, including Fiona Foley, Michael Riley and Brenda L Croft. The idea for Boomalli grew from a series of informal meetings where issues relating to the cultural authenticity of urban-based art were passionately discussed. Over the years, Boomalli has helped with bringing the Indigenous community together in events and exhibitions including social justice events, dance parties, International Women's Day events, youth arts workshops, and *The Pink, the Black and the Beautiful* – an exhibition coinciding with the Sydney Mardi Gras in 2006. In Brisbane, there is also the proppaNOW arts collective.

Advocates for art

The job at the Aboriginal Arts Board was a really good fit for me. I found myself in the midst of an explosion in Indigenous arts and culture. Indigenous creatives were thriving and changing the way Indigenous people and cultures were being seen and understood by others. In the 1990s, there was a shift away from the 'artist unknown' approach to makers and performers of craft and folklore. We were seeing leadership in the arts and creative industries. Aboriginal art centres formed a strong network and opened up opportunities for artists to exhibit their works in the big cities and internationally. The ethnographic lens, where culture was viewed through the eyes of the white 'other', was shifting to a strong, contemporary black expression. It had such an impact. The Aboriginal arts movement is one of the most significant in Australian arts history.

Indigenous art was outselling its non-Indigenous counterparts and artists were showing their works in amazing exhibitions overseas. *Aratjara: Art of the First Australians* (1993–94) was one of the big shows initiated by the Board. More than 100 Aboriginal artists were included, such as Judy Watson and Yolngu artist Dr David Malangi. It showed at three high-profile exhibition venues in Europe: the Kunstsammlung in Düsseldorf, the Hayward Gallery in London and the Louisiana Museum in Denmark.[4] There was success not just in visual art, but in dance and theatre companies like the now world-famous Bangarra Dance Theatre, and in literature too, with Indigenous writers like Sally Morgan, author of the autobiography *My Place* (1987), getting on bestseller lists.

I was the secretary to Lesley Fogarty, the Board director at the time. Lesley really advocated for me to do more work. I progressed from secretary to program officer, and became responsible for the implementation of funding programs for the Indigenous performing arts. It was a big responsibility and I was only in my early twenties. But I took it on, and the opportunities and experiences I had in working with Indigenous communities allowed me to commit to my career more deeply. I was on the road to a better understanding of myself and I was feeling connected. And it was a spiritual connection too, bringing a newfound sense of comfort and determination.

I remember my colleague, Jenny Pilot, a proud Torres Strait Islander woman, constantly calling for the inclusion of 'Torres Strait Islander' in the title of the Board. Sure enough, it soon became the Aboriginal and Torres Strait Islander Arts Board. Today, the Australia Council has the First Nations Arts Strategy Panel.

It was an exciting and eye-opening time. But it was when I attended a training session by the Australian Copyright Council that I really began to understand the importance of copyright for Aboriginal and Torres Strait Islander artists. Non-Indigenous people were trying to get in on the success of Aboriginal art and culture. Cultural artworks were being copied in poor quality; cultural designs were being stolen for cheap tourist souvenirs. The spiritual connection between the art and culture, and the land, was being degraded.

I started looking more deeply into copyright and rights for artists and became fascinated. When I returned to law school it was with a new energy, determination and strength. This time I was really focused, knowing that I wanted to be an advocate for Indigenous artists' rights.

Stamping out fake arts

Many people who travel around Australia are eager to experience the art and culture unique to the country. The number of arts tourists, from overseas and from Australia, has surged in recent years. It's pretty common for travellers to plan their trip around the different art shows and events they want to see. According to the Australia Council, a higher proportion of tourists visit our galleries and museums than they do wineries, casinos and sporting events. In 2017, 3.5 million arts tourists visited Australia.[5]

In the summer of 2019–20, I was in Circular Quay, the heart of Sydney tourism. The sun was shimmering off the harbour, the ferries sounded their horns and tourists were everywhere, posing to get that perfect picture of the Sydney Opera House and Harbour Bridge. As I entered one of the convenience stores, I overheard the conversation of a couple who were looking at miniature didgeridoos.

'Do you think these were made by Aboriginal people?' one asked.

'Maybe little Aboriginal people.'

I heard the answer. I didn't stick around to see if they bought one.

I had seen this scene countless times in airports, markets, souvenir shops and gift shops along the tourist strips of Melbourne, Surfers Paradise, Darwin and Cairns. They were all looking to sell travellers a little piece of Australia – something truly unique to remind them of their trip, a cute memento to give friends and family back home. It's hard to miss the fake Aboriginal souvenirs sold in these places. Brightly coloured dots and stolen cultural designs splashed across mugs, beach towels, calendars and coasters. Little didgeridoos made from plastic. Glossy boomerangs.

Kangaroo key chains. Stylised emblems on fridge magnets and bottle openers.

For the trained eye, it's easy to spot a fake. The mixing up of Indigenous designs and styles from different regions of Australia, the garish colours and the cheap materials are a dead giveaway. But if you were a tourist or someone unfamiliar with Indigenous art, maybe you wouldn't be able to tell.

The irony is that these cheap and nasty products disrespect and distort the very cultures they are trying to represent. By imitating the designs and stories of Aboriginal and Torres Strait Islander artists, the fake art and craft industry undermines thousands of years of culture and knowledge. It disrespects the rich cultural meanings and stories that the artists hold so close to their hearts within these objects and ignores the cultural obligations that come with them.

It also steals away economic opportunities from Indigenous peoples, deceiving consumers along the way, robbing us of the chance to enjoy authentic products. Laurie Nona, acclaimed printmaker from Badu Island in the Torres Strait, says, 'It really takes the core out from inside of you, it really dampens the spirit because you're telling your true story, and here are people taking patterns and colour just for the sake of creating a fake image so they can make money.'[6]

Speaking out: Wandjuk Marika

Laurie Nona isn't the first to have spoken out against the stealing of Aboriginal and Torres Strait Islander art and designs. In the 1970s, artist Wandjuk Marika was a particularly strong voice, and he did much for Indigenous rights related to copyright and fake arts. In 1974, he was passing through Cairns and saw a tea towel printed with his own sacred design in a tourist shop.[7] The design told an ancestral story his father had given to him about the Djan'kawu creation ancestors from Arnhem Land, and to copy this without permission was a serious offence.

The tea towel was being sold for $10, which was pretty expensive back then. It had been manufactured in the Netherlands without Marika's knowledge, and none of the profits were going back to him or his family. In his autobiography *Wandjuk Marika: Life Story* (1995), he says that he asked the shopkeeper if he could buy the tea towel at a discount, to pay for just the fabric, as it was his own copyright design.[8]

After seeing the tea towel, Marika was so devasted that he stopped painting for several years. He started advocating for the copyright protection of Aboriginal art, contacting the government to request reform. In 1974, he raised the issue of Indigenous copyright at a board meeting of the Australia Council for the Arts.[9] The message was that Aboriginal artworks aren't just generic pictures and patterns but unique cultural expressions that communicate specific stories and knowledge. Two years later, Marika became chair of the Aboriginal Arts Board of the Australia Council and continued his stance against the unauthorised copying of Aboriginal artworks. Marika pointed out that Aboriginal artists should be given the same respect as other Australian artists such as Sidney Nolan. Copying without asking is disrespectful. It also risks that special sacred works are reproduced irreverently. Instead, Marika called for Aboriginal artists to be acknowledged as the rightful owners of their artworks.[10]

Marika was speaking out in the 1970s when the Aboriginal land rights movement was gaining momentum. The Northern Territory's *Aboriginal Land Rights Act 1976* was the first law in Australia to recognise the Aboriginal system of land ownership, enabling Aboriginal people to claim rights to land based on proven traditional ownership. Aboriginal land councils were set up to represent the interests of Aboriginal people in different areas. The Act has enabled Aboriginal people in the Northern Territory to regain ownership of around 50 per cent of the interior land and 90 per cent of the coastline.[11] This reclaiming and return to home country allowed the nurturing of the creative arts that is so intimately intertwined with the land.[12] During this time, the Aboriginal Arts Board helped support the growth of an expanding network of community-based art and craft centres in northern and central Australia.

Calling in change: activists and advocates

The calls to protect Indigenous cultural heritage were getting louder. In 1975, the government set up a Working Party on the Protection of Aboriginal Folklore. The group comprised of representatives from the Attorney-General's Department, Australia Council, Australian Copyright Council, Department of Prime Minster and Cabinet, and Department of Aboriginal Affairs. Today, the term 'folklore' is considered outdated in Australia, but it is still used in some international discussions to describe the cultural heritage of traditional peoples.

In 1981, the Working Party released a report that recommended the creation of an Aboriginal Folklore Act. This special new law would prohibit offensive uses of Aboriginal arts and cultural material and set up a payment system to pay traditional owners for commercial use of their material. Although the law was never implemented, it shows that there was debate on Indigenous Cultural and Intellectual Property rights in these years.

During the 1980s, the popularity of Aboriginal art skyrocketed because of the Australian Bicentenary, marking 200 years since the arrival of the First Fleet in 1788. As the country prepared for the 'Celebration of a Nation', the fake art industry was growing. People wanted to sell products representing Australia, leading them into the realm of Indigenous designs. This is when the first Aboriginal copyright cases were being run – *Yangarriny Wunungmurra v Peter Stripes Fabrics* (1983) and *Bulun Bulun v Nejlam Investments Pty Ltd* (1989). These cases were showing that Aboriginal people were willing to take action against appropriation.

In the late 1980s and early 1990s, peak industry bodies such as Desart, APY Art Centre Collective, Ku Arts and ANKA (Arnhem, Northern and Kimberley Artists) began to form. To this day, they do much to support the Indigenous art centres and promote an ethical First Nations art market.

In the final year of my law degree in 1994, I was working at the National Indigenous Arts Advocacy Association (NIAAA), an Indigenous-run organisation advocating for the legal and cultural rights of Indigenous artists. The NIAAA had been given government funding to introduce a national labelling system to authenticate Indigenous art and craft products. Two labels were introduced: the Boomerang Tick – Label of Authenticity, which certified if a work was authentic, and the Collaboration Mark, which certified works produced through an ethical collaboration. When the NIAAA split up in 2002, the system stopped operating and was never re-implemented, despite discussions to bring back something similar.

In 2004, the Arts Law Centre of Australia established Artists in the Black (AITB), a program providing targeted legal services for Indigenous artists and arts organisations. The program was established under the leadership of Robyn Ayres, a lawyer and Arts Law's CEO. Prior to joining Arts Law, Robyn had worked extensively with Indigenous communities and saw the need to address the shortfalls in the law. 'Our aim is that any artist, no matter where they live, can get legal assistance … We want to assist First Nations artists and arts organisations to have strong and sustainable arts practices, with artists having money in the bank,' she says.[13] In 2019, lawyers and law firms contributed approximately a million dollars' worth of pro bono legal expertise through their program.

Considering their small resources, Artists in the Black has made a big difference thanks to the commitment of those who work there and support it. Since its inception, Artists in the Black has hired some very talented Indigenous staff in different roles. The original AITB team was Indigenous lawyer Samantha Joseph and AITB coordinator Blanch Lake. Indigenous lawyer Patricia Adjei, a Wuthathi, Mabuiag Islander and Ghanaian woman, made important contributions, and now continues her work at the Australia Council as the Head of First Nations Art and Culture. I met Patricia when she was completing her law degree in 2004 and we found out that we shared Wuthathi ancestry. She is now an internationally recognised expert in Indigenous Cultural and Intellectual Property.

Other former AITB staff who continue to make important contributions to the arts and cultural sectors include Kyas Sherriff, now senior commissioning editor at NITV; Beau James, now head of Indigenous programs at the Australian National Maritime Museum;

Bibi Barba, artist and arts officer at Create NSW; Sharna White, Indigenous lawyer now working in private practice; and the current Artists in the Black coordinator John Waight, who continues his remarkable career in the Indigenous arts industry.

The Indigenous Art Code (IartC) was launched in 2010 to set standards for fair and ethical trading in Indigenous art. It involves a voluntary Code that art dealers can sign up to, committing to standards of ethical and transparent treatment and fair pay of Indigenous artists. Gabrielle Sullivan has been the CEO since 2014. The logo of the IartC is displayed at the premises of galleries, art centres and art fairs. Look out for it when purchasing Indigenous art. Great work is done by the IartC to encourage and support art gallery and museum shops and buyers to consider the principles in their procurement and acquisition of Aboriginal and Torres Strait Islander art. But with continuing inequity, there is debate on whether a mandatory code should be created.

Stephanie Parkin, Quandamooka woman and Chair of the Indigenous Art Code, explains: 'The Indigenous Art Code promotes fairness and transparency in relation to the agreements between Aboriginal and Torres Strait Islander artists and the businesses who sell their work. Respecting and valuing an artist's Indigenous Cultural and Intellectual Property is crucial. To achieve this, the IartC is committed to working with artists to ensure they are able to exercise and maintain agency in decision-making processes which involve the sale and licensing of their artwork.'[14]

The resale of Indigenous art was another big problem in the art market. Galleries and resellers were making money when reselling Aboriginal and Torres Strait Islander artworks. A new resale royalty law was introduced around the same time the Indigenous Art Code was established. Copyright Agency was appointed by the federal Government to manage the resale royalty scheme, which sees artists receive a 5 per cent royalty on some resales of artworks that cost $1000 or more. Since the scheme began in 2010, approximately $8.5 million in royalties has been generated for almost 2000 artists, 64 per cent of whom are Indigenous.[15]

In 2016, the 'Fake Art Harms Culture' campaign was launched by the Indigenous Art Code, the Arts Law Centre and the Copyright Agency.

Instigated by artists, the campaign lobbies the government to address the proliferation of fake Aboriginal and Torres Strait islander art and craft products in the Australian market. With clever posters showing what fake art looks like, and slogans like 'Boomerangs that can go back to Bali' or 'From a very Northern Territory (called Indonesia)', there has been more public awareness and discussion on the issue.

The Hon. Bob Katter MP, federal Member for Kennedy in Queensland, is a strong supporter of the campaign. In 2017, he brought a draft law to federal parliament to deal with the sale of fake Indigenous art and souvenirs called the Competition and Consumer Amendment (Exploitation of Indigenous Culture) Bill 2017. This law would make it illegal to sell fake, imported Aboriginal-style art. It never made it through parliament, but was further developed in a bill Sarah Hanson-Young introduced in February 2019. There was an inquiry held, but this bill also failed to pass.

Meanwhile, a company called Birubi Art was supplying thousands of fake boomerangs, bullroarers, didgeridoos and message stones to retail outlets in Australia. These products featured Indigenous-style imagery like dot work, rarrk (crosshatching) and animal motifs, and were sold with labels claiming them to be 'Authentic Aboriginal Art' when they were in fact made in Indonesia.

The Australian Competition and Consumer Commission (ACCC), the government authority responsible for enforcing consumer law and fair trading in Australia, took Birubi to court. ACCC said that Birubi had misled consumers by falsely claiming that these products were made by Australian Aboriginal people. On these grounds, the Federal Court found Birubi to have breached Australian consumer law. In 2019, Birubi was fined a huge $2.3 million, sending a strong message that fake arts isn't to be taken lightly. This is unlikely to be paid, as the company went into liquidation.

Organisations have also been looking to innovative digital solutions. In 2018, the Australian Government provided Desart (the peak body for Aboriginal art centres in Central Australia) with funding to test the feasibility of using digital labels on Aboriginal and Torres Strait Islander products. The goal was to help consumers make informed choices, and to increase economic and cultural opportunities for Aboriginal and Torres Strait Islander artists and designers. Through the SAM Database, the Desart-owned online artwork management system for Indigenous art centres, QR codes were enabled and applied to products through the database, allowing consumers to scan the code on the product, linking them to information about the artist, their story and the item's provenance. This was trialled by three art centres, including Martumili Artists, which trialled it at Desert Mob 2019, a major Indigenous art fair held annually in Mparntwe (Alice Springs). The QR code technology continues to be taken up by art centres in 2021.

Another emerging approach for the supply of and trade in Indigenous art is the use of blockchain technology for the recording and tracking of sales. This has been trialled by the Copyright Agency to assist in the management of the resale royalty scheme and also forms the basis of First Nations Blockchain, a business established by Wakka Wakka man Shane Hamilton. Shane says, 'Our blockchain framework – essentially a database for recording transactions between parties – was drafted from scratch by senior technicians, built around protecting Indigenous Cultural and Intellectual Property rights. These records ensure transparency about the cultural connection of the work and the fair dealing of the work, knowing when it sells, for resale royalties.'[16]

Buying ethical Indigenous art

I met the late Lin Onus, a Yorta Yorta man, when he was chair of the Aboriginal Arts Board in the early 1990s. Yorta Yorta country crosses the border of southern New South Wales and north-eastern Victoria. Lin was committed to the issue of copyright theft of Indigenous arts and was an influential contemporary Australian artist in his own right, showing his work in Australia and overseas – in Madrid, Kyoto and New York.

You might know his sculpture *Fruit Bats* (1991) in the Art Gallery of New South Wales collection. It's one of Australia's most iconic contemporary Aboriginal works – a group of bats hanging upside down off a Hills Hoist clothes line. Lin painted their wings in rarrk, the traditional crosshatched design from Arnhem Land. He was closely associated with the Central Arnhem Land artists and had received permission to use the rarrk designs in his work.[17]

Lin was one of the first people I heard speak about the need for arts advocacy for Aboriginal artists in all areas of the art market throughout Australia, from fine arts to craft. When we met, Lin spoke to me of his father Bill's workshop in the Dandenong Ranges just east of Melbourne. In the 1950s, Bill Onus was carving and painting boomerangs and using his cultural designs to make ceramics, woomeras (spear throwers), fabrics and greeting cards for his business Aboriginal Enterprise Novelties.[18] These are types of cultural items that are most at risk from being copied by overseas imitation products.

Businesses like that still exist, such as Ngarga Warendj – Dancing Wombat started by Mick Harding, who makes wangim (boomerang), malgarr (shields) and dhaal galk (clapsticks). Mick says, 'When I create something I express my cultural integrity in place, be respectful of interpretation of my culture, and share my story as a Taungwurrung Kulin (Aboriginal man from my traditional country).'[19]

You can see that the cultural practice is a living one as it continues within families, and is a way they make a living. Finding places for selling art can be a hard thing for artisans. All year round there are Indigenous art fairs and markets like the Blak Markets, plus bigger art fairs like the Darwin Aboriginal Art Fair, Cairns Indigenous Art Fair, Meeanjin Markets in Brisbane and many more, where Indigenous art centres have stalls alongside other Indigenous businesses and independent artists. There is also the label Haus of Dizzy by Wiradjuri woman and designer Kristy Dickinson, who is known for her fun, glittery earrings with proud slogans like 'Deadly' and 'Blakfulla'. Gillawarra Arts by Worimi woman Krystal Hurst makes unique wearable art inspired by Krystal's cultural heritage, using echidna quills, quandong seeds and emu feathers.

The Haus of Dizzy was one of the many stalls buzzing with people at the National Indigenous Art Fair 2019, held in the Overseas Passenger Terminal at Circular Quay. As I walked around and took in all the great

HOW CAN I ETHICALLY BUY FIRST NATIONS ART?

- Learn about the diversity in Aboriginal and Torres Strait Islander art. If you aren't familiar with the different styles and traditions, visit museums and galleries to find out what you like.
- Research the artists and movements you like. Where do they come from and what are the stories in their art?
- Visit the galleries and stores that are members of the Indigenous Art Code.
- The Koori Heritage Trust in Melbourne operates a store with Aboriginal art products that are made under licence with Aboriginal artists.
- Look out for the Darwin Aboriginal Art Fair, Cairns Indigenous Art Fair, the Tarnanthi festival in South Australia and Desart Mob – visit those fairs to purchase art direct from the art centres. There are also Meeanjin Markets (Brisbane) and Blak Markets (Sydney).
- For extensive lists of Indigenous art centres in Australia, look at the peak bodies: Desart, APY Art Centre Collective, Indigenous Arts Centre Alliance (IACA), Ku Arts, Aboriginal Art Centre Hub of Western Australia (AACHWA) and Arnhem, Northern and Kimberley Artists (ANKA).
- For urban artists, go to Boomalli (Sydney) and proppaNOW (Brisbane).
- Ask where the artist comes from, how much are they getting paid and what the split is. Beware the bogus boomerang and ask questions about the work's source, artist and fair payment. If the tag says that 'royalties directly benefit the artists', ask more questions about these royalties.
- For fair licensing, talk to Copyright Agency to licence Aboriginal art from their artist members; use the Artwork Licensing Intellectual Property Toolkit for Indigenous Art Centres from the Arts Law Centre; Warlukurlangu Artists and Martumili Artists do good licensing; come to Terri Janke and Company.

stalls, I was captivated by a purple painting I saw hanging up at the Maruku Arts stand. I found out it was by Rene Kulitja, one of my favourite artists. Rene Kulitja is from the Mutitjulu community in the Northern Territory and is based at Maruku Arts.

That painting I fell in love with is called *Ancient Tracks and Waterholes*. Now it's framed and hanging up in my office. Just looking at it gives me energy. It is phenomenal. The work depicts the ancient waterholes of the land of the Central Australian desert where Rene's grandmothers and grandfathers lived. It tells a story of how when the waterhole dried up, they would walk until they arrived at the next one. Having this work in my office will always inspire me to continuously search for more answers and to keep moving forward.

Copyright in artworks

Whether you're Indigenous or non-Indigenous, if you make, buy or deal with art, it's worth knowing something about copyright. Copyright law protects works of art, literature, drama, music, film, sound recordings and broadcasts. In Australia, the law is a national one: the *Copyright Act 1968*. It grants rights to creators to control the use of their work and their copyright material. There is no need for registration. Copyright applies as soon as an original work (not one copied from other works) is created or made. The first copyright owner is generally the maker, but if the work was created during a term of employment in accordance with the contract of employment, the employer usually owns copyright. Written agreements can also change the general rules, and can specify who owns copyright if a person is paid to create a work. But once the work is created, the copyright will last for the life of the creator, plus 70 years following their death.

Unfortunately, as we have seen, copyright law does not protect all the rights of Indigenous creators. Intellectual property laws are based on Western ideas of originality and individuality, and focus on helping creators to capitalise on their creations. But, for Indigenous creators, there are also cultural interests at stake, and often the sharing of culture requires balancing the commercial with the cultural.

Sometimes, Indigenous art involves the continuation of an artistic tradition or pre-existing design or style that doesn't meet the originality requirement of copyright law. Some artists and communities therefore miss out on copyright protection. It is also problematic for protecting ancient works like rock art because this falls outside of the timeframe for protection. Indigenous art and cultural designs involve rights that go on forever. Understanding intellectual property laws such as copyright enables Indigenous people to make informed decisions about providing wide access to their material, and enables Aboriginal and Torres Strait Islander artists to take legal action against infringers.

Aboriginal art cases

The following cases tell the story about the exploitation of Indigenous art, including some groundbreaking legal cases where Indigenous artists looked to copyright law to protect their rights.

David Malangi's art stolen for the $1 note

In 1966, the Reserve Bank of Australia introduced the new decimal $1 note, the front bearing the coat of arms beside the face of Queen Elizabeth II. On the reverse were drawings of Aboriginal motifs – kangaroos, snakes, vessels, human figures and Mimi spirits – the sacred beings from Arnhem Land who live in the cracks and crevices of rocks. About half of this design had been copied from a bark painting by the Yolngu artist David Malangi. Malangi was from the Manharrngu clan, one of the many different Indigenous clans of the Yolngu people from northeast Arnhem land. The $1 note was already in circulation around the country before Malangi found out that his artistic design had been used on the note. But how did it get there?

A few years earlier, the Czech art collector Karel Kupka had bought the painting and given a photo of it to an officer in the Reserve Bank of Australia, who then passed it on to the designer of the note, Gordon Andrews. Throughout the process, no one had asked Malangi for permission to use his designs. He wasn't paid or even credited. Instead, Andrews' initials were at the bottom of the note. This approach reflected the view that, like the traditional lands which had been taken from Indigenous peoples, their arts and culture were also terra nullius, or 'nobody's land'. Clearly, the mindset was that Indigenous art was generic, anonymous and free to be taken.

Malangi's painting, *Mortuary Feast of Gurrmirringu, the Great Ancestral Hunter* (1963), tells a rich and unique cultural story that is deeply connected to his country and ancestors. It was also a work still in copyright under Commonwealth law, having been painted only a few years before the incident. However, as Malangi was a ward of the state, as was most of the Aboriginal population during this time, the copyright didn't belong to him but to the Director of Welfare, who was the legal guardian of his estate.[20] Not long after the note entered circulation, Malangi found out that his design had been copied and it surfaced in the media. HC 'Nugget' Coombs, then governor of the Reserve Bank, was quick to intervene, presenting Malangi with $1000, a fishing kit and an inscribed silver medallion.[21] This settled the incident and the note remained in circulation. Although there were no legal proceedings, this was a move in the right direction for Indigenous artists' rights.

The first Aboriginal copyright case: Yanggarrny Wunungmurra

The first Aboriginal copyright case took place in 1983 when Yolngu artist Yanggarrny Wunungmurra took the textile manufacturing company Peter Stripes Fabrics to court after they copied his artwork onto fabric without his permission.[22] His bark painting *Long-necked Freshwater Tortoises by the Fish Trap at Gaanan* (1975) reflected an important cultural story the artist had been given permission to depict by a senior member of the clan who had rights to the story under their laws. In his statement to the court, Wunungmurra pointed out that what had appealed to the designer as a pleasing border of diamond shapes and crosshatching was for him a profound statement of his cultural identity and custodianship of stories.[23]

The fabric company had taken these for their aesthetic appeal, ignoring the deep cultural significance of the work and the right of the artist to control its use.

Yanggarrny Wunungmurra showed the court that his painting had been copied from an exhibition catalogue. Although the painting involved pre-existing clan-owned designs, the artist had depicted the tortoise in his own unique style, making the work original and eligible for copyright protection. The court awarded damages of $1500 and account of profits as well as ordering the infringing fabric to be delivered up.[24] This case occurred during a time when many Aboriginal works in museums and galleries were still being treated as if they were made by anonymous Indigenous artists. Indigenous artists were now more aware of their stolen designs and the possibility of addressing the issue using Australian laws, and this propelled them to seek change. The case was not well known at the time, and it was another ten years or more before the courts would again look on Indigenous art and copyright in a way that favoured the artists.

The 'carpets case'

In my time working with the National Indigenous Arts Advocacy Association (NIAAA), my principal role was to provide general advice and information on copyright and cultural and intellectual property issues to Indigenous artists and arts organisations. Here, I worked alongside many influential and supportive people, such as Bundjalung woman Bronwyn Bancroft who was the Chairperson. I also worked with people who helped strengthen my understanding of intellectual property laws, including Michael McMahon, the NIAAA director, and barrister Colin Golvan, who I assisted in the copyright action of the 'carpets case'.[25] Lawyer Richard Crane, who worked for the North Australian Aboriginal Justice Agency (NAAJA, at the time called NALAAS) in Darwin, was another legal mind on the case. I found it fascinating how they set up their legal arguments, and took evidence from the artists and other witnesses – art historians like Vivien Johnson, anthropologists and Aboriginal art dealers, and of course the artists and their families. Meanwhile, I got to watch over their shoulders as I coordinated the travel for the artist and drove the minibus.

It was always good to hear Colin Golvan speak about the law and his work with Aboriginal artists. Colin says he came to work on Aboriginal art and copyright by complete accident. He heard the artist Lin Onus speaking on ABC Radio about the need for new laws to stop Aboriginal art being copied, and it motivated him to get in contact with Lin. They connected, and Colin's very first brief at the Victorian bar, in 1989, took him to Arnhem Land to meet with Aboriginal artist clients including John Bulun Bulun, whose work had been copied by a T-shirt manufacturer, to prepare for court. As a result of the case, the Federal Court granted an injunction to prevent the making and sale of the T-shirts.[26] An agreement was reached, a settlement of $150,000 was negotiated and the T-shirts were withdrawn from sale. Colin had established himself in the field, so when the NIAAA took up a case against an importer of carpets, they briefed Colin as barrister.

The carpets case of 1993 involved the unauthorised reproduction of Indigenous artworks onto carpets that had been made in Vietnam and imported into Australia by a company called Indofurn. The work of eight Aboriginal artists had been copied by the manufacturer. These artworks told significant creation stories belonging to the cultural groups of the artists, setting out the details of the birth of country and sacred places of belonging. Many of the carpets included images of waterholes, creation places, or goannas and snakes that held ancestral power, and in some of the carpets the images were altered, distorting the cultural meanings. Only three of the artists whose works were copied were living at the time of the case, and now only one remains alive: Banduk Marika, a Rirratjingu woman from Yirrkala in East Arnhem Land and younger sister of Wandjuk Marika. 'As an artist whilst I may own the copyright in a particular artwork under Western law, under Aboriginal law I must not use an image or story in such a way as to undermine the rights of all other Yolngu who have an interest whether direct or indirect in it,' she said. 'In this way I hold the image on trust for all the other Yolngu with an interest in the story.'[27]

The carpet importers argued that copyright didn't exist in the artworks because the works used pre-existing traditional designs and therefore didn't meet the originality requirement of copyright law. The Federal Court disagreed and found that if a design has intricate detail and complexity reflecting great skill and originality, it satisfies this requirement in the law, despite it drawing from a pre-existing design. The judge considered the reproductions to be a copyright infringement and the artists were awarded damages of $188,640.[28] This was a significant amount that took into account the amount for the sale of the items, but also included damages for the cultural harm caused to the living artists. The result showed how Indigenous artists whose works are directly copied without their permission could use copyright law to protect their rights.

In the end, the carpet company did not pay the full sum. There was an appeal of the judgment that held the directors should be liable personally for the award, which was won by the directors on the point of law. The carpets were handed over, which was the other important thing, and it was good to see Banduk Marika put her carpet in the local arts centre, Buku-Larrnggay in Yirrkala, sending a strong message for her community. One of the carpets is also on the floor of the Supreme Court in Darwin.

We both gave evidence at the 2018 inquiry into the Impact of Inauthentic Art and Craft in the Style of First Nations Peoples,[29] and still there is this continuing issue of copyright infringement and fake arts. And still there are no new laws.

The first Johnny Bulun Bulun case

Another important Aboriginal copyright case involved the artist Johnny Bulun Bulun of the Ganalbingu clan from Arnhem Land. In 1989, when the clothing manufacturer Flash Screen-printers copied his painting design onto T-shirts without his consent, Mr Bulun Bulun put forward a case that they had infringed on his rights under copyright and trade practices laws.[30] In his statement to the court, he said: 'This reproduction has caused me great embarrassment and shame, and I strongly feel that I have been the victim of the theft of an important birthright. I have not painted since I learned about the reproduction of my artworks and attribute my inactivity as an artist directly to my annoyance and frustration with the actions of the respondents in this matter.'[31]

Thirteen more Aboriginal artists whose works had also been copied to varying degrees joined the case. Like the Yanggarrny Wunungmurra fabric case, for the work to be eligible for copyright protection, it had to fulfil the originality requirement of copyright law. The case was settled with a $150,000 payout, which was split evenly among the artists, and the T-shirts were withdrawn from sale.[32] Once again, the idea that Indigenous art and designs do not have copyright was proved wrong.

Yumbulul's Morning Star Pole on the $10 note

In 1991, there was another copyright case concerning the reproduction of Indigenous art onto Australian currency, this time involving the $10 note that was introduced for the 1988 Australian Bicentenary. The front of the note depicted the First Fleet ship HMS *Supply* at Sydney Cove, and a group of settlers and immigrants. On the reverse was an illustration of an Aboriginal boy with body paint in front of an ancient Aboriginal rock painting and a Morning Star Pole. Morning Star Poles are traditionally used as funerary objects during the Morning Star Ceremony in Arnhem Land. This pole, by Terry Yumbulul, senior Yolngu elder and leader of the Warramiri clan, was made and sold to the Australian Museum for public display. The pole is made from wood, natural pigments, feathers and fibres, according to Yumbulul's design.

When the pole appeared on the note, Yumbulul was disheartened as, depicted in this way, his sacred work loses its true meaning and value.[33] While it was acceptable for the pole to be displayed in a museum to educate the public about Aboriginal culture, it was not considered culturally appropriate for such a sacred item to be reproduced on money.

In 1991, Yumbulul took action in the Federal Court against the Aboriginal Artists Agency and the Reserve Bank.[34] He argued that he wouldn't have authorised the licence had he fully understood the nature of it. The court ruled that there was insufficient evidence to establish this. In the proceedings, the judge did highlight the shortfalls in copyright law for the protection of Indigenous art: 'it may also be that Australia's copyright law does not provide adequate recognition of Aboriginal community claims to regulate the reproduction and use of works which are essentially communal in origin.' Nevertheless, this event and the difficulty it caused Yumbulul could have been avoided had the principle of consent and consultation been followed by those involved.

The second Bulun Bulun case

Johnny Bulun Bulun was involved in another groundbreaking case in 1998.[35] This time his designs had been reproduced without his permission on approximately 7600 metres of fabric that was made in Indonesia and imported into Australia by R & T Textiles. It was his ceremonial bark painting *Magpie Geese and Water Lilies at the Waterhole* (1980), an artwork depicting knowledge about Djulibinyamurr, a significant waterhole in the Arafura Swamp area of Ganalbingu country. Djulibinyamurr and the waterhole Ngalyindi are two very important cultural sites for the Ganalbingu people.[36]

Over half of the fabric had already been sold before the case began. The case was interesting because it considered not only the individual artist's copyright but also looked into the rights of a group when their communal ritual knowledge is embodied in a work. As the creator of the painting, Johnny Bulun Bulun is the copyright owner under Australian copyright law. But his painting embodied traditional ritual knowledge belonging to his clan group, the Ganalbingu people, that he was permitted to express under customary laws. Justice von Doussa, the same judge who had presided in the carpets case, found that there was a 'fiduciary relationship' between the artist and the clan. This meant that the artist had to discuss and negotiate the use of the work containing traditional knowledge with the relevant persons in authority within his clan.

Evidence given by artist Djardie Ashley showed how the Ganalbingu laws dealt with the consent procedures. He noted that in some circumstances, such as the reproduction of a painting in an art book, the artist might not need to consult with the group more widely. In other circumstances, such as its mass reproduction as merchandise, the artist may also be required to consult widely. The court found that the artist had a cultural obligation to the Ganalbingu people to deal with the work, and its reproduction, with the same integrity as the artist would for the knowledge. This means that the artist would have an obligation to guard the cultural integrity and to consult with the clan for any uses that might threaten the integrity and continued connection. For the first time, the Federal Court had given a judgment that offered a pathway for Indigenous clans to control how a copyright owner can deal with a work that embodies communally owned cultural knowledge.

Albert Namatjira's copyright returns to family

You can recognise an Albert Namatjira watercolour in an instant: the way he painted the rolling hills, waterholes and monumental ghost gum trees of his country in the Central Australian desert. Albert, a Western Arrarnta man, was born at the Hermannsburg Lutheran Mission outside Alice Springs in 1902. He passed away in 1959, leaving behind an incredible legacy of some 2000 paintings.[37] Albert's paintings depicted his spiritual connection with country even though his style of painting watercolours was different from traditional Aboriginal art styles at the time. But this legacy was under threat because of the copyright arrangements. In 1957, Namatjira entered into a legal agreement with Legend Press, a publishing company, allowing them to reproduce his paintings in return for royalties. After his death, Legend Press continued to manage his copyright, paying royalties to his family. But the administration of Namatjira's estate was passed to the Public Trustee for the Northern Territory Government following the death of his wife, to whom Albert had transferred his copyright under his will. His wife did not have a will and thus her estate, and the copyright of Albert, passed to the Public Trustee. When the legal agreement with Legend Press ended in 1983, the Public Trustee sold Namatjira's copyright for $8500 to John Brackenreg, the owner of Legend

Press. The Namatjira family was not consulted before this decision was made.

Not only was the value of Namatjira's copyright much higher than the sale price, but his family had lost control over the use of his works. For the next 34 years, Legend Press exercised full control over Namatjira's copyright and received royalties for the artworks' reproduction, money that it did not share with the family. The family didn't earn anything during this period from the use of Albert's copyright. The inequality of this arrangement was made public by curator Alison French in *Seeing the Centre: The Art of Albert Namatjira (1902–1959)*, a significant exhibition at the National Gallery of Australia that celebrated Namatjira's life and art.[38] This inspired calls for the copyright to be returned to the family, including by Indigenous former senator Aden Ridgeway.

Big hART (an Australian arts and social justice organisation) and the Namatjira Project held meetings with Namatjira's descendants to work out who were the beneficiaries. Copyright Agency and the Arts Law Centre of Australia were invited to assist too. In meetings, the secondary art market was discussed and explained, and the frequency of payments. Patricia Adjei, who was working as the Indigenous Engagement Officer with Copyright Agency at the time, says, 'It took a lot of explaining and breaking down concepts of copyright and resale royalty. People had expectations that they would get regular money every week.'[39] Namatjira family representatives discussed and agreed on who should benefit, signing a letter to confirm their agreement. The Namatjira Legacy Trust was then set up over four to five years by the Namatjira family, supported by Big hART, advocating for the return of the copyright to the family. The public campaign, which even saw the release of a feature documentary, generated a groundswell of support and public engagement. After further arrangements, including with the law firm Arnold Bloch Leibler and then philanthropist Dick Smith, the campaign led to Legend Press assigning Albert's copyright to the Trust.

Finally, in October 2017, three months after the release of the documentary and its associated social impact campaign, the Namatjira Legacy Trust, representing the family, became the copyright owner in

Albert Namatjira's works. 'It was a good win for the descendants of one of the most famous Aboriginal Australian artists whose legacy was taken advantage of. His landscapes are beautiful and timeless,' says Patricia.[40] The Namatjira family say, 'The most important thing to our family is keep our culture strong ... We are hoping that the Trust will help us to achieve better living conditions for our families, better schooling for our kids, and better resources for our art centre. We want to run the buses out and pick up the kids after school, and take them to paint on the country that we learnt to paint on from our fathers.'[41] The Namatjira Legacy Trust is now calling for Namatjira's work to remain in copyright indefinitely, to protect his ongoing legacy and use the funds to support the community. This would be similar to the way that the UK Government passed legislation to keep *Peter Pan* by JM Barrie in copyright, with royalties collected and paid to a children's hospital

The artistic and cultural legacy of Albert continues with the Hermannsburg School of painting, which Albert's family and relatives are a part of, continuing to paint watercolour landscapes as an important movement, represented by Iltja Ntjarra Many Hands Art Centre in Alice Springs. Albert's innovative artistic vision continues also with his grandson Vincent Namatjira, who creates unique portraits and won the Archibald Prize in 2020.

Exploitation of Australian Indigenous art

Around the world, Aboriginal and Torres Strait Islander art and culture continue to be exploited and commercialised without our consent. International companies cash in on artistic and cultural designs to sell their products. In 2003, ancient Aboriginal rock art paintings and motifs were copied onto Dutch chocolates. One of the chocolates depicted kangaroo rock art from Arnhem Land, taken from a research book published by the Australian Institute of Aboriginal and Torres Strait Islander Studies.[42] Ironically, the chocolate company was called 'Australian Homemade'. Rodney Dillon, Palawa elder, who was the Aboriginal and Torres Strait Islander Commission (ATSIC) Commissioner for Tasmania at the time, said, 'Once again we are seeing insult added to injury by this company's appropriation of Indigenous images. I have seen the company's promotional material which says in part "think Australian Homemade, think Aboriginals". It's a pity that the owners didn't follow their own advice and think about asking Aboriginals before they started making money both here and overseas, using our images.'[43]

Another example concerns the German ceramics manufacturer Villeroy & Boch that in 2019 released 'Rock Desert', a tableware line sold in Europe featuring Aboriginal-style dot painting on dinner plates, bowls and saucers. The company described the design as 'original Aboriginal art with a twist'. The problem was that they were not in breach of copyright law as their design was not a direct copy of an artist's work but mimicked the dot-painting style. Stephanie Parkin from the Indigenous Art Code (see page 67) called it 'a missed opportunity' for Villeroy & Boch to work with Indigenous artists.[44]

Another recent flare-up involved the popular Netflix series *After Life*, written, produced and directed by English actor Ricky Gervais. The show featured an Aboriginal-style painting in a lounge room set, but it had dubious origins: back in the 1990s, a non-Indigenous graphic artist had copied the artwork *Tingarri Dreaming* (1987) by well-known Papunya Tula painter Warlimpirrnga Tjapaltjarri, for use in the TV industry. (The original work is held by the National Gallery of Victoria.) Papunya artists of the Central Desert are known for using sinuous lines and dot work to express their cultural stories and knowledge. For the Papunya artists, it was like someone had stolen their story of place. Gervais's company Derek Productions then did the right thing, paying Tjapaltjarri an amount for compensation plus an ongoing fee to use an authorised print of the work, negotiated by the Copyright Agency. The print was used in the second series of the show that aired in 2020.

In Poland, Bibi Barba's painting *Desert Flowers* was copied throughout the interior designs of a hotel. Bibi discovered this while browsing the internet one night, when she saw photos of her artistic design reproduced extensively on carpets, wall panelling and pictures throughout the hotel.[45] She was devastated. The design was a very close copy of her original painting with its distinctive network of bright yellow and orange interconnected triangles. In a 2016 interview, Bibi said, 'I was gobsmacked ... The work was never supposed to be for that purpose ... It was the spiritual journey of the songline that was passed down from my grandmother ... All [the designer] had to do was ring me. Simple. Or send me an email.'[46]

When Bibi contacted the hotel, the Polish designer denied that it was a copyright infringement. The hotel had said that the design had been 'inspired' by Bibi's work, but it was clearly copied, and they had not paid her a fee or even asked for her consent. It is hard to imagine how shattering this would be. Bibi says, 'The value of free prior informed consent is priceless for all Aboriginal artists. It only takes a few moments to ask permission. This gives respect to 60,000+ years of cultural knowledge in any artform. Respect is earned and not to be taken lightly.'[47]

Protocols and licensing in the visual arts

Despite these examples of exploitation and stealing of culture, there are ways to ethically engage with Indigenous artists and their artworks. In 2002, the Australia Council for the Arts produced *Protocols for Producing Indigenous Australian Visual Arts*. I wrote these protocols with reference to an earlier document I had written for the National Association for the Visual Arts (NAVA) with Doreen Mellor, an Indigenous visual arts professional. That document was called *Valuing Art, Respecting Culture: Protocols for Working with the Australian Indigenous Visual Arts and Craft Sector*, and it was the first of its kind, written for galleries, organisations and event organisers in the visual arts to ensure that they understood the cultural issues that are often overlooked. It covered principles such as communication, consultation and consent, and also presented the legal considerations.

In 2002, artist and Pitjantjatjara woman Rene Kulitja, from the Northern Territory community Mutitjulu, was commissioned by the Australian airline Qantas to license her images to the artwork *Yananyi Dreaming*. The work depicts Uluru surrounded by kurkara (desert oak trees), tali (blue hills), mala (rufous hare-wallaby) tracks imprinted on the sand, and the lungkata (blue-tongue lizard) basking in the hot sun.[48] Qantas wanted to apply Rene Kulitja's images to the fuselage of an aircraft and entered into an agreement with Rene Kulitja and the Indigenous-owned design company Balarinji, which created the artwork design for the main body of the plane. The copyright licensing involved consultation with the artist and the community regarding the suitability of the iconography to be represented on the plane. Rene Kulitja owned the copyright in her artistic works, and the copyright in the design layout of her works on the aircraft belonged to Balarinji. The agreement involved commercial use of images captured of the plane, payment of a commission fee, payment of a licence fee based on the number of years the work will be applied to the plane, merchandising rights and rights of renewal.

Copyright Agency also licensed artwork for a Qantas plane by the late Emily Kame Kngwarreye, world-famous painter from the Utopia community in the Northern Territory, in another collaboration with Balarinji. The plane featured Emily's 1991 painting *Yam Dreaming*, and the project involved a long period of negotiation with the family. Patricia Adjei was involved in the licensing, and says that Qantas flew the plane into Alice Springs over the MacDonnell Ranges so all Emily's family and community could see it.

Licence agreements are an effective model for businesses seeking to engage with Indigenous artists, providing terms and conditions that, when respected, facilitate respectful and ethical engagement. Art licensing agreements can be used to create products featuring Indigenous art and designs. The works can be pre-existing or newly commissioned. They allow the Indigenous artist to retain copyright yet authorise others to reproduce their work, enabling the artist to gain exposure and develop ongoing relationships. The rights to use or reproduce the artwork on products should be done in a mutually beneficial manner that prioritises the ICIP rights of the artist. This can be implemented as part of a protocol framework. The granting of a licence is a contract and, like other contracts, it can be oral, implied or written, but it is best put into writing to set the terms and avoid future misunderstandings.

Labelling and certification

There is scope for the Indigenous arts industry to develop labelling, certification and geographic indications. In 1999, the 'Boomerang Tick – Label of Authenticity' certification was established by the NIAAA to protect Indigenous people's rights, culture, cultural respect, protocols and values through the promotion and protection of Indigenous arts and crafts.

The Label of Authenticity system made use of both a registered trade mark and a certification mark. The Label of Authenticity was the certification mark attached to works that were created by Aboriginal and Torres Strait Islander artists from start to finish. A second-level mark called the Collaboration Mark was designed to be affixed to products that were produced under licence with Indigenous artists.

The authentication mark scheme fell out of use following the dissolution of the NIAAA in 2002, though the mark had not often been used due partly to the costs and complexity associated with Indigenous artists gaining certification. This points to significant issues with the usability of the scheme, as well as with the level of education and promotion – and community acceptance.

Under the certification mark's rules, an 'Indigenous artist' was defined as a person of Australian Aboriginal or Torres Strait Islander descent, who identifies as such, and is accepted as such in an Indigenous community. This required the artist to prove their Indigeneity, resulting in more than 75 per cent of applications being rejected because of insufficient proof. The arrangement operated on a cost-recovery basis – NIAAA was a not-for-profit organisation – and charged an initial application fee of $30 and a yearly fee of $20.[49]

The scheme was also criticised for not taking into account region-specific styles of art, and it did not cater for dealing with potential misappropriation of styles between regions. For example, works by Indigenous artists in New South Wales using the dot style could be certified as authentic under the mark, even though the style is traditionally produced by Indigenous people in Central Australia. These aspects could be addressed more appropriately in a certification system, perhaps in a tiered scheme where it is relatively simple to use an Indigenous mark but more complex to use a region-specific marking.

Labels and certification marks are a good idea to stop the fakes. Swing tags alongside brands and other labelling help the discerning consumer pick the quality item over the cheap import.

A vision for a National Indigenous Cultural Authority

In 2008, I was invited to participate in the Kevin Rudd Government's 2020 Summit at Parliament House in Canberra. There were over 500 delegates, and the aim was to decide on a vision for a better Australia. We were each asked to bring one big idea. What would I contribute?

I had a chat to Kuku Yalanji woman Lydia Miller, then the Executive Director of the Aboriginal and Torres Strait Islander Arts team at the Australia Council. She was always supportive of my work. She said, 'You could talk about the idea for a National Indigenous Cultural Authority, an infrastructure organisation to hold rights.' I had written about this in *Our Culture: Our Future* and it was something that could be advanced to improve the protection of Indigenous culture and knowledge without the need to change any laws.

Walking inside the big house on the hill, I felt daunted. The likes of Cate Blanchett and Joel Edgerton were there to help set the future vision for the arts. My idea was on the back of the business cards that I sheepishly handed out to the big minds and movers at the event. The gist of the idea was that a National Indigenous Cultural Authority be established as a collective organisation to empower Indigenous artists, knowledge holders and communities to safeguard their cultures. The 2020 Summit Report included a recommendation to establish a National Indigenous Cultural Authority,[50] but the idea has not yet come to fruition.

More recently, Lydia Miller has led nationwide discussions on the formation of a National Indigenous Arts & Cultural Authority (NIACA). Lydia says, 'There's been discussion around how a body could uphold, protect, maintain and empower the national community through supporting activities, like operating a one-stop shop to advise artists about how to navigate their pathway through to an industry or being able to connect them with other industry bodies in relation to protecting and upholding the rights to their intellectual and cultural material.'[51] I participated in the well-attended Sydney forum, where there was a lot of support for the idea. A NIACA would be a useful organisation to support collaboration and Indigenous self-determination.

> **WHAT YOU CAN DO ...**
>
> - Buy authentic Aboriginal and Torres Strait Islander art and craft products from reputable sellers, including Aboriginal art centres (e.g. Desart, Indigenous Arts and Craft Alliance (IACA), Aboriginal Artists Co-operative). Look for the Indigenous Art Code logo on art and craft items.
> - Empower Indigenous-led and curated art projects.
> - Engage in genuine two-way collaborations that enable an Indigenous voice.
> - Use art licensing agreements that fairly seek the rights to use Indigenous arts for a negotiated fee. See also Copyright Agency, which provides licences on behalf of Indigenous artists.
> - Read and follow the Australia Council for the Arts First Nations protocols that are available online (see links below).
> - If you are a non-Indigenous artist, do not appropriate Indigenous art and designs, or adopt the 'style' of Indigenous art.
> - Consider Indigenous artists' moral rights – do not adapt or change works without consent, and consider communal moral rights. Always give attribution to the clan group.
> - If you want to commission or use an Indigenous artwork, consider ICIP issues, and then be aware that copyright should remain with the Indigenous artist.

Resources

Protocols for Using First Nations Cultural and Intellectual Property in the Arts (Australia Council, 2019): www.australiacouncil.gov.au/programs-and-resources/Protocols-for-using-First-Nations-Cultural-and-Intellectual-Property-in-the-Arts/
Indigenous Art Code (IartC): https://indigenousartcode.org
Fake Art Harms Culture campaign: https://indigenousartcode.org/fake-art-harms-culture/
National Indigenous Arts & Cultural Authority (NIACA): https://niaca.com.au/
First Nations Voice – National Association for the Visual Arts (NAVA): https://visualarts.net.au/advocacy/campaigns/first-nations-voice/
Artists in the Black (Arts Law Centre of Australia): www.artslaw.com.au/artists-in-the-black/
Indigenous Cultural Protocols and the Arts (case studies, Terri Janke and Company, 2016): www.terrijanke.com.au/indigenous-cultural-protocols-and-arts
Indigenous Knowledge: Issues for Protection and Management (Terri Janke and Company/IP Australia, 2018): www.ipaustralia.gov.au/sites/default/files/ipaust_ikdiscussionpaper_28march2018.pdf
First Peoples: A Roadmap for Enhancing Indigenous Engagement in Museums and Galleries (Terri Janke and Company, 2018): www.terrijanke.com.au/mga-indigenous-roadmap
Valuing Art, Respecting Culture (Doreen Mellor and Terri Janke, 2001): www.terrijanke.com.au/valuing-art-respecting-culture

Peak bodies

Aboriginal Art Centre Hub Western Australia (AACHWA): https://aachwa.com.au
Arnhem, Northern and Kimberley Artists (ANKA): www.anka.org.au
APY Art Centre Collective: www.apyartcentrecollective.com
Desart: https://desart.com.au
Indigenous Art Centre Alliance (IACA): https://iaca.com.au
Ku Arts: www.anangukuarts.com.au

Notes

1   Gough Whitlam, *Aboriginal Arts Board* [media release], Press Statement No. 83, 3 May 1973, <https://pmtranscripts.pmc.gov.au/sites/default/files/original/00002908.pdf>.
2   Dee Jefferson, 'Arnhem Land artist John Mawurndjul celebrated in his first major Australian survey', *ABC News*, 6 July 2018, <www.abc.net.au/news/2018-07-06/aboriginal-artist-john-mawurndjul-i-am-the-old-and-the-new/9948294>.
3   Lim Chye Hong and Lynnette Griffiths (eds), *Ghost Nets of the Ocean: Au Karem Ira Lamar Lu: Voices for the Sea from Australia's Torres Strait Islanders*, Asian Civilisations Museum, Singapore, 2017, p. 89.
4   Djon Mundine, 'Ich Bin Ein Aratjara: 20 years later', *Artlink*, June 2013, <www.artlink.com.au/articles/3952/ich-bin-ein-aratjara-20-years-later/>.
5   Australia Council for the Arts, *International Arts Tourism: Connecting Cultures*, Australia Council for the Arts, 2018, p. 6, <www.australiacouncil.gov.au/workspace/uploads/files/arts-and-tourism-report-pdf-5bf1f3c5079ac.pdf>.
6   Neda Vanovac, 'Indigenous artists battle mass-produced fakes, call for protection for their intellectual property', *ABC News*, 9 August 2017, <www.abc.net.au/news/2017-08-

09/indigenous-artists-battle-fakes-urge-consumers-to-buy-ethically/8788116>.
7   The unauthorised tea towel is in the National Museum of Australia collection: *Tea towel with design by Wandjuk Marika*, <http://collectionsearch.nma.gov.au/object/247396>.
8   Wandjuk Marika and Jennifer Isaacs, *Wandjuk Marika: Life Story*, University of Queensland Press, Brisbane, 1995, p. 118.
9   National Museum of Australia (NMA), *Yalangbara: Art of Djang'kawu*, NMA, 2010, <www.nma.gov.au/__data/assets/pdf_file/0012/303105/yalangbara-resource.pdf>.
10 Wandjuk Marika, 'Copyright on Aboriginal Art', *Aboriginal News*, vol. 3, no. 1, 1976, p. 7.
11 Joe Morrison, 'There's no conflict between Indigenous people, native title and development', *ABC News*, 16 November 2017, <www.abc.net.au/news/2017-11-16/no-conflict-between-native-title-and-development/9146346>.
12 Martin Hardie, 'What Wandjuk wanted?', in Matthew Rimmer (ed), *Indigenous Intellectual Property: A Handbook of Contemporary Research*, Edward Elgar, Cheltenham, UK, 2015, p. 156.
13 Robyn Ayres, *Robyn Ayres Speaks about AITB*, Arts Law, YouTube, 5 June 2019, <www.youtube.com/watch?v=A3OlUU63FfY>.
14 Stephanie Parkin, personal communication, 26 June 2020.
15 Copyright Agency, *10 Years of Resale Royalty for Australian Artists*, Copyright Agency, February 2020, <www.copyright.com.au/2020/06/10-years-resale-royalty/>.
16 Shane Hamilton, personal communication, 12 May 2020.
17 See Art Gallery of New South Wales, *Fruit Bats, 1991 by Lin Onus*, <www.artgallery.nsw.gov.au/collection/works/395.1993.a-c/>.
18 Ian Howie-Willis, 'Onus, William Townsend (Bill) (1906–1968)', *Australian Dictionary of Biography*, National Centre of Biography, Australian National University, Canberra, 2000, <http://adb.anu.edu.au/biography/onus-william-townsend-bill-11308/text20185>.
19 Ngarga Warendj –Dancing Wombat, *About Us*, Ngarga Warendj, 2021, <https://www.ngargawarendj.com/pages/about-us>.
20 Stephen Gray, '"Dollar Dave" and the Reserve Bank: A tale of art, theft and human rights', *The Conversation*, 22 March 2016, <https://theconversation.com/dollar-dave-and-the-reserve-bank-a-tale-of-art-theft-and-human-rights-56593>.
21 Stephen Gray, 'Government man, government painting? David Malangi and the 1966 one-dollar note', in Matthew Rimmer (ed), *Indigenous Intellectual Property: A Handbook of Contemporary Research*, Edward Edgar, Cheltenham, UK, 2015, p. 134.
22 *Yangarriny Wunungmurra v Peter Stripes Fabrics*, Federal Court of Australia, unreported, 1983.
23 Elizabeth Burns Coleman, *Aboriginal Art, Identity and Appropriation*, Routledge, London, 2016, section 4.2.
24 Vivien Johnson, 'The first copyright case', in *Copyrites: Aboriginal Art in the Age of Reproductive Technologies –Touring Exhibition 1996* [catalogue], NIAAA and Macquarie University, Sydney, 1996, p. 15.
25 *Milpurrurru and Others v Indofurn Pty Ltd and Others* (1994) 54 FCR 240; 130 ALR 659.
26 *Bulun Bulun v Nejlam Investments Pty Ltd*, Federal Court of Australia, unreported, 1989.
27 Banduk Marika, in Catherine Hawkins, 'Stopping the rip-offs', *Alternative Law Journal*, vol. 20, no. 1, 1995, p. 9, <www.austlii.edu.au/au/journals/AltLawJl/1995/4.pdf>.
28 *Milpurrurru and Others v Indofurn Pty Ltd and Others* (1994) 54 FCR 240; 130 ALR 659.
29 House of Representatives Standing Committee on Indigenous Affairs, *Report on the Impact of Inauthentic Art and Craft in the Style of First Nations Peoples*, Parliament of Australia, 2018, <www.aph.gov.au/Parliamentary_Business/Committees/House/

Indigenous_Affairs/The_growing_presence_of_inauthentic_Aboriginal_and_Torres_Strait_Islander_style_art_and_craft/Report>.
30   *Bulun Bulun v Nejlam Investments Pty Ltd*, Federal Court of Australia, unreported, 1989.
31   Terri Janke, *Minding Culture: Case Studies on Intellectual Property and Traditional Cultural Expressions*, World Intellectual Property Organization, Geneva, 2003, p. 52, <www.wipo.int/edocs/pubdocs/en/tk/781/wipo_pub_781.pdf>.
32   Colin Golvan, 'Aboriginal art and copyright: The case for Johnny Bulun Bulun', *European Intellectual Property Review*, vol. 11, no. 10, 1989, pp. 346–55.
33   Terry Yumbulul and Elena Wangurra, personal communication, 26 March 2021.
34   *Yumbulul v Reserve Bank of Australia* (1991) 21 IPR 481.
35   *Bulun Bulun v R & T Textiles Pty Ltd* (1998) 86 FCR 244.
36   Terri Janke, *Minding Culture*, p. 54.
37   Ausralian National Herbarium, *Namatjira, Albert (1902 – 1959)*, Australian National Botanic Gardens, 2015, <www.anbg.gov.au/biography/namatjira-albert.html>.
38   See Alison French, *Seeing the Centre: The Art of Albert Namatjira, 1902–1959* [catalogue], National Gallery of Australia, Canberra, 2009.
39   Patricia Adjei, personal communication, 6 January 2021.
40   Patricia Adjei, personal communication, 6 January 2021.
41   Namatjira Legacy Trust, *Why a Trust?*, Namatjira Legacy Trust, n.d., <www.namatjiratrust.org>.
42   EJ Brandl, *Australian Aboriginal Paintings in Western and Central Arnhem Land: Temporal Sequences and Elements of Style in Cadell River and Deaf Adder Creek Art*, Aboriginal Studies Press, Canberra, 1973.
43   Rodney Dillon, in 'Artful Dutch seek to sweet-talk furious Aborigines', *The Sun-Herald*, 7 September 2003, <www.smh.com.au/national/artful-dutch-seek-to-sweet-talk-furious-aborigines-20030907-gdhcj1.html>.
44   Caitlin Fitzsimmons, '"Devoid of any type of cultural value": Villeroy & Boch criticised for "misuse" of Aboriginal art', *Sydney Morning Herald*, 4 August 2019, <www.smh.com.au/entertainment/art-and-design/devoid-of-any-type-of-cultural-value-villeroy-and-boch-criticised-for-misuse-of-aboriginal-art-20190802-p52d8q.html>.
45   Copyright Agency, *Bibi Barba's Story*, Copyright Agency, <www.copyright.com.au/bibi/>.
46   ABC Radio, 'Case in Point: Bibi Barba', *AWAYE!*, ABC Radio National, <www.abc.net.au/radionational/programs/awaye/case-in-point:-bibi-barba/7878510>.
47   Bibi Barba, personal communication, 13 March 2020.
48   Qantas, *Flying Art Series*, Qantas, n.d., <www.qantas.com/au/en/about-us/our-company/fleet/flying-art.html>.
49   For an archived version of the NIAAA website, see the *Online Culture Portal*, <www.culture.com.au/exhibition/niaaa/>.
50   Commonwealth of Australia, *Australia 2020 Summit, Final Report*, Department of Prime Minister and Cabinet, 2009, pp. 273, 301, <https://apo.org.au/sites/default/files/resource-files/2008-06/apo-nid15061.pdf>.
51   Sabine Brix, 'The necessity of community consultations in helping to form a NIACA', *ArtsHub*, 20 March 2019, <www.artshub.com.au/education/news-article/sponsored-content/arts-education/sabine-brix/the-necessity-of-community-consultations-in-helping-to-form-a-niaca-257560>.

4
RESTRUCTURING INDIGENOUS ARCHITECTURE AND INDUSTRIAL DESIGN

In 2004–06, I was lucky enough to be part of a project that incorporated eight Australian Indigenous artworks into the architecture of a museum to be built on the banks of the Seine River. The Musée du quai Branly (MQB) in Paris was the vision of Jacques Chirac, the French president at the time. Chirac was passionate about non-Western art and cultures, and the value these bring to ways of seeing and understanding the world. The MQB had been previously called an 'ethnographic' museum. The new building and home on the bank of the Seine was an opportunity to shift to an inclusive model, which would involve the integration of some of the peoples whose artefacts were held at the museum. Housing thousands of cultural artefacts from Africa, Asia, the Near East, Asia, Oceania and the Americas,[1] including an important Indigenous Australian collection, the new museum building set the tone for a new approach where the source communities, like Australia, would have a greater connection with their works.

The Australian Indigenous Art Commission at the Musée du quai Branly

The French architect Jean Nouvel wanted to showcase the dynamism of contemporary Australian Indigenous art and culture within the new Musée du quai Branly building. With the help of the Australian architecture firm Cracknell & Lonergan Architects, and two of the country's leading Australian Indigenous curators – Brenda L Croft and Hetti Perkins[2] – Nouvel deliberately embedded the art of eight Australian Indigenous artists into the walls, columns, ceilings and façades of the museum. This was done in close consultation with the artists and/or their representatives who were from diverse urban and remote Australian Indigenous communities.

Brenda says, 'We were determined that the work would be a permanent part of the fabric of the administrative building; to remove it would require demolishing the building. It was essential that the work could also be viewed from the street and changed appearance depending on the time of day, the season and the light.'[3] On a tall stretch of wall inside the museum is the painting *Thoowoonggoonarrin* by the great artist Paddy Bedford, a Gija man (now deceased) from the East Kimberley region of Western Australia, the black-and-white forms showing his mother's country in the Kimberley landscape.[4] Works by artist Judy Watson of the Waayni people (north-west Queensland), *museum piece* (1998) and *two halves with bailer shell* (2002), were installed on a façade and ceiling, revealing organic forms of country and culture. The painting *Garak, the Universe* (2005), a mesmerising constellation of stars by the late Gulumbu Yunupingu, a Gumatj woman from north-east Arnhem Land, was installed on the ceiling and in the spaces between the windows of a long hallway overlooking the Parisian street below. The painting *Untitled (Wirrulnga)* (2000) by the late Ningura Napurrula, Pintupi woman from the Western Desert, was installed in a similar way, depicting an important women's site.[5]

Groundbreaking photographs by Michael Riley, Wiradjuri and Kamilaroi artist (who passed in 2004), from his *cloud* series of 2000 were reproduced in glass at street level, with natural and cultural objects hovering like clouds in a blue sky. The late Yannima Tommy Watson, a Pitjantjatjara man from the Western Desert, painted *Wipu Rockhole* (2004), a significant site on his grandfather's country.[6] It was installed at a large scale onto enamelled stainless steel tiles across a ceiling within the museum. Across the ceiling of the gift shop/bookshop is the work *Mardayin at Milmilngkan* (2006) by John Mawurndjul AM, a master of rarrk (crosshatching) painting from Arnhem Land, capturing the power of the land and his home at Milmilngkan on the Tomkinson River south of Maningrida.[7] A column installation features *Mardayin* (2005), a lorrkon or hollow log coffin. Renowned Gija artist Lena Nyadbi from the East Kimberley region painted the work *Jimbirla and Gemerre (Spearheads and Cicatrice)* (2005) that became a skin down the concrete façade of the building, evoking body scarification marks and the stone spearheads found on Nyadbi's country. Another one of her paintings, *Dayiwul Lirlmim*, was later reproduced on the 700 square metres of the external rooftop, visible from the top of the Eiffel Tower. 'The building became a canvas for the artists. They revealed their extraordinary imagination through this Commission – taking their art practice beyond what we imagined possible,' wrote Hetti Perkins.[8]

As the artworks convey important cultural stories and connections, there were many things to consider beyond the aesthetic outcomes. The overarching issue was how to keep the cultural integrity of the artworks intact as they were translated into new, larger forms. Where were the works going to be placed, and how would that affect their meanings? It was important that the works were used in a way that was appropriate to the stories and knowledge in them, especially if a work contained traditional cultural expressions requiring consent from the artist's family or clan.

Brenda and Hetti recommended that the Australia Council, a collaborator in the project, approach me for assistance with protocols, and with the processes of artist consultations and consent. Karilyn Brown at the Australia Council was my point of contact and was instrumental in overseeing the project. At the time, Karilyn was Executive Director of Audience and Market Development, responsible for major international projects including the Musée du quai Branly commission, and Australia's participation in the Venice Biennale. Our job was to develop the agreements between the artists and museum.

We drafted contracts in English and French that went back and forth between us and the French lawyers. The Australia Council's Indigenous protocols for visual arts were translated into French. We had to consider how to uphold the moral rights of the artists. Moral rights include the right of the artist and their community to be properly attributed, as well as the right to prevent derogatory treatment of a work that would harm the artist's reputation.

Even though the team was split between France and Australia, the artists were involved every step of the way, checking the drafts and design prototypes, even going over to Paris to see the building where possible. Using agreements made sure it was clearly understood how the works were going to be used in the building design and in any promotional and commercial material. We also worked out a system for royalty payments, which was important because artists, particularly Indigenous artists, often rely on royalties as a source of income.

The Musée du quai Branly's Australian Indigenous Art Commission set a benchmark for future collaborations of its kind. We had carefully negotiated the rights of the Indigenous artists rather than treating their designs as if they were in the public domain and free for the taking. On an international level, the project illustrated how protocols can enable the careful planning and execution of a major international collaboration.

The museum was officially launched in the Paris summer of 2006, with the likes of Nelson Mandela attending the opening. It is said that more than 1.3 million visitors have walked through the doors each year since then.[9]

Barangaroo's *Shell Wall*

Aboriginal and Torres Strait Islander artists, designers and architects help us understand and feel connected to place, story and culture. Just like in the Musée du quai Branly, their work feeds into the creation of Australian tourist sites too. On Gadigal land in Barangaroo on the Sydney Harbour foreshore there is *Shell Wall* (2015), designed by the talented senior shell artist Aunty Esme Timbery, a Bidjigal elder from La Perouse. Aunty Esme comes from a long line of shell workers and is best known for making shell sculptures of Sydney architecture. She has made works based on the Sydney Harbour Bridge, Sydney Opera House and Sydney Tower. Some of these are part of the Art Gallery of New South Wales collection.

The *Shell Wall* project was the first public art project at Barangaroo, and was commissioned by the property development and construction company Lendlease. The work is a magnificent, seven-storey vertical sculpture on the façade of an apartment building. It is made from thick aluminium panels, welded with giant cast shells in a pattern designed by Aunty Esme. You can see it when you walk along the southern end of the Wulugul Walk on Barangaroo's waterfront promenade.

Esme worked with the esteemed artist and curator Jonathan Jones, a Wiradjuri/Kamilaroi man. Jonathan says, 'Aunty Esme's practice and the production of this contemporary shell work is based on traditional knowledge and the maintenance of age-old cultural practices where shells were used for decoration. Collecting shells relies on ancestral knowledge and an intimate link to country, with knowing where and when to collect being handed down over generations. This work will hopefully create a locally relevant icon that will come to define the space and people's understanding of the Barangaroo site.'[10]

My firm was brought in to help with addressing the Indigenous Cultural and Intellectual Property issues the artists knew were at the heart of the project. Generations of cultural knowledge were behind the project. There was a need to consult with local Indigenous community groups. We consulted with the local Aboriginal land councils for La Perouse and the Sydney metropolitan areas. The design and creation of the artwork went ahead once all these processes had been completed. At the launch, with members of the La Perouse Indigenous community, we all admired the final work and ate fish and chips, their favourite meal.

Lendlease were so happy with the outcome that they asked us to develop their Indigenous protocols. They also wanted us to teach their staff about the importance of consulting with Indigenous people on place-based projects in the built environment. Annie Tennant, the manager of Lendlease's public art projects, was a strong champion for this. She understands that Indigenous-led design and sustainability principles are valuable when we are constructing the public domain. Annie says, 'Relationships and storytelling are at the heart of how to create great places, so for us, embedding a process that respects First Nations design principles and protocols has been critical. All projects, regardless of where they are, should be respectful, appropriate and enriched by the voices of Indigenous peoples and culture.'[11] Using the True Tracks framework, we wrote a *Place and Protocols* guide for Lendlease employees, consultants and contractors who work on projects involving Indigenous peoples and cultures.

Indigenous-led architecture and design

The Musée du quai Branly and Barangaroo projects are examples of how Indigenous art and culture can be embedded into architecture and public spaces. But what about Indigenous architecture itself?

It is a myth that there were no houses or architectural structures in Australia before invasion. In recent times, people have presented evidence to bust this myth, including Bruce Pascoe in *Dark Emu* (2014) and Paul Memmott in a hefty book on Aboriginal architecture called *Gunyah, Goondie and Wurley: The Aboriginal Architecture of Australia* (2007).[12] Memmott is an academic, architect and anthropologist, and the director of the Aboriginal Environments Research Centre at the University of Queensland.

Indigenous people have been architects for tens of thousands of years. Memmott's book puts the spotlight on Indigenous architecture, and how Indigenous people have managed spaces from gunyahs (shelters) to campsite villages. Memmott's book brings together more than 30 years of research, and explores permanent villages such as the stone houses of the Gunditjmara people in western Victoria. For Memmott, Indigenous architecture is an expression of a complex set of relationships between the physical and social environments.[13] I would agree that this remains the case for the Indigenous architects and designers who continue to innovate in Australia today. Kevin O'Brien, an Australian architect with Torres Strait Islander heritage, notes that the beehive huts on Mer (Murray Island) were some of the most amazing structures he's seen. His work is based on gaining an understanding of country first.[14] Alison Page, the well-known designer and former panellist on ABC TV's *The New Inventors*, examines space and identity in her work building contemporary spaces.

Dillon Kombumerri, a proud Yugembir Goori, is a trailblazer in Australian Indigenous architecture. Dillon was the first registered Australian Indigenous architect in Australia. In 1995 he founded the Merrima Aboriginal Design Unit within the NSW Department of Public Works and Services and was joined there by Indigenous practitioners Kevin O'Brien and Alison Page. Dillon says, 'Our aim was to design public buildings that responded respectfully to Indigenous culture and the Country it was being built on.'[15] These pioneers were working on Indigenous-themed projects in rural New South Wales such as the Girrawaa Creative Work Centre at Bathurst Correctional Centre, and the Wilcannia Health Service project. They understood that work requires co-design and collaboration with the community. Dillon is now a principal architect for the Government Architect NSW, working on projects to support better understanding of and response to Aboriginal culture in our built environment.

Wailwan and Kamilaroi man and architect Jefa Greenaway is a leader in Indigenous design thinking, and in 2018 he curated the exhibition *BLAK Design Matters* at the Koorie Heritage Trust in Melbourne.[16] The exhibition showcased the diversity of Indigenous cultural expressions within different design practices and featured landscape architecture by Paul Herzich, landscape architect and visual artist at the SA Department for Infrastructure and Transport. Paul is a descendant of the Kaurna and Ngarrindjeri people of South Australia. Work by Dillon Kombumerri and many others was also featured in the exhibition.

Concerned at the lack of Indigenous architects in Australia, Jefa Greenaway and Gunditjmara man Rueben Berg founded Indigenous Architecture and Design Victoria (IADV). IADV supports Indigenous students as they pursue a career in architecture. Rueben, a graduate architect, says that architects have a really big responsibility in shaping place in how they design a building and how they relate to the landscape, and that this can be done in a way that is culturally appropriate and sensitive to cultural practices. Another thing that's really important is the idea of environmentally sustainable design, he says, given that Aboriginal people have lived on this country for tens of thousands of years, we can design in a way that reinforces that cultural practice of living from the earth.[17]

Louis Anderson Mokak is a proud Djugun man from the West Kimberley. He is an interdisciplinary designer and a member of the First Nations Advisory Working Group and Cultural Reference Panel at the Australian Institute of Architects, the peak body for the architectural profession. Louis is concerned with the risk of cultural appropriation, as the interest in the cultural knowledge of Aboriginal and Torres Strait Islanders peoples grows within the architecture discipline. 'The sacredness of Aboriginal and Torres Strait Islander cultures should not be viewed as a smorgasbord in which you pick your favourite pieces and discard the rest,' he writes. 'There is an imperative, a responsibility, indeed an obligation for architects, and students of architecture living on these sacred lands, to themselves connect to place, community and cultures.'[18]

This is where protocols in architecture and design play an important role.

Protocols in architecture and design

The Australian Indigenous Design Charter (AIDC) was developed in response to the lack of guidance when it comes to the appropriate creation and commercial use of Indigenous arts in design practice. It sets out ten principles to follow when working on design projects involving Indigenous culture and knowledge, embodying principles to consider in projects, such as making sure Indigenous representation is Indigenous led, allowing for self-determination, ensuring that community-specific cultural protocols are followed and engaging in deep listening for better communication.

These guidelines fed into the creation of the International Indigenous Design Charter in 2018, a set of international protocols for working with Indigenous knowledge in commercial design practice.[19] The protocols guide respectful representation of Indigenous culture in design practice and education globally. 'The Charter has become a really useful document to normalise an understanding of the richness of culture and how Indigenous knowledge systems run parallel in equal value to Western knowledge,' says Jefa Greenaway.[20]

Indigenous architectural and design principles are relevant to education institutions too. The Department of Education and Training has put together a teaching and learning resource kit for professionals, academics and students working with Indigenous knowledge in the built environment. It's called *Indigenous Knowledge in the Built Environment: A Guide for Tertiary Educators* (2018).[21]

The sand-blasted pattern in the pavement of Cadigal Green at the University of Sydney responds to the history of the site – it was an Indigenous hunting ground for fish and a source of fresh water. The University of Sydney have developed the Wingara Mura design principles around the importance of honouring and using Indigenous narratives in design for universities. They want to apply these to the built environment to reflect Indigenous histories and values. The principles have won awards for reconciliation in architectural design. It is interesting to see how principles like these are setting best practice for working with Indigenous people and encouraging the shift to Indigenous-led architectural design rather than appropriation. They emphasise the underlying story, the deeper understanding of the Indigenous connection to a place, so that architecture and designs are not just colonial constructs with no meaning.

Patents, inventions and Indigenous knowledge

Every time I look at the image of David Unaipon (1872–1967) on the Australian $50 note, I am reminded that Indigenous knowledge is so rich and adaptable. David Unaipon, a Ngarrindjeri man born on the Raukkan (Point McLeay) Mission in South Australia, was the first Indigenous person to be a published author, and the first Indigenous person to own a patent. A patent is a form of intellectual property that gives rights to the creators of inventions.

Patents may be seen by Indigenous people as complex, inaccessible tools, or a way for people to exploit and capitalise on Indigenous knowledge, but Unaipon registered his patents almost 100 years ago.

In 1909, he developed and patented a modified hand piece for shearing sheep, and in the following decades he submitted patent applications for nine other inventions, including a centrifugal motor.[22] With no advanced education in mathematics, Unaipon devised his inventions based on his own research.[23]

Do patents protect Indigenous knowledge? They are strictly tools for commercialisation. Aboriginal and Torres Strait Islander people should not use the patent system to protect traditional knowledge that is not for wide exposure. This is because once that information is disclosed, it will be searchable in a database that is publicly accessible worldwide. This means that any secret or sacred knowledge would not be protected.

The other problem is that the term of a standard Australian patent is only 20 years. After this time, the patented invention becomes freely available. This is problematic for inventions based on Indigenous knowledge because Indigenous peoples' rights over their cultural knowledge need to extend indefinitely.

Even if an Indigenous group did want to go down the path of commercialisation, the costs of the patenting system is limiting. There are fees of thousands and even tens of thousands of dollars just to get the patent off the ground, coupled with further costs of maintaining patent rights. This means that many Indigenous communities simply cannot afford to apply for patents for inventions or resources that are based on their cultural knowledge.

In India, to stop the granting of patents based on traditional knowledge, the Traditional Knowledge Digital Library (TKDL) has been developed to document and publish all traditional knowledge so it can be used by a patent examiner to check the prior art. The TKDL provides details of scientific and traditional knowledge arranged according to the classification of international patents.[24] In Australia, this would be a big initiative, and given there are many different Indigenous groups, there would need to be extensive consultation. The patent disclosure provisions, however, may be a good step forward, if we can also manage to enact and implement effective laws relating to access and benefit sharing

HOW PATENTS WORK IN AUSTRALIA

In Australia, there is one type of patent: the standard patent. (The innovation patent, a faster and cheaper process, was phased out by the Australian Government in 2021.) Unlike copyright, patent protection is not automatic and, in Australia, the inventor must file an application and pay a fee to IP Australia. The patent must then pass an examination process before it is granted.

The patent specifications must clearly disclose the details of the invention so that the extent of the patent monopoly can be obtained. The applicant must show two things: novelty and inventive step. The reference point for assessing an invention's novelty is called the prior art base – that is, all the written scientific knowledge available. However, this is the catch for Indigenous knowledge holders: because the prior art base is *written* knowledge, the large body of oral and generationally transmitted knowledge is not part of this. This means that a person could get information from an Indigenous person about the healing properties of a plant, and then claim a patent.

Indigenous people have complained that this has happened in the past, and information taken from them has been used to identify potential plants for research and development. There is no requirement for the applicant to show they have consent from the Indigenous person who supplied the information.

In the WIPO IGC, there are discussions about requiring patent applicants to fully disclose the source of their inventions. Then, if traditional knowledge is used, this could trigger access and benefit sharing agreements made in accordance with the Nagoya Protocol and the Convention on Biological Diversity.

when plants are taken from Indigenous country, and when Indigenous knowledge is used in developing their use.

Traditional designs

A design in the context of traditional and Indigenous cultures is more complex than a design under Australia's intellectual property system. An Indigenous design refers to the styles, motifs, emblems, patterns and other cultural objects that signify belonging and connection to a clan group. Handed down through the generations, many Indigenous designs refer to creation beings and the journeys, places and events associated with them. Contemporary Indigenous artists draw from and reinterpret pre-existing designs, the most well known being rarrk (the fine, multicoloured crosshatching from Arnhem Land bark paintings), Wandjina figures (the ancestral creators of the Worrorra, Ngarinyin and Wunambal Gaambera people in the Kimberley region of north Western Australia), coiled basket designs and possum skin cloaks.

The Australian designs law, under the *Designs Act 2003* (Cth), protects approximately 7000 new products each year. The law protects the overall appearance of a product resulting from one or more visual features of it, as registered with IP Australia. Once the design has been examined and registered, you have the exclusive and legally enforceable right to use the product's design to gain a marketing edge in commercial production, and you can prevent others from using your design without permission. Registered designs may be applied to a range of products, including jewellery, textiles, household items and industrial items.

While a registered design can be a valuable commercial asset, it does not protect traditional Indigenous designs, motifs and symbols. The rarrk (crosshatching) pattern painted by Arnhem Land clans, for instance, could not be registered as a design in itself, but if it was applied to a product and met the requirements of 'new' and 'distinctive', it would be registrable.

Indigenous traditional design case studies

Wandjina sculpture: Sacred and not from this country

In 2010, a stone sculpture called *Wandjina Watchers in the Whispering Stone* was erected outside the ModroGorje Wellness and Art Centre in Katoomba in the Blue Mountains, New South Wales. It was commissioned by Vesna Tenodi, the gallery's non-Indigenous owner, and was created by a non-Indigenous sculptor.

The Wandjina is the sacred being of the Worrorra, Ngarinyin and Wunambal Gaambera people of the Kimberley region of Western Australia, and is often depicted on rock forms in the Kimberley. When it is used in inappropriate contexts, and in ways that sever the connection and spiritual significance of these ancestral beings, this causes a lot of distress to the custodians.

Wandjina Watchers was created without consultation with the three groups of traditional custodians on the other side of Australia. There was anger from both the Kimberley clans and the local Blue Mountains Aboriginal community, who wanted the sculpture taken down. Non-Indigenous people also found it disrespectful. Worrorra elder and renowned artist Donny Woolagoodja considered the sculpture to be a caricature of the powerful Wandjina, claiming it denigrated the spiritual beliefs of his people.[25] Given that copyright laws only protect expressions, not concepts or ideas, *Wandjina Watchers* was not copyright infringement. The Blue Mountains City Council prohibited the stone sculpture from being displayed on gallery grounds because it did not have a development permit. The gallery owners took action in the NSW Land and Environment Court, but the Council's decision was upheld.

This type of cultural appropriation of Indigenous designs is offensive and harmful to Indigenous peoples, undermining their cultural integrity. There have been many other incidences of unauthorised reproduction of the Wandjina, such as on a Wicked Campers van in 2014 and an exhibition by artist Driller Jet Armstrong in 2017.[26]

The Blue Mountains incident sparked the registration of a Wandjina trade mark by the Kimberley Aboriginal Law and Cultural Centre (KALACC), the organisation that represents the 30 language groups of the Kimberley. Their coordinator, Wes Morris, says that the trade mark is one tool, one mechanism, they use to engage in that advocacy to support the appropriate use of imagery. 'Yes, we hold the trade mark over the Wandjina. But this is completely secondary to the fact that senior cultural custodians hold cultural ownership of the Wandjina. They need support for the recognition of their cultural ownership and custodianship,' says Wes.[27] Unfortunately, the Australian legal system has been slow to address this and offers limited protection.

Revitalising possum skin cloaks

The possum skin cloak tradition of south-east Australia was recently revitalised by Gunditjmara and Yorta Yorta women artists. Possum skin cloaks were a vital part of life in pre-European times, used in daily activity, to keep warm, to sleep in, to carry babies and for many other purposes. They are made from pelts sewn together with animal sinew, incised with designs of country and clan.[28]

The revival was led by renowned artist Dr Vicki Couzens (Gunditjmara Keerray Woorroong) who, in 1999, encountered the historical Lake Condah Possum Skin Cloak with Lee Darroch (Yorta Yorta, Mutti Mutti, Boon Wurrung) in the Melbourne Museum collection during a workshop. Vicki recalls her first view of the cloak: '[It] was laid bare, without the usual barriers of a glass case ... I was enthralled. Emotions welled and swirled inside of me – awe, respect, love, yearning. This yearning was a physical sensation, a tugging of heart strings, a reaching of spirit, to know my Ancestors, a sense of loss, of knowledge, of language, of wanting to fill empty spaces.'[29] The Lake Condah Possum Skin Cloak, from Vicki's grandmother's country Gunditjmara, is one of two historical possum cloaks held by the Melbourne Museum. The other is the Maiden's Punt Cloak, of Yorta Yorta origin.

Vicki says that soon after this first encounter with the Lake Condah

Possum Skin Cloak, she experienced a vision granted by the ancestors of the cloak.[30] This led her to the idea of making 'copies' of the old cloaks as the first step of bringing the cloaks 'back to live in community'.[31] Lee Darroch and her cousin Dr Treahna Hamm (Yorta Yorta) recreated the Yorta Yorta cloak, while Vicki and her sister Debra Couzens recreated the Gunditjmara cloak. 'It was integral to our work to follow cultural protocol and seek support and permissions from Elders in our respective communities,' writes Vicki in her PhD.[32] The cloaks were shown at an exhibition at Melbourne Museum and were then acquired by the National Museum in 2004.[33] The revival of the tradition has been a great success, with community workshops and expanded interest ever since. As Lee Darroch says, 'Cloaks are powerful. They give people back their self-esteem and pride.'[34]

Aboriginal and Torres Strait Islander flags

The yellow circle against the red and black that is the Aboriginal flag is an unforgettable emblem of Aboriginal Australia. It became an official flag of Australia in 1995.[35] It's not only used as a flag but is put on T-shirts, bags, stickers, and temporary and real tattoos. Many Aboriginal businesses have adopted it in some way or other for their logos. In 2019, its copyright status was put in the spotlight. Is there copyright in the flag and, if so, who owns it? The story exploded in the media. I was getting countless calls from people asking about the copyright of the flag and how it would affect their business logo or product.

Harold Thomas, a Luritja artist from Central Australia, designed the flag in the 1970s. This makes him the owner of copyright under Australian copyright law, which will last for 70 years after his passing. As the copyright owner, Thomas has exclusive rights to reproduce the flag in material form, and to publish and communicate the flag to the public. He also controls the use of the flag by others and may grant them rights to the copyright in the flag. At the time of the media flare-up, it came to light that Thomas had granted exclusive licences to use the flag to three non-Indigenous companies: WAM Clothing, Flagworld and Gifts Mate.[36] To reproduce the flag on clothing, merchandise or flags, permission must be sought from WAM Clothing, Gifts Mate or Flagworld. To reproduce the flag for non-commercial and private use, permission must be given by Harold Thomas.[37]

This requirement for permission for its use has created widespread controversy. Given the history of the flag and what it holistically represents – that is, a symbol of protest and unification – there is a belief that the licensing arrangements in place tarnish the symbol and its significance to Aboriginal peoples and their lives. There has been growing distress in Indigenous communities as a result of the exclusive licensing arrangements that are held, and are subsequently being profited from, by non-Indigenous people.

Moreover, WAM Clothing sent cease and desist notices to a number of clothing companies, including Indigenous companies, for their use of the Aboriginal flag. The Australian Senate's Select Committee on the Aboriginal Flag, which undertook an inquiry into who has the right to reproduce the flag, heard submissions from many of these organisations and Indigenous people campaigning to 'free to flag'. This campaign was in response to what they considered a heavy-handed approach by WAM Clothing,[38] one of whose directors was an owner of Birubi Art, which was fined a record $2.3 million for misleading and deceptive conduct in selling Aboriginal products.

There's also the Torres Strait Islander flag that was similarly given legal recognition by the Australian Government in 1995.[39] The flag consists of green and blue stripes behind a white dhari (headdress) and star, designed by the late Bernard Namok from Thursday Island in 1992.[40] The five points on the star represent the Strait's five major island groups, and the star itself represents an unspecified navigational star.[41] It was the winner of a design competition. The copyright owner is the Torres Strait Island Regional Council (TSIRC) and its 15 communities. To reproduce it, you must request permission from the TSIRC.

These arrangements for the Aboriginal and Torres Strait Islander flags are different to the Australian national flag, which is considered to be in the public domain. The government allows anyone to use or reproduce the national flag for commercial purposes – no formal permission needed. They do give you a few guidelines, including that it should be 'used in a dignified manner' and 'reproduced completely and accurately'.[42] There are a range of flag images and template files for download on the Department of Prime Minister and Cabinet website.

Indigenous designs beyond country

When you look out from the top of the Eiffel tower, you can see the dazzle of Paris stretch out below you. Among the network of city buildings lies the art of Lena Nyadbi on the rooftop of the Musée du quai Branly, reproduced at 46 times its original size. The painting, *Dayiwul Lirlmim*, shares her ancestral dreaming story of Dayiwul, the barramundi whose scales created the diamonds that are embedded in Gija country. Now part of the Parisian landscape and seen by the 7 million people who climb the Eiffel Tower each year,[43] it is a long way from home, spreading the message of ancient Indigenous knowledge from the longest-living culture in the world. The power of its story emanates through this country and now it travels in the songlines through the ocean all the way to Paris, showing the strength of Indigenous culture that is here to stay.

WHAT YOU CAN DO ...

- Consider engaging and paying an Indigenous designer, architect, expert or cultural consultant for the project.
- Empower Indigenous-led architecture and design projects. Consider interpretation and relevance of sites, meanings and country and kin connected to place. This will require consultation and engagement.
- Engage in genuine two-way collaborations.
- Use written agreements to protect Indigenous Cultural and Intellectual Property rights.
- For artwork installed in buildings, or on public display, ensure that the artist consents to installation and is consulted during the installation. You must also consult the Indigenous artist or the community if the work is being removed, to give time for documentation. Seek advice on the cultural issues involved in your project.
- Identify cultural protocols specific to the place you are working in, or the people you are working with.
- Consider engaging and paying an Indigenous expert or cultural consultant for the project.

Resources

Bruce Pascoe, *Dark Emu: Black Seeds: Agriculture or Accident?*, Magabala Books, Broome, 2014

Paul Memmott, *Gunyah, Goondie and Wurley: The Aboriginal Architecture of Australia*, University of Queensland Press, Brisbane, 2007

Alison Page and Paul Memmott, *Design: Building on Country*, Thames & Hudson Australia, Melbourne, 2021

Indigenous Knowledge in the Built Environment: A Guide for Tertiary Educators (David S Jones et al., 2018): https://ltr.edu.au/resources/ID12-2418_Deakin_Jones_2018_Guide.pdf

Australian Indigenous Design Charter: www.design.org.au/documents/item/216

International Indigenous Design Charter: www.ico-d.org/database/files/library/International_IDC_book_small_web.pdf

Protocols for Using First Nations Cultural and Intellectual Property in the Arts (Australia Council, 2019): www.australiacouncil.gov.au/programs-and-resources/Protocols-for-using-First-Nations-Cultural-and-Intellectual-Property-in-the-Arts/

Connecting with Country: A Draft Framework for Understanding the Value of Aboriginal Knowledge in the Design and Planning of Places (Government Architect NSW, 2020): www.governmentarchitect.nsw.gov.au/projects/designing-with-country

Notes

1   Musée du quai Branly – Jacques Chirac (MQB), History of the Collections, MQB, n.d., <www.quaibranly.fr/en/collections/all-collections/history-of-the-collections/>.
2   At the time, Brenda L Croft (Gurindji | Malngin | Mudburra peoples; Anglo-Australian | Chinese | German | Irish heritage) was senior curator of Aboriginal and Torres Strait Islander Art at the National Gallery of Australia. Hetti Perkins (Eastern Arrernte and Kalkadoon peoples) was senior curator of Aboriginal and Torres Strait Islander Art at the Art Gallery of New South Wales.
3   Brenda L Croft, personal communication, 25 April 2020.
4   Musée du quai Branly, Australian Indigenous Art Commission: Musée du quai Branly, Art & Australia, Sydney, 2006, p. 23.
5   Art Gallery of New South Wales, Untitled (Wirrulnga), 2000, by Ningura Napurrula, <www.artgallery.nsw.gov.au/collection/works/151.2001/>.
6   Musée du quai Branly, Australian Indigenous Art Commission, p. 47.
7   Musée du quai Branly, Australian Indigenous Art Commission, p. 27.
8   Australia Council for the Arts, Australian Indigenous Art to become Parisian Cultural Landmark, Australia Council, 2006, <www.australiacouncil.gov.au/news/media-centre/media-releases/australian-indigenous-art-to-become-parisian-cultural-landmark-2/>.
9   Musée du quai Branly – Jacques Chirac (MQB), Key Figures, MQB, n.d., <www.quaibranly.fr/en/missions-and-operations/key-figures/>.
10 Jonathan Jones, personal communication, 31 March 2020.
11 Annie Tennant, email correspondence, 10 March 2020.
12 Bruce Pascoe, Dark Emu: Black Seeds: Agriculture or Accident?, Magabala Books, Broome, 2014; Paul Memmott, Gunyah, Goondie and Wurley: The Aboriginal Architecture of Australia, University of Queensland Press, Brisbane, 2007.
13 Paul Memmott, Gunyah, Goondie and Wurley, p. 4.
14 Margie Fraser, '20 Queensland designers: Kevin O'Brien', Design Online, n.d., <http://designonline.org.au/20-queensland-designers-kevin-obrien/>.
15 Dillon Kombumerri, personal communication, 17 June 2020.
16 Barnaby Smith, 'Jefa Greenaway on blak design and why it matters', Art Guide Australia, 19 July 2018, <https://artguide.com.au/jefa-greenaway-on-blak-design-and-why-it-matters>; Koorie Heritage Trust, Blak Design Matters, Koorie Heritage Trust, 2018, <https://koorieheritagetrust.com.au/whats-on/past-exhibitions/archive-2018/blak-design-matters/>.
17 Rueben Berg, FIL Rueben Berg Website, Fellowship for Indigenous Leadership, YouTube, 26 November 2013, <www.youtube.com/watch?v=qPRB88kQfvc>.
18 Louis Anderson Mokak, 'Architecture and appropriation', Caliper, no. 4, September 2018, republished in Assemble Papers, 2018, <https://assemblepapers.com.au/2018/09/20/architecture-and-appropriation/>.
19 Russell Kennedy, Meghan Kelly, Jefa Greenaway et al., International Indigenous Design Charter: Protocols for Sharing Indigenous Knowledge in Professional Design Practice, Deakin University, Geelong, VIC, 2018, <www.ico-d.org/database/files/library/International_IDC_book_small_web.pdf>.

20 Premier's Design Awards, *Design Strategy: International Indigenous Design Charter*, Premier's Design Awards, 2018, <www.premiersdesignawards.com.au/entry/international-indigenous-design-charter-2/>.
21 David S Jones, Darryl Low Choy, Richard Tucker et al., *Indigenous Knowledge in the Built Environment: A Guide for Tertiary Educators*, Department of Education and Training, Sydney, 2018, <https://ltr.edu.au/resources/ID12-2418_Deakin_Jones_2018_Guide.pdf>.
22 Reserve Bank of Australia, *David Unaipon (1872–1967)*, Reserve Bank of Australia, 2020, <https://banknotes.rba.gov.au/australias-banknotes/people-on-the-banknotes/david-unaipon/>.
23 National Portrait Gallery, *David Unaipon*, National Portrait Gallery, 2020, <www.portrait.gov.au/people/david-unaipon-1872>.
24 Sonal Sodhani, *India: Traditional Knowledge and Patents*, Mondaq, 30 May 2019, <www.mondaq.com/india/patent/810280/traditional-knowledge-and-patents>.
25 Melissa Davey, 'Gallery loses fight to keep controversial spirit statue', *Sydney Morning Herald*, 24 June 2011, <www.smh.com.au/national/nsw/gallery-loses-fight-to-keep-controversial-spirit-statue-20110623-1ghme.html>.
26 Kimberley Aboriginal Law & Cultural Centre, submission to House of Representatives Standing Committee on Indigenous Affairs, Inquiry into the Growing Presence of Inauthentic Aboriginal and Torres Strait Islander 'Style' Art and Craft Products and Merchandise for Sale across Australia, Submission 13, 2017–18, Submission 13, <www.aph.gov.au/Parliamentary_Business/Committees/House/Indigenous_Affairs/The_growing_presence_of_inauthentic_Aboriginal_and_Torres_Strait_Islander_style_art_and_craft/Submissions>.
27 Wes Morris (KALACC), teleconference, 6 January 2020.
28 Vicki Couzens, *Possum Skin Cloak Story Reconnecting Communities and Culture: Telling the Story of Possum Skin Cloaks*, PhD Thesis, RMIT University, Melbourne, 2017, p. 45, <https://researchrepository.rmit.edu.au/discovery/delivery?vid=61RMIT_INST:ResearchRepository&repId=12248272110001341>.
29 Vicki Couzens, *Possum Skin Cloak Story*, p. 25.
30 Vicki Couzens, personal communication, 5 January 2021.
31 Vicki Couzens, personal communication, 5 January 2021.
32 Vicki Couzens, *Possum Skin Cloak Story*, p. 28.
33 Vicki Couzens, personal communication, 5 January 2021.
34 Lee Darroch, personal communication, 26 February 2021.
35 This was under the law known as the *Flags Act 1953* (Cth).
36 Isabella Alexander, 'How easy would it be to "free" the Aboriginal flag?', *The Conversation*, 4 September 2019, <https://theconversation.com/how-easy-would-it-be-to-free-the-aboriginal-flag-145446>.
37 Isabella Alexander, 'How easy would it be to "free" the Aboriginal flag?'.
38 Select Committee on the Aboriginal Flag, Report (October 2020) p 67.
39 This was also under the *Flags Act 1953* (Cth).
40 AIATSIS, *Torres Strait Islander Flag*, AIATSIS, n.d., <https://aiatsis.gov.au/explore/torres-strait-islander-flag>.
41 Duane W Hamacher, Alo Tapim, Segar Passi et al., '"Dancing with the Stars": Astronomy and music in the Torres Strait', in Nicholas Campion and Chris Impey (eds), *Dreams of Other Worlds: Papers from the Ninth Conference on the Inspiration of Astronomical Phenomena*, Sophia Centre Press, Lampeter, UK, 2017, pp. 1–12, <https://arxiv.org/pdf/1605.08507.pdf>.

42 Department of the Prime Minister and Cabinet (DPMC), *Commercial Use of the Australian National Flag*, DPMC, n.d., <www.pmc.gov.au/government/australian-national-flag/commercial-use-australian-national-flag>.
43 Musée du quai Branly (MQB), *Aboriginal Works on the Roof and Ceilings*, MQB, n.d., <www.quaibranly.fr/en/public-areas/aboriginal-works-on-the-roof-and-ceilings/>.

5
FINE-TUNING: INDIGENOUS MUSIC, COPYRIGHT AND PROTOCOLS

Music is a powerful and timeless way of expressing cultural identity and cultural heritage for Indigenous peoples. It is enshrined in Indigenous Cultural and Intellectual Property (ICIP) rights, so it is crucial that Indigenous and non-Indigenous musicians, producers, record labels and listeners know these rights. Now more than ever – with the internet, music apps and the global appeal of Indigenous music and instruments – we need to protect the cultural links and keep them strong.

The first recordings of Indigenous songs date back to the 1790s, and were mainly manual transcriptions of music into Western notation, taken from live performances or observers' memories of songs. One of the first Aboriginal songs to be written down was 'Barrabu-la' in the early 1790s, sung by Bennelong and Yamroweny. This song was transcribed into written musical notation in 1811. The first mechanical recordings of Indigenous songs began in 1898, with sound recordings of the Meriam people of the Torres Strait collected that year.[1] Song remains a large part of Indigenous lifeways, but today we sing all genres, from traditional ceremonial song, playing didgeridoo or clapsticks, to rock, country, rap and folk – as well as dance music, my favourite.

The now passed Yorta Yorta musician, actor and teacher Jimmy Little was the first Aboriginal person to have a top 10 single in Australia, with 'Royal Telephone' in 1963. Bantamweight boxer Lionel Rose recorded and released the albums *I Thank You* (1970) and *Jackson's Track* (1971). Singer Bob Randall recorded 'Brown Skin Baby' in the 1970s, a song that canvassed the anguish of a mother whose baby was taken away from her.

Today, it is great to see Aboriginal and Torres Strait Islander musicians thriving in the music industry, sharing songs of culture, country, family and ancestors in a variety of genres. Traditional sounds intermingling with the contemporary have proved popular, as seen in the success of the great Yothu Yindi, who perform in Yolngu Matha and English. The beautiful songs of Yirrmal, the Yolngu songwriter, spread a message of unity on this land that connects all peoples. Yirrmal says, 'I am embracing my culture to tell deeper stories about the lore and about how Yolngu people see the land, nature and how First Nations people see things from a different perspective. They see and feel it with their hearts. I'm a storyteller. That's what my music is about.'[2]

There's also Yolngu rapper Baker Boy, who collaborated with Yirrmal in the much-loved song 'Marryuna'. Baker Boy raps in traditional language, celebrating cultural life and identity. In country and folk, we have heard the powerful music and storytelling of Kev Carmody, Archie Roach and Ruby Hunter.

Contemporary women performers like Jessica Mauboy, Leah Flanagan, Toni Janke, Deline Briscoe, Eleanor Dixon and Thelma Plum sing pop, soul and jazz, and express pride in their cultural heritage and identity. There are musicians who have broken new ground in other musical forms, such as Deborah Cheetham in opera and Eric Avery in contemporary composition and violin; these artists bring their families' songs, stories and language into the heart of their music. These deep cultural links to language, instruments, story and place bring heart and soul to the sound. Music is the energy with which they connect to their culture and identity.

Eleanor Dixon is a Mudburra woman from Marlinja in the Northern Territory and is part of the group Kardajala Kirridarra ('Sandhill Women') with Janey 'Namija' Dixon, Kayla Jackson and Beatrice 'Nalyirri' Lewis. She wants to make sure that the language, the voices, are protected. The group's self-titled album came out in 2017. Most of the sounds are in Mudburra language. The sounds are from country. Eleanor says, 'People need to understand the importance of language and not to use it without consent.'[3]

Miiesha is a proud Anangu and Torres Strait Islander woman from the small Aboriginal community of Woorabinda in Central Queensland. In mid-2020, aged only 20 years old, she released her first project *Nyaaringu*, Pitjantjatjara for 'what happened', telling stories of family, community and empowering yourself. The songs feature recordings of her grandmother speaking to her. Miiesha says, 'We set up the microphone and yarned for an hour. Nan let me use the recording throughout the project.'[4] Miiesha also included Pitjantjatjara language. In 2019, she had travelled to Central Australia, connecting with her grandfather and learning the language. In including the language on the album, she continually checked with her grandfather, sending him audio clips from the studio.

It's great to see how Indigenous people are playing key roles in the development of a strong Australian music scene.

Old music, respect for ritual

Old songs continue to be passed down from the ancestors, and new songs that follow the tradition closely are also sung. For Aboriginal and Torres Strait Islander people, new songs may have been made by human beings, or they may have been taught to living people in dreams by ancestral heroes, spirit familiars or recently dead ancestors.[5] There are songs that include ritual knowledge and have secrecy provisions attached, which means that they are not suitable to be sung outside of ceremonial contexts.

Yet the singing and playing of traditional Aboriginal and Torres Strait Islander song and music is under threat. The National Recording Project for Indigenous Performance in Australia (NRPIPA), which was launched by the Yothu Yindi Foundation and is now an initiative of the Musicological Society of Australia, aims to record the endangered performance traditions in a way that is led by elders and community interests.

A sweet lullaby that is not so sweet ...

In the 2000s, an American man named Matt Harding, known as 'Dancing Matt', left his job and began making videos of himself dancing in amazing cultural and tourist hotspots around the world. He danced at the archaeological site of Petra in the Jordanian desert, the Salar de Uyuni or salt flats of Bolivia, the streets of Sana'a in Yemen, among the elephants in Botswana, and even in Antarctica. The videos went viral. In the background of his videos, Harding included the hit single 'Sweet Lullaby' (1992) by the French electronic music duo Deep Forest (Michel Sanchez and Éric Mouquet).

Harding soon discovered that there was a controversy at the heart of the vocals in the Deep Forest track he had used. The beautiful singing in 'Sweet Lullaby' was from a traditional lullaby called 'Rorogwela', from the island of Malaita in the Solomon Islands. But how did 'Rorogwela' end up in a contemporary world music electronica song?

In the 1970s, the Swiss-French ethnomusicologist Hugo Zemp went to Malaita, the home of the Fataleka and Baegu peoples, and recorded a woman named Afunakwa singing the song. At the time, Zemp was working for the French National Centre for Scientific Research.[6] He had sought the right permissions from the Malaita authorities to research and record for the purposes of preserving culture.

Zemp's recording of 'Rorogwela' was included in an UNESCO traditional music album featuring an eclectic collection of recordings from all around the world – Africa, Tibet, Japan, India, Kurdistan and more. An album like this would usually have had a small circulation among interested ethnomusicologists and researchers. It was held in the UNESCO archives in Paris where it was later accessed, in the 1990s, by Deep Forest as they searched for field recordings of indigenous music for their new album.

Hugo Zemp did not give Deep Forest his permission to use the field recording, and the duo used the recording as a sample without consent from Afunakwa or her community.[7] They also failed to acknowledge the source of the song. The Deep Forest album was a worldwide hit, selling millions of copies, and some of the songs – including 'Sweet Lullaby' – were even licensed as background music for television commercials by big companies like Coca-Cola, Neutrogena, Porsche and Sony.[8] Although the lullaby resonated with worldwide audiences, Sanchez and Mouquet did not have permission to use it, or have any connection to the origins of the song back in the Solomon Islands.

Should there have been some sort of payment made to Afunakwa and her community? Musicians, producers and DJs run the risk of commodifying and misappropriating culture when they take sound recordings from other people to use as layers in their new songs. They also run the risk of infringing someone's copyright under the law. These are especially common issues now in the internet age, where content is so readily available and accessible.

Matt Harding says, 'After that 2006 video gained millions of views, I was made aware of its history. I realised I had taken something of value without compensating the right people.' Matt ended up going to the island of Malaita to visit Afunakwa's village. He met with her family and found out she had passed away. They discussed a way he could compensate the family, and resolved that he would pay the year's school fees for all of her school-aged descendants.[9] Afunakwa's story is told at conferences on indigenous intellectual property and traditional knowledge. It serves as a reminder for indigenous peoples to take care when their songs are recorded. World indigenous music that is recorded by researchers to 'preserve' culture ends up in archives spread out across the globe. The researchers and the archives must develop access processes and use protocols that consider the originating performers and their communities. It is good to see the NRPIPA developing protocols for recording, documenting and archiving Australian Indigenous music.[10]

Further, musicians who incorporate archival recordings of old song recordings must go back and seek consent, give attribution and share the benefits. There should be more collaboration with actual living Indigenous artists to enable them to continue their music as a living cultural practice.

The 1986 album *Graceland*, by American musician Paul Simon, presents a more palatable case study. For the album, Paul Simon hired

African musicians and paid them three times the fee of the American musicians he worked with. He also gave them strong credits as collaborators and paid royalties to the African performing artists.[11]

Who owns the recordings of traditional songs?

The traditional song 'Rorogwela' has been sung and handed down for generations. It comes from the island of Malaita, from the community; it is sung to children and during ceremonies. In this form, it is not protected by copyright due to the 'material form' requirement for copyright protection. But copyright does apply to Hugo Zemp's recording because now it is in material form. Zemp is the copyright owner as the maker of the recording and can now make copies and authorise others to use the recording. Australian copyright law protects musical works for 70 years after the death of the creator. A separate copyright exists in the music, the words or lyrics, the sound recording, and the performance of the song.

In Australia, we too have many recordings of Aboriginal and Torres Strait Islander music stored in archives and collections such as the National Film and Sound Archive (NFSA), or the sound collection at AIATSIS that houses 40,000 hours of audio.

But what about the local rights and obligations in communities for the use and transmission of sacred and ceremonial songs? The Western intellectual property system doesn't acknowledge communal ownership of cultural expressions that have been nurtured and passed down through the generations.

For bootleg recordings (unauthorised recordings of live performances or concerts), the performer will own half of the copyright with the maker of the recording. This creates an opportunity for Indigenous people to benefit from the sharing of their music.

There are many organisations, businesses, advertising agencies and filmmakers who want to use Indigenous music and sound recordings in their work, whether that be a short film, advertisement or educational video or for their website. This requires obtaining a licence and paying the necessary fees to the artist to use their music or sound recording. The licence may be required from the composer, lyricist, maker of the sound recording and performers with a copyright interest. Not clearing these rights may result in a copyright infringement. For this reason, if you are unsure, it is best to get legal advice before using music or sound recordings in your project – and engage Indigenous performers.

The popularity of the didgeridoo

The deep, resonant sounds of the didgeridoo (didjeridu) express connections to the land, story, knowledge and custom. The didgeridoo is originally from the north of Australia, where in Arnhem Land it is known to Yolŋu (Yolngu) people as the yidaki. In its cultural context, the didgeridoo is an instrument that only men played during ceremony, with rhythms and sequences passed down through the generations. Yolŋu man Djalu Gurruwiwi is the world's foremost authority on the yidaki. His story was featured in the exhibition *Yidaki* (2017) at the South Australian Museum in Adelaide.[12]

The band Yothu Yindi, formed in 1986 by Yolngu singer/songwriter Mandawuy Yunupingu, entwined the didgeridoo in music that draws from pop, rock and clan songs. With Indigenous and non-Indigenous musicians, the band sing in both Yolngu dialects and English, and play rock instruments and traditional instruments like clapsticks and didgeridoo.[13] They're probably best known for their famous song 'Treaty' from the album *Tribal Voice* (1991).

Today, it is common for the didgeridoo to be played by Indigenous male performers throughout the country. William Barton, a world-renowned musician and didgeridoo player, has played with Australian symphony orchestras and performs at international music festivals and concerts. The didgeridoo has also been keenly taken up by musicians and producers worldwide. This has generated debate about appropriation of traditional music and protocols, including whether women should play the instrument.

It is not my place to provide advice on specific protocols relating to the didgeridoo. A practical protocol that can also be used when playing other Indigenous instruments is to always acknowledge the source of the instrument and be respectful of its origins.

In recent times, the didgeridoo has also become a popular cultural product sold at markets for its aesthetic value rather than being played as an instrument. The rip-off market has produced overseas fakes that are imported into Australia and sold as Indigenous made. These fakes impact the sales of the many Indigenous hand-carved and hand-painted works of artistic craftsmanship, like the work of Lewis Burns, Wiradjuri man. In 2020, Lewis played didgeridoo on the Keith Urban song 'Tumbleweed', and he continues to make didgeridoos for sale.[14] If you are buying a didgeridoo, ensure you purchase one that is authentic and Aboriginal-made.

Growing national presence: Contemporary songs

When it comes to big national events, Australians want to celebrate what makes us so unique. I remember watching the closing ceremony of the Sydney Olympics in 2000. Torres Strait Islander singer Christine Anu sang 'My Island Home', a song first recorded by Warumpi Band. It's about the lead singer George Burarrwanga's home of Elcho Island off the coast of Arnhem Land, which he longed for during the time he spent living in the Central Australian desert.

Festivals around Australia and internationally like Survival Day (or Yabun), The Dreaming Festival and Laura Dance Festival are places where song is performed. Often this is where people record samples without the knowledge of the performer. It is important that Indigenous people are aware when audiences are recording their songs so they can make sure that their works are not stolen.

Embracing Indigenous song and themes in music connects us with the melody of what it means to be Australian. These are the songs our children should be singing in schools and choirs to learn about the uniqueness of their country. Gondwana Choirs, an Australian children's choir organisation, does this well and has helped to shape the Australian sound since it was founded in 1989 by Lyn Williams. In 2008, Lyn put together Gondwana Indigenous Choir to share the opportunity with Indigenous youth and to commission new works, many in Indigenous languages.[15] They follow a meaningful and engaged approach by developing relationships with Indigenous elders and cultural custodians to create new works with Indigenous content. They also have a group called Marliya made up of young Indigenous singers based in Cairns, born out of a collaboration between Gondwana Choirs and non-Indigenous musician Felix Riebl, of Australian band The Cat Empire.[16]

Gondwana Choirs follows cultural protocols for incorporating Indigenous content in its songs, focusing on consulting and involving Indigenous peoples. Their executive director, Bernie Heard, says, 'I am enormously proud of the work of Gondwana Choirs in supporting the preservation and sharing of Indigenous stories and languages. We have been honoured to work closely with the communities in the regions where we work, and our choristers view the performance of songs in Language as one of their greatest responsibilities. The *Protocols for Using First Nations Cultural and Intellectual Property in the Arts*, created by Dr Terri Janke, have been an essential framework for our extended team to refer to at every step of the process, and we also regularly refer our colleagues to consult these protocols.'[17]

The protocols in part responded to the fact that, in the past, people wrote music using Aboriginal words and themes without consulting Indigenous people. There were also songs that were offensive or not representative of Indigenous culture that were taught in schools for their 'Australiana' content. We are thankfully a long way from the Australiana song I learned to sing when I was at school, the music beamed in every week through the radio speaker at the front of the classroom. It was the song 'Tie Me Kangaroo Down, Sport' by Australian singer Rolf Harris, with its horrendous verse: 'Let me Abos go loose, Bruce ... They're of no further use.' This verse no longer appears in versions of the song and Harris later expressed regret about the racist nature of the original lyrics.[18] From the 1980s, Australian performers became more aware of Indigenous causes, with songs such as Goanna's 'Solid Rock', Midnight Oil's 'Beds

Are Burning' and Paul Kelly's 'Special Treatment' spreading the word for Indigenous rights.

As Australian creators became more aware of protocols, and the voices of Aboriginal and Torres Strait Islander musicians were empowered, the unearthing of hidden stories has continued to rise. In 2006, the Australian composer Paul Jarman wrote the popular choir song 'Pemulwuy'. Pemulwuy was the strong and fearless Eora man and leader who defended his country against the invading British in the late 18th century. However, as Paul remembers, there was little known about the story at the time. Paul was passionate about Australian history and had been writing about interesting Australian histories, including Irish, Chinese and Jewish immigrants. Yet he was conscious of the absence of Indigenous histories in compositions. He had been touring and working with Indigenous people and visiting communities, as well as working as musical director for the Deadly Awards. Paul also worked in collaboration with Gai-mariagal author and academic Dennis Foley. They got together and inspired schoolchildren from all over the Northern Beaches of Sydney to learn more about the local Indigenous history. With Dennis guiding him, Paul wrote three pieces that were sung by schools in that area.[19]

In 2006, Paul was commissioned to write a song for a small choir group in Canberra. Paul wrote a choir song about Pemulwuy, with lyrics that included some traditional language words. Paul consulted with Aboriginal friends about his work who gave him feedback to improve the song. His inspiration was a book by Aboriginal scholar Eric Willmot, *Pemulwuy: The Rainbow Warrior* (1987). 'I felt passionate about getting a history out there about Australia's first freedom fighter, an Indigenous hero,' Paul said. 'I felt slightly ashamed that our country had chosen in a way to "erase" his existence – that is the main reason I wrote the piece.'[20]

The song's first performance was in a church close to Parliament House, and it has now been performed by choirs across Australia and overseas. It opens up on a history that had been hidden. The story now reaches a wider audience, so that Pemulwuy the resistance fighter is remembered, honoured and celebrated.

Another interesting collaborative project was the song 'Yanada' by Australian indie rock band The Preatures, which features the Darug language (see chapter 2, page 44). The copyright to the song is jointly owned by Isabella Manfredi from The Preatures and Darug elder and songwoman Jacinta Tobin. They are joint composers, and royalties are shared between them. When The Preatures perform 'Yanada' on stage, they acknowledge the traditional owners. Isabella says:

> I began the process of writing 'Yanada' with question after question. There was nothing to do but ask, wait and listen. I had many reservations about writing and singing in Darug, given the complexities unique to the Sydney area's colonial history and the painful correlations between dispossession of language, culture and country. I knew it would be confronting for the music industry as well because, at the time, there was no support for Indigenous artists singing in their own languages on Triple J. The prospect of a white girl coming out and doing it would be provocative. Even with these complexities, the consensus from the Greater Sydney Indigenous community was very encouraging, and the feedback was that by following proper protocol, language can and must be cared for by everyone, no matter if you are Indigenous or non-Indigenous. Every time I sing 'Yanada' I do it from the position of being a guest. It is not my language, but I can still use the power I wield to honour it and make sure reparations are being made back to community.[21]

Protocols for better engagement

How can we best acknowledge the cultural links between traditional songs and the communities they come from? Do we recognise the performer of a traditional song as the owner of it? Is the song to be treated as folklore? The *Protocols for Using First Nations Cultural and Intellectual Property in the Arts* advises people who use old music to get permission from clan groups if the copyright owner is not known. These protocols focus on situations where traditional songs are incorporated into new music. In the past there has been a tendency for musicians to treat traditional songs as ethnographic, and not get consent to reuse them. A lesson about folk songs was learned recently from the 'Kookaburra Sits in the Old Gum Tree' case, a folk song I learned as a kid. In 2010 the Federal Court found that the band Men at Work had infringed copyright by incorporating the melody into their track 'Down Under' (1981). The original song had been written by a Melbourne teacher in 1934, but it was still in copyright, and the songwriters from Men At Work were ordered to pay a share of the royalties to the music publisher that now owned the copyright in the 'Kookaburra' song.

Ethical collaborations

We also have to consider the issues that arise now that Indigenous musicians are part of the contemporary music scene. Let's start with composing. A song can have two copyright components – the music and the lyrics – and different people may write each one. So, when Indigenous and non-Indigenous people collaborate, it is good to consider copyright ownership and ICIP protocols at the start of the writing. Who will own what? Who will sing the song? Is it appropriate for that person to sing the song?

There are many songs penned by non-Indigenous and Indigenous musicians together. APRA AMCOS, a music rights and licensing organisation for songwriters, composers and music publishers, has a composer agreement that sets out who owns what and in what percentages. However, APRA AMCOS also administers the mechanical copyright statutory licensing scheme, collecting and distributing those royalties. Many Indigenous musicians, songwomen and songmen are not members of APRA AMCOS and may get royalties collected for custodial groups. APRA AMCOS has developed protocols for collecting these royalties. In the past, traditional songs were treated as if they had no composer and were therefore in the public domain. Now these protocols recognise that royalties can be paid to the knowledge holder of the song.

Some examples of Indigenous artists collaborating on songs with non-Indigenous artists include Warumpi Band, the collaboration between Paul Kelly and Archie Roach on 'We Won't Cry' and 'Rally Round The Drum', and the Paul Kelly/Kev Carmody song 'From Little Things Big Things Grow'. It is important that collaborations of Indigenous and non-Indigenous people cover who would be recognised as composers and receive royalties.

SONGWRITING COLLABORATIONS WITH GROUPS

Songwriting collaborations often come about through youth arts programs, or other community projects. The question that arises when the song is finished and recorded is: who owns the copyright in the song? For example, a musician works with a class of schoolchildren to produce a song. They include the local language and one Indigenous girl recounts a story from her clan about a white-winged bird. The group workshops and brainstorms ideas, and the song is formed collaboratively, line by line. The song is then recorded by the musician and becomes popular. The girl's parents seek advice about whether their daughter should own copyright in the song as well. How much did the girl contribute to the finished words or music of the song? Was it more than just the idea?

This is not always clear and, as lawyers giving advice, we need to look at the facts – and any agreements that might be in place. What should the musician have done? What about the school? It can be a complex web of issues. This is why clarifying copyright is important for all musicians, but it plays out particularly for Indigenous performers, who often collaborate in groups and use music for social and cultural activities (for example, as a way to teach particular skills). They bring their own cultural stories, which only *they* may be able to use because of their link to a clan's culture. It is important to think about the copyright and the cultural protocols before embarking on these projects.

There are special issues that arise when composing and using Indigenous words (see also chapter 2). How can they be used? How should they be sung? Indigenous musicians who sing in language and share associated knowledge must be respected. What does this mean for the non-Indigenous collaborators? A song has reverence coming from country, sung in the language of ancient people. The custodians are the Indigenous collaborators, and to include the language in the song they have to broker cultural right via their obligations through a complex process. This is a fiduciary duty which so often gets left to the Indigenous partner, and it must be respected.

Agents, publishers and recording companies should also consider their approaches and look through an Indigenous lens. There have been a few agents and producers who have nurtured the talent of Indigenous musicians, such as Chryss Carr and Vicki Gordon.

Music publishers, recording companies and event promoters must consider ICIP protocols and how they engage with First Nations artists. There are growing numbers of Indigenous musicians getting signed to major record labels, performing on stages organised by big event promoters. But in bringing this cultural mix to the stage, there is a need for ICIP protocols. When collaborating with songwriting, consider the True Tracks protocols. For example, if there is Indigenous language or the song is about an Indigenous person in history or canvasses a theme, make sure you consult and engage. In live performance events, don't just bring Indigenous performers as an add-on, but make their inclusion meaningful. Bringing them on country to sing songs in another language may require consulting with local groups who are involved in the welcome to country. And it goes without saying that the Indigenous performers should be fairly paid. Another thing to look out for is the marketing of events and the inclusion of Indigenous performers. Check that your marketing and communications are presenting the Indigenous performing artists respectfully, and talk to the artist about any marketing ideas. It is offensive to make Indigenous cultures look cheap or tacky, or to present it as if it is imaginary folklore. The True Tracks principles provide a good guide – run through them as a checklist for every event. This is all part of a different, inclusive world which will see more Indigenous people bring their music to the world.

Songs of power and reclamation

Songs and music connect people, places and culture. They have the power to amplify voices, bring pride and open hearts. For people who have had their land and children taken from them, and their cultural practices threatened to near extinction, songs are a way to unite. The singer or musician can stand in their power to reclaim what was nearly obliterated from the face of the Earth during colonisation. Songs are like magical energy – a valuable currency to share and collaborate across cultures. This is where Indigenous voices must hit their heights, and should not be overshadowed but respected in collaborations.

Shellie Morris, a singer-songwriter with Wardaman and Yanyuwa roots, creates, records and performs with many different communities. Her stories are about sharing the opportunity. Since finding her birth families around 20 years ago, Shellie has spent much of her career working with remote Aboriginal communities, connecting languages to young people and celebrating languages through the creation of songs. 'My grandmother was part of the stolen generation – Borroloola stolen generation – and it was healing for me to return,' says Shellie. She has learned to sing in more than 20 Indigenous languages, many considered sleeping (see chapter 2, page 34), saying, 'We want to maintain First Nation languages and traditional song cycles.'[22]

Shellie was invited to collaborate on a music project with the Borroloola Songwomen from the Northern Territory, near the Gulf of Carpentaria, which led to the album *Ngambala Wiji li-Wunungu (Together We Are Strong)* (2012). The album features 58 traditional songs in the Yanyuwa, Garrwa, Gundanji and Marra languages, and ten contemporary songs in Yanyuwa and Gundanji language. Through a process of deep consultation, the copyright of each song was split between the women with cultural custodianship of songlines and, where applicable, Shellie Morris (in the case of the lyrics and composition of the contemporary songs). Royalties on the album sales and APRA AMCOS reporting are shared between the singers evenly. Overall copyright of the project sits with Barkly Regional Arts, Shellie Morris and the participating Borroloola songwomen.[23]

Jessie Lloyd is an Aboriginal and Torres Strait Islander musician who came to me a couple of years ago about reviving and recording contemporary Australian Indigenous mission songs from 1900 to 1999. She understood the need for proper protocols. Many of these songs had never been recorded or written down, having only been passed down orally through the generations.

Jessie started the Mission Songs Project because she wanted to bring to light the daily lives of Indigenous Australians who lived on Christian missions, reserves and state-run settlements. Throughout the project, Jessie travelled to Indigenous communities across Australia. In bringing the songs to life in her project, she sought permission from the originators and composers and, if they were deceased, their families. Face-to-face consultation was a strong part of the project, which involved consulting with families and senior Indigenous songmen and songwomen. The origin of the songs was acknowledged, and the arrangement reached was written in an agreement. Taking a cultural approach to the research process enabled elders to share their different experiences of living on missions and settlements in a culturally safe and respectful space. This approach also acknowledges the storytellers as the knowledge holders. The process of research and consulting took two years.[24]

Indigenous performing arts organisations like NAISDA Dance College and Bangarra Dance Theatre show us the connection between song and dance. When they include music in their performances, they acknowledge the connections and the custodians, and involve elders when they teach the songs to young people (see chapter 8, page 185).

The well-known Torres Strait Islander hymn 'Baba Waiar' was written by Miseron Levi of Moa Island and is performed widely, sometimes by large choirs. John Morseu, formerly at the National Library of Australia, described it as 'a little piece of Torres Strait that is spread around the world'.[25] The song was recorded by Christine Anu in the 1990s. Christine also wrote the beautiful, uplifting song 'Kulba Yaday' ('Old Talk') in the Torres Strait Kalaw Kawaw Ya language.

Indigenous singers performing and composing in their languages will gain even more recognition in the United Nations Decade of Indigenous Languages (2022–32). In the past, singing in language may have been considered a barrier for Indigenous performers, sidelining them as 'parochial'. But in the 2020s we see more opportunities for commercial use. This is where cultural protocols are a guiding framework that can assist when old songs are adapted for new songs, and can also set up consideration of the suitable use of the content, thereby respecting the cultural content.

Festivals, concerts and events

Convenors of festivals, concerts and events need to consider how they include Indigenous musicians in their line-ups. It should not be a last-minute thing or token gesture. The approach should be genuine inclusion, and musicians should be paid fairly.

Festival organisers need to think about how they engage with the traditional owners of the land that they are holding festivals on, and include an acknowledgement or welcome to country. They should also think about involving Indigenous producers and curators.

I've spoken to Indigenous performers who present at large festivals who do not feel culturally safe if there is no welcome to country or an acknowledgement of country – they do not feel comfortable singing their songs in their Indigenous language on other Indigenous peoples' land. For this reason, events and festivals that want to bring Indigenous performers should ensure connections with local Indigenous communities, and engage with them for welcomes and acknowledgements.

When promoting Indigenous musicians, festivals need to take care not to romanticise their Indigeneity, and ensure they are comfortable in how they are represented. Festivals can go too 'native' in their marketing and approach. It's important to be mindful of how Indigenous performers are juxtaposed with other themes Avoid stereotypes and romanticising culture. If you are organising a festival, be mindful of the context in which you promote Indigenous peoples and their cultures. This should be respectful – and, when in doubt, ask.

When performers are presenting traditional songs, there are protocols concerning who is allowed to perform the song, what the performer must do before they sing a song that belongs to someone else, and in what context the song can be sung. The song may have some personal, cultural or ceremonial background. Understanding that is key to how it is presented.

Of course, there have been many great Indigenous cultural festivals and gatherings that have set clear standards for the industry in programming and respect for traditional owners, elders and performers, presenting useful models for national and international events in supporting Indigenous performers. These include the Garma Festival of Traditional Cultures held in north-east Arnhem Land, and the Festival of the Dreaming directed by the talented Rhoda Roberts, a Bundjalung woman with extensive experience in bringing together Indigenous performance, including in her role as the first Head of First Nations programming at the Sydney Opera House from 2012 to 2021.

Recording and publishing agreements

There are only a small number of Indigenous record labels, such as CAAMA Music in Mparntwe (Alice Springs), which is run by an Aboriginal-owned and controlled media organisation. Performers including Letterstick Band, Lajamanu Teenage Band, Warumpi Band and Alice Skye have been recorded by CAAMA, including songs in language, covering country, pop and rock. CAAMA ensures that respect is paid to the sensitivities, cultural traditions and languages of Indigenous people, and this is reflected in their recording and production practices.

But now that Indigenous performers are getting deals with mainstream recording companies and publishers, there are a few issues to iron out. Indigenous musicians want to see publishing and recording agreements include cultural protocols – for instance, how the song might be used in the future. The context is important if you are giving rights to synchronise music in films or advertisements. Moral rights are often consented to in these agreements, but the composer of Indigenous cultural songs wants the right of integrity to continue. It must be used in the same spirit in which the song was shared.

But once recorded and published, other people can sing songs without permission, and can sing them as cover songs – so long as licensing fees are paid to APRA AMCOS. I love seeing community choirs sing songs written by Aboriginal and Torres Strait Islander musicians; they are respectful and inclusive in their approach. However, in the 1990s when I was at university, I watched a cover band perform Yothu Yindi's 'Treaty' in a pub in the Sydney's eastern suburbs, and heard them add the words 'Pass the flagon around' to the chorus. This was a song that Yothu Yindi had shared with strength. It was a call for our standing as Indigenous people to be recognised. It offended me and the other Indigenous students who were at the bar with me. We were not drunk and carrying on, but enjoying a quiet drink together. The inclusion of the extra lyrics was racist. We followed the band off stage to tell them that this was not on; they blew us off as angry blackfellas. I wrote a letter to the Sydney music magazine *On the Street* expressing my disappointment. It was published, and the week after the band's manager responded, arguing that I had no sense of humour, that it was a joke or a parody, and that Indigenous people should learn to laugh at themselves and not get so uptight. This example shows the stereotyping that we Indigenous people face, but also the way that our music can be taken and twisted away from the heart of the message.

National Indigenous Music Office

There are, however, opportunities for the respectful commercialisation of Indigenous music and song. APRA AMCOS has done work in developing Indigenous music, running programs and hiring Indigenous music officers to assist Indigenous members develop.

In 2020, APRA AMCOS established the National Aboriginal and Torres Strait Islander Music Office (NATSIMO), with musician

Leah Flanagan as national manager. The general vision for NATSIMO is to become an Australia-wide voice for Indigenous songwriters and composers. This includes advocating for cultural protocols and making sure that Indigenous people are properly paid for their work in the industry. NATSIMO also communicates with the wider music industry for collaborations and assists cultural creators.

There are many ways that the music industry can use the True Tracks principles to assist with making the industry more culturally appropriate for Indigenous musicians. It is all about recognising diversity but also about fine-tuning the industry to enable the unique sound and voice of First Nations musicians.

Where possible, the source of any Indigenous music, songs and traditional knowledge should be acknowledged, by stating the name of the performer and, if applicable, the relevant Indigenous community. This not only highlights the diversity of Indigenous communities but reinforces the autonomy and distinctiveness of Indigenous language groups across the country.

> **WHAT YOU CAN DO...**
>
> - Engage Indigenous composers and musicians for music projects, concerts and performances.
> - Discuss how Indigenous control over the music project will be exercised. Who can represent language groups and ensure clearance of traditionally and collectively owned material?
> - Talk to communities about how their traditional songs will be interpreted and represented.
> - Talk to people about the use of their names in music. If they have passed away, talk to their families.
> - Follow the Australia Council's *Protocols for Using First Nations Cultural and Intellectual Property in the Arts* and *Protocols for Producing Indigenous Australian Music*. Concerts and events should do welcome to countries or acknowledgment of

country and also have clear agreements that pay people fairly. Indigenous inclusion should not just be an afterthought.
- When you are recording Indigenous people and their traditional songs and music, get permission, and provide all the information about the intended use and future use of that recording.
- Do not record or commercialise Indigenous traditional songs, music and instruments without consent of the relevant traditional owners.
- If you do sample musical works, make sure you seek the copyright owner's permission, and seek the consent of relevant Indigenous people, including composers, songwriters (or next of kin if deceased) and custodians of the music.

Resources

Musicians and Composers: Useful Resources (Arts Law Centre of Australia): www.artslaw.com.au/information-sheet/musicians-and-composers-useful-resources/

Protocols for Using First Nations Cultural and Intellectual Property in the Arts (Australia Council, 2019): www.australiacouncil.gov.au/programs-and-resources/Protocols-for-using-First-Nations-Cultural-and-Intellectual-Property-in-the-Arts/

Protocols for Producing Indigenous Australian Music (Australia Council, 2007): www.australiacouncil.gov.au/workspace/uploads/files/music-protocols-for-indigenous-5b4bfc140118d.pdf

APRA AMCOS: https://apraamcos.com.au

National Aboriginal and Torres Strait Islander Music Office (NATSIMO): https://apraamcos.com.au/music-creators/natsimo/

National Recording Project for Indigenous Performance in Australia (NRPIPA): www.msa.org.au/Main.asp?_=NRPIPA

Notes

1. Work record, *A Song of the Natives of New South Wales*, AustLit, 2016, <www.austlit.edu.au>; Graeme Skinner and Jim Wafer, 'A checklist of colonial era musical transcriptions of Australian Indigenous songs', *Australharmony*, 2020, <https://sydney.edu.au/paradisec/australharmony/checklist-indigenous-music-1.php>.
2. Isabelle Oderberg, 'Yirrmal', *Beat*, n.d., <www.beat.com.au/yirrmal-2/>.
3. Eleanor Dixon, personal communication, 2021.
4. Miiesha, personal communication, 25 June 2020.
5. Jill Stubington, *Singing the Land: The Power of Performance in Aboriginal Life*, Currency House, Sydney, 2007.

6   Hugo Zemp, 'The/An ethnomusicologist and the record business', *Yearbook for Traditional Music*, vol. 28, 1996, p. 37, <www.posgrado.unam.mx/musica/div/pdf/GilBraga/The%20an%20ethnomusicologist%20and%20the%20record%20business.pdf>.
7   Hugo Zemp, 'The/An ethnomusicologist and the record business'.
8   Simon Frith, *Popular Music: Critical Concepts*, vol. 2, p. 72. This book has a section that goes into depth about the back and forth communications and confusion in the 'Sweet Lullaby' controversy.
9   Matt Harding, personal communication, 26 February 2021.
10 Allan Marett, Mandawuy Yunupingu, Marcia Langton, Joseph Gumbula, Linda Barwick and Aaron Corn (2006), 'The National Recording Project for Indigenous Performance in Australia: Year One in review', in Neryl Jeanneret and Gillian Gardiner (eds), *Backing Our Creativity: National Education and the Arts Symposium 2005*, Australia Council for the Arts, Sydney, pp. 83–89, <www.msa.org.au/edit/nrpipa/Backing_our_creativity_final_proceedings.pdf>.
11 Peter Munkacsi, *Freedom Cry – Cross Border IP Protection and Folk Music*, Introduction to Roundtable 1, WIPO IGC Folklore Seminar, Geneva, 23 June 2015, <www.wipo.int/edocs/mdocs/tk/en/wipo_iptk_ge_2_15/wipo_iptk_ge_2_15_presentation_peter_munk_csi.pdf>.
12 South Australian Museum, *Yidaki: Didjeridu and the Sound of Australia*, SA Museum, 2017, <https://samyidaki.com.au/>.
13 Karl Neuenfeldt (ed.), *The Didjeridu: From Arnhem Land to Internet*, John Libbey/Perfect Beat Publications, Sydney, 1997, p. 49.
14 Lewis Burns, <https://lewisburns.com>.
15 Gondwana Choirs, *Gondwana Indigenous Choir*, Gondwana Choirs, n.d., <www.gondwana.org.au/choirs/gicc/>.
16 Gondwana Choirs, *Marliya*, Gondwana Choirs, n.d., <www.gondwana.org.au/performance_choir/marilya/>.
17 Bernie Heard, personal communication, 22 February 2021.
18 Renee Switzer, 'Rolf's lyrics "a sign of the times"', *Age*, 7 December 2006, <www.theage.com.au/entertainment/music/rolfs-lyrics-a-sign-of-the-times-20061207-ge3qci.html>.
19 Paul Jarman, personal communication, 11 February 2021.
20 Paul Jarman, personal communication, 11 February 2021.
21 Isabella Manfredi, personal communication, 10 February 2021.
22 Shellie Morris, personal communication, 16 February 2021.
23 Shellie Morris, personal communication, 16 February 2021.
24 Jessie Lloyd Music, *The Research*, Mission Songs Project, n.d., <www.missionsongsproject.com/blank-page-1>.
25 John Morseu, in *Baba Waiar Composed by Miseron Levi: A Collection Conversation*, National Library of Australia, YouTube, 28 May 2017, <www.youtube.com/watch?v=nAJnJPla7KM>.

6
CROSS-CULTURAL LENS: SHIFTING THE FOCUS IN AUSTRALIAN FILM AND TELEVISION

When we were kids in Canberra in the 1970s, my dad took us to the movies to see *Storm Boy* (1976). Yolngu man David Gulpilil played Fingerbone Bill, the wise Aboriginal custodian of the land, looking after the pelican and helping the small boy who was the hero. I was happy to see an Indigenous person on the big screen for what was probably the first time. Gulpilil went on to star in many iconic Australian films, including *Crocodile Dundee* (1986), *The Tracker* (2002) and *Rabbit-Proof Fence* (2002), but back in the 1970s, Indigenous representation in film was only just starting to develop.

Fast forward to today and there is a much stronger Indigenous presence, not only in front of the camera but behind it as well. Many Indigenous filmmakers and actors are making their mark in the Australian television and film industries, creating, directing and starring in feature films, documentaries, short dramas and TV series. Actor Rob Collins, known for starring in the TV series *Cleverman* and *The Wrong Girl*, reflects on his time in the industry:

> I'm fortunate to have entered the film and television industry at a time when there's a real appetite for Aboriginal faces and stories both at home and overseas, and finally some recognition that Aboriginal filmmakers – the likes of Warwick Thornton, Leah Purcell, Wayne

Blair, and Rachel Perkins – are up there with the world's best. My first serious TV job boasted an 80 per cent Indigenous cast, an Indigenous creator and producer, and Indigenous directors and writers re-imagining Indigenous Dreamtime stories. And while there's still some ground to cover, the appetite right now for Aboriginal faces and stories is leaning toward an industry where this may become the rule rather than the exception.[1]

For Indigenous people, storytelling is a tradition that goes back for many generations, where we sat by the campfire hearing stories from elders. Storytelling in film is something Indigenous filmmakers excel at, like the internationally acclaimed artist Tracey Moffatt, known for the horror film *Bedevil* (1993), which showed at the Cannes Film Festival, the Dia Centre for the Arts in New York and the National Centre for Photography in Paris,[2] or Ivan Sen, who directed *Beneath Clouds* (2002), a story about two Indigenous adolescents escaping from their hometown in remote New South Wales. Warwick Thornton, a Kaytetye man from Alice Springs, is another acclaimed filmmaker known for the critically lauded films *Samson and Delilah* (2009) and *Sweet Country* (2017), and documentaries *We Don't Need a Map* (2017) and *The Beach* (2020). Warwick says:

> As Indigenous filmmakers we're kind of rebuilding our library at the moment, we're finally getting our voice back. And the novelists as well, and musicians and songwriters, Indigenous people artistic across the board, we're starting to actually talk our truth, an oral history that's been passed down and a different version of history – what *we* know our history as … As Indigenous filmmakers we have to be incredibly succinct and precise because this is *our* history and we don't want to go and fantasise. We've got an opportunity to speak the truth and have a dialogue.[3]

RACHEL PERKINS AND BLACKFELLA FILMS

It's true: the past few decades have seen the rise of many acclaimed Indigenous actors and filmmakers in Australia. A standout is the acclaimed writer/director/producer Rachel Perkins, an Arrernte and Kalkadoon woman and member of the Australian Heritage Council. Rachel founded Blackfella Films, one of Australia's leading Indigenous production companies. Rachel says, 'Certainly up until the '80s, the only films that were made about Aboriginal people were by non-Aboriginal people, and Aboriginal people were trying to get a bit of participation in that or control of that. And a lot of the images that had been made of Indigenous people were stereotypical, fantasies, you know. So it was very important for Indigenous people to intervene in that process, to have some sort of self-representation.'[4] Many of these films pushed the popular racial stereotypes that were offensive and mythologised Aboriginal people and culture: the 'noble savage', the 'point-the-bone native', the 'cute piccaninny' and 'going walkabout'.

Rachel has worked on major film and television productions such as *Jasper Jones*, *Redfern Now* and the pinnacle documentary series *First Australians*. After Rachel set up Blackfella Films in the early 1990s, she was later joined by the filmmaker Darren Dale, a Bundjalung man with the same passion for supporting Indigenous people to share their stories on screen. Their contribution to the Australian film and television industry has been huge, with the production of award-winning documentary series and groundbreaking dramas, championing a highly consultative approach and following protocols to protect ICIP rights.

Protocols in the film and television industries

Back in the 1990s, I worked at a small but well-known film and entertainment law practice, then called Michael Frankel and Company. My boss Michael Frankel, a respected media and entertainment lawyer, asked me to speak at a national film conference about Indigenous cultural protocols. Michael was one of the first lawyers to include ICIP clauses in contracts to provide scope for Indigenous peoples' rights in a system that favoured the legal rights holders. I remember being very nervous that day, about what I should say about the need for changes to recognise ICIP. I talked a bit too fast and couldn't wait to get off the stage, but people were pretty interested, and there were questions from the floor that I tried my best to answer.

By following protocols, we can prevent stereotypical representations and misappropriation of Aboriginal and Torres Strait Islander cultures. 'Films, video and television are powerful media: it is from these that most Australians "know" about Aboriginal people,'[5] wrote Indigenous academic Marcia Langton in her 1993 paper for the Australian Film Commission. This paper was a pivotal point for understanding the use of film and television in shaping peoples understanding of Indigenous Australia.

Historically, non-Indigenous filmmakers have not always represented Aboriginal and Torres Strait Islander people accurately or fairly. Yolngu man, painter and activist Wandjuk Marika and his community were angered by the film *Where the Green Ants Dream* (1984) by German director Werner Herzog.[6] It was a fictitious story based on real events, including the *Milirrpum v Nabalco Pty Ltd* (1971) land rights case, in which the Yolngu peoples unsuccessfully challenged the Nabalco mining company that was operating on their land. Herzog was criticised for misrepresenting Aboriginal groups, inventing Dreaming stories and incorrectly using Indigenous names. His film made heavy use of stereotypes, portraying Aboriginal culture as timeless and romantic, and Aboriginal people as silent and stoic. Most of the time the white characters, such as the biologist, speak for the Aboriginal characters while they sit in stony silence.

Another example is the film *The Chant of Jimmie Blacksmith* (1978), an adaptation of the 1972 novel of the same name by Thomas Keneally. It told the story of the Indigenous bushranger Jimmy Governor, who went on the run after committing a series of murders in response to racist maltreatment. As well as being a big-screen depiction of a violent Aboriginal man, the film and the novel generated controversy because the non-Indigenous author and director told the story from the perspective of the Aboriginal protagonist. Whose story is this to tell?

You couldn't make films like that today. The standard is much higher, with directors and film companies involving Indigenous cultural consultants and following proper protocols. As Rachel Perkins explains, 'Indigenous people are now making most of the drama, most of the documentaries themselves, and non-Indigenous filmmakers consider those issues before they go into making films on Indigenous people. They'll either employ Indigenous people as consultants or they'll employ them in key creative roles or, you know, film agencies now have Indigenous assessors on all their projects.'[7]

I once got a call from a filmmaker who was literally driving into an Indigenous community about to start filming. He had heard that he should be dealing with protocols and getting clearances before he started. His film was about body scarification practices – a sacred and secret cultural practice in some communities. Scarification is like a language inscribed on the body, with each scar carefully and deliberately placed to tell of story and identity.[8]

On the phone, the filmmaker told me that a colleague had suggested he call me about protocols. It was clear that he hadn't really considered if this was an appropriate topic for him to be exploring, let alone to speak with Indigenous people for consent. I told him to speak with a person with cultural authority and to slow it down. However, he was getting ready to film the next week. I wasn't all that surprised at his conduct – disheartened, sure, but not surprised. There have been many, many cameras pushed in Indigenous peoples' faces in communities.

Australian Rules: *The importance of consultation*

There was controversy when the film *Australian Rules* (2002) was created and released. The film was an adaptation of non-Indigenous writer Phillip Gwynne's literary hit *Deadly, Unna?* (1998), a novel based on Gwynne's experience growing up in the coastal town of Port Victoria, South Australia. The novel is a work of fiction that drew from some real events, including a traumatic incident that happened in Port Victoria in 1977, when a publican shot two Aboriginal boys who had allegedly been trying to break into his hotel.[9] Gwynne had sent the manuscript to members of the community for their input, and also copies of the book to the community,[10] but it possibly did not reach everyone.

Four years later, the making of the film and its release caused backlash from some of the Indigenous community. Some people were deeply distressed and offended that they weren't consulted in the creation of the book and the film, when the events portrayed were based on incidents that had happened to their family and friends. Despite these complaints, the film still went ahead, and the conflict it caused teaches us a lesson about the importance of following protocols. It was soon after this that Screen Australia commissioned me to write *Pathways & Protocols: A Filmmaker's Guide to Working with Indigenous People, Culture and Concepts* (discussed below).

Developing protocols

In the 1990s, a production company called Aboriginal Nations, then working with the NSW Aboriginal Education Consultative Group (AECG), developed protocols for Aboriginal Dreaming stories. Jeffrey Samuels, a Ngemba artist and friend who I had worked with at the Australia Council, was involved with them. Jeffrey was a founding member of the Boomalli Aboriginal Artists Co-operative in Sydney. The Aboriginal Nations protocols ensured that Indigenous people would be the storytellers of the Dreaming stories, and that the stories would be owned by them.

The idea of controlling the story in the film industry is one that is fraught with issues. Filmmakers are often required to acquire all the rights before they can seek financial investment in their project. Bodies like Screen Australia as well as private film investors want all rights to be clearly owned by the production company. So how does this work when an Indigenous person is sharing their story? Release forms given to Indigenous people who are telling their stories often seek rights in perpetuity for that story to be reproduced and adapted in the future. They may even waive the story owner's moral rights to the story.

For Indigenous people, signing these release forms is always a dilemma. These rights to cultural heritage are explored by the late Barry Barclay, acclaimed Māori filmmaker, in his book *Mana Tuturu* (2005).[11] If Māori are asked to sign away their stories and all rights now known and yet to be developed, he asked, how can they still be connected to that story? How can they trust the filmmaker, those who see the film and those who want to use the footage? How can they be sure that their story is not damaged in any future reproductions?

Some years later, in 2008, trailblazing creative film executive Sally Riley – head of the Indigenous branch at Screen Australia – asked me to write protocols for working with Indigenous people and culture in the film industry. Sally, a Wiradjuri woman, has done a lot of work to nurture Indigenous film and television in Australia. Sally, Nicole Stevens, Erica Glynn, Gillian Moody and Juliane T'oa from the Indigenous branch provided guidance and expertise during the project.

In preparation for the Screen Australia protocols, we embarked on a consultation process, holding workshops around the country. We talked with people in the film industry and those in front of the camera who had been asked to be part of documentaries. We asked, 'What are the issues the protocols should cover?'

Our consultations and other research resulted in a guide called *Pathways & Protocols: A Filmmaker's Guide to Working with Indigenous People, Culture and Concepts* (2009).[12] Drawn from the True Tracks principles, the guide addresses the ethical and legal issues involved in transferring Indigenous cultural material to the screen, whether writing a film from scratch or making one based on a pre-existing text – transferring story to a new medium may introduce new considerations that the written work didn't involve. The guide also built upon the work done by Bundjalung man Lester Bostock, a media pioneer who was the first Indigenous presenter on SBS Radio, who wrote a set of protocols and guidelines for SBS in 1997.[13]

Film presents challenges because it is a medium that may be widely disseminated, and because footage can be edited and reused. Films can be made of people, places and objects – both sacred and secret – and many Aboriginal and Torres Strait Islander people view this medium as a risky way of recording cultural knowledge and expression. If Indigenous people exercise their prior informed consent to the filming of Indigenous Cultural and Intellectual Property, and filmmakers follow protocols, then filming can accommodate Indigenous and non-Indigenous aspirations.

For example, in the epic historical drama film *Australia* (2008), Baz Luhrmann worked with cultural consultants for the creative elements involving Indigenous content. The film also included a warning at the start about deceased Aboriginal people. As Marcia Langton wrote, 'I was thrilled with Baz Luhrmann's compassion and good humour, and his visionary way of overcoming the guilt complex that poisons our national debate.'[14] There are other positive examples of non-Indigenous filmmakers respecting protocols and working in partnership with Aboriginal people, as described below.

The *Pathways & Protocols* guidebook also asks filmmakers to consider at the outset how their films might impact Indigenous people, how the cultural material will be respectfully presented, and how benefits will be shared with communities. There are also considerations for filming on Indigenous lands, national parks and urban areas.

Before advancing a film project, Dunghutti woman and award-winning filmmaker Darlene Johnson recommends filmmakers consider the question: 'Am I the best person to tell this story?' Indigenous writers and directors often bring specialist cultural knowledge to their work, and have experience in cultural heritage management and cross-cultural exchange.[15]

It is always important to uphold cultural protocols when filming Indigenous people. This should never occur without consent, especially when it concerns Indigenous elders. There are mourning protocols that make the display of deceased people's images inappropriate. Many Aboriginal people do not want images or voices of deceased people to be seen or heard. Many ABC and SBS programs and news stories include a warning about depictions of people who have passed, as do some more commercial films. Release forms should always include a clear warning to the family if the footage will be used beyond the life of the Indigenous person who appears in the film. What happens if someone dies when you are filming? Filmmakers need to think about these things; they need to answer these questions and establish clear protocols before filming begins, and definitely before screening. The time required to negotiate and clarify these issues needs to be factored into the filmmaking schedule.

Lynette Wallworth's Collisions

Collisions (2016) is a 17-minute virtual reality (VR) film directed by Lynette Wallworth, acclaimed Australian artist and director known for using emerging technology. Created in close consultation with the Ngaanyatjarra and Martu people, *Collisions* tells the story of Nyarri Morgan, Ngaanyatjarra elder living on Martu lands, and the Martu people of the Pilbara region in Western Australia. When Nyarri was a kid in the 1950s, he witnessed a British atomic bomb test at Maralinga in the South Australian desert. To experience the film, you wear a virtual reality headset, entering the landscape and Nyarri's world.

It was always really important to Lynette to build the project around the protocols, and really embed the protocols at every stage of the project. She is especially careful to give proper attribution to the Indigenous owners of the stories she engages with. 'This film followed protocols. I can't just arrive there, I have to be invited, someone has to ask me to come and there has to be a reason for my coming. So that's in the beginning of this film: I say "Nyarri has a story he wants to share and that's why we're travelling."'[16]

Terri Janke and Company helped Lynette with the protocols that would make Nyarri the main storyteller and also involve members of his family. His grandson Curtis Taylor, a Martu artist and filmmaker who narrated the film with Lynette, was a Director's Attachment and adviser helping with locations, story development and translation, and he travelled to the US to view the finals of the work. We wrote a contract to protect Nyarri's cultural heritage rights. The shot lists were drafted in advance and reviewed by Nyarri and his family.

Protocols were also important because Lynette was using new technology. As she explains, 'VR will soon hit in a big way, very possibly to become ubiquitous. In the window of time that exists before then I wanted to make a work that has protocols of meeting at its core. Nyarri's world is only available to me to visit, and in this work through the technology, that invitation is extended to the viewer.'[17] Nyarri and his family got a chance to familiarise themselves with the drones that would be used for the project – so they had a complete understanding of what Lynette was planning to shoot and how. This then also meant that Nyarri and elders of Parnngurr community could provide feedback on how high or low the drone should go, to avoid secret or sacred sites. As Lynette explains, 'The agency in *Collisions* belongs to Nyarri. When I put the camera down in front of him, he said, 'It has sixteen eyes.' I replied that it has sixteen eyes and four ears. From that moment, Nyarri [and elders of Parnngurr community] become the one who decided what was seen and what was not to be seen, what was told and what was not told.'[18]

Collisions toured internationally and won many awards, including a Sundance/Skoll Stories of Change Impact Award and a News & Documentary Emmy Award. The project was also a chance for Nyarri to advocate for his country and his culture, and raise awareness on the dangers of nuclear weapons. It was screened as part of a disarmament film series alongside the UN General Assembly's First Committee on Disarmament and International Security meetings in 2016 – after which the UN voted for the first time in favour of a global ban on nuclear weapons. Lynette went on to use these protocols to make *Awavena* (2018), a VR film about the Amazonian Yawanawa people. *Collisions* is a really good illustration of a project that uses protocols to create a deeper impact. It's not a linear checkbox exercise – Lynette understood that the principles such as self-determination should be embedded at every stage.

Cleverman: *Dynamic consent*

Film and television writer/director and Kamilaroi man Ryan Griffen says, 'At a time when unique stories are in demand, this country holds 60,000 years worth of stories that will blow the world's audiences away.'[19] Adapting his own comic book series, Ryan created *Cleverman*, a six-part sci-fi television series that combines Dreaming stories and sci-fi. He wanted to create an Indigenous superhero who his son could look up to, the Cleverman, based on the Hairypeople in Dreaming stories. He worked with Goalpost Pictures producer Rosemary Blight to produce the series. The Indigenous creative team included Ryan, writer Jon Bell, directors Wayne Blair and Leah Purcell, and production designer Jacob Nash. The series boasts an 80 per cent Indigenous cast, including Hunter Page-Lochard, Rob Collins, Tysan Towney and Deborah Mailman.

The series includes tales about totems, such as the story that follows the relationship between a boy and a willie wagtail. Ryan spent seven years obtaining permission to use these cultural stories, and said that protocols were a way that he could speak to elders. Shows like *Cleverman* are years in the making. The Indigenous storyteller must earn the trust of the Indigenous knowledge custodians and obtain the right to play with themes and adapt them into new stories.

Because the show was inspired by Indigenous Dreaming stories, extensive consultation was undertaken with individual knowledge holders, language centres and communities to bring the language, creatures and messages onto screen in a culturally appropriate way. The Hairypeople in *Cleverman* speak the Gumbaynggirr language, from the mid-north coast of New South Wales, alongside the northern NSW language of Bundjalung, which was taught to the actors in those roles. The Kamilaroi language was also included for the character names. Ryan met with me in my office just before the filming of the first series. He wanted to ensure that the trust people put in him was covered in his agreement with the production team. He was assigning over the rights to make the story, but he wanted to make sure there was integrity and attribution.

Ryan's creative process demonstrates how filmmakers can use the protocols of dynamic consent and ongoing consultation, while always showing respect, to maintain Indigenous culture into the future. All of these protocols are in line with the True Tracks principles.

Ten Canoes: *Collaborative filmmaking*

The critically lauded 2006 film *Ten Canoes* is perhaps the most trailblazing example of an Indigenous/non-Indigenous partnership on a big-screen production. It is the result of a collaboration between Dutch-Australian director Rolf de Heer, co-director Peter Djigirr, and the north-east Arnhem Land community of Ramingining. The making of this film demonstrated that it is possible to integrate Indigenous intellectual and property rights into the filmmaking process. The copyright in the film is shared between de Heer and the Ramingining community; they are recognised as co-producers. *Ten Canoes* went on to inspire community projects which they called *11, 12, 13* and *14 Canoes*. These community-led initiatives included art exhibitions and filmmaking projects for youth. What I like about the film is its telling of a pre-colonisation story of an intertribal conflict in northern Australia. It's an Indigenous story, with an all-Indigenous cast, told in an Indigenous language.

Ten Canoes was a good illustration of how a filmmaker can engage in positive and productive collaborations with Indigenous people. Belinda Scott, who has a long association with the artists of Ramingining, assisted with the making of *Ten Canoes* and was an 'integral associate' of the project.[20] She was very committed to it. The story focuses on ten men from Ramingining, who make canoes so they can hunt for magpie goose eggs. Minygululu is the group's leader and elder, and he has three wives. The young man Dayindi, the main character, covets Minygululu's youngest wife. Minygululu deals with this potential conflict by telling Dayindi an ancestral story that involves a similar scenario. The film touches on many more cultural issues, covering aspects of cultural lore including payback (makaratta), canoe making and ceremony. It is set both in the past (centuries ago, before the coming of white people to Australia) and in the Ganalbingu mythical past.[21] To include these cultural concepts in the film, the directors and producers needed to constantly consider protocols, involving many consultations with the Ramingining community.

The idea for the film sprang out of connections between Rolf de Heer and David Gulpilil, the internationally acclaimed Yolngu actor who narrates *Ten Canoes*. The pair met while making another film, *The Tracker*, in 2000. David invited Rolf to Ramingining where they spent time and decided to make a film together.[22] The film was inspired by a photograph of ten canoeists taken by Donald Thomson,[23] an anthropologist who spent time working in Ramingining in the 1930s. Thomson's work includes 2500 photographs and documents recording Yolngu customs, ceremonies, hunting and daily survival.[24]

Rolf de Heer visited Ramingining a number of times before filming started. This was so the community could become more familiar with him and to broaden community consultations.[25] Rolf consulted the community about the storyline. There were essentially three storytelling problems. First, some of the essential elements of the story had to be clarified. For example, the goose egg–gathering expedition (depicted in the photographs) was no longer practised, and it had been decades since a swamp canoe had been made. Rolf discussed this with the community at length, and the community agreed to make the canoes. Senior men used the Thomson photographs to work out how to sew the canoes, which was also an act of cultural revival.

Second, the story needed to have drama so that it would accommodate the cinematic expectations of a western audience. However, this was complicated by the fact that the Ramingining community had valued the time when Thomson had lived with them. They did not want it portrayed as a time of conflict. Third, the Thomson photos, highly valued recordings of the people's cultural history, were in black and white. The Ramingining community was eager to have the film's representation of the photographs remain faithful to their original colour scheme. But the film had to be in colour because of the investment agreement.

The colour-film problem was solved by the addition of a creative narrative device. It was decided that the dramatic part of the story would be set in mythical times. According to Yolngu community members, 'anything was allowed to happen' during the mythical times, so deviating from the black-and-white colour scheme of the Thomson pictures was allowed. This creative adaptation of Yolngu custom made it possible for the character Minygululu to relate a dramatic and cautionary tale to Dayindi (and the audience) during the goose egg hunt, which was filmed in black and white. In this way, 'a script which pleased both cultures' was made possible.[26] Rolf de Heer's respect for protocols, specifically for upholding Yolngu cultural integrity, made this cross-cultural creative process a success.

The film was the first to strongly feature an Aboriginal language, a Yolngu language, predominantly Ganalbingu – although David Gulpilil, the narrator, speaks in English. The Ramingining community is made up of 16 clans which speak up to eight Indigenous languages. Some of the actors in *Ten Canoes* came from different clans, and spoke different languages, but they could all understand each other. Several cast members could speak English well, and as filming commenced, they would work through communications problems with the others.[27]

The filmmakers had to factor in cultural considerations in the casting. The ten men in Thomson's canoes photograph have been identified over the years, and many people in Ramingining are related in some way to at least one of them. Those with the strongest claims to heritage chose themselves to play their ancestor, as they saw it, and that was the end of that. The women were chosen because of their kinship relationships to the main men.[28]

Before the public release of *Ten Canoes*, the filmmakers held a screening for the community in Ramingining in December 2005. It was a chance for the community to see the film on country and to experience it with those who had contributed to it. For the official launch, Ramingining community members were flown to Adelaide to attend the world premiere of the film. At the Adelaide Festival, it screened in two sell-out sessions.

To amplify the benefits generated for the Yolngu creative collaborators, the filmmakers facilitated the development of seven other projects of interest to the Ramingining community. These included *11 Canoes*, a video-making and editing course for young people; *Twelve Canoes*, a website about the culture, people and environment of Ramingining;[29] *13 Canoes*, a multimedia arts and cultural project that featured the objects and artefacts made for the film; and *15 Canoes*, a music preservation project. These additional projects are evidence that Rolf de Heer and the other non-Yolngu creative partners were committed to honouring their cultural and ethical obligations to share the benefits equally with their Yolngu partners.

Through consultation with the relevant Indigenous people on issues to do with casting and storyline, the filmmakers were able to resolve a number of conflicts. Art, props and photographs made by local women were also used in the film. For example, woven bags, spears and woomeras were included via the exhibition at Bula'bula Arts, the local Aboriginal art centre, and this was a great way of ensuring community control and ownership.[30] *13 Canoes*, the exhibition of the art, props and photographs from the film, toured after its release, giving Ramingining artists even broader exposure and recognition.

Sydney Olympics: Sacred Wandjinas in film

Wandjinas are the sacred creator beings of the Kimberley Aboriginal people. Worrorra, Ngarinyin and Wunambal Gaambera people have painted images of Wandjinas on the walls and ceilings of rock shelters and continue to depict the Wandjina in art today. In the opening ceremony of the 2000 Sydney Olympics, film recordings of Wandjina paintings were featured, beaming across the world. Bundjalung arts director Rhoda Roberts was involved with the Sydney Organising Committee for the Olympic Games (SOCOG). Her influence ensured that the use of the Wandjina images followed protocols and that they were used in the right context. There were limits on what the images could be used for and where they could be displayed. The footage couldn't just be used for anything that the filmmakers wanted.

Torres Strait Islander filming and BBC protocols

The 'Australian art' episode in the BBC series *Hidden Treasures of ...* (2011) followed Welsh comedian Griff Rhys Jones as he travelled to the Torres Strait.[31] Rhys Jones took with him a photograph of a mask held in the British Museum. He travelled from island to island in search of the mask's origin and the answer to his question: 'Can traditional arts survive in the modern world?' Looking for proof, the producers wanted to film the sacred rocks on one of the islands. They needed permission to film on Island land. The Island committee elders met to discuss the request. On film, we see the elders talking in language with knitted brows, heads down. Griff Rhys Jones looks on nervously, then says to the camera, 'It doesn't look to be going very well.' The elders decided not to allow filming because they want to keep their rock art secret. They were worried that their art would be copied without reference or respect – not by the filmmakers, but by others who might see it, who they would never know.

The BBC now has its own protocols that guide journalists and filmmakers in their engagements with indigenous peoples all over the world. These protocols outline the importance of obtaining consent and respecting indigenous peoples' privacy. The guidelines recommend, 'If a community has indicated either verbally or by other actions that they wish to be left undisturbed, their wishes normally should be respected.'[32] They also outline the need to ensure accuracy in reporting, especially in translating the words of indigenous peoples and representing the traditional elements of indigenous cultures. The guidelines also counsel filmmakers to examine their preconceptions about indigenous peoples, reminding them of the damage that can be done to indigenous peoples by stereotyping. It is good to see that some of the most powerful and recognisable names in global television are now creating formal protocols for filming indigenous peoples.

Legacy films: Films made before protocols

In the very early days of the film camera, indigenous peoples and their cultures were recorded by outsiders conducting anthropological research expeditions. In Australia, the first capture of Indigenous culture through the lens of a film camera occurred on Mer (Murray Island) in the Torres Strait. It was 1898 and the English scientist and anthropologist Alfred Cort Haddon was documenting life in the Torres Strait Islands as part of a Cambridge University anthropological expedition. As well as collecting cultural artefacts and genealogies, the researchers used early movie cameras and wax cylinders to make the first film and sound recordings of the region.[33] Since then, cameras have captured a lot of Indigenous content ranging from ethnographic accounts of culture, to sacred ceremonial practices, personal histories and Indigenous knowledge about the land, animals, plants and important events.

When Blackfella Films made *First Australians* (2008), a documentary series on Indigenous stories from the start of colonisation, Darren Dale said they 'looked for the Aboriginal voice' in the film archives.[34] Rachel Perkins says, 'Mostly we are known as natives, blacks, savages and at best Aboriginals or Islanders. The bulk of the early written records are from non-Indigenous Australians. So of course, whatever snippets of evidence there is or reporting of voices is skewed through a certain view. Our challenge was to use the records, but to bring a contemporary Indigenous interpretation to them.'[35] Similar to the way Bruce Pascoe offered an Indigenous reinterpretation of colonial documents for his book *Dark Emu*, the makers of *First Australians* used non-Indigenous recordings to tell Indigenous stories on film.

Archival films

Archives and collections have inherited a lot of films with significant Indigenous content and are now faced with the issue of how to best manage the material and access to it. Often, the copyright owners are not the Indigenous people captured on film, even though they are the owners of the cultural expressions embodied in the film. (See chapter 14 for more on the management of archives.) This is because under Australian copyright law, the filmmaker is recognised as the owner of the copyright in the film – or, when films are made for another person and fees are paid, the copyright belongs to the person who commissioned it. This is a concern for Indigenous people whose stories and knowledge have been recorded in the past without proper consent. Filmmakers owned the films and were in control of crafting the stories.

An interesting story told by Dr Jane Anderson clarifies the sorts of cross-cultural issues that arise when dealing with the Indigenous film archives. Anderson is an Associate Professor of Anthropology and Museum Studies at New York University, and has a background in IP and the protection of Indigenous cultural heritage. Anderson accompanied her friend Dr Joe Gumbula (now passed) of the Gupapuyngu clan in the Northern Territory on a visit to the National Film and Sound Archive in Canberra to look at the collections related to his community. They came across a film recording of Joe's father Djawa teaching a ceremony to some children, including Joe, in the 1950s.[36] Fifty years on, Joe was able to view the film, his father and, for the first time, himself as a child. Joe, like other Indigenous Australians, was able to reclaim this material, taking it back to his community so that they could establish their own archive.[37] For Indigenous Australians, there are concerns about the use of film footage of ceremonies. From a legal standpoint, the copyright owners and depositors have the right to control access, but the Indigenous cultural owners do not. Indigenous people seek to have a say over how these important materials are used, and who gets access to them.

Archives like the NFSA that hold significant Indigenous content in their collections have developed policies and protocols for access and reproduction. The NFSA Collection holds more than 25,000 Indigenous related works, including films, photographs, videotapes, audio tapes and other forms of media, some containing culturally sensitive materials that depict traditional cultural ceremonies or practices. As a storehouse of information related to family, ancestors and traditions that are being revitalised, the NFSA benefits greatly from using ICIP guidelines and

ICIP protocols to ensure this material is stored and accessed in a respectful way.[38]

The Australian Institute of Aboriginal and Torres Strait Islander Studies (AIATSIS) Audiovisual Archives has an Access and Use Policy for their collection, which includes film and television materials (see chapter 14, page 309). The policy covers sensitive content, restricting access to materials containing secret and sacred information, and information that is personal or defamatory.[39]

Indigenous themes in Hollywood movies

Hollywood's use of indigenous themes in movies and cartoons, its savage representations of world indigenous peoples in tales of 'cowboys and Indians' and the romanticised mythologies surrounding the 17th-century Powhatan woman Pocahontas have all been of concern for Native Americans. Famously, the Native American actor and activist Sacheen Littlefeather stood on stage at the 1973 Academy Awards ceremony and declined the Best Actor award that Marlon Brando had just won, on Brando's behalf, making a political statement about Hollywood's poor treatment of Native Americans on film. (Brando boycotted the awards in protest over the issue.) Older cinematic representations of indigenous peoples such as the 1950s TV series *The Lone Ranger* and Disney's 1937 cartoon *Little Hiawatha* heavily relied on negative and/or simplistic stereotypes. More recent depictions are starting to change this, such as in *Lilo & Stitch* (2002) and *Moana* (2016), where indigenous people were consulted in the production process.

In 2019, Disney released a statement about its past use of indigenous story in its films. The company stated that it would treat indigenous stories in a respectful way and consult with indigenous people. This took place with the sequel to the hugely popular film *Frozen*. A written agreement was signed between the Walt Disney Company and the Sámi people.[40] The Sámi people's lands cover parts of what is now Finland, Russia, Sweden and Norway. The agreement set out Disney's 'desire to collaborate with the Sámi in an effort to ensure that the content of *Frozen*

2 is culturally sensitive, appropriate and respectful of the Sámi and their culture.'[41] The agreement also referenced free, prior and informed consent (FPIC), and benefit sharing. These are principles that are also included in the True Tracks principles. It is good to see a leading film studio changing its approach to working with Indigenous stories and peoples.

Back in 2009, the film *Avatar*, directed by James Cameron, was released globally. The film drew on Indigenous themes to create the plotline, characters, costumes and even the language of the Na'vi people. *Avatar* was very much a film about world indigenous cultures. Although it's not clear how, it is said that James Cameron did undertake some consultation, such as with the United Nations Permanent Forum on Indigenous Issues (UNPFII). The film went on to make over A$4 billion worldwide at the box office. It was considered a leader in 3D technology. There were Blu-ray releases, extended cuts, books and merchandise released. Cameron, the director, presented his film at the UNPFII, and has been praised by some Indigenous groups as an advocate.

However, other commentators slammed *Avatar* for perpetuating stereotypes of Indigenous peoples by creating a mishmash – a fictional 'faux indigenous world' drawn from commonalities of world indigenous cultures. It does not copy one indigenous cultural group but takes the concepts of indigenous languages, cultural expressions and traditional knowledge and adapts them to create an anthropology of the Na'vi and their environment in the land of Pandora. *Avatar* has also been characterised as another 'white saviour film', with Māori academic Dr Rawiri Taonui saying, 'The white guys and the neo-liberals save the people rather than the indigenous people saving themselves.'[42] There is very little depiction of indigenous resistance in the film, yet we know that indigenous peoples resisted and survived colonisation all over the world.

After the film's release, I read of several claims against Cameron's company that alleged copying. In 2010, I came across a blog by the artist Christine Sherry, a young Canadian artist who claimed that James Cameron had appropriated artworks of blue people that she had created and posted on her website. Sherry's figures are blue but do not look like the Na'vi people. I noticed that the blog was taken down shortly after.

Cameron has said that the idea of tall blue people came from a dream his mother had. It is unlikely that a person could claim that the idea to make the people blue had been copied. The Smurfs are blue, and Hindu deities are depicted with blue skin.

The paraplegic theme was alleged to have been taken from the short story 'Call Me Joe' (1957) and novella *The Avatar* (1978) by American writer Poul Anderson. The 1957 story has as its main character a paraplegic who can telepathically connect with an artificially created life form in order to explore the planet Jupiter.[43] The cover of the short story was also reported to have a blue alien figure on it. While several film websites allege similarities between Anderson's works and the *Avatar* film, as far as I can ascertain, there has been no legal action commenced by the estate of Poul Anderson.

Nevertheless, the film is considered to be aligned to environmental and indigenous rights movements. *Avatar* has been labelled anti-mining and anti-American, and criticised by conservative commentators as pushing a left-wing anti-American agenda.[44] Protestors for environmental rights painted themselves blue. In addition, jumping on its pro-environment reputation, eco-friendly tourism experiences also make connections to the film. Films of this magnitude do bring attention to indigenous peoples and the impact of colonisation through a fictional lens, which hits at the heart rather than head and can support indigenous rights.

Celebrating David Gulpilil

At the 2019 NAIDOC Awards in Canberra, David Gulpilil won the Lifetime Achievement Award. He wasn't present because he is not well. We all stood up for a standing ovation when the breathtaking montage of his acting career was screened. Then his two beautiful daughters went up on stage to receive the award and gave such a heartfelt speech that there was not a dry eye in the house. They formally acknowledged Rolf de Heer in their acceptance speech on behalf of their father. Rolf has become a good friend of the family and they were very respectful of Rolf's contributions to Gulpilil's life and career. Their meaningful and highly productive working relationship is evidence of all that can be achieved when protocols are respected and negotiated between Indigenous and non-Indigenous film artists.

> **WHAT YOU CAN DO ...**
>
> - If you are a non-Indigenous filmmaker, ask if you should be the one to tell this story through film.
> - Enable Indigenous creatives, filmmakers and actors to tell their own stories.
> - Ensure appropriate negotiation of rights for the Indigenous stories shared, particularly traditional stories that are used as narrative threads on screen.
> - Do not romanticise and mythologise Indigenous culture and people. Speak to Indigenous people or, better still, work with Indigenous writers and advisers to develop appropriate stories.
> - Use of languages should be checked, as should uses of art and music. Check all licences for content in a film.
> - Use releases that list details rather than being too vague. Ensure that Indigenous people who are being filmed understand rights, and that all clearances are properly understood and in writing.

Resources

National Film and Sound Archive of Australia (NFSA): www.nfsa.gov.au

Marcia Langton, 'Well, I heard it on the radio and I saw it on the television': An Essay for the Australian Film Commission on the Politics and Aesthetics of Filmmaking by and about Aboriginal People and Things, Australian Film Commission, Sydney, 1993.

Michael Leigh and Walter Saunders, Hidden Pictures: Colonial Camera, Australian Film Commission, Sydney, 1995.

Pathways & Protocols: A Filmmaker's Guide to Working with Indigenous People, Culture and Concepts (Terri Janke for Screen Australia, 2008): www.terrijanke.com.au/pathways-protocols

Guidance: Reporting and Portrayal of Tribal Peoples (BBC, 2019): www.bbc.com/editorialguidelines/guidance/reporting-tribal-peoples/

Susan Goldberg, 'For decades, our coverage was racist. To rise above our past, we must acknowledge it', National Geographic, 12 March 2018: www.nationalgeographic.com/magazine/2018/04/from-the-editor-race-racism-history/

Marcia Nickerson, *On-Screen Protocols & Pathways: A Media Production Guide to Working with First Nations, Métis and Inuit Communities, Cultures, Concepts and Stories*, imagineNATIVE, Toronto, 2019: https://iso-bea.ca/download/on-screen-protocols-pathways/

Notes

1. Rob Collins, personal communication, 9 March 2021.
2. Art Gallery of New South Wales, *Tracey Moffatt*, AGNSW, n.d., <www.artgallery.nsw.gov.au/collection/artists/moffatt-tracey/>.
3. Warwick Thornton, *Warwick Thornton on the Role of Indigenous Filmmakers | TIFF 2017*, TIFF Originals, YouTube, 16 September 2017, <www.youtube.com/watch?v=YmAvnfdYMVs>.
4. Rachel Perkins, *Rachel Perkins Discusses Indigenous Filmmaking in Australia* [2004], National Film and Sound Archive (NFSA), YouTube, 27 February 2014, <www.youtube.com/watch?v=tDtEHA6_0d8>.
5. Marcia Langton, 'Well, I heard it on the radio and I saw it on the television': *An Essay for the Australian Film Commission on the Politics and Aesthetics of Filmmaking by and about Aboriginal People and Things*, Australian Film Commission, Sydney, 1993.
6. Wandjuk Marika and Jennifer Isaacs, *Wandjuk Marika: Life Story*, University of Queensland Press, Brisbane, 1995, pp. 138–40.
7. Rachel Perkins, *Rachel Perkins Discusses Indigenous Filmmaking in Australia*.
8. Australian Museum, *Aboriginal Scarification*, Australian Museum, 2018, <https://australianmuseum.net.au/about/history/exhibitions/body-art/aboriginal-scarification/>.
9. Stephen Gray, 'Shaking the skeleton of principles: Teaching Indigenous legal issues in intellectual property law', *Ngiya: Talk the Law*, vol. 4, 2012, p. 9, <www.austlii.edu.au/au/journals/NgiyaTLaw/2002/9.pdf>.
10. Phillip Gwynne, personal communication, 19 February 2021.
11. Barry Barclay, *Mana Tuturu: Maori Treasures and Intellectual Property Rights*, Auckland University Press, Auckland, 2005.
12. Terri Janke, *Pathways & Protocols: A Filmmaker's Guide to Working with Indigenous People, Culture and Concepts*, Screen Australia, Sydney, 2009, <www.terrijanke.com.au/pathways-protocols>.
13. Lester Bostock, *The Greater Perspective: Protocol and Guidelines for the Production of Film and Television on Aboriginal and Torres Strait Islander Communities*, SBS, Sydney, 1997, <http://media.sbs.com.au/home/upload_media/site_20_rand_1000072370_the_greater_perspective_sbs.pdf>.
14. Marcia Langton, 'Why Greer is wrong on Australia', *Sydney Morning Herald*, 23 December 2020, <www.smh.com.au/politics/federal/why-greer-is-wrong-on-australia-20081222-73kk.html>.
15. Terri Janke, *Pathways & Protocols*, p. 21.
16. Lynette Wallworth, *Discussion: 'Collisions' tell tales with VR*, CGTN, YouTube, 8 August 2016, <www.youtube.com/watch?v=e1C5lxD3P7k>.
17. Lynette Wallworth, 'Collisions: "This story I carry is until the end"', *World Economic Forum: Agenda*, 22 January 2016, <www.weforum.org/agenda/2016/01/collisions-this-story-i-carry-is-until-the-end/>.
18. Lynette Wallworth, 'Collisions: "This story I carry is until the end"'.

19 Ryan Griffen, 'Imagine the untold stories we'll find with more people of colour on television', *The Guardian*, 13 July 2017, <www.theguardian.com/commentisfree/2017/jul/13/imagine-the-untold-stories-well-find-with-more-people-of-colour-on-television>.
20 'The Crew', *Ten Canoes Press Kit*, n.d., p. 35, <www.metromagazine.com.au/tencanoes/pdf/TheCrew.pdf>.
21 Vertigo Productions, *Ten Canoes Production Notes*, Vertigo Productions, n.d., <www.vertigoproductions.com.au/ten_canoes_production_notes.php>.
22 Vertigo Productions, *Ten Canoes Production Notes*.
23 The image was DF Thomson, *Goose egg hunters poling themselves through the Arafura Swamp*, April 1937.
24 Susan Jenkins, 'Colliding Worlds at Tandanya; *13 Canoes* at the South Australian Museum', *Art Monthly Australasia*, no. 189, May 2006, pp. 16–21.
25 Vertigo Productions, *Ten Canoes Production Notes*.
26 'A story to please two cultures', *Ten Canoes Press Kit*, n.d., p. 11, <www.metromagazine.com.au/tencanoes/pdf/background.pdf>.
27 Vertigo Productions, *Ten Canoes Production Notes*.
28 Terri Janke, 'Avatar dreaming: Indigenous cultural protocols and making films using Indigenous content', in Matthew Rimmer (ed), *Indigenous Intellectual Property: A Handbook of Contemporary Research*, Edward Edgar, Cheltenham, UK, 2015, p. 182.
29 *Twelve Canoes*, <www.12canoes.com.au>.
30 Rolf de Heer, speech at the Sydney Film Festival, 2006.
31 Modern Television (Producers), 'Australian Art', *Hidden Treasures Of ...*, episode 1, 2011, <www.bbc.co.uk/programmes/b00z09hp>.
32 BBC, 'Guidance: Reporting and portrayal of tribal peoples', *Editorial Guidelines*, BBC, 2019, <www.bbc.com/editorialguidelines/guidance/reporting-tribal-peoples/>.
33 Queensland Government, *Mer (Murray Island)*, Queensland Government, 2018, <www.qld.gov.au/atsi/cultural-awareness-heritage-arts/community-histories/community-histories-m/community-histories-mer>.
34 Australian Screen, *First Australians (2008–2008)*, NFSA, n.d., <https://aso.gov.au/titles/series/first-australians/>.
35 Rachel Perkins, keynote address, *2Deadly: The 2006 ATSILIRN Conference*, University of Technology Sydney, 21 November 2006, <https://atsilirn.aiatsis.gov.au/conferences/conf06/papers/Rachel%20Perkins.pdf>.
36 Jane Anderson, 'Access and control of Indigenous knowledge in libraries and archives: Ownership and future use', paper presented at *Correcting Course: Rebalancing Copyright for Libraries in the National and International Arena*, American Library Association and The MacArthur Foundation, Columbia University, New York, 5–7 May 2005, p. 3, <https://ccnmtl.columbia.edu/projects/alaconf2005/paper_anderson.pdf>.
37 Jane Anderson, 'Access and control of Indigenous knowledge in libraries and archives', p. 3.
38 NFSA, *Indigenous Connections*, NFSA, n.d., <www.nfsa.gov.au/about/what-we-collect/indigenous-connections>.
39 AIATSIS, *Access and Use Policy: AIATSIS Collection*, AIATSIS, 2018, p. 8, <https://aiatsis.gov.au/sites/default/files/2020-09/aiatsis-access-and-use-policy-2018.pdf>.
40 Aroha Awarau, 'Disney embraces indigenous peoples and their stories', *Te Ao Māori News*, 24 November 2019, <https://teaomaori.news/disney-embraces-indigenous-peoples-and-their-stories>.
41 Bailee Abell, 'Disney agreed to respectfully portray indigenous people in "Frozen 2"', *Inside the Magic*, 20 November 2019, <https://insidethemagic.net/2019/11/disney-

frozen-2-cultural-appropriation-indigenous-people-ba1/>. The signed agreement between Disney and the Sámi people can be found online at: <www.samediggi.fi/wp-content/uploads/2019/09/Agreement_WDAS_SAMI.pdf>.

42   Charlie Gates, '*Avatar* recycles indigenous "stereotypes"', *Stuff*, 14 January 2010, <www.stuff.co.nz/entertainment/3201437/Avatar-recycles-indigenous-stereotypes>.

43   Max Kennerly, 'Does copyright law care if James Cameron's *Avatar* ripped off parts of "Call Me Joe"?', *Litigation & Trial* [blog], 2 November 2009, <www.litigationandtrial.com/2009/11/articles/the-law/for-people/does-copyright-law-care-if-james-camerons-avatar-ripped-off-parts-of-call-me-joe/>.

44   Miranda Devine, 'Hit by the leftie sledgehammer', *Sydney Morning Herald*, 2 January 2010, <www.smh.com.au/opinion/hit-by-the-leftie-sledgehammer-20100101-llpp.html>.

7

HOW THE STORY GOT ITS BLACK VOICE BACK: AMPLIFYING INDIGENOUS VOICES IN WRITING

Stories are the heartbeat of Aboriginal and Torres Strait Islander cultures. They encode knowledge and hold messages of law, country and kinship. They pass on our memories of the past, our experiences and our triumph of survival. They connect us to each other, the land and the seas. Our cultural continuum, from one generation to the next, owes its existence in part to the power of story – spoken, danced and, more recently, written down and published. More than words, stories are a cultural code, a passport, an inheritance and a treasure for those who have faced near-devastation. For me, stories keep me strong. They can share so much, and empower us to do great things. Our Indigenous stories are *our* stories, when so much has been taken from us.

My friend Professor Anita Heiss, Wiradyuri woman, has always known about the power of story to empower people and to bring about social change. As Anita writes, 'I want to create resources that encourage young Aboriginal people to read. I think it's important Aboriginal people today can see themselves in the Australian literary landscape. I want to empower other young Australians to tell stories important to them as well. There are so many gaps in the published story of Australia today – I am motivated to fill those gaps.'[1]

I have known Anita since university and have watched her continuously work hard to advance Indigenous voices in the Australian literary scene. The author of over 15 books, from non-fiction and poetry to 'chick lit', Anita advocates for other Indigenous writers and is a Lifetime Ambassador of the Indigenous Literacy Foundation. Anita's main mantra is 'our stories, our way'. This is because so much past writing on Indigenous themes has been cultural appropriation – Indigenous stories used by non-Indigenous authors. These stories have been told in ways that are offensive and that diminish culture. Indigenous storytellers speaking their words or performing their culture have had their stories written by others; these writers then become the owners of our stories through the workings of copyright law.

There is a need for greater understanding to enable the true voices to speak, and to access the economic, social and cultural benefits that go with authorship. The Indigenous story is getting its black voice back, and protocols have been – and continue to be – instrumental in delivering this.

The rise of Indigenous writing

When I was a kid, there were not many books written by Indigenous people. There were some about Indigenous people by non-Indigenous authors. Colin Thiele's children's book *Storm Boy* (1964) featured the Aboriginal character Fingerbone Bill. Other books by non-Indigenous writers that included Indigenous characters were Jeannie Gunn's *We of the Never Never* (1908), Katharine Susannah Prichard's *Coonardoo* (1929), Xavier Herbert's *Capricornia* (1938), Mary Durack's *Kings in Grass Castles* (1959) and Thomas Keneally's *The Chant of Jimmie Blacksmith* (1972).

Publishing has become more accessible to Indigenous people in the past 20 years, and it has been great to see the rise of Aboriginal and Torres Strait Islander authors publishing books, from children's books to romance, history and fiction. Many have achieved national recognition and awards for their works, including Noongar author Kim Scott (*Benang: From the Heart*, 1999), Wiradjuri author Tara June Winch (*The Yield*, 2019) and Waanyi author Alexis Wright (*Carpentaria*, 2006), all of whom have won the Miles Franklin Award.

There were a number of trailblazers before them, and we should all be thankful to them for the hard road they had to travel. The social activist Oodgeroo Noonuccal (Kath Walker), a descendant of the Noonuccal people of Minjerribah (North Stradbroke Island), is recognised as the first published Indigenous Australian poet. Other early writers include David Unaipon, the first published Indigenous author; Kevin Gilbert, the Indigenous playwright known for *The Cherry Pickers* (1968); and Dick Roughsey, known for writing children's picture books in the 1970s.

In the 1980s and 1990s, there was a surge of Aboriginal and Torres Strait Islander life writing. Sally Morgan's *My Place* (1987), an autobiography of finding Aboriginal heritage, was a bestseller that opened up an understanding of the complexities of Indigenous identity. There was also the honest and open-hearted memoir *Don't Take Your Love to Town* (1988) by Ruby Langford Ginibi, Bundjalung woman. *Follow the Rabbit-Proof Fence* (1996), by Doris Pilkington Garimara, was loosely based on the experiences of her mother, and detailed the long walk of three children from a children's home back to their family country in Western Australia after being taken from their families. The book was adapted into a very successful 2002 film directed by Phillip Noyce. Kenny Laughton's *Not Quite Men, No Longer Boys* (1999) is an autobiographical account of Laughton, an Aboriginal boy from the bush, who undertook a tour of duty in Vietnam. The story of *Auntie Rita* (2005), told by her daughter Jackie Huggins, was a respectful way for an author to share the memories of her mother.

Since 2000 there has been a great acceleration of writing as we have continued to publish and share our stories with the world. Some other prominent writers in the Indigenous Australian literary scene include Melissa Lucashenko, Kim Scott, Ali Cobby Eckermann and Larissa Behrendt, to name just a few. Up-and-coming writers in the spotlight include Jannali Jones and award-winning poet Ellen van Neerven. Ellen says, 'I was the only Aboriginal student in my year in my creative writing degree. I thought I had to follow the group but suddenly I had this feeling of another approach, a sort of stronger way that I could reclaim who I was and write myself on the page.' Ellen's collections of poetry *Comfort Food* (2016) and *Throat* (2020) explore family, memory and cultural belonging. Ellen says, 'There's a lot of things that I want to write about. I feel like there's so much injustice in this country and I wish that poetry and writing were ways to combat that injustice, or to heal. I'm not sure if it can ever be enough. So I just do the little bits that I can.'[2]

Indigenous authorship and identity

I want to address a controversial area: Is claiming another's identity in the narrative of a book a literary device? Should a non-Indigenous writer be able to fictionally take on an Aboriginal character identity in a narrative? These questions present interesting challenges.

In the past, publishers have been caught out. One of the most memorable literary scandals involved *My Own Sweet Time* (1994), published by Magabala Books, a prominent Indigenous Australian publishing house based in Broome, Western Australia. *My Own Sweet Time* was believed to be the autobiography of the author, Wanda Koolmatrie, a Pitjantjatjara woman from South Australia and member of the stolen generations. In 1996, the book won the Dobbie Literary Award for women writers, the judges praising it as a 'distinctive new voice in the growing genre of Aboriginal women's writing'.[3] It was also a prescribed text for Aboriginal studies in high school and university, and was even included in a NSW Higher School Certificate exam.[4]

On the eve of the award ceremony, Magabala Books discovered that it was a hoax – the author was actually non-Indigenous man Leon Carmen, a taxi driver from Sydney writing under a pseudonym. Carmen had carefully mimicked the style of life writing by Indigenous women who were gaining literary acclaim at the time. Carmen's book worked to confuse the publisher and the award conveners. He took on the last name of a well-known SA Aboriginal family, and he never disclosed he was the author when he applied for an award that had been established to encourage the voices of Indigenous women to be published.

An 'Indigenous' person is an Aboriginal or Torres Strait Islander person. The definition used since the 1980s contains three parts:

1. descent – you have Indigenous ancestors
2. identification – you must identify with this heritage
3. community – you must be accepted by the community that you live in or come from.

It is generally standard for arts funding bodies, like the Australia Council for the Arts, to ask for written confirmation in the form of a letter from an Aboriginal or Torres Strait Islander organisation or a certificate of Aboriginality, which requires sign-off by an Indigenous organisation. This practice aims to stop false claims. Some Indigenous artists and writers are offended when they are asked for written proof of Aboriginality. It takes them back to the 'dog tag' days when Aboriginal people were required to carry a Certificate of Exemption, which was an assimilationist tool. However, certificates of Aboriginality can be useful to avoid confusion and hoaxes like the Leon Carmen example. Many Indigenous literary award panels now also require letters of Aboriginality or statutory declarations to be provided for a book to be eligible for an Indigenous award.

Don't turn sacred culture into fantasy!

Non-Indigenous writers, historians, editors and journalists have a history of representing Indigenous people in extremely offensive and harmful ways. Indigenous people have been described in the diaries of early European settlers and explorers, including those who sailed on James Cook's *Endeavour*, and First Fleet officers like Watkin Tench; in books by non-Indigenous authors and historians; and in journalism and politics. Whether these are personal histories or shared cultural stories, Indigenous peoples are concerned about their stories being made publicly available without prior consultation and consent. Even more troubling is the possibility of these stories being distorted and misconstrued. Worse still, Indigenous themes and stories have been exploited for a quick buck by authors who ignore how their work may misrepresent and offend the living people and culture.

An example of what not to do concerns the bestseller *Mutant Message Down Under* (1994) by Marlo Morgan, a non-Indigenous writer from the United States. Originally self-published in 1992 as *Walkabout Woman: Messenger for a Vanishing Tribe*, the novel was marketed as a true account of Morgan's own spiritual experiences with a group of Indigenous people in Central Australia who she called the 'Real People'. She writes about learning how to communicate through hand signals and mental telepathy, as well as learning body transformation and being initiated to enter a sacred site. Having transferred this knowledge to Morgan, the Indigenous group decide to die out as they are upset with the way the world is going.

Morgan has made a living travelling around the United States to give lectures on the novel[5] and she was even featured on *The Oprah Winfrey Show*. She eventually admitted that the work was fiction and apologised to 'any Australian Aboriginal person if she has offended them in any way'.[6] HarperCollins is reported to have bought the rights to the book for US$1.7 million and republished it as fiction, this time including a disclaimer at the beginning that states 'This book is a work of fiction inspired by actual events.' However, Morgan maintained this was only to protect the identity of the tribe. It has been translated into over 20 languages and sold millions of copies worldwide.

Understandably, the book deeply offended Indigenous people. Indigenous Australian lawyer and writer Professor Larissa Behrendt, a Eualeyai/Kamillaroi woman, was scathing of Morgan: 'Morgan manipulates our culture's values and ideas in support of her own beliefs, hoping her audience will know no better. That's reprehensible, even when disguised as fiction … I am angered by her lame, hideous attempt to cloak her lack of integrity in fiction.'[7]

This is an example of what not to do when writing about Indigenous culture. The sacred in Indigenous cultures shouldn't be tampered with. White people should not write about the sacredness of Indigenous spirituality or ceremonial beliefs, especially in ways that are romanticised to fit into some idea of an ancient quest for self-enlightenment through finding a 'spirit guide'. We also find offensive stories that make sacred themes part of their storyline but do not allow enough time to unravel the deep nature of this business. For instance, if you are writing a story that uses the action of pointing the bone, or mentions a sacred ceremonial cave, perhaps you should stop and consider if you should be telling this story. You should at least speak to living Aboriginal people about your writing. In the New Age realm, where people feel spiritually drawn to the sacred and mystical dimensions of indigenous cultures, it's very common for these sorts of things to happen. People feel connected to indigenous cultures at a deep spiritual level but use them in a way that is extremely inappropriate and derogatory.

While it's common for writers to dream up imaginary characters and take on different voices in their novels and stories, this isn't necessarily appropriate for depicting the life experiences of Indigenous peoples whose voices have been ignored and silenced in the past.

Copyright favours the person with the pen

It was once common for outsiders to write down and publish Indigenous stories without consent in 'myths and legends' books that contribute to Western concepts of the Dreaming. Traditional stories transferred through the generations for thousands of years, with no single creator, were often treated as free for the taking by non-Indigenous authors, editors and publishers with an interest in Indigenous culture. When they do not properly attribute the source or the Indigenous storyteller, publications of this kind suggest the stories are from a bygone culture of a distant time and place. The New Zealand publisher Alexander Wyclif Reed published a collection of Aboriginal creation stories in the book *Aboriginal Legends: Animal Tales* (1978).[8] In the introduction, Reed describes the stories as 'coming from tribes scattered across the continent', but there is no mention of which tribes. Reed also retold stories from other cultures, like those of Polynesia. Because they are so old, the stories weren't subject to Western copyright laws, so it was unlikely that permission was obtained, and I assume that no royalties were shared.

Under Australian copyright law, the copyright owner will automatically be the person who wrote the story down into material form. Clearly this is problematic when Indigenous stories and knowledge belong to the Indigenous storyteller and their family or clan group.

An interesting example concerns David Unaipon, the Ngarrindjeri man featured on the Australian $50 note who is celebrated as the first published Indigenous author. He is also one of the first victims of literary theft. Unaipon focused on creation stories, highlighting the similarities between Aboriginal and European spirituality. In the 1920s he submitted his writing material section by section to the publishers Angus & Robertson, who paid him a sum of £150 and edited the material into book form.[9] In 1930, it was published in England as *Myths and Legends of the Australian Aboriginals*, with the authorship and copyright assigned to William Ramsay Smith, a Scottish anthropologist and physician. It wasn't until the 1990s that the appropriation of the work was discovered by Adam Shoemaker and Stephen Muecke, who arranged for the copyright to be legally transferred back to Unaipon's family. In 2001, the original manuscript was republished under David Unaipon's name, with his original title *Legendary Tales of the Australian Aborigines*.[10]

Intellectual property laws do not protect oral-based cultures, but in fact allow the taking of them. Copyright is the relevant intellectual property law that allows authors to own their stories, and control how they can be reproduced, used or adapted. The foundations of copyright are built on the invention of the printing press. The written word is the currency of copyright. So, writing down Indigenous stories takes us into a culturally risky space where authors can write and own stories in which they have no claim, no connection and no responsibility. This situation is shared by other indigenous peoples around the world who have oral cultures, and whose traditional knowledge and stories have been reproduced and written as fables by writers not from that culture. This is why in the WIPO Intergovernmental Committee (IGC) there is a move to include folk tales, folk poetry and riddles as traditional cultural expression, which will therefore require consent before publishing and reproducing. African and Native American stories are often retold around the world without any connection to the story owners, and they are changed along the way, adding insult to injury. In some instances, the attribution falls away or is too generic, and this is where the cultural connection starts to be severed.

The *Copyright Act 1968* (Cth) provides creators of literary works with the rights to own and control their written stories. Although you don't have to register your work for it to be protected by copyright, it must be written down or put in material form. Oral stories, the main form of many Indigenous stories, are not protected by copyright. So, when an Indigenous story is written down, copyright will come into play, but it will belong to the person who is reducing the story to the written form.

Ultimately, it's ideal for the Indigenous person to be the copyright owner of the work. An example of this is the life story of Hazel McKellar, an Indigenous woman, that was written down by Kerry McCallum from tapes of Hazel recounting her life experiences. This resulted in the book *Woman From No Where* (2000), with the copyright in the book owned by Hazel. This shows the willingness of a non-Indigenous author – Kerry McCallum was a friend of the family – to tell Hazel's story while recognising the importance of not alienating her or her family from the story. Hazel died in 2003 but her family continues to be in control of that story and is still friends with McCallum.

International appropriations of story

Indigenous people see stories as part of culture that are owned communally and passed down, an approach that is at odds with Western notions of individual ownership and authorship. Worldwide, indigenous peoples call for recognition that the ownership of traditional stories is collective and continuing, and that permission for publishing such collectively owned material should be sought – with cultural integrity and proper attribution.

Cultural appropriation is the adoption of elements of a minority culture by members of the dominant culture. It is not cultural exchange. It perpetuates the unequal balance that stems from colonialism and the continuing imbalance of power that pervades those societies. Non-Indigenous people writing about Indigenous people should be aware of this power dynamic and challenge themselves – first, to ask if they should be writing this story, and second, if they should ask an Indigenous cultural adviser about a character or story that is included.

I recommend that you recognise the power imbalance and respect the True Tracks principles. Specifically, consider if there are any restrictions in telling a particular story to the public. When working with Indigenous stories, you need to consult directly with us. Don't assume you have expertise.

A common issue for non-Indigenous people writing about Indigenous peoples is the use of inappropriate technology. Terms such as 'full blood' and 'half-caste' are offensive. Words like 'gin', 'savage' and even 'tribe' can be seen as outdated. There are guides that can help you with this; some are listed at the end of this chapter. Challenge your writing skills and find alternatives. And remember to always use capitals for 'Aboriginal' and 'Indigenous' when writing about Indigenous Australians.

Non-Indigenous writers and protocols

At the Sydney Writers' Festival in 2010, I gave a talk on how the right to tell and guard stories is an Indigenous cultural right. I spoke about how Indigenous peoples' stories shouldn't be treated as being in the public domain, and that consultation and consent is needed to include their life stories and histories in books. It isn't enough to slightly alter a story and use different names because you could still harm culture and offend people. This happened when Phillip Gwynne's literary hit *Deadly, Unna?* (1998) was adapted into the 2002 film *Australian Rules* (see chapter 5, page 141). The protocols I wrote for Screen Australia not long after this – called *Pathways & Protocols: A Filmmaker's Guide to Working with Indigenous People, Culture and Concepts* – are applicable even when a film is based on a pre-existing text, as transferring the story to a new medium may introduce new considerations that the written work didn't involve.

Given the problematic history of Indigenous representation and misappropriation in Australian literature, can non-Indigenous writers depict Indigenous culture and people in their work today?

I think the answer is yes, if you carefully take the right steps, following protocols such as proper consultation and consent procedures. This not only keeps culture strong and prevents the misappropriation of Aboriginal and Torres Strait Islander cultures, but leads to creating meaningful relationships between Indigenous and non-Indigenous people.

Non-Indigenous Australian author Kate Grenville wrote the award-winning novel *The Secret River* (2005).[11] Grenville consulted with members of the Darug community, including Uncle Colin Gale and Auntie Edna Watson, respected Darug elders, during the writing of the book. The draft of the novel was read by Melissa Lucashenko, an Indigenous writer, and John Maynard, an Indigenous historian. Grenville said that they 'tactfully pointed out several big mistakes I'd made (e.g. having Darug play didgeridoos in 1816)'.[12] The process enhanced her understanding of cultural issues and made her book richer and more sensitive to the issues. While the book still received some criticism, her approach showed a keen willingness to do the right thing when writing about Indigenous culture and histories.

Paruku: The Desert Brumby (2014) by the Australian author Jesse Blackadder is a children's book based on a true story of a 12-year-old non-Indigenous girl who travels to the remote Kimberley desert. The girl is travelling with her father, a horse vet employed by the crown prince of Dubai to capture wild brumbies for his stables. As the novel progresses, the girl becomes attached to a majestic young stallion named Paruku and is faced with the reality that the horse will soon lose his freedom. Although Blackadder was non-Indigenous, she included a substantial amount of Indigenous content such as the word 'Paruku', the Indigenous name for Lake Gregory, where the brumbies live. There are also Indigenous characters in the story. Blackadder, who died in 2020, adopted an approach to consultation with the Indigenous community that successfully implemented writing protocols for a non-Indigenous author, and her approach offers guidance to other non-Indigenous writers wishing to make use of ICIP in their works.

In 2018, there was a difficult lesson for NewSouth, the publisher of this book, involving the book *Deadly Woman Blues: Black Women & Australian Music*. Written by Clinton Walker, a non-Indigenous Australian music journalist, it profiled many Aboriginal and Torres Strait Islanders who have contributed to the Australian music scene over the years. Walker had previously written a book called *Buried Country: The Story of Aboriginal Country Music* (2000) that shone a light on the history of Aboriginal country music in Australia. This book was well received and was accompanied by a music album and documentary film. When *Deadly Woman Blues* was released, some of the Indigenous women musicians who were featured were surprised as there had been no contact with them. Some, including Nardi Simpson from the Stiff Gins and Jessie Lloyd of the Mission Songs Project, were outraged that the book had been published when they hadn't been properly consulted. This meant that their voices were not included and they had no control over how their personal stories were represented. The book included errors in their biographies and interpretations that were offensive to the women.

Deborah Cheetham AO, Yorta Yorta Opera singer, composer and founder of Short Black Opera, slammed the book for its inaccuracies, poor research and offensive tone. The book got Cheetham's birthplace wrong, stating she was born in Cummeragunja. This was particularly distressing for Cheetham as it denies the true story of her birth. Given that Cheetham was stolen from her mother from a hospital in Nowra, this error and the interpretation of her feelings around first meeting her mother were disrespectful. The book described Cheetham as an 'Opera Snob' and also depicted Cheetham as wearing a suit, which she rarely wears. Cheetham says, 'he chose to show me in a suit and tie to illustrate his point that he believes me to be a cross-dresser'.[13] Cheetham spoke out, naming the issue clearly: 'The problem was not the book. The problem was the process and set of assumptions, not the concept of the book itself. It is lazy and it takes liberties.'[14] Walker said, 'I should have followed protocols and consulted and checked and am now reflecting on my processes as a writer. Given all this, withdrawing the book from sale is the right decision. I apologise unreservedly to the women for any hurt I have caused.'[15] NewSouth Publishing also apologised to the women, withdrew the book from circulation and began reviewing its editorial guidelines. This included the development of clear processes and ICIP protocols for the publisher and its authors. We were able to work with them on the development of these protocols.

Secret and sacred information

In the 1970s, anthropologist Charles Mountford caused a stir when he published *Nomads of the Australian Desert* (1976), a book that exposed sacred and secret information about the Pitjantjatjara people of Central Australia. The Pitjantjatjara people had showed him this information in confidence. He had taken lots of photos in his field work in the decades prior and compiled them in this 600-page publication, of which he was now the copyright owner. Here there are two problems: Mountford had exposed secret cultural information, and he was now the copyright owner of the book under copyright law. The Pitjantjatjara Council took him to the Supreme Court of the Northern Territory on the grounds that he had shared confidential information that was restricted to a group of initiated men. The Council won the case, stopping publication in the Northern Territory. But it continued to be distributed in wider Australia and internationally, and you can still find that book with its offensive cover in some libraries.

There are many language dictionaries and texts by anthropologists about Aboriginal people that include detailed content about Aboriginal culture that is of a sacred, secret, sensitive or personal nature. Incredible amounts of Indigenous knowledge and cultural expressions have been recorded in books, field notes, reports and language dictionaries by a range of outsiders – linguists, anthropologists and university researchers. You may still come across these sorts of books in second-hand shops. The right of knowledge holders to maintain the secrecy of their knowledge and other cultural practices is important. Protocols should be followed before Indigenous knowledge is shared in writing.

Protocols for sensitivity readers

We get emails from all around the world from authors who want to write about Indigenous themes and characters and want an Indigenous person to read their work for advice. An Indigenous cultural sensitivity reading

ENGAGING INDIGENOUS SENSITIVITY READERS

1. **Choose the right person**
   - They should be Indigenous – Aboriginal or Torres Strait Islander.
   - They should have connections to the topic/subject matter.
   - They need familiarity with the proposed market, such as young adult fiction, or history.
   - Check with Indigenous organisations like the First Nations Australia Writers Network (FNAWN) or other organisations related to the topic.

2. **Give them a brief and negotiate a fee**
   - The reader will not rewrite, but they can help identify any parts that might be offensive.
   - Lead the sensitivity reader to any particular concerns that you have.
   - Keep it highly confidential – trust that the reader will keep it confidential.

3. **Dealing with feedback**
   - The reader only gives feedback. If issues are identified, they must discuss these with the author/publisher. Can the material be changed or dealt with? Are there risks that need to be managed?
   - You can engage more than one reader if needed.

refers to the process of having an Indigenous person (or people) read a manuscript and check the cultural content. It is a good idea to have someone read the manuscript for this purpose, but also to make it better. This is not censorship; it enables writing that is better informed. They are experts that can help the book be better.

Indigenous writers and protocols

Indigenous writers also follow cultural protocols when writing about Indigenous culture and themes. For us, there can be repercussions with family and community. Dr Jared Thomas, Nukunu man, has written several books, including *Calypso Summer* (2014) and *Songs That Sound Like Blood* (2016). Jared says that it is important to always ask permission to represent the things you wish to. This becomes part of the process of writing about culture. 'You get to know the sensitivities that you may not have been aware of when you started. For instance, secret sacred areas are not pointed out to people so it's important to ask permission to include certain places in your narrative.'[16] Asking people helps you navigate any sensitivities within your narrative.

In *Calypso Summer*, Calypso, a young Nukunu man, works at a health food shop where his boss pressures him to collect native plants for natural remedies. Calypso then visits family in the Flinders Ranges to learn more about the cultural knowledge of his ancestors. Jared was careful not to name any Nukunu plants that had healing or medicinal properties. He explained, 'I didn't want foragers, particularly commercial foragers, looking for Indigenous plants for new medicines or foods, so I intentionally did not name any Nukunu plants to protect the knowledge and to protect the cultural eco-systems.'[17] The book has been a success and is being developed into a television series, which will take the story to an even wider audience. There will be more consultation as the story moves from the page to the screen..

Professor Anita Heiss followed protocols in writing *Yirra and Her Deadly Dog, Demon* (2007) with students from La Perouse Public School to co-create a story. Heiss ensured that the principles of attribution, and recognition and protection were paramount in *Yirra*, with its copyright being jointly held by Heiss and La Perouse Public School. Heiss also upheld the principle of benefit sharing: a clause was included in her contract with the publishers to ensure that the royalties for the novel (including the advance) would be split 50/50 with La Perouse Public School. Students at the school also received complimentary copies of the book on the launch day. Other key principles that shine throughout *Yirra* are those of interpretation and integrity, with Heiss consulting with the student co-authors to break down negative stereotypes of Indigenous peoples, and showcasing the lives and experiences of the young Aboriginal children who helped create the novel.

Ryan Griffen, who wrote the *Cleverman* comic book series inspired by Dreaming stories and adapted it to a television series (see chapter 6, page 146), spent several years consulting with community elders on how he should appropriately depict Indigenous stories in a new work that would have mass appeal.[18] Ryan talks about getting permission:

> I travelled a long way into the centre of Australia to seek permission from an elder to share a story of that Country in *Cleverman*. I sat with the elder on Country. We spoke about the songline and listened to the river. The power of the story struck me with awe. I was so honoured to be given the right to transfer it to the screen.[19]

Wiradjuri author Tara June Winch was mindful of respecting culture in her book *The Yield* (2019). *The Yield* looks at the effects of dispossession on Indigenous culture, land and familial connections. She includes the story of Albert 'Poppy' Gondiwindi, a grandfather who is working to pass on the Wiradjuri language and stories of his people as he approaches his death. He is writing a dictionary that she includes at the end of the novel. Many language words and phrases also appear throughout the narrative. To include Wiradjuri language, Tara made sure she consulted with the broader community. She also consulted with Wiradjuri language practitioners who are experts in the field. Connecting with language custodians and knowledge holders ensured that her use of Wiradjuri aligned with the broader interests of the community. (See chapter 2, page 41.)

In 2021, Anita Heiss released her novel *Bila Yarrudhanggalangdhuray (River of Dreams)*, the first Australian work of commercial fiction with an Aboriginal title. Reimagining life in the time of the great flood in Gundagai in 1852, Anita wanted to honour her Wiradyuri ancestors. She drew her inspiration from the story of Wiradyuri men Yarri and Jacky Jacky saving townspeople as the flood waters rose. The use of traditional language, culture and knowledge in the novel were all carefully considered in line with the *Protocols for using First Nations Cultural and Intellectual Property in the Arts*. This was very important for Anita. She felt the responsibility to write authentically to reflect her ancestors in an honourable way. I think she achieved this. This is my favourite book of Anita's. There are so many intertwining story circles, like ripples in water. The themes of love, place and belonging are positioned with the images of the Wiradyuri people, animals and plants, the references to family cultural themes and the river itself. *Bila Yarrudhanggalangdhuray* is an excellent example of how protocols can enable a work to flourish with cultural vitality.[20]

Indigenous publishing

Indigenous publishing houses such as Magabala Books in Broome do much to support Indigenous storytellers and advocate for protocols. Magabala, Australia's oldest independent Indigenous publishing house, was first established in the 1980s by Kimberley elders who had noticed the increasing number of non-Indigenous writers and PhD candidates recording Indigenous stories in the Kimberley region. Elders were particularly concerned about poor practices regarding copyright, royalties, and failure to return resulting publications and storyteller materials back to communities. They decided to establish their own publishing house to take control of their stories. Nimunburr and Yawuru woman Rachel Bin Salleh is the publisher at Magabala. Rachel says, 'As an Aboriginal publisher, I believe in deep listening [to our creators].

There is as much said in cultural silence as there is in the noise of words and white-speak.'[21]

Anna Moulton, the Magabala CEO, says, 'In collaborative projects it's crucial that the Indigenous storyteller is determining the story they want to tell and how it is told. While the story may be written in collaboration between an oral storyteller and non-Indigenous writer, our contracts ensure copyright belongs to the storyteller and/or their community, as appropriate to the project.'[22]

Other Indigenous publishing houses include Aboriginal Studies Press in Canberra, IAD Press in Alice Springs and Batchelor Institute Press in Batchelor, Northern Territory. These Indigenous publishing houses follow protocols to help keep the cultural essence of a story intact. At Batchelor Institute Press, 'Elders, communities and protocols guide where copyright is assigned. For clan-owned stories, ICIP may be attributed to the clan, and copyright to a community organisation and/or creators. Each community has a different approach, which is why proper consultation is so crucial.'[23] An ICIP statement sits alongside the copyright statement for publications that include traditional knowledge.

Butterfly Song: *Writing my own family's stories*

I grew up listening to stories about my family. These stories became the fabric of my imagination and my identity. They were about strong women who lived in times of limited choices. I saw my own life experiences reflected in theirs, although in many ways they seemed worlds apart.

The connections went through my pen and onto paper when I wrote my novel *Butterfly Song* (2005). I wrote a fictional story based on family history, on my mother's recollection of her life and the lives of her parents. But it is also my story. It is part of my heritage. Do I have the right to tell my mother's stories? Do I inherit them? Do I pass them on to the next generation of my children?

I was lucky enough to be given a mentorship with the Australian Society of Authors in 1992, which enabled me to work with the skilled and patient mentor Pearlie McNeill. Pearlie imparted so many tips and was able to get me to write a book at a time when I had a young family and a growing legal practice. The process of writing took more than five years and involved a lot of talking with my mother, Joanna Janke, because the story of my grandparents was told through her eyes. I worked closely with her; she read lots of drafts and receives some of the royalties. While some events and literary sequences in the novel are not based on fact, much of the story is autobiographical and includes characters based on family members or events drawn from family experiences. In order to include this material, which is not only my story but my family's story, I had to consult with all family members referred to in the book, even if I used different names or contexts in the novel.

What I loved the most about the whole process was how it contributed to healing for my mother, for me and for our family. When she received a copy of the final book, she spent the day reading it in bed and said it was a very emotional experience for her to relive the deeply buried family memories and reflect on how these are still felt in our lives today. She loved it because revisiting the stories helped her to mourn the death of her parents and heal. Writing that story made me stronger, and it made my relationship with my mother stronger too. When the book was launched in Sydney, my mother came down from Cairns to celebrate.

Butterfly Song was published in Australia and also translated into French (as *La Chanson du Papillon*) for publication in Tahiti and France. I was ecstatic when I found out that Tahitian students had created a photograph inspired by the first passage of the book. The work was featured in an award-winning collection by students completing their Master of Education degrees at the University of French Polynesia, in 2018. I was very honoured that they were moved by the experience, and I hope that the voice and strength of the story will inspire others to create and share their own – and be strong in their Indigenous cultural identity.

I wanted to share the power of story with my children too. When my daughter Tamina was a young child, we wrote a book together called *What Makes a Tree Smile?* (2003). Some years later, my son Jaiki and I wrote *Kin Island* (2011) about a trip he took to the Torres Strait Islands to connect with his heritage. *Kin Island* was part of an Indigenous education series called Yarning Strong that was commissioned by Laguna Bay Publishing. The writers of the series closely followed writing protocols, and the books are used in classrooms as teaching resources.

Respecting Indigenous stories

What are the standards that Indigenous writers, authors, journalists, publishers and editors should be following to respect Indigenous rights to story? The Australia Council for the Arts' *Protocols for Using First Nations Cultural and Intellectual Property in the Arts* are a good start. Based on the True Tracks framework, they aim to recognise Indigenous ownership of traditional stories. The protocols state that if writing up traditional stories involves the verbatim transcription of an oral story from specific informants, then permission, attribution and ownership of the material should always be recognised.[23] This is also the case for using Indigenous languages in your writing – it is necessary to consult and work with Indigenous communities about the use of language in your writing work (see chapter 2).

The protocols promote working respectfully with authors. I think the key point to remember is the storyteller's connection to the story is a very important thing to respect. Indigenous people guard their right to their stories; these stories are like cloaks of identity. We understand that the story is a connection tool, an identifier, and that it holds power. Editing and altering this can be problematic.

Life stories should be treated carefully. Have the people who the story is about been involved? Have they had a chance to approve and review the stories about them? The writer and the story owner should be on the same page about how the story is represented. It can be deeply troubling for Indigenous people when writers and publishers engage with their stories without respecting their wishes. One recent example is a commissioned local Aboriginal history, the story of two elderly people, that a company paid a historian to write. The historian and the elderly people disagreed on the voice, and there was a difference of values. This deeply upset the people whose story was being told, and their health was affected. The historian thought she was writing the historical truth. However, given that the story was told through the eyes of the elders, they wanted to put their own interpretation on it. It is not resolved. The elders do not want the story published.

Lucy Treloar, a non-Indigenous Australian author, knew she was on controversial ground when she was figuring out how to include an Indigenous story in her novel *Salt Creek* (2015). Although she was drawing from her own family history, it involved a history and a past connected to the Ngarrindjeri people of the Coorong, South Australia, and surrounding areas. She said, 'I felt filled with conflict the whole time and worried whether I was re-enacting that cultural thing which I was also critiquing, that idea that I could just march in and do what I wanted.'[24]

Treloar looked to the Australia Council's protocols, then wrote to Indigenous leaders to talk about including a strand of non-fiction about the Ngarrindjeri people. They responded enthusiastically and were looking to negotiate the final approval of the manuscript in line with the Australia Council protocols. But after learning more about Ngarrindjeri culture, Treloar decided that it wasn't her story to tell and focused on the non-Indigenous narrator's perspective instead.[25] This, I think, exercises a deeper understanding that Indigenous voices need the space to be amplified.

WHAT YOU CAN DO ...

When writing about Indigenous people, it is important to always communicate and consult with the relevant Indigenous people in authority and seek their consent for your project. Even if the author is Indigenous, there is still a need to consult with traditional owners and knowledge holders when writing about their knowledge and culture. Indigenous people have identified a number of particularly important protocols when engaging in the communication, consultation and consent process:

- Identify the relevant people to discuss the intended use of Indigenous knowledge in the writing. Consent should be sought from each custodian – this may mean asking different communities for permission.
- Be prepared for the possibility of consent being withheld. For example, there may be more than one group with custodianship of a creation story, so all groups must be consulted, and consent obtained from each one. Also note that if a creation story is written from a verbatim transcription, then permission, attribution and ownership of the oral story must be recognised.[26]
- Take thorough notes when interviewing informants, and return all photographs, news clippings, recordings and artworks.
- Keep the relevant Indigenous people informed and provide regular updates.
- Go back and seek approval and confirmation of facts once the first draft is completed.
- Be flexible with time. The consultation process requires patience and time. Remember that people have to speak to others – your writing may impact a whole community.

When a non-Indigenous writer includes Indigenous content, the True Tracks principles should be considered, especially:

- **Respect**: Is the writer following the protocols, and can they demonstrate that they have followed them? Have they understood the issues?
- **Consent and Consultation**: Have Indigenous people been consulted?
- **Interpretation**: Should the non-Indigenous writer be the person to tell the story, or refer to that knowledge in that way? Are they telling a whole story, or including a character? What is the point of view being represented? How is the knowledge represented?
- **Maintaining Indigenous Cultures**: How will this publication impact on the culture of Indigenous people?

Resources

Protocols for Using First Nations Cultural and Intellectual Property in the Arts (Australia Council, 2019): www.australiacouncil.gov.au/programs-and-resources/Protocols-for-using-First-Nations-Cultural-and-Intellectual-Property-in-the-Arts/.

Protocols for Producing Indigenous Australian Writing (Australia Council, 2007) www.australiacouncil.gov.au/workspace/uploads/files/writing-protocols-for-indigeno-5b4bfc67dd037.pdf

Indigenous Cultural Protocols and the Arts (case studies, Terri Janke and Company, 2016): www.terrijanke.com.au/indigenous-cultural-protocols-and-arts

More than Words: Writing, Aboriginal and Torres Strait Islander Culture and Copyright in Australia, Australian Society of Authors (Terri Janke and Company, 2021): https://www.asauthors.org/products/asa-resources-and-guides/more-than-words

Guidelines for the Ethical Publishing of Aboriginal and Torres Strait Islander Authors and Research from Those Communities (AIATSIS, 2015): https://aiatsis.gov.au/sites/default/files/2020-09/ethical-publishing-guidelines.pdf

Anita Heiss, 'Writing about Indigenous Australia – Some issues to consider and protocols to follow: A discussion paper', *Southerly*, vol. 62, no. 2, 2002, pp. 197–205.

Jared Thomas, 'Respecting protocols for representing Aboriginal cultures', *Journal of the Association for the Study of Australian Literature*, vol. 14, no. 3, 2014, pp. 1–13, https://openjournals.library.sydney.edu.au/index.php/JASAL/article/view/9907

Devon Abbott Mihesuah, *So You Want to Write about American Indians? A Guide for Writers, Students and Scholars*, University of Nebraska Press, Lincoln, NE, 2005.

Notes

1. Anita Heiss, *Anita Heiss*, Copyright Agency, 2020, <www.copyright.com.au/profile/anita-heiss/>.
2. Ellen van Neerven, in 'Episode 14: Ellen van Neerven' [podcast episode], *The Real*, 2019, <www.the-real.com.au/podcast/>.
3. Maggie Nolan, 'In his own sweet time: Carmen's coming out', *Australian Literary Studies*, vol. 21, no. 4, 2004, <www.australianliterarystudies.com.au/articles/in-his-own-sweet-time-carmens-coming-out>.
4. Neil Löfgren, 'The unbearable whiteness of being: The Wanda Koolmatrie fraud', *Polemic*, vol. 8, no. 2, <www.austlii.edu.au/au/journals/PolemicUSyd/1997/22.pdf>.
5. Susan Wyndham, 'The mystery of Marlo Morgan down under', *The Australian Magazine*, 29–30 October 1994, pp. 26–28.
6. 'Mutant author says she's sorry', *The Weekend Australian*, 27 January, 1996, p. 11.
7. Larissa Behrendt, 'Dark places in a country built on lies', *Sydney Morning Herald*, 15 October 1994, Spectrum, p. 11A, <http://wmuma.com/mutantmessage/mutantmessagebooknews3.html>.
8. AW Reed, *Aboriginal Legends: Animal Tales*, Reed Books, Sydney, 1978.
9. Melissa Jackson, 'David Unaipon 1872–1967', in State Library of New South Wales, *The Heritage Collection 2004: Nelson Meers Foundation*, SLNSW, Sydney, 2004, p. 42, <https://www2.sl.nsw.gov.au/archive/events/exhibitions/2007/heritage/docs/heritageguide2004.pdf>.

10 David Unaipon, *Legendary Tales of the Australian Aborigines* (Stephen Muecke and Adam Shoemaker, eds), Melbourne University Press, Melbourne, 2001.
11 Kate Grenville, *The Secret River*, Text Publishing, Melbourne, 2005.
12 Australia Council for the Arts, *Protocols for Producing Indigenous Australian Writing*, 2nd ed, Australia Council, Sydney, 2007, p. 7, <www.australiacouncil.gov.au/workspace/uploads/files/writing-protocols-for-indigeno-5b4bfc67dd037.pdf>.
13 Deborah Cheetham, in Aaron Corn and Marcia Langton, 'A post-mortem of a pulped book: Making sense of the missed opportunities of *Deadly Woman Blues*', *Musicology Australia*, vol. 40, no.1, 2018, p. 66.
14 Deborah Cheetham, in Bhakthi Puvanenthiran, 'Deborah Cheetham is done with "cleaning up the mess of a white man"', *Crikey*, 14 March 2018, <www.crikey.com.au/2018/03/14/cleaning-up-mess-deborah-cheetham-deadly-woman-blues/>.
15 Clinton Walker, in NewSouth Publishing, *Deadly Woman Blues*, 6 March 2018, <www.newsouthpublishing.com/articles/deadly-woman-blues/>.
16 Jared Thomas, personal communication, 19 November 2020.
17 Jared Thomas, personal communication, 18 February 2021.
18 Ryan Griffen, 'We need more Aboriginal superheroes, so I created *Cleverman* for my son', *The Guardian*, 27 May 2016, <www.theguardian.com/tv-and-radio/2016/may/27/i-created-cleverman-for-my-son-because-we-need-more-aboriginal-superheroes>.
19 Ryan Griffen, personal communication, March 2021.
20 Anita Heiss, 'Want to write the great Australian novel? You need to engage with Indigenous Australia first', *The Guardian*, 28 April 2021 <https://www.theguardian.com/books/2021/apr/28/want-to-write-the-great-australian-novel-you-need-to-engage-with-indigenous-australia-first>.
21 Australian Book Review (ABR), 'Publisher of the month with Rachel Bin Salleh', *ABR*, no. 413, August 2019, <www.australianbookreview.com.au/abr-online/archive/2019/371-august-2019-no-413/5669-publisher-of-the-month-with-rachel-bin-salleh>.
22 Anna Moulton, personal communication, 11 March 2021.
23 Karen Manton, personal communication, 23 February 2021.
24 Australia Council for the Arts, *Protocols for Producing Indigenous Australian Writing*, p. 15.
25 Richard Lea, 'Lucy Treloar on writing about Indigenous Australians: "I felt filled with conflict"', *The Guardian*, 28 September 2017, <www.theguardian.com/books/2017/sep/28/lucy-treloar-salt-creek-indigenous-settlers-south-australia-emily-hack>.
26 Richard Lea, 'Lucy Treloar on writing about Indigenous Australians'.
27 Australia Council for the Arts, *Protocols for Producing Indigenous Australian Writing*, pp. 14–15.

8
DANCING COUNTRY AND ACTING UP

Aboriginal and Torres Strait Islander performing arts are connected to ceremony and country, the heart and the sacred, and the painting of skin, all of which link us to kin. In some communities, a complex system of dances, songs, stories, body designs and dress has developed in association with belonging to country.

With ancient roots reaching back through time, the performing arts continue to play an influential role in recording and interpreting contemporary Indigenous lives, allowing for reflection and renewal. The dancers, choreographers, actors and directors of today work with an innovative combination of Indigenous knowledge sources, drawing from pre-existing cultural works, family and community histories, biographies and archives to create new expressions. Indigenous contemporary theatre of dance and drama continues to do what it has always done: to strengthen our culture and identity, and to shine a light on issues that offer life lessons for those to come.

Dance companies: Connecting with culture

Bangarra Dance Theatre: Protocols in practice

Have you ever been lucky enough to experience a Bangarra Dance Theatre performance? Bangarra is the highly sought-after Australian Indigenous dance company that performs all around the world. I am grateful to have enjoyed their shows over the years, including their 30th anniversary show in 2019, *Bangarra: 30 years of sixty five thousand*. It was a proud moment for the company. From the technical prowess behind the choreography and composition to the innovative costume and set designs, their shows are dazzling.

Stephen Page, a descendant of the Nunukul people and the Munaldjali clan of the Yugambeh Nation from south-east Queensland, has been the company's artistic director for more than 25 years. As Stephen writes:

> The work Bangarra creates is only possible due to the incredible trust and generosity of the many Elders, Song Men and Women and Cultural Custodians who share their cultural knowledge with us. These relationships are built up over many years, formed through connections within the Company. Each Bangarra Dancer has a proud Aboriginal and/or Torres Strait Islander heritage, and we support the Dancers to learn, rekindle and strengthen their own cultural knowledge and traditions. Like so many of my generation, I am in a constant process of rekindling and reclaiming my own heritage, the saltwater and freshwater cultural traditions of my mother and father. It fills me with such hope to see the younger generations coming up now who are speaking Language, and proudly representing and carrying their culture forward.'[1]

The Bangarra dancers have their cultural roots in many different Aboriginal and Torres Strait Islander groups throughout Australia. Elma Kris, from the Torres Strait Islands, is their longest serving dancer, appearing with the company for more than 20 years before her retirement from the permanent ensemble.[2] Given her history within the company as a dancer, cultural adviser and creative collaborator who carries with her more than 20 years of entrusted cultural knowledge, she is often invited back to perform as a guest artist. In doing so, she works with the younger dancers to pass on that cultural knowledge to the next generation of artists and future cultural leaders. A bold photo of Elma, mid-dance, surrounded by red light, is on the front cover of the *Protocols for Producing Indigenous*

Australian Performing Arts, which Terri Janke and Company prepared for the Australia Council for the Arts. Based on True Tracks principles, the protocols guide dance and theatre companies, performing artists, directors and choreographers to maintain a strong link between the cultural material behind the work and its new expression. The choreographers at Bangarra do this really well, working closely with Indigenous custodians and families to create new works. Our firm helped them to develop an ICIP policy, which includes taking on cultural advisers to oversee ICIP used in the performances, including story, dance, set design, language and music.[3]

Bangarra's approach involves closely engaging with various Indigenous communities and respecting cultural authority in the creation of new works, including elders and cultural consultants. This has been the key to their success – keeping the cultural integrity of traditional knowledge intact and the links to culture strong. For example, Bangarra has significant links with Mer (Murray Island), and also the Wangurri clan of north-east Arnhem Land, that have enabled the company to perform and adapt traditional dances and songs by following cultural protocols. An important part of this cultural exchange is Bangarra's 'Return to Country' practice, which ensures that works return to their cultural origins 'as a sign of respect for the communities whose stories and spirits inspire Bangarra productions'.[4] This sees the continuity and deepening of Bangarra's relationships with communities, developed over many years.

NAISDA Dance College

You can see these links between cultural and contemporary dance, performance and storytelling clearly at NAISDA Dance College's annual Sydney performance seasons. Situated on Darkinjung land (Central Coast, New South Wales), NAISDA is Australia's only nationally accredited dance and performance training college specifically for Aboriginal and Torres Strait Islander young people. Over the past 44 years, NAISDA has been the training ground for the majority of Aboriginal and Torres Strait Islander dance artists. It has been the birthplace and bedrock of Australian contemporary Indigenous dance and the generator of a creative industry that has had worldwide success.

'NAISDA's connection to cultural practice and Indigenous knowledge, through remote communities, Elders, cultural tutors and a unique cultural residency program, is at the core of our teaching practice and performative response,' says Kim Walker, respected arts practitioner and CEO of NAISDA. 'We are proud to be both a cultural catalyst and cultivator for the nation, providing students with training connected to country, culture, identity and wellbeing.'[5] Graduates include Stephen Page (Bangarra's Artistic Director), Frances Rings (Bangarra's Associate Artistic Director), dancer Elma Kris, singer Christine Anu, director Jacob Boehme, Karul Projects co-artistic directors Thomas ES Kelly and Taree Sansbury, independent choreographer and director Vicki Van Hout, and there are many more alumni who are award-winning leaders in their disciplines, empowering and inspiring the next generation of artists.

BlakDance

BlakDance is a national industry and producing organisation for First Nations contemporary dance. It was founded by Marilyn Miller of Kuku Yalanji and Wanji heritage, a veteran of Indigenous Australian performing arts. It provides a voice for Indigenous dancers and producers. Through working with BlakDance, I have been able to listen to the concerns of Indigenous choreographers and practitioners they represent. BlakDance convened a National Indigenous Dance Forum (NIDF) in 2017 that highlighted ICIP as a key issue. The practical steps of acknowledging elders and dance custodians are taken, and the links between them and the new contemporary innovators is maintained, to guide and bring authenticity to Indigenous dance practice. A Cultural Council is also embedded in the governance structure of BlakDance for cultural guidance and the discussion of cultural matters.

Performance, dance and the law

Indigenous groups follow strict guidelines around who can perform traditional dance because of the deep cultural and spiritual significance. Respecting these guidelines keeps culture strong. When dance styles are copied without permission, or when Indigenous stories are told in theatre without Indigenous involvement, this silences Indigenous voices and belittles cultural practice. The problem is that there is currently no legal requirement in Australia to follow cultural protocols or consult with Aboriginal people when performing Aboriginal dance.

The traditional owners of Indigenous dance seek to have the cultural integrity of their dance performances respected. Dance comes from country and encodes stories for survival, food and plants and deeper knowledge of ceremony. They seek the right to be consulted and to give consent when their important dances are performed outside the cultural setting, or by others who have no cultural connection. Issues that have arisen for Indigenous clans include seeing their traditional dances adapted in derogatory or demeaning ways or used by other Indigenous groups and non-Indigenous people without permission.

Russian figure skaters: Ice-cold on cultural competency

In 2010, at the European Figure Skating Championships and the Winter Olympic Games, a Russian figure-skating duo had prepared to perform 'Aboriginal Dance', a routine supposedly inspired by Australian Aboriginal dance and culture. The Russian figure skaters wore dark skin-toned body suits marked with white paint. Fake leaves hung off them, flapping in the air as they moved around the ice rink. Their movements played into stereotypical ideas of tribal dance and culture. At one point, one skater led the other around the ice by her ponytail.

There was no Indigenous input in the development of the routine, costumes or music. Indigenous leaders in Australia heavily criticised the performance. Bev Manton, then chair of the NSW Aboriginal Land

Council, wrote in response: 'From an Aboriginal perspective, this performance is offensive ... They are wearing white body paint in designs they dreamed up after reading about Aboriginal Australians on the internet.'[6]

Kim Walker of NAISDA Dance College reached out to me for assistance to write a letter to the president of the International Olympic Committee in Switzerland. In the letter, we explained how the dance routine was a form of cultural misappropriation that overlooked the cultural heritage rights of Indigenous peoples, such as the right to consent for use of culture, and the right of attribution.

The Russian duo ditched their costumes for their appearance at the Winter Olympics, which Bev Manton said was a step in the right direction; however, there was no acknowledgement from the skaters of the issues raised. There was no legal recourse for Indigenous people, and no apology or public statement was made.

The haka: Cultural strength not cultural theft

In New Zealand, the haka is a ceremonial dance that involves chanting, fierce movements and wide eyes. There are many hakas, which come from different *iwi*, or tribes of Māori. The haka was used on the battlefield, and today it is performed for special occasions such as birthdays and weddings.[7] The Ka Mate haka, composed by the Ngāti Toa rangarita (chief) Te Rauparaha around 1820, has become one of the most well known. It was made world famous by New Zealand's national rugby team, the All Blacks, who perform it before each match begins.

The Ka Mate haka has been misappropriated by advertisers and others without any link to Māori. When British company Bass Breweries produced an advertisement featuring women wearing bikinis on a beach performing a haka to advertise an alcoholic fruit drink, it caused some controversy. The New Zealand High Commission in London wrote to the manufacturer of the drink to ask that the advertisement be withdrawn immediately on the basis that the use of the haka in a context involving women and alcohol was offensive to Māori culture. The advertisement was reportedly withdrawn following many complaints received by Britain's Independent Television Commission.[8] Others who have used the haka in questionable ways include the Spice Girls, a German insurance company,[9] a car advertisement for the Italian Fiat[10] and a Japanese Coca-Cola advertisement.[11] There is now a special law for the Ka Mate haka, the *Haka Ka Mate Attribution Act 2014* (NZ), which protects the haka as *taonga* – that is, a cultural treasure. The Act requires attribution be given to the origin of the haka if it is used in a commercial context.

Culture at festivals: Sharing with sensitivity

Does the law offer any protection? Dance is an interesting example because it illustrates so many of the shortfalls in copyright law. In Australia, copyright doesn't protect the dance unless it is put into material form – for example, when the choreography is written down as notation. The same goes for film recordings. Filming of dance performance creates copyright in the film, and allows the film to be circulated without the permission of the Indigenous performers, and without any connection to the custodians of the dance and encoded knowledge.

These are the sorts of issues raised in public performances and cultural festivals. I have advised the Festival of Pacific Arts and Culture, an Indigenous festival that occurs in the Pacific every four years, on these issues. Countries and performers attending the Festival are proud to attend and share their cultures, but the increasing appropriation of culture at these events was a cause for concern. I was lucky enough to be engaged by WIPO and the Secretariat of the Pacific Community as a consultant to assist with intellectual property management of the festival when it was held in American Samoa in 2008, and with developments towards the Solomon Islands event in 2012. We were faced with the issue of protecting the dances, stories, cultural expressions and knowledge that are shared at the festival from appropriation by outsiders. A question for the participants and the countries that convened the delegation was how to stop cultural copying by outsiders – the cheap, imitation art – and the theft of knowledge, such as craft and medicinal properties of plants, that might be shared at such public events, and attended by tourists wishing to experience Indigenous Pacific cultures?

The issues that had occurred over the years of running the festival included the illegal filming and pirating of the festival's official broadcast signal, which included live performance of song and dance along with traditional knowledge displays. It also included the sale of fake festival merchandise such as offensive copies of sacred symbols, postcards that reproduced dancers without permission and commercial use of a video clip of a traditional ceremony. Traditional dance costumes, body and face painting, tattooing, carving and cultural remedies had also been copied.

In the lead-up to the festival in the Solomon Islands in 2012, I was asked by the local coordinating team to visit the Islands and assist them with information about copyright, contracts, protocols and changes to local laws. One humid day, typical of the region, I presented a workshop and consulted artists and performers in the National Museum in Honiara. It was so hot the sweat was dripping from my skin. I spoke about how when performances are captured through film and photography, they are owned by the filmmaker, photographer or production company, due to copyright laws requiring the work to be in material form. I wrote an intellectual property guide for the festival that set out the use of protocols, contracts, notices and systems.[12]

Each year, about 2500 guests from all over Australia attend the Garma Festival. The Garma Festival is an immersive celebration of Yolngu art, culture and ceremony held near Yirrkala in north-east Arnhem Land. There are sharings of culture by way of knowledge, song and dance, as well as art. Aboriginal leaders attend to discuss current political themes, and non-Indigenous leaders in the Australian corporate and government worlds also attend to gain a greater understanding of Indigenous culture. The red dirt, the salt pans, the ochre, and the sounds of the Yolngu people and their country provide the perfect cultural environment for non-Indigenous and Indigenous people to come together for focused discussions. Knowledge is shared through weaving, fishing and storytelling. The organisers, the Yothu Yindi Foundation, have developed strict guidelines for filming and recording during the festival that are in line with Yolngu cultural protocols.

For instance, attendees must follow the right process and seek permission of the Yothu Yindi Foundation and subjects when taking photographs and recordings during women's and men's programs.

Indigenous peoples may find it inappropriate and offensive to capture images and footage of traditional dance, performance and ceremony. It is particularly offensive if the content is misappropriated in a way that does not link back and respect the cultural connection. These days, it is so easy for audiences to capture a dance performance on their phones or cameras. Uploads on YouTube, Facebook and other social media mean that the dance can go to a wider audience. Performers have the right to control recordings of their performances, to say who can and cannot film them, but this right must be exercised at the time the recording is taken. Where do the recordings go? Who can access them? Are we keeping track to make sure that the source is recognised, and the culture respected?

The filmmaker controls the way a performance is interpreted and narrated by choosing what to film and how to film it, and what to alter or omit during the editing process. When this takes place without the input of the relevant Indigenous community, the cultural material may not be portrayed in a respectful way. An Indigenous performer may think they are consenting to a film for one idea only (such as archival purposes), but then find the film has altered the meaning of their performance or has been circulated to a much wider audience than expected. There are cultural issues in some communities where it is against customary practices for images of deceased persons to be circulated.

Old film recordings that are out of copyright

Many old ethnographic recordings of ceremonial material are now held in archives and libraries. Some depict ceremonies and images that would be considered offensive today. The recordings and photographs are old, and may now be in the public domain – that is, it has been 70 years since the publication of the recording and the copyright has expired, and they are now free for all to use (in a copyright sense) without the need to seek consent. Indigenous people are concerned that these kinds of materials, often holding important or sensitive cultural information, are now at risk of being misappropriated and exploited. For example, the filming of an Indigenous ceremony that took place in the 1940s could be reproduced and commercialised in a music video by an outsider with no connection to the cultural expression in the recording. The display, public communication and broadcast of these films are against customary law, and their wider dissemination will have great impact on the culture contained in them.

Proactive institutions require consent from Indigenous communities before allowing this material to be published. Often, Indigenous people do not know this material is held in the archives, or find it difficult to access. This is changing as there are more repatriation projects such as the Returning Photos: Australian Aboriginal Photographs from European Collections project, bringing historical photos held in European collections into the hands of Aboriginal communities in Western Australia and Arnhem Land.[13] With greater access to visual collections, Indigenous peoples and communities are able to amalgamate the visual images with their oral stories and histories.[14]

There are also the old film recordings that depict content that is sacred and not for public viewing. Some of these are now stored in archives. These films were taken at a time when consent was not properly given, and when it was never considered by the community or performers, or even the filmmaker, that the content would be viewed or re-used. Much of this content might not have been checked or properly identified. Some recordings might hold ceremonies, or information that is secret or sacred. So there is a need for community members to visit film archives so they can identify material. This can serve the purpose of making the information available for the community to reinvigorate cultural practice. Also, the community can give direction on whether the film should remain closed, and to provide consent if further use by others is requested.

Traditional dance and copyright

Traditional Aboriginal and Torres Strait Islander dance that originated many centuries ago will not be protected by copyright – it is old and, further, there is a lack of material form, which is a key requirement for a copyright work.

There is also, usually, no individual choreographer of a traditional dance; rather, it is culturally owned by a community. Different communities have different dances, each telling different stories and holding particular knowledge. The dances cover stories about the community, land, seas and environment. They tell us about people, relationships and ways of life – including food collection and other survival skills.

Any copyright in recordings and film belongs to the sound recording or filmmaker. Depending on when it was made, that person may still control its reproduction. In the past, depending on the deposit agreement with the archive, that person would have had most of the say over how the film or sound recording was used. (If a film or sound recording was made more than 70 years ago, generally it lies outside of the copyright protection period.)

Indigenous cultural laws recognise ownership of the dances by the relevant groups, and certain dances may only be performed or viewed by initiated men or women. Many dances have been passed on through time and refined, and it's important to recognise the source – to recognise the group of origin, as the dance is still important today. This means that if you want to dance a dance that doesn't belong to your cultural group, you need to get permission.

Drama and theatre

Rachael Maza, a Yidinji and Meriam woman, is the artistic director of Ilbijerri Theatre Company in Melbourne. Rachael wants to champion an Indigenous way of developing theatre productions that takes into account the cultural authority and ownership of personal stories. She feels that the

Western structure of the playwright owning all the copyright in the script is not suitable for First Nations works, for example, in a play about an Indigenous person's life. 'There needs to be a more cultural model where the First Nations person and their family or community have more of a stake,' Rachael says. 'The general Western model of the playwright holding all control needs to be challenged when the Indigenous people contribute so much, such as the story, the cultural information and the language that is used.'[15] We have been assisting Ilbijerri to develop processes and cultural contracts for productions that include traditional stories and present the lives of Indigenous people.

Copyright and Indigenous theatre

Under the Copyright Act, a work of 'joint ownership' refers to a work produced by the collaboration of people working on the material form of the work. In many instances dramatic works have more than one contributor – for example, a play that has been workshopped by writers, actors, directors and community members. What if you want to develop a play about the life of a famous Indigenous person? The person – or if they have passed away, the family members – play a big part in telling the story, but is it enough for that person or family to be called 'co-writer'? Who should own the story?

Copyright only protects the person who wrote down the work, and this is generally the playwright. Conventionally, there is no allocation of rights to other people whose ideas have informed the final work. But agreements can be used to ensure that collaborators share in the copyright or benefit from the use of the story or information. The agreement should be in writing to enable copyright assignment and to avoid misunderstanding.

Workshopping material raises issues about who owns the content that is developed. Ilbijerri worked with the Arts Law Centre of Australia to develop a workshop participants' agreement to be signed by each participant. It acknowledges that the participant owns the copyright in the material they create in the workshop; however, in participating, they also agree to give an exclusive, royalty-free licence to Ilbijerri to perform the material for an agreed length of time internationally. This means that once the season ends and the performance is no longer produced, the participants can freely adapt and use their materials towards performance pieces of their own.[16]

Indigenous playwrights and theatre companies

Theatre refers to the live performance of plays and may even include improvisations. This type of performance-based culture has been widely used in Indigenous cultures throughout the millennia. The ceremony and replaying of events in front of a fire, or under a rock shelter, was a way Indigenous people entertained each other and passed on information. Contemporary Indigenous culture has continued this genre. A number of Indigenous playwrights – such as Kevin Gilbert, Jack Davis, David Milroy, Eva Johnson, Jane Harrison and Andrea James – penned theatre works that have developed the art form and provided social and political commentary.

Indigenous theatre companies such as Yirra Yaakin Theatre Company, Moogahlin Performing Arts, Ilbijerri Theatre Company and the no-longer-operating Kooemba Jdarra Indigenous Performing Arts Company were established during the past 30 years. These companies have developed significant Aboriginal and Torres Strait Islander theatre that draws from cultural heritage, traditional and personal stories, and the experiences of Indigenous people such as the stolen generations, deaths in custody or prevailing health issues.

Strong theatre performance pieces have been developed by Indigenous playwrights including Wesley Enoch, a Noonuccal Nuugi man, who has contributed to the development of Indigenous theatre through his direction of classic Indigenous plays such as Kevin Gilbert's *The Cherry Pickers* (1968), first performed in the early 1970s, and Jack Davis's *No Sugar*, first performed in 1985.[17]

There are also theatre collaborations, such as *Namatjira*, a play co-directed by Scott Rankin and Wayne Blair, the lead role played by acclaimed

MOOGAHLIN PERFORMING ARTS: *BROKEN GLASS*

Broken Glass was a significant project by First Nations performing arts company Moogahlin Performing Arts, in partnership with Blacktown Arts, for Sydney Festival in 2018. A collaborative performance and installation work, it explores the rituals of death and mourning in First Nations communities of New South Wales and Victoria through the perspectives of First Nations women artists Lily Shearer, Liza-Mare Syron, Andrea James, Aroha Groves, Katie Leslie and Brenda Gifford. It reflected on how First Nations knowledges and practices regarding death and ceremony have adapted in the post-invasion contemporary era. The work was shared with the public at St Bartholomew's Church and Cemetery on Darug country in Prospect, western Sydney, and supported by Create NSW, Blacktown City Council, Australia Council for the Arts, the Crown Resorts Foundation and Joseph Medcalf Funeral Services.

Broken Glass involved a series of seven visual and sound performances staged in and around the St Bartholomew's Church and Cemetery complex. Audiences were immersed in these intimate experiences as they moved through the site, following a spirit guide performed by the artists at various stages of the performances throughout the site. The idea for the production was informed by conversations with Dunghutti man Robbie Dungay, the longest serving First Nations funeral director in Australia, and other research undertaken by the artists from archival materials.[18] The project carefully followed cultural protocols, with the artists consulting with elders and community members during the research phase of the project and making sure to not disclose secret and confidential information.

actor Trevor Jamieson, telling the story of the famous watercolourist Albert Namatjira. The play was created with the Namatjira family and is part of the Namatjira Project, run by the production company Big hART. The play opened in 2010 and toured the nation. As part of the project, the Namatjira Legacy Trust was assisted pro bono by law firm Arnold Bloch Leibler to secure the return of the copyright in Albert Namatjira's lifetime works to his descendants, as well as compensation from the Northern Territory Government. The lawyers involved included ABL's senior partner Mark Leibler, partners Zaven Mardirossian and Peter Seidel, and senior associate Gabriel Sakkal. The copyright had been sold to Legend Press when Namatjira's wife died without leaving a will (see chapter 3).

Nakkiah Lui, the Gamillaroi/Torres Strait Islander actor and award-winning playwright, has been instrumental in bringing an important female Indigenous voice to the stage with *Black is the New White* (2017), a lively and hilarious play about love, race, class and politics. Commissioned by the Sydney Theatre Company, the play was a big hit, performing for two seasons in Sydney as well as travelling to Brisbane, Canberra and regional theatres, and later published as an award-winning book.

Issues in Indigenous theatre can arise when a play is performed, or an improvisation occurs. Theatre companies must consider the collective issues and cultural protocols when a play is workshopped and developed. Who should be recognised as the owner of copyright of a performance developed collectively from the cast's experiences of dealing with a common issue, or retelling a particular event in history? It is ideal to have the framework worked out before writing begins.

Producing great content

The work of Indigenous festival directors such as Wesley Enoch and Rhoda Roberts has changed the game. Where Indigenous people were once just seen as tick-the-box add-ins, with no fees paid for performers, now Indigenous productions and events have become a mainstay of Australian festivals. Sydney Festival is an example. With Wesley Enoch as the director in recent years, Indigenous content is integral to the festival. Indigenous stories and voices have been strong: in 2020, Jimmy Chi's 1990 Aboriginal musical *Bran Nue Dae* hit the stage, and Archie Roach sang his latest album, *Tell Me Why*, at the City Recital Hall in Sydney.

Rhoda Roberts has consistently produced high-standard Indigenous content that breaks new ground for Australian performance, including the Festival of the Dreaming that began in Sydney in 1997 before relocating to Woodford in Queensland. She was the first head of First Nations programming at the Sydney Opera House, where she was responsible for the development of *Badu Gili*, the light installation of Indigenous art on the sails of the Opera House (badu gili means 'water light' in the language of the traditional owners of Bennelong Point, the Gadigal people), and Dance Rites, the Indigenous dance competition that started in 2015. 'Dance Rites was really an initiative about reclamation and ensuring that the traditional aspects of our culture were kept alive and revitalised,' Rhoda says. 'It's so important for our communities. It really shows us the intergenerational exchanges that occur. You've got elders and custodians who remember the old songlines or the dances or indeed the costumes that they wore ... passing them on to the next generation in a really culturally safe space. It is a competition, but most of the entrants see it as a great gathering.'[19]

Performing for Indigenous excellence

The best way to ensure respect for Indigenous Cultural and Intellectual Property in performing arts is to empower Indigenous performing artists, theatre companies, playwrights, dancers and actors. Then there must be more collaborations with the performing arts organisations and theatre companies to work together. Some of the key issues will be how works are to be created or composed and generated when using existing content that is ICIP. There is a need for collective processes to be recognised, by bringing in the people whose stories are being told, and maintaining integrity by allowing them to contribute to the storytelling process and presentation. The performing arts industries need to be more attuned to how they commission works, how they accept writers' agreements in collaborations, payment of Indigenous cultural advisers, and the ownership of copyright.

The recognition of Indigenous performance should also address welcome to country and acknowledgment of country protocols, how performing arts companies work with Indigenous talent, and how roles should be treated in terms of cultural consultants, advisers and collaborators.

> **WHAT YOU CAN DO ...**
>
> - If you want to work with Indigenous cultural heritage in your performance or choreography, consider if it is appropriate. What is the cultural connection? Are you respecting the cultural heritage?
> - Seek consent from performers before filming or taking photographs. Although consent may be oral or implied, it's best that rights are put into writing so that the terms can be clearly understood.
> - Use written agreements to set out processes for checking materials with ICIP; collaboration; payments to Indigenous cultural advisers; recognition of clan stories or key people; and future adaptations, share of box office and earnings.

Resources

Protocols for Producing Indigenous Australian Performing Arts (Australia Council, 2007): www.australiacouncil.gov.au/workspace/uploads/files/performing-arts-protocols-for-5b4bfd3988d3e.pdf

Protocols for Using First Nations Cultural and Intellectual Property in the Arts (Australia Council, 2019): www.australiacouncil.gov.au/programs-and-resources/Protocols-for-using-First-Nations-Cultural-and-Intellectual-Property-in-the-Arts/

Bangarra Dance Theatre eResources: www.bangarra.com.au/learning/resources/eresources/

Bangarra Dance Theatre Knowledge Ground: https://bangarra-knowledgeground.com.au/

BlakDance: www.blakdance.org.au

Ilbijerri Theatre Company: https://ilbijerri.com.au

NAISDA Dance College: https://naisda.com.au

Notes

1. Stephen Page, personal communication, 23 March 2021.
2. National Indigenous Australians Agency, *Elma Gada Kris: 2019 Artist of the Year*, NAIDOC, n.d., <www.naidoc.org.au/awards/winner-profiles/elma-gada-kris>.
3. Bangarra Dance Theatre, *Indigenous Cultural & Intellectual Property Policy*, Bangarra, 2015, <https://bangarra-knowledgeground.com.au/icip>.
4. Bangarra Dance Theatre, *Terrain | Return to Country*, Bangarra, n.d., <https://bangarra-knowledgeground.com.au/productions/terrain/terrain-return-to-country>.
5. Kim Walker, personal communication, 8 March 2021.
6. Bev Manton, 'Russian ice dancers should rethink their routine', *Sydney Morning Herald*, 21 January 2011, <www.smh.com.au/politics/federal/russian-ice-dancers-should-rethink-their-routine-20100121-mnwj.html>.
7. Tourism New Zealand, *The Haka*, 100% Pure New Zealand, n.d., <www.newzealand.com/int/feature/haka/>.
8. WIPO Intergovernmental Committee on Intellectual Property and Genetic Resources, Traditional Knowledge and Folklore (IGC), *Fourth Session: Presentations on National and Regional Experiences with Specific Legislation for the Legal Protection of Traditional Cultural Expressions (Expressions of Folklore)*, IGC, Geneva, 9–17 December 2002, p. 6, <www.wipo.int/edocs/mdocs/tk/en/wipo_grtkf_ic_4/wipo_grtkf_ic_4_inf_2-main1.pdf>.
9. 'German advertisement criticised for using Maori haka', *BBC Newsbeat*, 11 May 2017, <www.bbc.co.uk/newsbeat/article/39883154/german-advertisement-criticised-for-using-maori-haka>.
10. 'Italians drive ahead with Car Mate haka [video clip]', *NZ Herald*, 4 July 2006, <www.nzherald.co.nz/nz/news/article.cfm?c_id=1&objectid=10389619>.
11. Kelly Burns, 'Japanese Coke haka has Rugby Union fizzing', *Stuff*, 23 February 2010, <www.stuff.co.nz/sport/rugby/3357486/Japanese-Coke-haka-has-Rugby-Union-fizzing>.
12. Terri Janke, *Intellectual Property and the 11th Festival of Pacific Arts, Solomon Islands, 2012*, World Intellectual Property Organization, Geneva, 2012, <www.wipo.int/edocs/pubdocs/en/tk/tk_fpa/tk_fpa_2012.pdf>.
13. University of Western Australia (UWA), *Returning Photos: Australian Aboriginal Photographs from European Collections*, UWA, n.d., <https://ipp.arts.uwa.edu.au>.
14. Donna Oxenham, 'The return of photographs – What does it mean for Aboriginal people?' [news post], *Returning Photos: Australian Aboriginal Photographs from European Collections*, UWA, 28 August 2015, <https://ipp.arts.uwa.edu.au/post-2/>.
15. Rachael Maza, teleconference, 4 May 2020.
16. Arts Law Centre of Australia, *Ilbijerri Theatre Company – Copyright Ownership and Contract*, Arts Law Centre of Australia, 18 April 2011, <www.artslaw.com.au/case-studies/ilbijerri-theatre-company-copyright-ownership-and-contract-2/>.
17. Jack Davis, *No Sugar*, performed by the Playhouse Company in association with the Australian Theatre Trust, Festival of Perth, 1985.
18. Liza-Mare Syron, personal communication, 24 March 2021.
19. Rhoda Roberts, in ABC Radio, 'Dance Rites 2020', *Speaking Out with Larissa Behrendt*, 25 October 2020, <www.abc.net.au/radio/programs/speakingout/phonda-roberts/12807456>.

9
THE RAINFOREST IS OUR SUPERMARKET: BUSH FOODS AND TRADITIONAL MEDICINE

I was born in the tropical green humidity of Cairns in Far North Queensland. During the wet season, the rainforest drips with plant life and sun showers that take you by surprise. Thick vines seem to hang from the sky and connect the trees together when you look up. The waterfalls are at their fullest, flowing down streams and weaving around boulders.

As a young child, when my eczema was really bad, an uncle mixed traditional bush medicine to heal my flaking skin. He collected leaves to make special mixtures that I would soak in. This knowledge can be traced back to not just a few hundred or thousand years, but more than 65,000 years. I think that's pretty incredible.

Indigenous peoples' deep connection with the land and the plants stretches back through the ages. This is about respecting Indigenous custodianship and stewardship, and recognising the responsibility of caring for country that is deeply felt by indigenous groups all over the world. However, for all the recent interest in using Australian plants for new foods, medicines and cosmetics, few of these ventures are owned and managed by Indigenous people. We need to recognise Indigenous peoples' cultural heritage rights and generate opportunities for them to be part of the research, use and commercialisation of these plants, and to benefit from the wealth their knowledge provides.

In Cairns, the Tropical Indigenous Ethnobotany Centre (TIEC) at the Australian Tropical Herbarium at James Cook University is the first Indigenous-driven centre in Australia dedicated to the study of ethnobotany. Ethnobotany is the study of people, plants and culture. It looks at how different cultures use plants for food, medicine, shelter and tools, and in ceremony and spirituality. Usually a Western ethnobotanist, an outsider, looks in on the Indigenous context. But the TIEC has changed that, and its manager, Gerry Turpin, is leading the way. Gerry is a Mbabaram traditional owner and ethnobotanist with family links to Far North Queensland. The main aim of the TIEC is to record Indigenous biocultural knowledge. Gerry explains that the best part of his job is being 'out on country with traditional owners, listening to stories, learning about their knowledge, their culture, camping under the stars at night'. He notes the continuing connection that traditional owners have: 'Traditional owners are still connected to their land and culture. They're still passing on that knowledge to the younger generation.'[1] The uses of the different plants, and the names of animals and places, are learned by children from their elders out on country. This knowledge has been learned over thousands of years.

I met Gerry at the National Seed Science Forum of 2016 at the Australian Botanic Garden in Mount Annan, south-west Sydney. We were on a panel put together by Ninti One and the University of New England's Australian Centre for Agriculture and Law. Law academic and Torres Strait Islander woman Dr Heron Loban was also on the panel, as was Clarence Slockee. Clarence is a Bundjalung man and director of Jiwah, a cultural landscape and design company. A popular presenter on *Gardening Australia* and a key creator of native urban green space, he does much to connect people with Aboriginal plant knowledge.

The panel was one of the first times Aboriginal and Torres Strait Islander people had spoken at a national event like this, and it had been brought together by the award-winning Australian academic Dr Kylie Lingard, a friend of mine who has done a lot of research on Indigenous plant use and the law, and how to empower Aboriginal people in the commercialisation of native plants.[2] In our panel discussion, we talked about the importance of plants and seeds to living cultures and practices. Heron spoke about how plants remain relevant to Indigenous people, and have different names and various contexts – like the seed pods used for kulaps (seed shakers), instruments played by Torres Strait Islanders. I spoke about the importance of protocols and the growing legal rights for Indigenous people under international law, and presented the True Tracks principles.

Biopiracy: What is it and how can we prevent it?

Australia is known for its brilliant plant diversity. The myriad of environments, from the desert to the rainforest and coastlines, are home to more than 20,000 different species of native plants.[3] Many of these have been carefully cultivated, used and traded in for millennia by Aboriginal and Torres Strait Islander peoples. Sophisticated bodies of knowledge related to these plants have been transmitted from generation to generation, along with cultural responsibilities to nurture and respect different species. This knowledge transforms the land into a vast supermarket and pharmacy with fully stocked shelves.

To trained eyes and hands, these trees, shrubs, grasses, flowers, vines and seeds hold vital nutrients, flavours, medicines and stories. For many Indigenous communities, plants are used in a holistic way, with ceremony, song and story used to unlock the knowledge and powerful healing effects of the plant. Indigenous groups know what is available in what season and how each plant relates to the other parts of the ecosystem. This has produced sophisticated fields of knowledge intimately linked to both diverse cultural geographies and the natural environment across the country.

Western scientific, government and commercial institutions have been collecting Australian plant material for more than 200 years. Sometimes, such collectors obtain Indigenous knowledge along with the plant material: where and how it is grown, the method of caring for the plant and so on. Examples include Duboisia, a tree from Queensland, whose leaves are now used for alleviating travel sickness; smokebush, which is used in medicines; and tea-tree, a traditional remedy of the Bundjalung people from the north coast of New South Wales.

On occasions, the culturally based Indigenous ownership of that knowledge has been acknowledged by collectors. However, in the majority of instances, that has not been the case. Different Western institutions take different approaches to the collection, management and use of Australian plant material and associated Indigenous plant knowledge. A particular challenge in this arena is the lack of a shared understanding of intellectual property issues related to Indigenous knowledge, and how those might best be addressed. But momentum is gathering, from diverse quarters, to face such challenges.

The early European settlers did not see the value in Indigenous plant applications. Indigenous people were seen as primitive and not intelligent cultures. Scientists and researchers ignored Indigenous peoples' role in identifying biological resources and providing related information. This, inevitably, led to biopiracy, where Indigenous people's knowledge of biological resources such as plants were taken and commercialised without Indigenous people's consent, and without any profits or benefits going back to their communities. This topic has been written on by notable academics and experts in the area including Professor Daniel Robinson from Australia and Vandana Shiva from India.[4]

Currently, in Australia, Indigenous knowledge is in demand by bioprospectors, and heavily sought by medical researchers and pharmaceutical companies in their quest to develop new medicines and products for commercial exploitation. There are currently no laws or policies that clearly define and protect the extensive amount of knowledge held by traditional owners that feeds into the creation of these products. Indigenous people report the looting of their knowledge and resources including plants, animals, hair, blood and genes. Indigenous Australians, and indigenous peoples worldwide, are concerned that their knowledge is being appropriated without their consent or knowledge and for little or nothing in return. Of greater concern are the threats these interests pose to the continuance of Indigenous cultures.

The good news is that, despite all this, there are ways that we can apply Indigenous plant knowledge in commercial industries without harming culture. In fact, when done right, by following the correct protocols, we can strengthen culture, empower communities and protect the knowledge for the next generations of Indigenous knowledge holders. This is for the benefit of all, as plant knowledge clearly feeds into and enriches so many areas of society such as horticulture, cooking, health and environmental conservation.

But it is crucial that throughout commercialisation, Indigenous peoples stay in control of their knowledge and resources, to protect them for future generations, keeping culture vibrant and intact, and ensuring the equitable sharing of commercial benefits.

The problem of patents

A patent is a form of intellectual property that aims to protect the rights of inventors by allowing them exclusive control over the use of their invention for a limited time frame. (See also chapter 4, page 102.) In Australia, this occurs under legislation known as the *Patents Act 1990* (Cth).

WHAT CAN BE PATENTED?

Standard patents last for 20 years. To have a standard patent application approved by IP Australia, an inventor or organisation needs to demonstrate that their invention is new and involves an 'inventive step'. This means that a plant existing in nature or a mere discovery is not patentable, nor is a way of doing something that is already obvious to an expert in the field. A new method of extraction of a particular plant enzyme with analgesic qualities could be protected with a patent, however.

Indigenous peoples may face difficulties obtaining standard patents for their methods of bush food harvesting, cooking and production due to the 'inventive step' requirement of patents. Also, applying for protection, or applying to oppose a patent, is costly and involves substantial financial and legal resources that may not be available to Indigenous communities. But why shouldn't the Indigenous peoples who have nurtured the plant and known of its properties for thousands of years share in the benefits that come from that knowledge? There is a need for the Australian patent system to change to uphold Indigenous cultural heritage rights.

In New Zealand, however, the intellectual property recognises the importance of Māori traditional knowledge. Māori patent officers (the Patents Māori advisory committee) monitor the use of Māori knowledge in patents and advise on whether a claimed invention is derived from traditional knowledge, or from indigenous plants or animals. They also advise if the commercial exploitation of that invention is likely to be contrary to Māori values.[5]

The smokebush story

I first heard the story of the smokebush plant (genus *Conospermum*) in 1996, at an Indigenous intellectual property conference in Brisbane. Predominantly found in the coastal areas between Geraldton and Esperance in Western Australia, the smokebush plant is traditionally used by Aboriginal people as medicine for many ailments.[6] Two speakers at the conference referred to smokebush – Henrietta Marrie, a Yidinji elder and Indigenous rights activist from Cairns, and Professor Michael Blakeney, then an intellectual property lecturer with the University of Western Australia. Henrietta spoke about an unscrupulous scientist who had taken smokebush samples back to his home country.

From the 1960s, smokebush specimens were collected by the US National Cancer Institute (NCI) for cancer research via a licence granted to them by the Western Australian Government. In 1981, the NCI tested 17 specimens of the smokebush plant for cancer application. The tests were negative. In the late 1980s, the US Government screened the stored specimens again for treating HIV. This time the screening of the plants struck gold. Out of 7000 plants screened internationally, the smokebush was one of only four plants found to contain the active property conocurovone. Laboratory tests showed that conocurovone had potential for treating the HIV virus. The US Government's Department of Health and Human Services then filed for a US patent in 1993 (granted in 1997 as US patent 5672607) and for an Australian patent in 1994 (granted in 1997 as Australian patent 680872).

The smokebush patents gave the US Government the exclusive right to use the compounds from the smokebush for the treatment of AIDS, and to license its use to others for terms they saw fit. The Western Australian Government negotiated a commercial deal with the NCI to license the patent rights to AMRAD, an Australian pharmaceutical company. According to Professor Blakeney, AMRAD paid $1.65 million to the WA Government for research and access rights to the plant. Blakeney estimated that if conocurovone was successfully commercialised, the WA Government would recoup royalties of up to $100 million per year by 2002.[7] No royalties or other compensation, or even acknowledgment, were forthcoming for Aboriginal people of Western Australia, highlighting the shortfalls in patent law in protecting traditional knowledge. This was in spite of the fact that their intergenerational nurturing of the plant had resulted in knowledge of its current potency as a healing plant.

At that 1996 conference in Brisbane, similar biopiracy stories were told by our Pacific neighbours, and US and Canadian indigenous brothers and sisters. Professor Kamal Puri, then a legal academic at University of Queensland, spoke about the Neem plant (*Azadirachta indica*), a tropical evergreen tree that is native to India. The Western world was alerted to the Neem's wonders in 1959, when a German entomologist reported that Neem trees were spared during a locust swarm that devoured all other crops.[8] Although the Neem tree has been used for centuries by Indian farmers and doctors, its chemical properties are exploited by US multinationals who have patented its properties.[9] Indian scientists, farmers and political activists assert that multinational companies have no right to expropriate the fruit of centuries of Indigenous experimentation.[10]

The Pacific Islanders have a similar story about their plant kava (*Piper methysticum*). Kava is highly valued as the source of a ceremonial beverage in Fiji, Vanuatu, Samoa, Hawaii and Tonga, among other Pacific nations.[11] Its effect on the limbic system of the brain – the system associated with emotions, along with other functions – means it has attracted the attention of Western medicine to treat anxiety, the side effects of menopause and other conditions. The plant has now been patented by companies in Germany, the United States and France; for example, the French company L'Oreal has patented kava as a treatment to reduce hair loss and stimulate hair growth. In 1997, the US market generated $30 million from the use of kava,[12] yet Pacific Islanders did not reap any benefits from this. The patent laws in the 1990s did not protect the traditional knowledge, and Pacific Islander countries were not able to challenge these patents.

In Samoa, the *Intellectual Property Act 2011* made changes to cover traditional knowledge. Each new patent application has to state whether or not the invention is based on local or Indigenous community knowledge. This aims to trigger permission to be sought, and deal to be struck, so that hopefully Samoans will benefit. However, there are limitations beyond borders. The patents laws of the world still allow kava derivative patents, because applicants are able to show inventive step and novelty with reference to prior art that has already been published.

However, the Nagoya Protocol (2010), a supplementary agreement to the Convention on Biological Diversity of 1992, provides some direction. The Protocol aims to facilitate benefit sharing for the use of genetic resources such as plants, animals, microorganisms, and even genes and molecules. It also aims to support the conservation and sustainable use of biological resources. In Article 12, it directs parties to the Protocol to take the customary laws of Indigenous people into consideration, along with community protocols and procedures, to respect traditional knowledge associated with genetic resources.

The Gumby Gumby story

For thousands of years, plants known by the name Gumby Gumby (also Gumbi Gumbi) have been used for medicine and healing by Indigenous people in Western Australia, South Australia, Queensland and New South Wales. In recent years, non-Indigenous people have grown their businesses around Gumby Gumby, such as the owners of a business based near Yeppoon, Queensland. This business sells health products derived from Gumby Gumby and the Indigenous knowledge associated with it, such as liquid extracts, soap, tea and powder. In 2008, the business successfully registered a patent for the exclusive rights to produce Gumby Gumby leaf extracts and their use in medicine.[13] This greatly undermines the cultural rights of Indigenous groups who may wish to also share in the commercial benefits of the plant and medicinal knowledge associated with it.

Palawa woman Lee Doherty owns and runs Bushfoods with Benefits, a business specialising in Gumby Gumby products such as capsules, tinctures, tea, soap and balms. The non-Indigenous Gumby Gumby business from Yeppoon sent her a 'cease and desist' letter, claiming she was in breach of their patent. But the patented extraction process was not the same as the traditional method Lee uses to create her products. In an interview on podcast *The Wire*, Lee said, 'Back in 2006 they put in a patent for an extraction process [for] Gumby Gumby. Because the extraction process was ethanol extraction [which] has never been done with traditional bush medicine, it was actually allowed to go through on the basis that it was "novel".'[14]

In 2020, academics with expertise in the protection of Indigenous knowledge, including Professor Daniel Robinson and Yamatji-Noongar woman Dr Margaret Raven from the University of New South Wales, lodged a formal request that IP Australia re-examine the grant of the patent. The inquiry is still in progress.

The Yeppoon business also attempted to trade mark the words 'Gumby Gumby', an Indigenous name that has been around for thousands of years. Lee says, 'For companies to come in and [find] our traditional medicine that's been around for 50,000 plus years, to put patents and trade marks on it, to me is morally and ethically really wrong. We need to be able to be self-sustaining and be able to commercialise our own traditional bush medicine however we wish to.'[15] Luckily, this trade mark application was not accepted. However, the business owners were successful in registering a composite trade mark consisting of the words 'Gumby Gumby' and an image of two hands cupping a pile of Gumby Gumby leaves.[16]

The trouble with trade marks

A trade mark is another type of intellectual property. It is a distinctive sign used by a person or business to identify itself to consumers and set apart its products or services from those of other traders. A trade mark can be a letter, number, word, phrase, sound, smell, shape, colour, logo, picture, movement, aspect of packaging, or a combination of these. In essence, trade marks are all about marketing and gaining a competitive edge in the market. The *Trade Marks Act 1995* (Cth) is the Australian law that provides protection for a registered trade mark against unauthorised misuse. Like patents, trade marks are registered with IP Australia.

Indigenous culture and trade marks

There are some aspects of the registered trade mark regime that may allow Indigenous people, including artists, creators and business operators, to protect aspects of their cultural expressions. But the flip side of this is that Indigenous language words, imagery and emblems may be used by non-Indigenous entities without permission of Indigenous people who are the owners of these cultural expressions. For example, a non-Indigenous person wants to name their jam and chutney business with an Indigenous language word from the region in which they live. They then decide to trade mark this so no one else can use the name – not even the Indigenous people whose are the custodians of that language. Is this fair?

Indigenous language and traditional plant names are not always appropriate in the labelling and marketing of food and health products. Some uses are culturally offensive, and even the general use of words and emblems may have an impact on Indigenous cultures separated from their original context. And critically, as with patents, what if an Indigenous person wanted to use their assets for their own commercial purposes but were prevented because it had been already been patented or trade marked by an outsider?

An alternative to this is engaging in an honest process of reflecting on whether the Indigenous language word is suitable to use. Do not use Indigenous language words for your bush products without considering whether it is appropriate, discussing it with Indigenous people and asking for permission. It is critical to consult and seek consent – the third True Tracks principle.

Indigenous people argue that they should have the right to provide consent before their culture is registered for IP rights such as trade marks and patents. But in Australia, there is currently no legal requirement to obtain consent.

Māori trade marks

New Zealand has recognised Māori ICIP in their trade mark law. The law provides that trade marks cannot be registered if they are offensive to Māori. The *Trade Marks Act 2002* (NZ) mandates that the Commissioner must appoint an advisory committee to advise whether a proposed use or registration of a trade mark that is derived from a Māori sign, text or imagery is, or is likely to be, offensive to Māori.[17] According to Aroha Mead, Māori ICIP advocate and member of the Māori Trade Marks Advisory Committee, there has been an increased number of trade marks containing Māori elements. The Committee has worked with the NZ Trade Mark Office to set up systems to manage this, including assessing against four different Māori dictionaries upon submission of the application.[18] The Māori Trade Marks Committee has also developed educational resources, such as guides on Māori imagery and concepts, and Māori designs and words that can freely be used (for example, the word 'kiwi', and the fern-leaf motif koru design, which can be used freely to describe goods and services or in designs).[19]

Reforms to the IP system in Australia

IP Australia has considered the establishment of an Indigenous Advisory Panel, similar to the Māori advisory committees in New Zealand, to assist with the protection and handling of Indigenous knowledge by the Australian IP system. This would provide greater protection for Indigenous people and their cultures.

At the time of writing, discussions have been held around the country to get feedback and explore options for how the system can be changed to better protect Indigenous knowledge rights. The Indigenous Knowledge Work Plan 2020–2021 includes proposals such as creating a Dictionary Database for trade mark and design examiners to refer to.[20] This would help prevent the misuse of Indigenous knowledge, and improve access to Indigenous knowledge information resources.

In the meantime, until the system is changed, people should carefully consider if the use of Indigenous language and knowledge is appropriate to commercialise, and consult with the relevant custodians.

Bush foods and products

What about bush foods? So far, the industry has latched on to just a handful. Around 18 Indigenous foods have been commercialised; these are in high demand in Australian and also internationally. People are going crazy over lemon myrtle, finger limes, Davidson plum, Kakadu plum, quandong, wattleseed and macadamia. These are increasingly being stocked in health shops and bulk food stores, often marketed as 'superfoods' due to their outstanding nutritional benefits. The Kakadu plum (*Terminalia ferdinandiana*), for instance, contains the world's highest known level of naturally occurring vitamin C in a fruit, with over 900 times more vitamin C than blueberries.[21]

Native ingredients are springing up in cafes, bars and fine-dining restaurants around the country. Native herbs like pepperberry are being sprinkled on plates, sprigs of the coastal succulent plant known as pig face tossed in salads and warrigal greens used in place of English spinach. I've also seen lemon myrtle cocktails and wattleseed lattes. Ironically, these native ingredients have an exotic allure because we are so much more familiar with produce from Europe. However, as Bruce Pascoe writes in the foreword to Indigenous cookbook *Warndu Mai*, 'Australian Aboriginal people domesticated, cooked and cared for foods which are adapted to our country's climate and fertility ... And we did it for around 100,000 years.'[22]

Australian Indigenous chefs are leading the way in raising the profile of native ingredients. Grounded in culture and family, they innovate the traditional and the contemporary. One renowned chef is Bundjalung man Mark Olive, who also goes by the name 'The Black Olive'. 'I was introduced to Indigenous ingredients by my elders and have been using them my whole life. Coming out of a chef apprenticeship and starting my career, I wanted to infuse all the amazing produce from this land into everyday cooking,' says Mark.[23]

Mark has achieved a lot and is now a highly sought-after celebrity chef who makes appearances at cultural festivals and events worldwide. He ran the successful Black Olive Catering in Melbourne, working with large corporates like Qantas and Tourism Australia and catering for events such as Oprah Winfrey's visit to Australia. Mark's training in performing arts and film production feeds into his natural flair as a television producer and host, such as the hit 2004 television series *The Outback Café* that shared his travels to remote Aboriginal communities and led to the publication of a recipe book with the same name. He even collaborated with gourmet ice cream company Peter's Connoisseur brand in 2019 to make a range of ice-creams featuring native ingredients like Davidson plum, cinnamon myrtle and wild hibiscus, saying, 'This can help Australians become more familiar with ingredients that are unique to our country, which deserve to be tasted and celebrated.'[24] The list of achievements go on, and Mark continues his passion in showcasing Indigenous foods with his restaurants south of Sydney – Dapbeto's Midden and Olive's on Wodi Wodi, in Dapto.

In 2017, Mark was joined by Derek Nannup, Whadjuk, Bindjareb, Yued and Wardarndi man of the Noongar nation, to co-present *On Country Kitchen*. One episode in the SBS TV series included a visit to Yuin country, where they harvested and cooked local shellfish – bimbalas and oysters – with elder Noel Butler. 'You don't take anything in a breeding cycle. It's got to reproduce first, it's continued on and you've always got it,' Noel says in the episode. 'People are not aware that we've got over 4500 different native plants that are edible, and yet we're not utilising them ... only about a dozen or fifteen plants, because that's all you can get, unless you can go out into the bush and get it. It's important for everybody to learn the real value of our country.'[25]

Clayton Donovan is another internationally acclaimed chef who is passionate about native ingredients. He starred in the ABC TV series *Wild Kitchen*, travelling country and visiting farms to source ingredients for his recipes. After running his own restaurant, Jaaning Tree, in Nambucca Heads, Clayton now cooks for corporate, public and private functions, and also teaches in schools. He says, 'Bush tucker is an important part of my cooking. At Jaaning Tree, it was about placing native ingredients in contemporary fine dining, showcasing and enjoying culture.'[26]

Many more talents have run restaurants, such as Aunty Beryl Van-Oploo, who had a popular café in Redfern and now runs Biri Biri Catering. Kieron Anderson, a proud Quandamooka, Kullilli and Wakka Wakka man, runs Yalabin Dining. After having worked in significant Brisbane restaurants, he now runs his restaurant on Minjerribah (North Stradbroke Island), his grandmother's homeland. His passion has developed towards private dining experiences which focus on sharing cultural knowledge of native foods and ancient cooking techniques learned from his family and elders. Alongside this, he creates educational food spaces to engage the wider community of Greater Brisbane, the Gold Coast and the Sunshine Coast in bush foods and Aboriginal customs.[27]

A lot of non-Indigenous chefs are jumping on board and using bush foods in their restaurants and recipes too. It is no surprise that Indigenous ingredients are taking off. They have highly unique and complex flavours, are extremely rich in nutrients and require the exact growing conditions the Australian climate provides. But the rise of Indigenous bush foods in the modern Australian culinary palette has largely been at the cost of Indigenous participation. A good idea is heard by an entrepreneurial visitor and then the opportunity is gone.

The question is: how can we respectfully integrate Indigenous knowledge into the Australian cuisine and food industry? We need to respect the wishes of the communities who are growing and looking after the plants and knowledge, and ensure that they share in the economic benefits too.

Indigenous growers and harvesters

The macadamia is a prime example of how the commercialisation of Australian bush foods can escape the involvement of Indigenous peoples. Macadamia trees are native to the rainforests of eastern Australia where Indigenous communities traded in and used the nut for its high energy content, oil and healing powers. As a delicacy, they were highly valuable. Aboriginal names for the nut include boombera, jindilli and others.

The macadamia is one of the few native Australian foods that is now a staple commercial product worldwide. It has been commercialised in Hawaii, South Africa, Brazil, Costa Rica, Kenya, Guatemala, New Zealand and more. This can all be traced back to the late 19th century when a small handful of macadamias were taken from some wild trees in south-east Queensland and sent to Hawaii.[28] Today, the Australian macadamia industry is enormous, worth over A$280 million annually, with over 700 growers.[29] A better outcome for Indigenous communities would have been being involved in the expansion of the industry, through benefit sharing and consent processes. Indigenous people could have been included in supply chains, or marketing and telling the origins of the nut.

A younger industry involves the Kakadu plum (*Terminalia ferdinandiana*), a small tree native to the Top End of the Northern Territory and the Kimberley region of Western Australia. The Kakadu plum has many other names, depending on the region, like 'gubinge' for the Bardi people of the western Kimberley. It has been used as food and medicine for thousands of years by Indigenous Australians. Interest in its nutritional power is growing rapidly, especially its vitamin C content. It's sold as a powder and put into products like juices, energy drinks, jam and cosmetics.

The Indigenous families who grow and harvest Kakadu plums across northern Australia have come together to strengthen their standing in the supply chain. This led to the formation of the Northern Australia Aboriginal Kakadu Plum Alliance (NAAKPA), a network of Aboriginal corporations.

NAAKPA was formed to support Indigenous leadership, economic independence and self-determination in the Kakadu plum industry. In the 2019 season, NAAKPA enterprises harvested over 20 tonnes of Kakadu plum, with a farm gate value of more than $A600,000.[30] NAAKPA also aims to help protect the traditional knowledge and cultural practices in the commercialisation of the plant, looking to the framework of the United Nations Declaration on the Rights of Indigenous People (UNDRIP – see chapter 1), especially Article 31, and the Nagoya Protocol. NAAKPA encourages the use of Nagoya to ensure that the benefits from using native plants and animals are shared with Aboriginal people who have the knowledge related to those resources.[31]

Mayi Harvests is one of the businesses within NAAKPA. It is owned and run by Pat (Mamanyjun) Torres, who is of Djugun, Yawuru, Ngumbarl/Jabirr-Jabirr, Nyul Nyul, Bardi and Karajarri descent, in Western Australia's Kimberley region. The company wild-harvests on their traditional family lands in Ngumbarl and Jabirr-Jabirr country. As Pat says, 'Every bush food has its own creation story, its own song and dance and cultural knowledge that has been handed down by our ancestors for thousands of years ... The challenge for us is how do we bring our ancient foods into a contemporary industry while maintaining our connection to our culture, because for us, it's not just about money, it's about our identity.'[32]

Rayleen Brown is a Ngangiwumirr/Arrernte woman who started her catering business, Kungkas Can Cook, in Alice Springs in 2000. Rayleen has done much to raise the profile of bush foods in a way that supports the livelihoods of the women she works with, and respects connection to story and country. 'When I first started buying bush foods, I was really interested to find out more about the women who wild harvest these beautiful products,' she writes on her website. 'Growing up myself in the bush, living off these bush foods, I wanted to link up with these women who had such a rich knowledge about plants and stories and Country and the environment. We are so lucky to have these women ... this knowledge is something they can use to produce an economy they and their communities can benefit from.'[33]

Rayleen says that the Indigenous people in the industry – the wild harvesters, growers and suppliers – deserve a bigger portion of the benefits. She also insists on better protection for the ecological knowledge rights of those who have sustained their communities for thousands of years using these foods.[34]

In Sydney, Peter Cooley has established IndigiGrow, an Aboriginal social enterprise that leads environmental projects and includes a native plant nursery.[35] On the island of Groote Eylandt, in the Gulf of Carpentaria, there is Bush Medijina, a business that draws from traditional plant medicine to create bush remedies like balms, soaps and oils. It was the vision of Warningakalina women elders, who saw the need to build culture and capability across the islands to support livelihoods of women, children and families, and to pass their knowledge down to the younger generation.[36]

Anika Valenti, senior solicitor at Terri Janke and Company, has been providing legal support to Bush Medijina for the last few years. As Anika says, 'Bush Medijina have worked really hard to build a sustainable business supporting local women and based on traditional knowledge and traditional bush medicine. The difficulty for Bush Medijina, and a lot of Aboriginal businesses with products using medicinal plant knowledge, is the prohibitive regulatory requirements of the *Therapeutic Goods Act 1989* and having to alternatively market their products as cosmetics. The TGA makes legal compliance very difficult, forcing them to deny the deep cultural significance of the work they do.'[37]

One possible solution to the free-riding of Indigenous knowledge and exclusion of Indigenous people in the growing and harvesting side of the bush foods industry could be a certification or collective trade mark for specific industries such as the Kakadu plum. These could be Indigenous-owned and Indigenous-managed, providing local producers with an opportunity to come together and set their own standards based on the needs of their region.

This system can be thought of in a similar way to geographical indications (GIs), a form of intellectual property that benefits the original manufacturers of a product linked to a geographical region. Like a brand or label, they can also enhance the market value of products. Champagne, Scotch whisky, Darjeeling tea and Roquefort cheese are all well-known examples of GIs. GIs are not only applicable to agricultural products like liquor, coffee and cheese, but also to art and crafts. There is an opportunity for Indigenous-grown food to be protected under GIs. This would require local producers to come together and set rules as a group to implement their collective trade mark.

Indigenous wholesalers, businesses and buyers

Sharon Winsor is a Ngemba Weilwan woman who runs Indigiearth, a thriving bush products business. Sharon's story is inspiring. As a friend and business peer, I am constantly impressed by her drive and passion. Sharon says, 'I've enjoyed setting up a business than enables Indigenous producers to have an outlet for their produce.'[38] A key to her success has been knowing what to sell and who to buy from. She thoughtfully sources her products from Indigenous growers all over the country. Indigiearth sells many different native ingredients for cooking, such as lemon myrtle and roasted wattleseed, as well as beautiful loose-leaf teas, skin care products and condiments.

There are many more like Sharon who have created innovative businesses. Jesse Gurugirr, a Guringai man, owns LORE Australia, a health and wellness company using native bio-foods, selling native-infused kombucha and a special Guradji tea. Robert Dann, a Nyul Nyul man from the Kimberley region, started the business Bindam Mie. At the heart of this business is the boab tree, native to the region where Robert is from, which has been used by his ancestors for thousands of years. As well as the vitamin- and mineral-rich boab powder made from the nuts of the tree, Bindam Mie sells boab beverages like iced tea and ginger beer, boab syrup and a skin ointment too.

When you want to support Indigenous businesses such as these, it's sometimes hard to tell whether a business is actually Indigenous-owned, or just using Indigenous ingredients. To find certified Indigenous-owned and operated businesses, go to the Supply Nation database.[39] Supply

Nation is an important organisation that certifies Aboriginal and Torres Strait Islander businesses in Australia, keeping the Indigenous business ecosystem strong and healthy (see chapter 16).

Indigenous health and wellbeing businesses

Removal from traditional lands, along with alienation from land, resources and cultural practices, have had direct effects on the health and wellbeing of Indigenous people, who face significantly lower life expectancy than non-Indigenous people. There is potential for Indigenous bush foods to improve this situation, and for benefits to flow back to Indigenous peoples, whose knowledge and resources underlie the bush foods industry. As Gamilaroi woman and nutritionist Tracy Hardy says, 'I realised the effect our bush foods have on our physical, emotional, social and cultural health, as well as our spiritual connection to Country.'[40] Sharon Winsor, who runs Indigiearth, also focuses on health. She does this well by offering ingredients and recipes that are nutritious and healthy. Gamilaroi man Clinton Schultz of Sobah promotes wellbeing and sobriety in his alcohol-free beer infused with native ingredients.

Researching bush foods

Scientists are also researching the composition, and health and nutritional benefits of bush products – for example, replacing salt with saltbush to reduce sodium intake for high blood pressure. Wattleseed has high levels of protein; is a good source of zinc, iron and dietary fibre; and has a low glycaemic index, which makes it ideal for diabetic and other specialty diets.[41] Twelve native fruits – Kakadu plum, Illawarra plum, Burdekin plum, Davidson plum, riberry, red and yellow finger limes, Tasmanian pepperberry, brush cherry, Cedar Bay cherry, muntries and Molucca raspberry – have been identified as having significantly higher antioxidant and vitamin capacities than the blueberry, which has long been renowned for its high antioxidant levels.[42]

However, this kind of scientific research into bush foods needs to embody a more collaborative approach, marrying traditional knowledge with the health, science and food sectors in a way that benefits community.

Kakadu plum: Collective knowledge

In 2016, Terri Janke and Company advised scientists from the University of Western Australia, who were looking to collaborate with Aboriginal communities to work out the genetic make-up of the Kakadu plum. Although the project did not go ahead, we developed a framework for access and benefit sharing. This shift to a collaborative approach is needed in research policies within all universities, to consider the *collective* knowledge of Indigenous people and how benefits are going to be shared with the communities where, for example, the plants are situated.

Rooibos tea: A South African case study

Rooibos tea is made from the leaves of the shrub *Aspalathus linearis*, endemic to the Cederberg mountains, north of Cape Town, South Africa. Research has suggested that the San and Khoi people, indigenous inhabitants of South Africa, discovered rooibos centuries ago, using it as a tea and herbal remedy. The San people's origins in southern Africa are understood to date back to 100,000 years ago, with the Khoi arriving much more recently, around 2000 years ago. It is said that Carl Thunberg, a Swedish botanist, first recorded the use of rooibos as a beverage by these communities in 1772.[43] Communities also report using rooibos to manage high blood pressure and treat various medical conditions such as stomach ailments and skin disorders.[44] Passed through the generations, the traditional knowledge behind these uses has been associated with the San and Khoi people. However, the rooibos industry has shown a perception that there is no conclusive evidence that traditional knowledge of rooibos rests with any particular community.[45]

The commercial value of rooibos grew in the 20th century and it is now a popular alternative to black tea and coffee, as it is caffeine free and high in antioxidants. It is also used as an ingredient in cosmetic and skin products.[46] Today, commercial rooibos farming is worth an estimated 500 million rand (A$43.6 million) a year, with Germany, the Netherlands,

UK, Japan and the US representing 86 per cent of the export market in 2010.[47]

Following disputes involving the filing of trade marks in the US using the word 'rooibos', the South African Rooibos Council (SARC) and the rooibos industry championed for the registration of rooibos as a geographical indication (GI).[48] This is a label for products that are only produced in specific geographic locations. GIs help protect the misuse of the name and creates guidelines for how it should be produced to ensure quality. They also add value and support marketing.[49] In 2014, South Africa developed a geographical indication (GI) for rooibos. Now, the term rooibos can only be used for products from the designated geographical area.

In late 2019, after almost a decade of negotiation, South Africa's rooibos tea industry entered into an agreement with the San and Khoi communities to share the profits. Under the agreement, the San and Khoi communities will receive 1.5 per cent of the value that the farmers get when they sell to the tea processor, which is estimated to amount to 12 million rand (A$1 million) for the year 2019.[50] The proceeds of the agreement will be split evenly between the San and Khoi communities, with a third group of small-scale rooibos farmers in the region disadvantaged under apartheid sharing in the Khoi portion.

This is a landmark agreement, being the first industry-wide Indigenous benefit sharing agreement following the ratification of the Nagoya Protocol. This agreement is the largest of its kind between indigenous peoples and a bush food industry, and provides a model for other countries and industries that rely on indigenous traditional knowledge in bush food production. Significantly, it acknowledged San and Khoi as holders of the traditional knowledge associated with rooibos. Overall, the rooibos agreement represents an incredible achievement for the compensation of indigenous communities in their ownership and passing down of traditional knowledge, and recognising indigenous contribution to the development of bush food industries.

Although this arrangement is largely a successful outcome of nearly a decade of negotiations, questions still remain regarding how the funds are to reach the San and Khoi people, as many are not well-connected with their communities' leadership.[51] As a result, the parties have agreed to revisit the agreement. Despite the agreement, however, the precise origins of rooibos tea and its use are still contentious. This disagreement is a substantive reason as to why the rooibos agreement took so long to make, eventually leading the government to advise the tea industry that it needed to pay the communities.

Indigenous leadership in the bush foods industry

In 2019, I went to the first National Bushfood Symposium hosted by the Aboriginal charity First Hand Solutions. The first of its kind, the symposium aimed to bring Aboriginal and Torres Strait Islander communities together to discuss how to increase Indigenous participation in the bush foods sector, in all levels of the supply chain – from growers and harvesters to farm managers, exporters and businesses. One of the main aims was to identify and address the barriers that prevented Indigenous peoples' involvement in the industry. Peter Cooley, First Hand Solutions CEO, noted that even though the bush food industry was valued at A$20 million each year, 'it is estimated that Aboriginal and Torres Strait Islander people make up only 1–2% of the market presence and we're keen to work together to improve this percentage.'[52]

'We put together the symposium because the bush food industry … is quite a large industry at the moment, and it's on the verge of getting much, much bigger. Aboriginal people have such a small presence in the industry and we need that to change, in a way that Aboriginal people benefit much more from our knowledge and our culture – and in a way that it's also protected,' says Peter.[53] It was a groundbreaking event for many of the attendees who shared their wisdom over the two days. It was inspiring to see so many businesses making their bush products with so much heart and passion for keeping culture alive.

At the end of the symposium, the attendees created a National Indigenous Bushfood Statement. The statement carries a strong message of self-determination and Indigenous empowerment when it comes to using Indigenous knowledge in industries such as food, pharmaceuticals, cosmetics and agriculture. The First Nations Bushfood & Botanical Alliance Australia was formed to work on key recommendations, including:

- establish national protocols (based on the True Tracks principles) across the industry to promote Indigenous values and protect cultural integrity
- develop a certification mark and/or geographical indications to benefit Indigenous producers and recognise Indigenous custodianship
- set up a national Indigenous-controlled industry body
- promote changes to the law to protect Indigenous knowledge in the bush foods industry
- educate others to respect Indigenous knowledge, values and protocols.[54]

Along similar lines, the Federation of Victorian Traditional Owner Corporations (FVTOC) developed a Native Food and Botanicals Strategy and a program named Djakitjuk Djanga (meaning 'Country's food' in the Dja Dja Wurrung language) for supporting Aboriginal-owned businesses and organisations in the industry. The FVTOC want to make sure that traditional owners and other Aboriginal people in their communities receive the economic benefits from the commercialisation of knowledge, products and land use – through employment and training, capacity building for Aboriginal business, or by placing profits from commercial activities into a trust for community.

As the stewards and custodians, Indigenous people should be the people who take Indigenous plant knowledge to market. Though neglected in the past, today the preparation of plants generates much more interest. Indigenous people have always known about the foods and medicines available from the rich plant life in the environment. They have also known that preparation is important – for example, which plants can kill you if you do not strain them in a dillybag in cool, fast-flowing water to remove toxins. They know what parts of the plant to use and how to prepare them, just as a seasoned chef does in a supermarket, or a pharmacist does in a pharmacy. But Indigenous people are always mindful that the land and waters give life, and will continue to do so for thousands of years to come.

> **WHAT YOU CAN DO ...**
>
> If you are thinking about commercialising plants based on Indigenous knowledge, consider:
> - Why have I selected this plant resource based on Indigenous knowledge, or a connection with Indigenous people? What are my intentions behind using, adapting and marketing it?
> - How can this project be about enabling and enhancing Indigenous opportunity?
> - How am I engaging and involving Indigenous people in the process?
> - How am I accessing this resource from Indigenous country? If you access traditional knowledge and plants from Indigenous land or waters, you should enter into access and benefit sharing (ABS) agreements with regional alliances, and form collective growing cooperatives.

Resources

Supply Nation: https://supplynation.org.au
Indigenous Business Australia (IBA): www.iba.gov.au
First Nations Bushfood & Botanical Alliance Australia: www.firstnationsbushfoods.org.au
Northern Australia Aboriginal Kakadu Plum Alliance (NAAKPA): https://naakpa.com.au/
Daniel F Robinson, *Confronting Biopiracy: Challenges, Cases and International Debates*, Earthscan, London, 2010
Ikechi Mgbeoji, *Global Biopiracy: Patents, Plants, and Indigenous Knowledge*, Cornell University Press, Ithaca, NY, 2006
Vandana Shiva, *Biopiracy: The Plunder of Nature and Knowledge*, North Atlantic Books, Berkeley, CA, 2016
Bruce Pascoe, *Dark Emu: Black Seeds: Agriculture or Accident?*, Magabala Books, Broome, 2016
Nelly Zola and Beth Gott, *Koori Plants, Koori People*, Koorie Heritage Trust, Melbourne, 1992
Indigenous Knowledge: Issues for Protection and Management (Terri Janke and Company/ IP Australia, 2018): www.ipaustralia.gov.au/sites/default/files/ipaust_ikdiscussionpaper_28march2018.pdf

Terri Janke, 'From smokebush to spinifex: Towards recognition of Indigenous knowledge in the commercialisation of plants', *International Journal of Rural Law and Policy*, no. 1, 2018, 5713, <www.austlii.edu.au/au/journals/IntJlRuralLawP/2018/1.pdf>

Mark Olive, *Mark Olive's Outback Café: A Taste of Australia*, 3rd ed, RM Williams Publishing, Sydney, 2011

Damien Coulthard and Rebecca Sullivan, *Warndu Mai (Good Food)*, Hachette, Sydney, 2020

Notes

1. Gerry Turpin, *A Bridge Between Two Worlds: Gerry Turpin, TEDx JCU Cairns*, TEDx Talks, YouTube, 29 November 2016, <www.youtube.com/watch?v=hE7KKBC1vMM>.
2. For example: Dr Kylie Lingard, 'Making "bush food" markets fair', *Farming Matters*, vol. 32, no. 2, 2016, pp. 31–32.
3. Arthur D Chapman, *Numbers of Living Species in Australia and the World*, 2nd ed., report for the Australian Biological Resources Study, Australian Biodiversity Information Services, Canberra, September 2009, <www.environment.gov.au/system/files/pages/2ee3f4a1-f130-465b-9c7a-79373680a067/files/nlsaw-2nd-complete.pdf>.
4. See Daniel F Robinson, *Confronting Biopiracy: Challenges, Cases and International Debates*, Earthscan, London, 2010; and Vandana Shiva, *Biopiracy: The Plunder of Nature and Knowledge*, North Atlantic Books, Berkeley, CA, 2016. I have also written about these issues: see Terri Janke, 'From smokebush to spinifex: Towards recognition of Indigenous knowledge in the commercialisation of plants', *International Journal of Rural Law and Policy*, no. 1, 2018, 5713, <www.austlii.edu.au/au/journals/IntJlRuralLawP/2018/1.pdf>.
5. New Zealand Intellectual Property Office (NZIPO), *Māori IP*, NZIPO, n.d., <www.iponz.govt.nz/about-ip/maori-ip/>; *Register IP that has a Māori element*, NZIPO, n.d., <www.iponz.govt.nz/about-ip/maori-ip/register-ip-that-has-a-maori-element/>.
6. Phillip G Kerr, 'Bioprospecting in Australia: Sound biopractice or biopiracy?' *Social Alternatives*, vol. 29, no. 3, 2010, p. 44; Ellen Reid and TJ Betts, 'The records of Western Australian plants used by Aboriginals as medicinal agents', *Planta Medica*, vol. 36, 1979, pp. 164–73.
7. Michael Blakeney, *Bioprospecting and the Protection of Traditional Medical Knowledge*, paper presented at the Symposium on Intellectual Property Protection for the Arts and Cultural Expression of Aboriginal and Torres Strait Islander People, Brisbane, 28 September 1996, p. 196.
8. Kamal Puri, 'Indigenous knowledge and intellectual property rights – The interface', in Pradip Ninan Thomas and Jan Servaes (eds), *Intellectual Property Rights and Communications in Asia: Conflicting Traditions*, Sage, New Delhi/London, 2006, p. 122.
9. Vandana Shiva and Radha Holla-Bhar, 'Intellectual piracy and the Neem tree', *The Ecologist*, vol. 23, no. 6, 1993, p. 223.
10. Vandana Shiva, *Protect or Plunder? Understanding Intellectual Property Rights*, Zed Books, London, 2002, p. 60.
11. Kanchana Kariyawasam, 'Protecting biodiversity, traditional knowledge and intellectual property in the Pacific: Issues and challenges', *Asia Pacific Law Review*, vol. 16, no. 1, 2008, pp. 73–89.
12. Kanchana Kariyawasam, 'Protecting biodiversity, traditional knowledge and intellectual property in the Pacific'.

13. IP Australia, *2008300612: Production of Leaf Extracts of Pittosporum phillyraeoides and the Use Thereof in Medicine*, AusPat, 2009, <https://pericles.ipaustralia.gov.au/ols/auspat/applicationDetails.do?applicationNo=2008300612>.
14. Lee Doherty, in 'A war of words over the trademarking of traditional bush medicine' [podcast episode], *The Wire*, 16 June 2016, <http://thewire.org.au/story/a-war-of-words/>.
15. Lee Doherty, 'A war of words over the trademarking of traditional bush medicine'.
16. IP Australia, *Trade Mark 1760850*, Australian Trade Mark Search, 201, <https://search.ipaustralia.gov.au/trademarks/search/view/1760850>.
17. *Trade Marks Act 2002* (NZ), section 178.
18. Aroha Mead, Member, NZIPO Māori Trade Marks Committee, personal communication, 10 August 2020.
19. NZIPO, *Māori Words and Designs*, NZIPO, n.d., <www.iponz.govt.nz/about-ip/maori-ip/words-designs/>.
20. IP Australia, *Protection of Indigenous Knowledge in the Intellectual Property System: Work Plan 2020–2021*, IP Australia, 2020, <www.ipaustralia.gov.au/sites/default/files/ip-australia-indigenous-knowledge-work-plan-2020-2021.pdf>.
21. Ian Cock and Shimony Mohanty, 'Evaluation of the antibacterial activity and toxicity of *Terminalia ferdinandia* fruit extracts', *Pharmacognosy Journal*, vol. 3, no. 20, 2011, p. 72, <www.kimberleywildgubinge.com.au/application/files/9214/8116/9190/Kakadu_journal_proof.pdf>
22. Rebecca Sullivan and Damien Coulthard, *Warndu Mai (Good Food): Introducing Native Australian Ingredients to Your Kitchen*, Hachette, Sydney, 2019.
23. Mark Olive, email correspondence, 28 January 2021.
24. Remedios Lucio, 'Connoisseur champions native ingredients in latest range', *FMCG*, 13 August 2019, <https://insidefmcg.com.au/2019/08/12/connoisseur-champions-native-ingredients-in-latest-range/>.
25. Noel Butler, in SBS, *On Country Kitchen*, season 2, episode 9, 2019, <www.sbs.com.au/ondemand/program/on-country-kitchen>.
26. Clayton Donovan, personal communication, 16 March 2021.
27. Kieron Anderson, personal communication, 23 February 2021.
28. Jennifer Nichols, '"Shocking" DNA discovery traces most of the world's macadamias back to one Australian tree', *ABC Rural*, 30 May 2019, <www.abc.net.au/news/rural/2019-05-30/macadamia-research-nuts/11160786>.
29. Australian Macadamia Society, *About the Macadamia Industry*, Australian Macadamia Society, n.d., <www.australianmacadamias.org/industry/about/about-the-macadamia-industry>.
30. NAAKPA, *NAAKPA 2019 Kakadu Plum Harvest Update*, NAAKPA, 2019, <https://naakpa.com.au/NAAKPA%20harvest%20update>.
31. NAAKPA, *Nagoya Protocol and Access and Benefit Sharing Agreements*, NAAKPA, n.d., <https://naakpa.com.au/nagoya-protocol-and-access-and-benefit-sharing-agreements>.
32. First Hands Solutions, *Bushfood Symposium*, First Hands Solutions, 2019, <www.firsthandsolutions.org/bushfood-symposium>.
33. Kungkas Can Cook, *The First Farmers* <https://kungkascancook.com.au/first-farmers>.
34. Kungkas Can Cook, *Rayleen Brown: Founder & Owner*, Kungkas Can Cook, n.d., <https://kungkascancook.com.au/rayleenbrown>.
35. IndigiGrow, *What We're All About*, Inidgigrow, n.d., <www.indigrow.com.au/about>.
36. Anindilyakwa Services Aboriginal Corporation, *Bush Medijina: Our Story*, Bush Medijina, 2020, <https://bushmedijina.com.au/pages/our-story>.

37 Anika Valenti, personal communication, 25 June 2020.
38 Sharon Winsor, personal communication, 28 January 2021.
39 Supply Nation, <www.supplynation.com.au>.
40 Tracy Hardy, personal communication, 23 February 2021.
41 AgriFutures Australia, *Wattleseed*, AgriFutures Australia, n.d., <www.agrifutures.com.au/farm-diversity/wattleseed/>.
42 Michael Netzel, Gabriele Netzel, Qingguo Tian et al., 'Native Australian fruits – A novel source of antioxidants for food', *Innovative Food Science and Emerging Technologies*, vol. 8, 2007, pp. 339–46.
43 South African Department of Environmental Affairs, *Traditional Knowledge Associated with Rooibos and Honeybush Species in South Africa*, October 2014, p. ii, <www.environment.gov.za/sites/default/files/reports/traditionalknowledge_rooibosandhoneybushspecies_report.pdf>.
44 South African Department of Environmental Affairs, *Traditional Knowledge Associated with Rooibos*; Boris Gorelik, *Rooibos: An Ethnographic Perspective*, Rooibos Council, Pniel, South Africa, 2017, pp. 22–23, <https://sarooibos.co.za/wp/wp-content/uploads/2018/10/20180723-SARC-format-TK-Paper-SU-1.pdf>.
45 South African Department of Environmental Affairs, *Traditional Knowledge Associated with Rooibos*; Boris Gorelik, *Rooibos: An Ethnographic Perspective*, Rooibos Council, Pniel, South Africa, 2017, p. 38, <https://sarooibos.co.za/wp/wp-content/uploads/2018/10/20180723-SARC-format-TK-Paper-SU-1.pdf>.
46 South African Department of Environmental Affairs, *Traditional Knowledge Associated with Rooibos*, p. 22.
47 Elizabeth Joubert and Dalene de Beer, 'Rooibos (*Aspalathus linearis*) beyond the farm gate: From herbal tea to potential phytopharmaceutical', *South African Journal of Botany*, vol. 77, no. 4, 2011, p. 869.
48 WIPO, *Disputing a Name, Developing a Geographical Indication*, WIPO, 2011, <www.wipo.int/ipadvantage/en/details.jsp?id=2691>.
49 WIPO, *Disputing a Name, Developing a Geographical Indication*.
50 Linda Nordling, 'Rooibos tea profits will be shared with Indigenous communities in landmark agreement', *Nature*, 2 November 2019, <www.nature.com/articles/d41586-019-03374-x>.
51 Linda Nordling, 'Rooibos tea profits will be shared with Indigenous communities in landmark agreement'.
52 First Hand Solutions, *National Indigenous Bushfood Symposium*, First Hand Solutions, 2019, <www.firsthandsolutions.org/bushfood-symposium>.
53 Peter Cooley, in *Inaugural National Indigenous Bushfood Symposium*, First Hand Solutions, YouTube, 21 December 2019, <www.youtube.com/watch?v=MDx1FljGvnU>.
54 First Hand Solutions, *Statement from the National Indigenous Bushfood Symposium*, First Hand Solutions, 2019, <www.firsthandsolutions.org/national-indigenous-bushfood-statem>.

10

CULTURAL COGNISANCE: BRINGING ANCIENT KNOWLEDGE AND SCIENCE TOGETHER

In 2016 I gave a TEDx talk at James Cook University in Cairns. I spoke about creating a culture of innovation with Indigenous knowledge and the immense value this could bring to wider knowledge systems in Western society, particularly in science. As I was preparing, I was interested in including knowledge of Mer (Murray Island), so I contacted Falen D Passi.

Falen is the chair of Mer Gedkem Le (Torres Strait Islanders) Corporation based on Mer, the subject of the 1992 Mabo case. He is also skilled at natural resource management, with great knowledge of the island and the environment. Falen explained to me how everything is interconnected, how the seasonal shifts show the ebbs and flows of all life on the island, and how this extends to the Pacific and the world. He explained how the Meriam people know that the nesting season of the Toli bird (eastern curlew) has begun by paying attention to the turtle:

> Meriam people call the bird Toli. We don't see that little brown bird lay its eggs on the island or the sand cay, not like the frigatebird or the booby. In Meriam we say toli ra ardar kak wer, meaning we don't see the eggs or the nesting of the toli. During turtle season, when the turtles come up to lay their eggs on the beach, the toli begins to sing and fly around and around like a whirlwind. Now the islanders say the bird is being chased by somebody, it must be the turtle. Western science tells us that they fly high due north all the way to Siberia for nesting. They then fly due south back to Mer and the sand cay.[1]

Cultural cognisance: Bringing ancient knowledge and science together

I love this example because it demonstrates how Indigenous science considers the whole picture of how life interacts on the land and in the sea. It also shows us the connections between knowledge, story and language. Western scientists may have the technology to generate extremely detailed information about the biology and reproductive behaviour of the toli, but this may not enable them to predict when they will start nesting. Yet Indigenous science gives us the answer, based on observing the behaviour of the turtle.

The knowledge system of the Islanders is also connected to the flickering stars in the night sky, including the Tagai constellation. The Southern Cross forms part of this large constellation. Falen says, 'For us on Mer, Tagai shows us many things, from navigation to leadership, gardening, turtle season, changes in the seasons and the weather, when to plant food, the low and the high tides.'[2]

This wealth of scientific information and know-how in Indigenous knowledge systems stems from thousands of years of intergenerational teaching and interaction with the land and sea. It is grounded in the interconnectedness of all things and an understanding that human beings are part of the ecosystem, not separate from it. You could say that Indigenous world views are deeply holistic. In the past, Indigenous ways of understanding the natural world were rarely acknowledged as equal to Western science. Mainstream scientists and academics treated Indigenous science as something that fell outside the boundaries of what was strictly classified as 'science'. Indigenous people were viewed as only informants or consultants, rather than as scientists and experts, perhaps because their knowledge wasn't acquired through a university degree or in a laboratory.

Indigenous science has deep historical and spiritual roots, connecting to ancestral and intergenerational ways of understanding and caring for country and people. As Corey Tutt, Kamilaroi man and founder of the educational charity Deadly Science, says, 'Aboriginal people were the first scientists, with tens of thousands of years of trial and error.' For example, Corey says resin has been used by Aboriginal people for thousands of years, but commercial glue was only invented around the 1500s.[3]

Understanding of Indigenous science is growing in mainstream academia and in the public mind, as the success of Bruce Pascoe's popular book *Dark Emu* (2014) shows. Bruce explores evidence of the scientific and agricultural practices that existed across the Australian continent before invasion, illuminating the cultivation of native plant food crops like grains and tubers, and Indigenous aquaculture – the eel farming by the Gunditjmara people of south-west Victoria, and the stone fish traps on the Barwon River at Brewarrina, for example. As Bruce, in his 2014 TEDx Talk, said, 'Let's get rid of the idea of the hapless hunter-gatherer and recognise the ingenuity of the First Australians.'[4] Corey Tutt wants every remote Australian school to have a copy of *Dark Emu* to help educate them about Australia's history of Indigenous land management and cultivation. He wants Indigenous children to believe in themselves and understand their environment for the benefit of all Australians.[5]

Indigenous science goes far beyond boomerangs and spears, says Joe Sambono, a Jingili man with a background in zoology:

> This is not an issue of Western science vs Indigenous Science. It is simply a matter of understanding that all groups of humans around the world and throughout history have hypothesised, experimented, made empirical observations, gathered evidence, recognised patterns, verified through repetition, made inferences and predictions, and developed branches of knowledge that helped them to make sense of the world around them and their place within it.[6]

Indigenous people are increasingly being included in the science-based system. Marcus Hughes is a strong supporter and advocate. Marcus says, 'Let's celebrate and share the sophistication, richness, and leadership of Australia's First Peoples within the scientific domain.'[7] Marcus, former Head of Indigenous Engagement and Strategy at the Museum of Applied Arts and Sciences (MAAS), established the MAAS Indigenous Sciences Symposium, bringing together Aboriginal and Torres Strait Islander academics, theorists, researchers, designers, engineers, educators and students to discuss current and future scientific research agendas and investigations.

People like Falen D Passi, Corey Tutt, Bruce Pascoe and Joe Sambono know that Indigenous knowledge of country presents an enormous opportunity to develop alliances with scientists, universities and organisations seeking positive change. Indigenous knowledge and science can help us find solutions to caring for country. It can help us manage fires, water, and invasive weeds and animals. We could see more breakthroughs in medicine, health and astronomy too.

Science and research also offer opportunities for Indigenous people to develop culturally based businesses; there is serious potential in creating equal partnerships with Indigenous communities within scientific research contexts. This will not only enrich the Western scientific contexts, but support Indigenous employment and help to keep cultural practices alive. I believe that if we can share Indigenous science within the right ethical and legal frameworks, we can create pathways to empower Indigenous peoples and positively impact the Earth – and everyone on it.

Integrating Indigenous and Western science: Legal considerations

Patents legislation in Australia – under the *Patents Act 1990* (Cth) – focuses on inventors being the first creators of patent ideas. The novelty and inventive step needed to file a patent, which then enables exclusive rights to exploit an invention, are based on Western knowledge systems that favour written knowledge. (See chapter 9, page 207.) In the past, Indigenous people were seen as the informants, not the inventors. This has led to much exploitation, and Indigenous people have become understandably sceptical about sharing their knowledge. Their knowledge could assist many things in the world, from health and medicines to technology and shelter – almost everything in innovation.

We have only just begun to scratch the surface of applying Indigenous knowledge in scientific growth. What if we were to unlock this potential? What would happen if we were to harness that knowledge and engage Indigenous people as an integral part of the new knowledge economy?

We might see more medical breakthroughs involving plants like

Barringtonia acutangula – the mudjala tree, or freshwater mangrove – that has been used for generations by the Nyikina Mangala community from the Kimberley region of Western Australia for its healing properties. This came to light in 1986 when Paul Marshall, a former Kimberley Land Council CEO, was in the Kimberley interviewing senior elders for an Aboriginal oral history book project,[8] at the request of respected elder John Watson, a former Kimberley Land Council Chair. By coincidence, a freshwater crocodile John Watson had been hunting had recently removed the top of his finger and he told Paul how he had used mudjala to treat the pain. Following discussions on its commercial potential, the Nyikina Mangala elders appointed Paul to start exploring whether it could be commercialised to the benefit of the Nyikina Mangala people. Acutely aware of biopiracy (see chapter 9) and the unethical exploitation of Indigenous knowledge, Paul first consulted an old friend, Greg Woods QC, who referred him to a patent attorney for further guidance. Then, after an investigation into the capabilities of research institutions, Paul approached Professor Ron Quinn of Griffith University, a leader in natural product discovery and commercialisation.

This led to an Intellectual Property and Confidentiality Agreement in 1987 and the start of a groundbreaking research partnership between the Jarlmadangah Burru Aboriginal Corporation and Griffith University, with Ron Quinn winning two NHMRC grants to support a chemistry PhD scholar to isolate and identify the active analgesic compounds in the plant. By 1998 it became clear that mudjala contained novel analgesic compounds and had potential for patenting. The traditional owners and Griffith University began a long journey to do this as equal partners. What followed was years of research, interspersed with grant applications (some successful and many not), partnership agreements, non-disclosure agreements, commercial negotiations, meetings and more meetings, exchange visits, ongoing partnership-building and community capacity building that continues to this day.[9] Jarlmadangah Burru has benefited from considerable pro bono support – including from commercial and IP lawyers – as well as a strong research partnership with Griffith University.

In 2003, Jarlmadangah Burru and Griffith University were certified as co-owners of the Indigenous biotechnology patent that came out of the research.[10] This collaboration reflects the growing trend for Indigenous people to be involved in the management of their ecology and the recognition of their sciences in the established science and research system. The issue here is that patent rights give the rightsholder the ability to exclusively commercialise the invention, but those rights only last for 25 years. Once this period ends, the patent information can be used by anyone. This is problematic for protecting Indigenous knowledge in the long term.

As Indigenous science collides with Western science, we need to make sure that we follow ethical protocols so Indigenous people can take part in the knowledge economy without culture being harmed. Scientists and researchers can look to frameworks such as the United Nations Declaration on the Rights of Indigenous Peoples (UNDRIP), that covers cultural heritage rights, and the Convention on Biological Diversity (CBD), which relates to conserving genetic resources. The Nagoya Protocol of 2010 (see chapter 9, page 210) addresses benefit sharing with indigenous communities in the use of genetic resources. These frameworks guide government agencies and universities in ensuring the outcomes of their research projects benefit local indigenous communities.

In 2020, the final report by Professor Graeme Samuel on the review of the *Environmental Protection and Biodiversity Conservation Act 1999* (Cth) noted that there was limited engagement with Indigenous knowledge, and reported the need for more.[11] The EPBC Act is Australia's implementation of the CBD and the Nagoya Protocol at a national level. But the legal landscape is a mix of state and Commonwealth laws, as states control lands and things on them. The Northern Territory and the Commonwealth have biodiscovery laws that establish access and benefit sharing arrangements, but they have had very little practical application. Indigenous groups call for more legal protection. Queensland has amended its biodiscovery laws to cover use of traditional knowledge; anyone engaging in biodiscovery must take all reasonable measures to form agreement with the custodians of the Indigenous knowledge being used. Western Australia is looking to make similar changes.[12] In reality, ethics play a big role in this, as do university policies, but projects that are not government funded can still exploit Indigenous knowledge without legal ramifications. There is not enough education and awareness for researchers, who need guidance and support. Many want to do the right thing, but need guidance on how to engage, identify people in authority and get consent from a group, or groups.

For more about ethics guidelines in scientific and other research, including the *AIATSIS Code of Ethics for Aboriginal and Torres Strait Islander Research*,[13] see chapter 11.

Caring for country: Applying Indigenous knowledge in environmental management

Indigenous peoples' lands guard over 80 per cent of Earth's biodiversity.[14] The biodiversity in Australia is rich, with eucalypt forests, mangroves, rainforests, deserts, heathlands, rivers, salt lakes, seagrass meadows and coral reefs – and all the plants and animals that live in them. For thousands of years, Indigenous Australians have honed holistic land management practices to keep country strong. This knowledge, developed over time and passed through the generations, is sometimes referred to as Indigenous ecological knowledge (IEK).

Aboriginal and Torres Strait Islander traditional owners and land management experts seek to sustainably manage and heal their country as they have done so for so many generations. Many Indigenous people call the land 'our mother'. The connection to country and all things on it is about relationships – totems and inherent responsibilities to guard the land and seas. Stories of country, dancing up country and walking country are ways to express and strengthen this connection. If you look after country, country will look after you and your kin. This concept of caring for country is a cultural practice.

OUR KNOWLEDGE, OUR WAY

The CSIRO document *Our Knowledge, Our Way* is a set of protocols that support Indigenous-led approaches to strengthening and sharing knowledge for land and sea management. These cultural protocols can be negotiated when sharing knowledge, and can include:
- agreement on the activities, responsibilities and contributions of each partner
- acknowledgement and consideration of background intellectual property (IP)
- considering how the research IP will be shared.

Formalised research agreements between institutions offer a higher level of protection to IP because they are binding.

The protocols also advocate respect for Indigenous data sovereignty, recommending that data needs to be returned in an accessible format, and that agreements are essential to ensure data is collected, analysed, kept and shared according to cultural protocols.[15]

Indigenous fire management

In the summer of 2019–20, Australia witnessed some of the most devasting wildfires we have ever seen. Out-of-control fires raged across the country, hitting the south-east coast of New South Wales more intensely than anywhere else. Lives were lost, thousands of homes were destroyed and ecosystems turned to ashes. One billion or more animals were killed.[16] The sky was so thick with smoke haze that it covered up the sun, and the floating ash particles collected on the surface of my car as I drove to work in the busy Sydney traffic. Burnt gum leaves and bark washed up on the sand of our beaches and even fell into our urban backyards.

At the time, Victor Steffensen was due to release *Fire Country*, his book about the fire management practices that have existed on this continent for thousands of years.[17] Victor is a descendant of the Tagalaka people of northern Queensland and is a passionate Indigenous fire practitioner, who believes in the power of reviving this knowledge to heal country and reconnect people to culture and spirit. In an episode of the ABC series *Australian Story*, Victor says, 'Fire is beautiful. It's like water. It trickles through the landscape and the right fire protects the trees, and it brings food and encourages new life. It takes away all the rubbish that's suppressing the landscape, it looks after our animals, and even the animals know fire. It is something that belongs in this landscape. But when people don't know the fire and they disconnect themselves from the landscape, then that's when we have trouble.'[18]

As a young man, Victor lived in the small town of Laura in Far North Queensland, where he was mentored by two Awu-Laya Elders, the late Dr George Musgrave and Dr Tommy George, who taught him how to read the land and apply fire. In *Fire Country*, Victor writes:

> Those two old people, old man TG and Poppy, took me under their wing and shared their world with me … The main thing they wanted was to practise culture and get back onto their country. They wanted to apply their knowledge back onto the land, the fire, the water, looking after the story places. But most of all they wanted their younger ones to learn the language and get back onto country. It was vital because the two men were the last of the Awu-Laya Elders who knew the traditional knowledge and stories of that country.[19]

Victor has been travelling around the country for many years, conducting fire workshops and reintroducing cultural burning into the Australian landscape with Indigenous communities. He is a co-founder of Firesticks Alliance, an Indigenous-led network creating cultural learning pathways to fire and land management.[20] Even in the face of the catastrophic fires of 2019–20, Victor has not lost hope. But we must take real action – now, he says. 'Now more than ever it is vital to be working together to bring cultural burning back into the landscape.' In *Fire Country*, he writes that the country 'is where the knowledge comes from', noting the expertise that can only come from tens of thousands of years of knowledge: 'Applying fire or any other cultural practices to the landscape is done by the country communicating with the custodian ... Reading the landscape is a skill where the land is the boss and tells us what to do. Aboriginal people have perfected this technique in synergy with the environment for thousands of years.'[21] Managing fire-dependent landscapes is crucial, he says, to 'opening other doors of cultural knowledge', like accessing materials for basket weaving, or plants for medicine and food.[22]

Working with water

Indigenous science can help us manage the waterholes, streams, rivers and oceans in Australia and around the world that are in a state of crisis with water pollution, scarcity and drought. Our economy and our lives are dependent on river health. A big issue concerns water management in the Murray-Darling basin and Indigenous peoples' rights to water. The drying up of the river, and the mass fish deaths that have occurred, are environmentally disastrous.

Yorta Yorta woman Sonia Cooper is the Living Murray facilitator with the Yorta Yorta Nation Aboriginal Corporation. She talks about the delicate balance of caring for water on country, and the importance of personal connection. 'When we look at country, it's really how your connection is to country. Outside of my boundaries I wouldn't comment on somebody else's connection to country, because they certainly might do something quite different,' Sonia says. 'For me it's about leaving the water in the forest or the bush ... it's about just leaving things the way they are.'

In her role, Sonia believes it is really important to understand the environment from both sides – using the Yorta Yorta approach at Yorta Yorta Nation and through what she is taught by the elders, and also using the Western perspective through her Bachelor of Science degree at university.[23] 'Obviously the elders have been here a lot longer than I have so they have seen a lot more change, not only environmental change but cultural changes occurring because certain things are getting washed away,' she says. '[An] example of that is with the river widening, the Murray [River] widening, you'll also have a lot of midden sites and burial sites near the waterways, and so that tends to get impacted because of the water.'[24]

'When we see country, sometimes we can see the pain in country,' Sonia continues. 'And when you see the pain in country, it makes you feel really upset. You get upset, you feel quite unwell, and you feel like you have to fix it. So that's the hard thing about looking at country. You might have a connection, but if that connection dies, and that knowledge dies with it, then we can't pass that on.'[25]

Kamilaroi man Bradley Moggridge works in a similar way. He is a water scientist working to integrate Indigenous cultural values into Western science. Bradley is an Associate Professor in Indigenous Water Science at the University of Canberra, and an Indigenous liaison officer at the National Environmental Science Programme (NESP) Threatened Species Recovery Hub. Bradley says, '[Indigenous people] are scientists in ourselves because we have survived. We have tested this dry landscape to get the most out of it, to be here after thousands of generations. That's one of the things that excited me most, [but] I got a bit upset because [the knowledge] wasn't being used and I thought, "How can I have impact to make sure that this knowledge doesn't go to waste?" If we are caring for country, we are healthier.'[26]

There is a science to this knowledge which we can learn from if we draw upon it and respect it. This was noted in Professor Graeme Samuel's recent review of the *Environment Protection and Biodiversity Conservation Act 1999* (Cth) (EPBC Act).[27] The final report stated that the EPBC Act is not fulfilling its objectives in relation to Indigenous Australians in protecting biodiversity and the respectful use of Indigenous knowledge. It proposes to enable Indigenous views and knowledge to be better incorporated into regulatory processes, and recommends that Indigenous knowledge and Western science should be considered on an equal footing when advising the environment minister. We should be looking to

Indigenous peoples' knowledge, the report states, and we should allow for collaboration and joint decision making in environmental management.[28]

Indigenous seasonal knowledge

In 2017, I attended a powerful lecture called 'Sea Country, Hear Country' by Chels Marshall, a Gumbaynggirr woman and scientist from the mid-north coast of New South Wales.[29] Chels spoke about Indigenous ways of understanding the sky, the sea and the cycles of life. The lecture was part of a launch of a new digital exhibit at the Australian Museum – an Aboriginal seasonal calendar that shares this knowledge.

Chels grew up on country and has dedicated her life to championing holistic land management, working between Indigenous and Western sciences and knowledges. Chels says that in the past, it was commonly believed that Aboriginal culture and knowledge in New South Wales was no longer alive. A key intention of the seasonal calendar project was to show that Indigenous knowledge *is* alive, and that ICIP protocols still apply.

Indigenous knowledge of the seasons differs from the typical Western seasonal structure of summer, autumn, winter and spring. Different Indigenous groups have their own seasonal calendars that reflect centuries of observations and understandings of climatic changes and environmental activities in their country. These calendars indicate past, current and future food sources and weather conditions, and aim to protect the environment for the community. Chel's calendar is an interpretation of the traditional knowledge systems and understanding passed down orally for thousands of years by the Gumbaynggirr people. The calendars share Indigenous knowledge such as understanding what is happening under the sea by what is happening on the land; for example, when the cicadas start calling, this means that garfish are plentiful and ready to eat.[30]

CSIRO has also worked with some different Indigenous language groups including Larrakia, Ngan'gi, Tiwi and Kunwinjku to create a series of calendars showing their knowledge of the seasons and ecology.[31]

It is important to see the link here between Indigenous languages and Indigenous ecological knowledge. Language is embedded within the connections between kinship, country, ceremony and the law. The use of language in environmental management is also very important – in the names of plants and areas, and in the names of the seasonal stages.

North Australian Indigenous Land and Sea Management Alliance (NAILSMA)

Around Australia, there is a growing workforce of Indigenous rangers and ranger programs that manage ancestral lands and seas, undertaking activities such as cultural site maintenance, fire management, weed and feral animal control, visitor management, biodiversity, and habitat mapping and protection.[32] One helping factor in this has been the North Australian Indigenous Land and Sea Management Alliance (NAILSMA), an Indigenous not-for-profit that helps Indigenous people manage their country across northern Australia. Established in 2001, Aboriginal and Torres Strait Islander man Joe Morrison was the founding CEO.

NAILSMA designed the Indigenous-Tracker or I-Tracker app, a data collection and mapping tool to help Indigenous rangers manage country. It has been used for monitoring turtles and dugongs, and for mapping seagrass. Traditional owners were consulted in making the apps, and the traditional owners collectively developed a set of overarching guiding principles for using the applications. Key components of the principles are informed consent of traditional owners for data collection, and consultation with traditional owners on the appropriate use and sharing of collected data. This helps ensure that the I-Tracker apps meet the priorities of the particular communities using them, and that Indigenous people retain control of the knowledge recorded. ICIP protocols and release forms were important elements in this. NAILSMA also developed a data safekeeping policy that allows for high-quality data storage if a ranger organisation has issues with mould, cyclones or other conditions that would threaten their data.

NAILSMA monitors downloads of the apps, and all users are made aware of the guiding principles. NAILSMA also trains Indigenous rangers to use the applications. (See chapter 13, page 297, for more on I-Tracker.)

Holistic healing: Indigenous medical doctors in Australia

Dr Mark Wenitong, Kabi Kabi man, works as a GP and is a leader in Indigenous health. Mark was one of the founders of the Australian Indigenous Doctors' Association (AIDA) that was set up in 1998. Mark says, 'A key goal of AIDA is to ensure medical and cultural approaches are articulated. That is part of our role. We have always accepted, acknowledged and worked with our Traditional Healers … When I'm asked about Traditional Healers, I usually start by saying, I studied medicine for five years, but they've been doing it for over 90,000 years, to put it into some perspective.'[33] AIDA have been working to increase the number of Indigenous doctors. They support Indigenous medical students and doctors in the Australian health workforce.

In 2015, just 0.5 per cent of employed medical practitioners in Australia identified as Aboriginal or Torres Strait Islander.[34] On top of this, most of us know that Aboriginal and Torres Strait Islander peoples today face lower life expectancies and higher rates of chronic illnesses, diabetes and child mortality compared with non-Indigenous people. Worimi man Dr Kelvin Kong is an ear, nose and throat, head and neck surgeon (an otorhinolaryngologist) who is passionate about eliminating the gap in ear health. He wants to help bring Indigenous Australian children to the same level of wellbeing and health care access as non-Indigenous children. 'The rates of ear disease are much higher for Aboriginal and Torres Strait Islander children across Australia. The dichotomy is alarming, with hearing loss affecting learning, language and social skills lifelong,' he says.[35]

Indigenous peoples deserve access to a health care system that is culturally safe and in tune with their needs. Recently there was a major Indigenous-led study on Aboriginal and Torres Strait Islander wellbeing called *Mayi Kuwayu*. The name broadly means 'to follow Aboriginal people over a long time' in Ngiyampaa language, the language of the Wongaibon people of New South Wales.[36] Importantly, it was designed and led by Indigenous researchers and staff at the Australian National University, including Ray Lovett, a Ngiyampaa/Wongaibon man and epidemiologist. The study looked at how Indigenous health and wellbeing are closely linked to culture, explaining how so often in public health we look at just the presence (or absence) of disease, rather than the cultures within which disease occurs. Indigenous wellbeing is in fact linked to things like connection to country, cultural practices, spirituality and language use.[37]

The 2020 Close the Gap report *We Nurture Our Culture for Our Future, and Our Culture Nurtures Us* also reflected on the reciprocal relationship between culture and wellbeing. It was prepared by The Lowitja Institute, Australia's national institute for Aboriginal and Torres Strait Islander health research. The report explains how the Aboriginal and Torres Strait Islander concept of health has always been holistic, encompassing mental, physical, cultural, environmental and spiritual health.[38] More integrated approaches, like this one, are starting to regrow. For example, the Anangu Ngangkari Tjutaku Aboriginal Corporation (ANTAC) in South Australia has partnered with a public hospital in Adelaide to provide holistic treatments by Ngangkari traditional healers to Indigenous patients.[39]

Gazing at the sky: Indigenous astronomy

There's a Meriam song that tells us when the monsoon season is coming. It tells us to look at the way the stars are twinkling and the clouds moving in the sky. The stars' brightness changes as a result of moving pockets of air that bend the starlight in different directions, and the faster these pockets move, the faster stars twinkle. The Meriam people observe this to predict weather and seasonal changes. If the stars are twinkling fast and are bright blue in colour, this indicates storms are approaching.[40] There is science in this song.

Astronomy has been a vital part of Indigenous cultures for thousands of years. This is being recognised more and more; for example, the Sydney Observatory developed its Dreamtime Astronomy program that explores the diverse astronomies of Aboriginal people and the ways in which stars have been used for navigation, seasonal calendars, food economics, ceremony and social structure.[41]

In 2015, there was a star officially dedicated to Eddie Koiki Mabo, the famous Meriam land rights activist.[42] The star 'Koiki' is next to the tail of the iconic Southern Cross constellation and also forms part of the much bigger Tagai constellation that is significant to Torres Strait Islander people (see page 231).[43] Just as these stars have helped Torres Strait Islanders to travel across the sea and know the seasons, Eddie Koiki Mabo's light illuminated the night sky too; he led us down a new pathway and was a personal inspiration to me, giving me belief that the Australian legal system could deliver justice for Aboriginal and Torres Strait Islander peoples.

There are many more stars out there shining their light and continuing the legacy – like Wiradjuri woman Kirsten Banks, an astrophysicist and finalist in CSIRO's Indigenous STEM Awards (2017). Another shining star is Krystal De Napoli, a Kamilaroi woman from rural northern Victoria studying astrophysics at Monash University. She has also been speaking about Indigenous astronomy, presenting research and Indigenous knowledge gathered from elders that describes First Nations peoples' complex understanding of the sky and its objects. She has been doing research into Muruwari astronomy with Muruwari man William (Willy) Stevens. She has also been creating a public database of Indigenous science knowledge, covering topics like astronomy, agriculture, aquaculture, medicine, food, engineering, plants and animals.

Karlie Noon, an astrophysicist and Gamilaraay woman from Tamworth, New South Wales, is also deeply passionate about Indigenous astronomy. 'A lot of discoveries in science are pinned to Europeans; however, this is not the case when you consider the vast amount of discoveries Indigenous Australians have made and are still making,' she says. 'We knew the Earth was not flat and we knew tides were influenced by the moon way before Galileo.'[44] Karlie has worked with Duane Hamacher, an associate professor in cultural astronomy at the University of Melbourne, to research how Indigenous people used moon halos – rings around the moon formed by ice crystals – to predict storms.[45]

Indigenous science in the classroom

Kamilaroi man Corey Tutt is deeply passionate about improving science education to empower Indigenous youth. He established the Deadly Science initiative to tackle the lack of resources in Indigenous communities, and has distributed more than 16,000 books and 500 telescopes, and engaged with more than 100 schools around Australia, especially in remote areas. In a recent survey, these schools showed a 25 per cent increase in engagement in STEM-related subjects. Pia Wadjarri school in remote Western Australia had a 40 per cent increase in attendance due to the science equipment provided by Deadly Science. Celebrity scientists Professor Brian Cox and Dr Karl Kruszelnicki have supported his cause and provided copies of their books. In 2020, Tutt was awarded NSW Young Australian of the Year for his hard work.[46] In that year he was also named a human rights hero by the Australian Human Rights Commission for his advocacy work in providing STEM education to Aboriginal and Torres Strait Islander students.

What about science class more generally in schools? Should Australian students be learning about Indigenous science? Joe Sambono works at the Australian Curriculum, Assessment and Reporting Authority (ACARA), the organisation in charge of the Australian Curriculum. He has been helping to develop the curriculum so that teachers can draw from Indigenous knowledges when teaching science. In 2019, ACARA released 95 new science 'elaborations' (examples) that apply Aboriginal and Torres Strait Islander history, culture and knowledge in the explanation of scientific concepts for students from Foundation to Year 10. For example, in understanding how the Earth's surface changes over time as a result of natural processes and human activity, a Year 4 student will learn about Indigenous fire management practices that took place over tens of thousands of years to change the distribution of flora and fauna in many regions of Australia.[47]

The South Australian Department of Education, and the Narungga, Ngarrindjeri and Kaurna communities were involved. The project involved working with elders, teachers and the South Australian Museum to make sure that the lessons reflected a well-rounded and culturally appropriate approach, and to ensure the content was ethically approved, and okay to teach and share widely. There is potential to expand this to other areas of learning.

What else is happening in science education? There have been efforts to increase the number of Aboriginal and Torres Strait Islander students in the science, technology, engineering and mathematics (STEM) industry via the CSIRO Indigenous STEM Education Project. The project involves primary, secondary and tertiary students all across Australia, and it shows how the link between traditional knowledge and the science curriculum can be made stronger. Traditional knowledge holders, elders and community leaders are all part of the program. Another initiative is the National Indigenous Science Education Program (NISEP), aimed at creating pathways to tertiary education and employment in STEM.[48]

A vision for a First Peoples Science Centre

How can we create a space for First Nations science in Australia? In 2016, Wamba Wamba man Steven Ross and Alicia Talbot began developing the idea for a national First Peoples Science Centre as part of their work with the City of Paramatta in western Sydney. A First Peoples Science Centre could highlight the value of Indigenous science and strengthen the critical connection between scientific research and traditional knowledge.[49] Importantly, it could empower Indigenous communities and encourage ICIP protocols, advance the role of Indigenous scientists, and lead culturally sensitive projects to improve health, education, employment and the economy.

In 2020, we worked on the project and consulted with local Darug people, Indigenous and non-Indigenous scientists and other stakeholders for the report *Finding a Space for First Peoples' Science: A Vision for a National First Peoples Science Centre*. There was overwhelming support for the Centre to assist Indigenous communities to develop their own science knowledge, store it, and work with scientists to develop it and learn more – and, if they want to, explore commercial means, or share opportunities through education. After an implementation plan was commissioned by the Museum of Applied Arts and Sciences (MAAS), undertaken by Yuin woman Sonja Stewart (then working with Arrilla Consulting), MAAS employed an Indigenous project officer, Yirrganydji woman Sarah Szydzik, to drive the development of the Centre.

Indigenous science meets Western science head on

Australia's first peoples have been innovating for more than 40,000 years. As Indigenous science meets Western science head on, we need to see not only how Indigenous communities can benefit from the knowledge that they have nurtured, but also how that can become part of the wider knowledge economy. This is already happening in a few places, but there is the potential for so much more. We are at just 1 per cent of applying Indigenous knowledge in technological growth. What if we were to unlock this?

With the proper protocols and rights recognition in place, and ensuring that Indigenous people have access to benefit sharing agreements, there could be incredible outcomes. The key to unlocking this knowledge is about genuine partnerships. At its heart, this means a shift away from the focus on material form and outcomes, towards a process of recognising cultural value, respecting protocols and building relationships for mutual benefit.

Indigenous communities are amazingly adaptable. You have to be to survive on this continent and be the oldest living culture on the planet.

WHAT YOU CAN DO

- Follow the True Tracks principles when setting up and working on collaborations between Indigenous knowledge and Western science.
- Read the UNDRIP and the Nagoya Protocol, and develop systems to implement and respect these documents. The Nagoya Protocol should be implemented by government, and the UNDRIP should be supported by legislation.
- Focus on the process and not just the outcomes of any scientific project.
- Enable Indigenous people to be in key decision-making positions and to co-design projects.
- Disclose the origins of traditional knowledge (TK) and resources used in patents, and enable Indigenous people to share ownership in rights to patents using their TK, and to have power of veto over the commercialisation of their scientific knowledge. Patent disclosure of TK should be made part of the application process.
- Encourage the use of ICIP protocols within research practices (see also chapter 11). While every university has IP policies and research and ethics committees, these usually lack ICIP processes. Look to developing your own protocols, and use the *AIATSIS Code of Ethics for Aboriginal and Torres Strait Islander Research* to implement best practice.

Resources

AIATSIS Code of Ethics for Aboriginal and Torres Strait Islander Research: https://aiatsis.gov.au/sites/default/files/2020-10/aiatsis-code-ethics.pdf

We Nurture Our Culture for Our Future, and Our Culture Nurtures Us (The Lowitja Institute): www.humanrights.gov.au/our-work/aboriginal-and-torres-strait-islander-social-justice/publications/close-gap-2020

Bruce Pascoe, *Dark Emu: Black Seeds: Agriculture or Accident?*, Magabala Books, Broome, 2014

Victor Steffensen, *Fire Country: How Indigenous Fire Management Could Help Save Australia*, Hardie Grant, Melbourne, 2020

National Indigenous Science Education Program (NISEP): https://nisep.org.au

CSIRO Indigenous STEM Education Project: www.csiro.au/en/Education/Programs/Indigenous-STEM

NPY Women's Council Aboriginal Corporation, *Traditional Healers of the Central Desert: Ngangkari*, Magabala Books, Broome, 2013

Indigenous Ecological Knowledge and Natural Resources in the Northern Territory: Report on the Current Status of Indigenous Intellectual Property (Terri Janke and Company, 2009): www.terrijanke.com.au/iek-management

Indigenous Knowledge: Issues for Protection and Management (Terri Janke and Company/IP Australia, 2018): www.ipaustralia.gov.au/sites/default/files/ipaust_ikdiscussionpaper_28march2018.pdf

Finding a Space for First Peoples' Science: A Vision for a National First Peoples Science Centre (Terri Janke and Company, 2020): www.terrijanke.com.au/national-first-peoples-science-know

Notes

1. Falen D Passi, personal communication, 30 March 2021.
2. Falen D Passi, personal communication, 30 March 2021.
3. Paul Brescia, 'Citizen scientist Corey Tutt wins NSW Young Australian of the Year', *Innovation Intelligence International*, 11 November 2019, <www.innovation-intelligence.com/citizen-scientist-corey-tutt-wins-nsw-young-australian-of-the-year>.
4. Bruce Pascoe, *A Real History of Aboriginal Australians, the First Agriculturalists: Bruce Pascoe, TEDxSydney*, TEDx Talks, YouTube, 24 July 2018, <www.youtube.com/watch?v=fqgrSSz7Htw>.
5. National Australia Day Committee, *Corey Tutt: Indigenous Mentor and Fundraiser*, Australian of the Year Awards, 2020, <www.australianoftheyear.org.au/recipients/corey-tutt/2207/>.
6. Joe Sambono, 'Indigenous science goes far beyond boomerangs and spears', *IndigenousX* (11 November 2018) <https://indigenousx.com.au/indigenous-science-goes-far-beyond-boomerangs-and-spears/>.
7. Museum of Applied Arts and Sciences, *MAAS Indigenous Sciences Symposium 2018*, MAAS, 2018, <https://maas.museum/event/maas-indigenous-sciences-symposium-2018/>.
8. Paul Marshall (ed), *Raparapa: Stories from the Fitzroy River Drovers*, Magabala Books, Broome, 1989.
9. Paul Marshall, personal communication, 9 February 2021.
10. Virginia Marshall, Terri Janke and Anthony Watson, 'Community economic development in patenting traditional knowledge: A case study of the Mudjala TK Project in the Kimberley region of Western Australia', *Indigenous Law Bulletin*, vol. 8, no. 6, 2017, pp. 17–21, <www.austlii.edu.au/au/journals/IndigLawB/2013/21.pdf>.
11. Graeme Samuel, *Independent Review of the EPBC Act – Final Report*, Department of Agriculture, Water and the Environment, October 2020, <https://epbcactreview.environment.gov.au/resources/final-report>.
12. David Jefferson, Daniel Robinson, David Claudie et al., 'Australia's plants and animals have long been used without Indigenous consent. Now Queensland has taken a stand', *The Conversation*, 16 September 2020, <https://theconversation.com/australias-plants-and-animals-have-long-been-used-without-indigenous-consent-now-queensland-has-taken-a-stand-144813>.

13 AIATSIS, *AIATSIS Code of Ethics for Aboriginal and Torres Strait Islander Research*, AIATSIS, 2020, <https://aiatsis.gov.au/research/ethical-research/code-ethics>.
14 United National Environment Programme (UNEP), 'Indigenous Peoples: The unsung heroes of conservation', UNEP, 9 January 2017, <www.unep.org/news-and-stories/story/indigenous-peoples-unsung-heroes-conservation>.
15 Emma Woodward, Rosemary Hill, Pia Harkness et al. (eds), *Our Knowledge Our Way in Caring for Country*, CSIRO, 2020, <www.csiro.au/en/Research/LWF/Areas/Pathways/Sustainable-Indigenous/Our-Knowledge-Our-Way/OKOW-resources>.
16 Lesley Hughes, Will Steffen, Greg Mullins et al., *Summer of Crisis*, Climate Council of Australia, 2020, <www.climatecouncil.org.au/resources/summer-of-crisis/>.
17 Victor Steffensen, *Fire Country: How Indigenous Fire Management Could Help Save Australia*, Hardie Grant, Melbourne, 2020.
18 Victor Steffensen, 'Fighting fire with fire', *Australian Story*, ABC TV, 13 April 2020, <https://iview.abc.net.au/show/australian-story/series/2020/video/NC2002Q009S00>.
19 Victor Steffensen, *Fire Country*, p. 10.
20 Firesticks Alliance, <www.firesticks.org.au>.
21 Victor Steffensen, *Fire Country*, p. 145.
22 Victor Steffensen, *Fire Country*, p. 172.
23 Sonia Cooper, in 'Episode 2: Part 2 – Water law, traditional owner knowledge and rights with Dr Emma Carmody' [podcast episode], *STREAMing Podcast*, 28 February 2021, <www.rbms.org.au/media/podcast/>.
24 Sonia Cooper, 'Episode 2', *STREAMing Podcast*.
25 Sonia Cooper, 'Episode 2', *STREAMing Podcast*.
26 Bradley Moggridge, *Indigenous Water Research Specialist – Bradley Moggridge*, Questacon, YouTube, 3 July 2014, <www.youtube.com/watch?v=YkMFehIfT-4>.
27 Graeme Samuel, *Independent Review of the EPBC Act*.
28 Graeme Samuel, *Independent Review of the EPBC Act*.
29 Chels Marshall, 'Sea Country, Hear Country' [lecture], Australian Museum, Sydney, 8 July 2017.
30 Australian Museum, *Garrigarrang Sea Country: Secondary Education Kit*, Australian Museum, Sydney, 2015, p. 7, <https://media.australian.museum/media/dd/documents/Garrigarrang_Secondary_Ed_Kit_20Mar2019.b740946.pdf>.
31 CSIRO, *Indigenous Seasons Calendars*, CSIRO, 2020, <www.csiro.au/en/Research/Environment/Land-management/Indigenous/Indigenous-calendars>.
32 Rod Kennett, 'Caring for Saltwater Country', *SAMUDRA Report*, no. 58, 2011, p. 26, <www.icsf.net/en/samudra/article/EN/58-3562-Content.html>.
33 Dr Mark Wenitong, email correspondence, 17 March 2020.
34 Australian Institute of Health and Welfare (AIHW), *Medical Practitioners Workforce 2015*, AIHW, 24 August 2016, <www.aihw.gov.au/reports/workforce/medical-practitioners-workforce-2015/contents/who-are-medical-practitioners>.
35 Kelvin Kong, email correspondence, 25 November 2020.
36 Mayi Kuwayu, <https://mkstudy.com.au>; Minette Salmon, Kate Doery, Phyll Dance et al., *Defining the Indefinable: Descriptors of Aboriginal and Torres Strait Islander Peoples' Cultures and Their Links to Health and Wellbeing*, 2nd ed, report commissioned by Mayi Kuwayu and The Lowitja Institute, Melbourne/Canberra, September 2019, <https://openresearch-repository.anu.edu.au/bitstream/1885/148406/8/Defining_the_Indefinable_WEB2_FINAL.pdf>.
37 Minette Salmon, Kate Doery, Phyll Dance et al., *Defining the Indefinable*, p. v.

38 The Lowitja Institute, *We Nurture Our Culture for Our Future, and Our Culture Nurtures Us*, report commissioned by the Close the Gap Steering Committee, Close the Gap Campaign Steering Committee for Indigenous Health Equality, 2020, <www.humanrights.gov.au/our-work/aboriginal-and-torres-strait-islander-social-justice/publications/close-gap-2020>.
39 Rhett Burnie, 'Aboriginal healers treat patients alongside doctors and nurses at Lyell McEwin Hospital', *ABC News*, 20 February 2019, <www.abc.net.au/news/2019-02-20/aboriginal-healers-treat-patients-alongside-doctors-and-nurses/10826666>.
40 Anna Salleh, 'Indigenous song Twinkling Stars tells science of the seasons', *ABC Science*, 16 September 2016, <www.abc.net.au/news/science/2016-09-16/twinkling-stars-song-from-murray-island-tells-science-of-seasons/7754054>.
41 Geoffrey Wyatt, Toner Stevenson and Duane W Hamacher, 'Dreamtime Astronomy: Development of a new Indigenous program at Sydney Observatory', *Journal of Astronomical History and Heritage*, vol. 17, no. 2, 2014, p. 4, <https://arxiv.org/ftp/arxiv/papers/1405/1405.2506.pdf>.
42 Luke Briscoe, 'A star is named: Eddie Mabo honoured in star dedication', *NITV News*, 3 June 2015, <www.sbs.com.au/nitv/article/2015/06/03/star-named-eddie-mabo-honoured-star-dedication>.
43 Cristina Briones, 'The man, the stars, the land', *MAAS Magazine*, 28 August 2017, <https://maas.museum/magazine/2017/08/the-man-the-stars-the-land/>.
44 Karlie Noon, personal communication, 25 February 2021.
45 Australian National University (ANU), *Karlie Noon*, ANU, n.d., <https://rsaa.anu.edu.au/study/student-profiles/karlie-noon>.
46 National Australia Day Committee, *Corey Tutt: Indigenous Mentor and Fundraiser*.
47 ACARA, 'F-10 Australian Curriculum: Science elaborations for the Australian and Torres Strait Islander cross-curriculum priority', Australian Curriculum, 2018, <www.australiancurriculum.edu.au/media/5644/new-content-elaborations-for-the-australian-curriculum-science-f-10.pdf>.
48 CSIRO Indigenous STEM Education Project, <www.csiro.au/en/Education/Programs/Indigenous-STEM>; National Indigenous Science Education Program (NISEP), <https://nisep.org.au/>.
49 Terri Janke, Carla Wilson and Ruby Langton-Batty, *Finding a Space for First Peoples' Science: A Vision for a National First Peoples Science Centre*, paper commissioned by City of Parramatta and University of Sydney, Terri Janke and Company, 2020, <www.terrijanke.com.au/national-first-peoples-science-know>.

11
RETHINKING INDIGENOUS RESEARCH

I was about 15 when someone asked me to be involved in their research project. A woman in a brown turtleneck jumper came to our house to interview me for her PhD on Indigenous education. She asked me questions about my studies. How was I finding it? What were the challenges and what were my future goals? I don't really remember what I said. My mum tells me that I was researched as a baby. There were some vaccines for smallpox they wanted to trial on Aboriginal and Torres Strait Islander newborns. I obviously don't remember that either.

Indigenous people are the most researched people in the world. I first heard this from Yidinji woman Henrietta Marrie, who was speaking at a conference in Brisbane in the 1990s. Henrietta, a leader in the area of Indigenous cultural rights, was an inspiration to me in my early career. She has done much to speak out and create change around the use of Indigenous knowledge in science and research, and in institutions such as museums and archives. In a 1989 article called 'Who owns the past?', Henrietta quoted the American historian WT Hagan, who first described Native Americans as 'archival captives' in 1978.[1] By referring to Indigenous peoples in this way, WT Hagan and Henrietta Marrie – and all others who have used the term since – are saying that we Indigenous people have been viewed as subjects of study by curious outsiders. We have been documented, etched, photographed and filmed. Our behaviour has been probed and interpreted. Our belongings have been taken as arte-facts; our ancestors have been treated as human remains for scientific testing; our DNA is seen as a genetic resource. But we are captives because we do not own the archives, written records and documents about our lives. Our stories are not told by us.

We can turn this around by championing ICIP protocols in our collecting and educational institutions, and by supporting Indigenous people to design and lead research projects that involve and affect them.

A difficult history

Research is a universal problem for Indigenous peoples. The vast amount of information collected about us has been obtained without permission and told in a way that is tainted with stereotypes and preconceptions. Since British invasion, Aboriginal and Torres Strait Islander peoples and cultures have been researched by outsiders in fields like anthropology, sociology, history, science, psychology and health. Indigenous cultures were often viewed as if they were going extinct, steeped in antiquity and mystery, with the researchers passing judgment on their humanity. Outsiders have entered Indigenous people's homes and lands to take samples and stories, then spread them across the world where their sacred origins are no longer known or even cared about. Karen Martin (Booran Mirraboopa), academic and Noonuccal woman with Bidjara ancestry, has used the term 'terra nullius research' to describe the research conducted on or about Aboriginal people without permission, consultation or any involvement of the people being studied.[2]

Māori academic Linda Tuhiwai Smith calls the word 'research' one of the dirtiest words in the indigenous world's vocabulary. When mentioned in many indigenous contexts, it stirs up silence, it conjures up bad memories, and it raises a smile that is knowing and distrustful.[3] Indigenous people continue to be concerned that non-Indigenous researchers are exploiting Indigenous people by obtaining their knowledge, taking it back to their universities only to acquire degrees and advance their careers.[4] It is rare that these researchers stay connected or share benefits with the communities whose knowledge they use.

AIATSIS published their first ethics guidelines for researchers in 1999; at the time, they represented a new approach to research ethics, repositioning Indigenous peoples as partners in research rather than subjects. In 2020, the guidelines were replaced with the AIATSIS Code of Ethics for Aboriginal and Torres Strait Islander Research.[5] The Code's framework is guided by four principles: Indigenous self-determination, Indigenous leadership, impact and value, and sustainability and accountability. Supplementing the Code, AIATSIS developed a guide to applying the Code of Ethics, which benefits people wanting to publish Indigenous authors or material written about their histories and cultures.[6]

Thankfully, there are also many Indigenous academics now working in the research sector. This has led to many changes that enable better practices, and a centring of Indigenous voices. However, there is much work yet to be done in the way that intellectual property laws, university policies and practices, and ethics processes deal with Indigenous research. The topic of Indigenous research raises many issues around epistemology, ethics and consent processes. There are many great books on research written by esteemed Indigenous authors that can guide you through these topics.[7] In this chapter, I have chosen to focus on intellectual property, and the protection of traditional knowledge and traditional cultural expressions that are shared in the context of research.

The problems encountered during Indigenous research

There are some common issues that arise in research about Indigenous peoples. First, let's discuss the ownership issues.

When outsiders come into the lives of Indigenous people with their pens, computers, cameras and recording devices, they are bringing the tools with which to create intellectual property rights that are recognised in the Western system. As discussed in previous chapters, copyright ownership of these materials is often legally vested in the person who puts the knowledge into material form, usually the researcher or the non-Indigenous author. So Indigenous people often have no stake in the legal ownership of their oral stories, knowledge and cultural expressions when these are captured by outsiders in sound recordings, films, books and records. The underlying traditional knowledge and cultural expression are not protected under copyright law.

Indigenous people have also struggled to gain access to these records, or to use them and publish them without the permission of the copyright owners. They have not been able to control who can access the materials, even if they contain secret or sacred knowledge belonging to ancestors.

Maybe the outsiders who studied Indigenous people were driven by the desire to capture what they thought of as the last embers of Indigenous life, preserving the remnants of a soon-to-be-dead culture. But the living descendants of those knowledge holders are now pushing for their ownership to be recognised.

Copyright, sacred knowledge and uses of research

Reproducing sacred imagery was the issue in the 1970s when Riptide Churinga, a Sydney-based manufacturer, produced T-shirts featuring Mimi figures from the rock art in Arnhem Land. Mimi spirits are the sacred creator beings from this region, and the use of their image is carefully guarded under customary law. Although painted tens of thousands of years ago, rock art remains highly significant to contemporary Indigenous life and has been heralded as the world's longest continuing art tradition.[8] The discovery of these T-shirts at Sydney's Paddy's Markets by Dr Vivien Johnson and her student 'copyright detectives' came after a tip-off from Jabiru traditional owner Mandy Muir. Vivien did much work to look further into the incident, researching the sources of each image and preparing an extensive report for AIATSIS to use to confront the manufacturers. Because these images are so ancient, they are no longer the subject of Western copyright laws.

Indigenous Australians have often complained about their rock art being photographed and reproduced by graphic designers and artists who are not entitled to depict the imagery. Images are exploited commercially without their permission and without any royalties returned to them. In many instances, the use has been derogatory and without attribution. But where had these T-shirt images come from?

In the late 1960s, researcher Eric Brandl was funded by the Australian Institute of Aboriginal Studies, now AIATSIS, to record rock art in Arnhem Land. During several field trips to the area between 1968 and 1972, Brandl took photographs of rock art of the Badmardi clan in the Deaf Adder Creek region, in places that were very difficult to access. He then returned to his office, where he projected the images onto paper and traced the figures by hand. These drawings were then published by the Institute in a book with copyright belonging to Brandl.[9] As images of the Deaf Adder rock art sites are rare and the sites are restricted from public access, it was highly likely that the T-shirt manufacturers copied the images directly from this book, although the manufacturer never admitted this.

The underlying works, and the rights of the Badmardi clan, were not protected by copyright. But Eric Brandl's work was, which meant the Institute, the Brandl Estate and the Badmardi clan had grounds to demand the T-shirt company stop production. They entered a settlement that included damages and the delivery of unsold items, and the T-shirt maker posted a national public apology in *The Australian*.

This incident illustrates that *copyright* owners had the rights, and by virtue of this the *cultural* owners were able to enlist them to commence action, even though the cultural owners had no copyright ownership rights. Dr Jane Anderson, a law and museum studies scholar, notes that 'had the images of the Mimi reproduced on the tee-shirts been copied straight from the rock-art itself, there would have been no grounds for complaint by AIATSIS, the Brandl Estate or the [Badmardi] clan, for the material would be classified as being in the public domain and therefore open to use. The problem of protecting rock art has existed as a persistent complaint about the biases of copyright.'[10]

A related case was the 1976 publication *Nomads of the Australian Desert* by anthropologist Charles Mountford, which exposed confidential information about the Pitjantjatjara people of Central Australia. Mountford owned copyright, but the Northern Territory Supreme Court did rule that the book could not be sold in the Northern Territory. (See chapter 7, page 173.)

We need more Indigenous researchers

Professor Linda Tuhiwai Smith, mentioned earlier in this chapter, argues that there is a growing 'international community of Indigenous scholars and researchers' who are 'talking more widely about Indigenous research, Indigenous research protocols and Indigenous methodologies'.[11] Her work is so influential because it not only exposes the flaws in past Western research practices, but shines the light on the way forward, outlining cultural protocols that would reclaim Indigenous control over research practices.

As Professor Lester-Irabinna Rigney from the Narungga, Kaurna and Ngarrindjeri nations in South Australia sees it, the growing numbers of First Nations people undertaking higher degrees and conducting research at universities around the world are breaking the mould. In 2006, he wrote:

> Until recently, Indigenous Australians did not have equal opportunity and access to a university education. Indigenous Australian involvement in research has been at the imposition of Western non-Indigenous researchers' agendas and their universities. Throughout history, Indigenous peoples have been the objects of research and never the initiator, manager or co-investigator of research. Similarly, knowledge productions about Indigenous worldviews and realties have always been obscured by the 'cultural' and 'race' bias of the non-Indigenous interpreter.[12]

Professor Rigney is part of a growing cohort of Indigenous academics who are campaigning to make university campuses more accessible for Indigenous students and scholars, and more inclusive of Indigenous ways of knowing.

A best practice approach

Dr Payi Linda Ford is an Aboriginal academic who identifies as Rak Mak Mak Marranunggu, from Kurrindju on the Finniss River, Northern Territory. Growing up with her ala – her mother – and uncles, aunties, grandparents and extended family around, she was educated in a traditional Aboriginal cultural context. Her ala, Ngulilkang Nancy Daiyi, authorised her to use the Rak Mak Mak Marranunggu epistemology and ontology in her work as an academic and her PhD about traditional knowledge. Payi was mindful to acknowledge her ala's contributions to the research, in keeping with the right to attribution in the True Tracks protocols.

Payi was one of the first Indigenous PhD students to engage an Aboriginal elder for her higher degree by research supervisory panel, to embed Rak Mak Mak Marranunggu knowledge in her research, and this was acknowledged internationally. Her PhD was also extraordinary because it was the first to be supervised by a person without academic qualifications. Payi had started her doctoral study at Charles Darwin University in the Northern Territory in late 1998, but there were no senior Indigenous academics with a sufficient understanding of the issues that she was tackling. She transferred to Deakin University in 1999, where she completed her undergraduate and masters degrees. Later in 2002, during her confirmation of candidature for her PhD, Payi had to convince her review panel that her ala should be on her supervisory team, because she was the only person who had the required Marranunggu knowledge. With her ala's guidance and support, Payi graduated with her doctorate in 2006.

Payi's thesis was about traditional knowledge, and her ala's knowledge. When Payi graduated, she gave her ala a copy of her thesis, *Narratives and Landscapes: Their Capacity to Serve Indigenous Knowledge Interests* (2005). Her ala was very proud. Her ala also wanted a shiny-covered book, so Payi published her first solo publication: *Aboriginal Knowledge Narratives and Country: Marri kunkimba putj marrideyan*, in 2010. Her ala, an invaluable Marranunggu knowledge custodian, passed away in 2007.

Payi advocates that Australia should embed Indigenous knowledge into its formal systems and structures for pre-service teachers in the Bachelor of Education (Primary) at Charles Darwin University. Higher education institutions are supposed to be the best at recognising and respecting Indigenous knowledge. Payi says that by excelling in universities, Indigenous people can have a presence in the knowledge space, and we can continue to chip away at the structures that exclude us and kept us invisible for the last 250 years. By increasing Indigenous enrolments and employment in universities and by producing more Indigenous academics, we can break down those barriers of exclusion, she says.[13]

Currently, Payi teaches postgraduate students and does a lot of Indigenist research. She draws strength from her Indigenous theoretical base of Mirrwana and Wurrkama theory to bridge diverse disciplinary fields, including aquaculture, plant biosecurity, ethnomusicology, education, health, and land and sea management. Her research passion includes Indigenous knowledges, education, language, culture, and society. These elements rarely stay neatly boxed into their own disciplines. Her research can cross traditional Western knowledge boundaries because of her holistic way of thinking, which is typical of Indigenous epistemologies – they emphasise respect, relationships and connections that underpin multidisciplinary research.

Professor Reuben Bolt, a descendant of the Yuin/Wandandian and Ngarigo peoples, is the Pro Vice-Chancellor Indigenous Leadership and Regional Outreach at Charles Darwin University; previously he was the director of the Nura Gili Indigenous Programs Unit at the University of New South Wales. He conducts his own research projects, often involving direct interaction with Indigenous people. This necessarily involves approval from relevant research ethics committees, which has become somewhat a source of frustration. Reuben says, 'It has been many years now that Indigenous peoples have advocated for research that benefits Indigenous communities, and importantly, that such research does not solely benefit the career of non-Indigenous researchers. This was common practice in years gone-by, but now the standard for research to involve

Indigenous communities has come under intense scrutiny. Adopting this same logic, the careers of Indigenous academics should not benefit, if such research is detrimental to the community, or does not benefit the community".[14]

University policies

Universities have intellectual property policies that manage the ownership of the products they produce, like journal articles, photos, films and books arising from research, and other academic activities. There is an urgent need for these policies to expand to include ICIP rights. Some universities in Australia are already on board, such as the University of Wollongong. Terri Janke and Company helped the university to update their IP policy in 2019; researchers are now required to seek permission for research conducted about Indigenous peoples, and to enter into access and benefit sharing agreements when they are accessing Indigenous land and resources in research. Other universities have also included clauses around ICIP in their policies.

Indigenous people are calling for new laws to cover their IP, as ethics committees and their processes are not legally binding. What happens if someone breaches the ethics guidelines? In the US, Native Americans have taken action against a university for misuse of gene samples taken in genetic research.[15] Members of the Havasupai Tribe of the Grand Canyon, northern Arizona, gave blood for diabetes research. However, the consent forms used were deliberately vague, and research samples were used without their knowledge for studies on schizophrenia, inbreeding and ancient-human migration – all stigmatised research topics that participants would never have consented to. This use of their blood caused them great distress.

In 2004, the Havasupai Tribe brought claims against the scientists and the university, and the Arizona Board of Regents, the governing body for Arizona's public university system, for breach of fiduciary duty due to a lack of prior informed consent.[16] Further, the Havasupai claimed negligence, trespass, and intentional or negligent infliction of emotional distress. The Havasupai's claim centred the invasion of privacy that resulted from the misuse of their genetic information, giving rise to 'deeply personal and subjective injury'.[17] The parties settled out of court.

This case highlights the importance of appropriate use of research. Researchers should always have consent forms signed by subjects, and they should seek re-approval for any future use of genetic or other materials beyond the original approved uses.

Research partnerships: Positive potential

Partnerships between Indigenous communities, researchers and educational institutions can lead to innovative and sustainable solutions in health and medicine, environmental conservation, resource use and preservation, energy production and more. There is potential to solve some of the most pressing problems facing our world. Empowering research partnerships require outside investigators to work with local Indigenous peoples as skilled researchers in their own right, and to support Indigenous research and economic goals. Better still, institutions and researchers can champion projects that are Indigenous designed and Indigenous led. Following cultural protocols is critical for success.

The Madjedbebe research project

Researchers from the University of Queensland worked on a project with the Gundjeihmi Aboriginal Corporation (GAC), a traditional owner organisation representing Mirarr people, to excavate and date cultural artefacts at the Madjedbebe rock shelter, an important cultural site in western Arnhem land. The project made international headlines in 2017 as the findings showed that Aboriginal people have been living in Australia for at least 65,000 years.[18]

To ensure Mirarr people had control over the excavation and the analysis of its results, the university and GAC entered into a research agreement. This put into writing that GAC, on behalf of the Mirarr people, had the right to halt the excavation under certain circumstances, maintain control over artefacts and comment on the publication of findings. The agreement also covers the eventual repatriation of excavated objects and artefacts back to Mirarr people. In February 2020, a group of scientists and GAC knowledge holders published a paper outlining the excavated plant foods, which illustrated a broad plant food diet at Madjedbebe. The paper included a notice of ownership and control over the material by GAC, asserting the ICIP rights of the Mirrar people and the need for consent to publish or use the Indigenous knowledge in the publication.[19]

GAC has been able to position itself as an owner of the intellectual property generated from the Madjedbebe site, as well as mark out its conditions for retaining Indigenous knowledge control. This, like Western legal systems of intellectual property, provides a means for GAC to establish future opportunities using this knowledge as a base. This is unique because in many other Indigenous communities where similar cultural sites are situated, the knowledge and artefacts are not under any control of the Aboriginal people. In this respect, GAC has been able to negotiate the control of cultural heritage research activities; these are cultural assets for the community, but can also create economic opportunities for Mirarr people. The world significance of the site means that it attracts archaeologists from around the globe and other related research areas. GAC's control of the ICIP will enable future benefits to flow to the community.

Access to land and resources

One way that Indigenous peoples have restricted access to their ICIP for the purposes of research is through regulating access to land. For instance, the *Aboriginal Land Rights (Northern Territory) Act 1976* (Cth) establishes a system of regulated access to Aboriginal land in the Northern Territory. People who wish to enter Aboriginal land require a written permit to do so.[20] People who propose to conduct research projects on Aboriginal land or with Aboriginal communities, for example, first require a permit to enter their land, and also require a permit to undertake research activities.

By making such permits conditional upon the observance of cultural protocols, traditional landowners can ensure that they have continuing legal rights to their ICIP and biological resources. Fundamentally, this is about asserting Aboriginal self-determination in research.

Another relevant law is the *Environment Protection and Biodiversity Conservation Act 1999* (Cth), also known as the EPBC Act. This law regulates all access to biological resources and Indigenous knowledge in Commonwealth areas by establishing a permit system.[21] The law only protects Indigenous knowledge where biological resources to be accessed are in Commonwealth-owned areas; the access sought is for commercial purposes; and there is Indigenous knowledge associated with the access and use of the biological resources.

However, the EPBC Act does not require benefit sharing agreements where access to the land is sought for non-commercial purposes, such as research. But Bininj, who have lived in Kakadu for some 65,000 years, can attach conditions to the access permits that require the researchers to enter into research agreements that protect ICIP, assign copyright over research results and materials to Bininj or their organisations, and require research to be conducted in accordance with community protocols.

Researchers who partner with Bininj to conduct research have responsibilities to obtain free, prior and informed consent from Bininj individuals and groups they work with, and to support Bininj self-determination by developing the research proposal and ethics protocols in collaboration with the people involved in the research. Consent and self-determination are both True Tracks principles. The research proposal should address Bininj research priorities and ensure proper attribution and benefit sharing.

Indigenous-led research

Indigenous-designed and Indigenous-led research can help solve some of the most pressing problems facing our world. Partnerships between Indigenous communities, researchers and education institutions like universities can find innovative and sustainable solutions to global problems in areas like health and medicine, environmental conservation, resource use and preservation, and energy production.

Spinifex partnership: A positive collaboration

In 2015, I attended the *Ochre, Spinifex & Foil* symposium and exhibition at the University of Sydney that explored how the two-way exchange of Indigenous and non-Indigenous science can create new pathways in Australian design knowledge. Professor Paul Memmott, architect-anthropologist, presented a paper about a partnership involving the University of Queensland and the Dugalunji Aboriginal Corporation. Professor Colin Saltmere, a proud Indjalandji-Dhidhanu man, is the managing director of the Dugalunji Aboriginal Corporation which is part of the Myuma Group of not-for-profit Aboriginal corporations. Colin is instrumental in leading the Myuma Group that champions many significant initiatives in industries such as construction, science, research and tourism.

The spinifex partnership falls under the research arm of the Myuma Group. The project is developing commercial applications for spinifex, a native Australian grass. Traditionally, Aboriginal Australians widely used spinifex as waterproof roof-thatching as well as adhesive gum produced from a carefully controlled heating technique, practices which were once widespread but declined in the latter 20th century.[22] This knowledge is being revitalised through this collaborative research project, which has proven spinifex to be a strong and flexible material that has potential for a number of applications, including building technology.

In 2015, a patent was registered over a composite material comprising an elastomer and nanocellulose derived from spinifex plants.[23] Initially solely owned by the university, with reports stating that benefits were shared with the community, the patent is now jointly owned with the Dugalunji Aboriginal Corporation, meaning the royalties and commercial outcomes are split equally. The research partnership is still going today, and is just a slice of the innovative work led by Colin Saltmere and the Myuma Group. Research partnerships such as this one have the potential to create a powerful synergy between Western and Indigenous scientific knowledges to solve shared problems and empower Indigenous communities.

Strehlow Research Centre: Repatriation of sacred objects

The Strehlow Research Centre in Mparntwe (Alice Springs) manages one of Australia's most important collections of film, sound, archival records and museum objects relating to Indigenous ceremonial life.[24] The collection was put together by Professor TGH Strehlow, an anthropologist who researched the Arrernte people of Central Australia. The Arrernte people are arguably the most documented Aboriginal group in Australia; their language and ceremonies have been subject to intensive documentation by missionary and anthropological scholars. This archive now constitutes a treasure trove of linguistic detail, song texts, detailed descriptions of ceremony and Indigenous toponymy (the study of place names).[25]

In 2005, a change to the Northern Territory's *Strehlow Research Centre Act 2005* allowed for the return of sacred objects from the collection to their custodians,[26] where custodians could be identified and there was evidence to substantiate the claims of ownership. Today, the Arrernte community play a central role in the research and repatriation process.

Shaun Angeles Penangke, Arrernte and Kungarakany man, was the cultural repatriation manager at the Strehlow Research Centre. During his time there, he conducted a lot of research into the collection, particularly the Artwe-kenhe (Men's) Collection that saw him closely engage with Indigenous elders and men from the community. 'The knowledge the Elders possess can never be learnt through courses or universities, but only through our ancient "schools" of ceremony that have been passed down through generations,' Shaun writes. 'They make sense of artefacts and collections where nobody else can, and they are the only people on earth who can enrich the existing knowledge held within museums.'[27] This is one archive that is slowly unshackling our cultures and objects. Shaun now continues this important work in repatriation with the

AIATSIS Return of Cultural Heritage project that facilitates the return of Aboriginal and Torres Strait Islander cultural materials from overseas.

Indigenous genomics

In 1999, I gave birth to my son Jaiki in a Sydney hospital. The nurse asked me if I wanted to donate the umbilical cord blood. She told me that the genetic research team were specifically looking for Aboriginal and Torres Strait Islander donors because such specimens were considered rarities. I said no. Although I understood the need for life-saving medical research, how was I to know, five minutes after having a baby, the implications of saying yes? Would my DNA, and my baby's, become the property of a medical researcher? Who would own the actual blood tissue sample? What information was being sourced from the sample and what conclusions were going to be made about Indigenous people? Were the samples being used to find information for a patentable invention?

This experience opened my eyes to the fact that genetic researchers often target Indigenous people as a sample group, and that few details are provided about the use of our tissues, blood and genetic information. Genomics – the study of genes – is a quickly expanding area of science in the 21st century. Studying genes and DNA can help researchers understand how these components function and can help scientists develop medications, and treat genetic disorders and diseases. But when geneticists are interested in Indigenous peoples' DNA, there is a need to follow ICIP protocols to make sure the research is done ethically. There is a need to stop and ask: 'What does it mean to take someone's blood, study it and store it in a science lab off country?' The taking of genetic samples could upset people and communities if it isn't done ethically. And when the future uses of those samples are yet to be imagined, this is another concern. Consent and consultation, and cultural integrity are key principles here.

There are IP and ICIP issues arising from the collection and use of Indigenous health-related genomics information in clinical and research settings. Moral issues arise when researchers assert their exclusive ownership of and right to commercially exploit genetic material, for example in patents. Put simply, gene patenting is controversial, and is even more concerning for indigenous peoples. An intellectual property system that allows the patenting of unique human genes could expose indigenous communities to exploitation. The Havasupai Tribe case, mentioned earlier, is an example of this; it also happened with the Hagahai tribe of Papua New Guinea, whose genetic material was patented without their prior consent or consultation.[28]

The collection of Indigenous genes raises issues of identity, cultural rights and human rights. There are added layers of complexity that arise from the issue of privacy for Indigenous people – not just individual privacy. Indigenous peoples' rights to control communal data, and how genetic information is referred to and reported, are key areas that genetic researchers need to understand. It also raises the issue of discrimination, because genetic research might reinforce some people's negative assumptions about disempowered racial groups, or be misinterpreted as evidence of the racial inferiority of Indigenous peoples. So researchers must first consider why genomics is important to Indigenous people, the values and cultural norms that surround it, and the potential risks and benefits to Indigenous people. Processes of dynamic consent should be implemented throughout these projects.

Other issues relate to the long-term storage of gene specimens collected from Indigenous people. Terri Janke and Company has been following the approach taken by the ANU National Centre of Indigenous Genomics (NCIG) in Canberra. We attended presentations by Mick Gooda and Dr Simon Easteal on the importance of dynamic consent and community engagement. The NCIG was set up to deal with legacy blood samples that the Australian National University collected in research from the 1960s to the 1990s. Free, prior and informed consent is required for access and use of material in the collection.

In the NCIG's 2017 annual report, Mick Gooda, who was chair of the Governance Board at the time, wrote of the 'immense cultural, historical and scientific importance' of Indigenous genomics research. His vision of ethical genomics research was for 'a proper partnership between the

THE LOWITJA INSTITUTE: GUIDELINES FOR INDIGENOUS HEALTH RESEARCH

Long before the first hospital was built, long before the first medical doctor, the First Australians developed a sophisticated system of health, medicine and physical and emotional wellbeing practices.[34] Building on this foundation of health knowledge, the Lowitja Institute was established in 2010. It is now Australia's national institute for Aboriginal and Torres Strait Islander health research.

This Indigenous-led research institute is a glowing example of Aboriginal and Torres Strait Islander people developing their own health research projects and conducting them in culturally safe ways. This is research by Indigenous people for Indigenous people, with an aim to conduct research that has a clear and positive impact on the wellbeing of Indigenous people.[35]

The Institute's publication *Researching Indigenous Health: A Practical Guide for Researchers* (2011) offers guidance in Indigenous health research.[36] It highlights the need for Aboriginal and Torres Strait Islander health research to be driven by Indigenous priorities. It is a very useful resource for those seeking to educate themselves about culturally acceptable research, and how to improve how they carry out research on Indigenous health.

---

original donors, their families, descendants and communities, and the University'.[29] This comes back to True Tracks principles, particularly the principle of consent and consultation – the need to put Indigenous people in control of the research about their lives.

As well as the potential health benefits that genomics research and precision medicine can deliver, genomics could potentially assist Indigenous people in tracing their ancestry. For example, members of the stolen generations who don't have information about their Indigenous families and ancestors may be able to use genetics to reconnect with their family.[30] Additionally, the NCIG annual report explains that genomics research could help 'identify the geographical origin of human remains, allowing repatriation from museums and other institutions all over the world back to Country'.[31] Genomics research could be part of the unlocking of the Indigenous archives. There are many potential benefits to Indigenous genomics research, but it has to be conducted respectfully and it must give Indigenous people the right to say no. It must also deliver benefits to the Indigenous people being researched. Training Indigenous people in genomics research techniques will create employment opportunities and enable them to conduct the research for themselves.[32]

The pace of research is also a factor. Dr Misty Jenkins, a Gunditjmara woman and immunologist, says that many Indigenous people do not trust scientists because of past experiences and communal memory of exploitation.[33] It takes time to build trusting relationships, and research time frames need to account for this.

Indigenous data sovereignty

With all the research that has been done on Indigenous people, and the development of digital means of collecting, sharing and analysing collected data, Indigenous people are calling for data sovereignty. What is Indigenous data sovereignty? It is the right of Indigenous peoples to determine the means by which data about or related to Indigenous people is collected, accessed, interpreted, analysed, managed, shared and reused. In early 2017, the Maiam nayri Wingara Indigenous Data Sovereignty Collective was formed in Australia. They have been promoting good data practices and developing protocols and principles (see also chapter 13). ANU Associate Professor Ray Lovett (Wongaibon/Ngiyampaa) is one of the founding members.

The data sovereignty movement is worldwide. In Aotearoa (New Zealand), Te Mana Raraunga Māori Data Sovereignty Network was established in 2015 to advocate for Māori data rights. Te Mana Raraunga have a set of Māori Data Sovereignty principles. The principles deal with the recognition of ICIP rights, and protocols for maintenance and long-term data storage, highlighting the need for indigenous peoples to be in control of these. Indigenous data governance means decision-making power. Australia is also developing Indigenous data sovereignty as a framework for Indigenous rights.[37]

The research approach: Working together

Henrietta Marrie oversees the First People's Think Tank and Research Centre at Central Queensland University, also known as the Yei-Nie Institute (after Yei-Nie, a warrior known as 'the King of Cairns' or 'the Peace-maker').[38] Henrietta explains the importance and goals of the project: 'We want to bring together community leaders and experts from across the world, and pursue social justice, economic independence, innovation, and growth opportunities for Indigenous communities.'[39] The Institute is building partnerships between researchers and Indigenous communities, so that the most pressing issues facing Indigenous peoples can be solved.

Professor Martin Nakata is a Torres Strait Islander academic who has worked in several Australian universities. In his book *Disciplining the Savages: Savaging the Disciplines*, he uses the term 'cultural interface' to refer to the space where Western and Indigenous knowledge systems meet and interact. This is a complex and challenging space, one that many Indigenous peoples navigate. As a society, we can ethically work through the research issues that arise at this cultural interface by following protocols, such as the True Tracks principles, that uphold Indigenous cultural heritage and knowledge rights.

There is a need for clear guidance and standards when it comes to the use of ICIP in research. The IP Australia Indigenous knowledge discussion paper, which Terri Janke and Company wrote for IP Australia, offers the following recommendations:

- Standardise research protocols and guidelines.
- Develop and promote standard research and commercialisation agreements to vest traditional knowledge rights with traditional owners.

- Include free, prior and informed consent as a requirement for Australian Government–funded research programs.[40]

Even if a researcher is Indigenous, there is still a need to consult with traditional owners and knowledge holders when working with their knowledge and culture. Protocols should be discussed and drawn up in research agreements that outline how the ICIP will be used, whether there is an opportunity for review, and what attribution should be given. The protocols should also address clearances for future use of the research, as well as benefit sharing – such as payment, and copies of (or access to) research outcomes like books, publications, photographs, recordings and films.

Fundamentally, Indigenous people have the right to control the research that is conducted about them. This is underwritten by their right to self-determination. Consent and consultation are integral principles when it comes to working with Indigenous people in a research context. Indigenous people have a right to know what is being written about them, and what is happening to the genetic and cultural material and knowledge that is gathered from them by researchers. Aboriginal and Torres Strait Islander peoples expect that when research is conducted about their lives, it is done in a culturally appropriate way that respects and preserves their cultural integrity and humanity. But above all we expect that all research conducted about Indigenous peoples should deliver some benefit. It can't just be research for the sake of curiosity or interest. Researchers have an ethical obligation to collaborate with and listen to Indigenous people so that the research of the future strengthens our societies and our cultures. It should never again demean us or hold us captive.

WHAT YOU CAN DO

- First, ask: 'Am I the one to do this research? Is it suitable that this body of knowledge be interpreted through my lens?'
- Follow ethics guidelines published by Indigenous research organisations, such as the Lowitja Institute and the Aboriginal Health and Medical Research Council of NSW.
- Identify the relevant custodians to discuss the intended use of Indigenous knowledge in the research work. Seek consent from each custodian – this may mean asking different communities for permission. Ensure that research is only conducted where Indigenous research partners have given their free, prior and informed consent to participate. Be prepared for the possibility that consent may be withheld.
- Consult the relevant Indigenous groups about ethical ways to document and database Indigenous knowledge.
- Be flexible with time – consultation processes may take a while.
- Give proper attribution to and acknowledge Indigenous cultural custodians for their contributions to research.
- Take good notes when interviewing informants, and return all photographs, news clippings, recordings and artworks.
- Negotiate on an ongoing basis with Indigenous research partners wherever research involves data collection and storage, and Indigenous knowledge management. Keep going back to seek approval throughout the project.
- Keep relevant Indigenous people informed on the progress of the research, and provide regular updates.
- Give Indigenous research partners appropriate time to review and give feedback on research publications, books and presentations before they are released.
- Create opportunities for consultation at all stages of the research process, even after it has been completed.
- Engage Indigenous people as researchers wherever possible.
- Train Indigenous people in research methods, data collection and report writing.

Resources

Linda Tuhiwai Smith, *Decolonizing Methodologies: Research and Indigenous Peoples*, Zed Books, London, 1999

Martin Nakata, *Disciplining the Savages: Savaging the Disciplines*, Aboriginal Studies Press, Canberra, 2007

Martin Nakata, 'The cultural interface', *Australian Journal of Indigenous Education*, vol. 36, no. 1, 2007, pp. 7–14

Jo-Ann Archibald, Jenny Lee-Morgan and Jason De Santolo (eds), *Decolonizing Research: Indigenous Storywork as Methodology*, Zed Books, London, 2019

Tyson Yunkaporta, *Sand Talk: How Indigenous Thinking Can Save the World*, Text Publishing, 2020

Ambelin Kwaymullina, 'Research, ethics and Indigenous peoples: An Australian Indigenous perspective on three threshold considerations for respectful engagement', *AlterNative: An International Journal of Indigenous People*, vol. 12, no. 4, 2016, pp. 437–49

Henrietta Marrie, *Emerging Trends in the Generation, Transmission and Protection of Traditional Knowledge*, paper presented to United Nations Permanent Forum on Indigenous Issues, 18th Session, 2019: www.un.org/development/desa/indigenouspeoples/unpfii-sessions-2/18-2.html

AIATSIS Code of Ethics for Aboriginal and Torres Strait Islander Research: https://aiatsis.gov.au/sites/default/files/2020-10/aiatsis-code-ethics.pdf

A Guide to Applying the AIATSIS Code of Ethics for Aboriginal and Torres Strait Islander Research (AIATSIS, 2020): https://aiatsis.gov.au/sites/default/files/2020-10/aiatsis-guide-applying-code-ethics_0.pdf

Guidelines for the Ethical Publishing of Aboriginal and Torres Strait Islander Authors and Research from Those Communities (AIATSIS, 2015): https://aiatsis.gov.au/sites/default/files/2020-09/ethical-publishing-guidelines.pdf

Indigenous Knowledge: Issues for Protection and Management (Terri Janke and Company/IP Australia, 2018): www.ipaustralia.gov.au/sites/default/files/ipaust_ikdiscussionpaper_28march2018.pdf

Researching Indigenous Health: A Practical Guide for Researchers (Lowitja Institute, 2011): www.lowitja.org.au/content/Document/Lowitja-Publishing/Researchers-Guide_0.pdf

AH&MRC Ethical Guidelines: Key Principles (2020) V2.0 (Aboriginal Health and Medical Research Council of NSW, 2020): www.ahmrc.org.au/publication/ahmrc-guidelines-for-research-into-aboriginal-health-2020/

Ethical Conduct in Research with Aboriginal and Torres Strait Islander Peoples and Communities: Guidelines for Researchers and Stakeholders (National Health and Medical Research Council, 2018): www.nhmrc.gov.au/about-us/resources/ethical-conduct-research-aboriginal-and-torres-strait-islander-peoples-and-communities

Lester-Irabinna Rigney, 'Indigenist research and Aboriginal Australia', in Julian E Kunnie and Nomalungelo I Goduka (eds), *Indigenous Peoples' Wisdom and Power: Affirming Our Knowledge Through Narratives*, Ashgate, Aldershot, UK, 2006, pp. 32–50.

Notes

1 Henrietta Fourmile (Marrie), 'Who owns the past? Aborigines as captives of the archives', *Aboriginal History*, vol. 13, no. 1, 1989, pp. 1–8.

2   Karen Martin – Booran Mirraboopa, 'Ways of knowing, being and doing: A theoretical framework and methods for Indigenous and indigenist re-search', *Journal of Australian Studies*, no. 76, 2009, pp. 203–14.
3   Linda Tuhiwai Smith, *Decolonizing Methodologies: Research and Indigenous Peoples*, Zed Books, London, 1999, p. 1.
4   Alison Laycock with Diane Walker, Nea Harrison and Jenny Brands, *Researching Indigenous Health: A Practical Guide for Researchers*, The Lowitja Institute, Melbourne, 2011, p. 7, <www.lowitja.org.au/content/Document/Lowitja-Publishing/Researchers-Guide_0.pdf>.
5   AIATSIS, *AIATSIS Code of Ethics for Aboriginal and Torres Strait Islander Research*, AIATSIS, 2020, <https://aiatsis.gov.au/research/ethical-research/code-ethics>.
6   AIATSIS, *A Guide to Applying The AIATSIS Code of Ethics for Aboriginal and Torres Strait Islander Research*, AIATSIS, 2020 <https://aiatsis.gov.au/sites/default/files/2020-10/aiatsis-guide-applying-code-ethics_0.pdf>.
7   See, for example, Linda Tuhiwai Smith, *Decolonizing Methodologies*; Martin Nakata, *Disciplining the Savages: Savaging the Disciplines*, Aboriginal Studies Press, Canberra, 2007.
8   George Chaloupka, *Journey in Time: The World's Longest Continuing Art Tradition: The 50,000-Year Story of the Australian Aboriginal Rock Art of Arnhem Land*, Reed New Holland, Sydney, 1993, p. 15.
9   EJ Brandl, *Australian Aboriginal Paintings in Western and Central Arnhem Land, Temporal Sequences and Elements of Style in Cadell and Deaf Adder Creek Art*, Aboriginal Studies Press, Canberra, 1973.
10 Jane Anderson, 'Access and control of Indigenous knowledge in libraries and archives: Ownership and future use', paper presented at *Correcting Course: Rebalancing Copyright for Libraries in the National and International Arena*, American Library Association and The MacArthur Foundation, Columbia University, New York, 5–7 May 2005, p. 24, <https://ccnmtl.columbia.edu/projects/alaconf2005/paper_anderson.pdf>.
11 Linda Tuhiwai Smith, *Decolonizing Methodologies*, p. 4.
12 Lester-Irabinna Rigney, 'Indigenist research and Aboriginal Australia', in Julian E Kunnie and Nomalungelo I Goduka (eds), *Indigenous Peoples' Wisdom and Power: Affirming Our Knowledge Through Narratives*, Ashgate, Aldershot, UK, 2006, p. 32.
13 Dr Payi Linda Ford, personal communication, 19 May 2021.
14 Professor Reuben Bolt, personal communication, 19 February 2021.
15 *Havasupai Tribe v. Ariz. Bd. of Regents*, 204 P.3d 1063 (Ariz, Ct App 2008); appeal denied, 2009 Ariz. LEXIS 82 (20 April 2009).
16 *Havasupai Tribe v. Ariz. Bd. of Regents*, 204 P.3d 1063 (Ariz, Ct App 2008).
17 *Havasupai Tribe v. Ariz. Bd. of Regents*, 204 P.3d 1063 (Ariz, Ct App 2008).
18 Genelle Weule, 'Indigenous rock shelter in Top End pushes Australia's human history back to 65,000 years', *ABC News*, 20 July 2017, <www.abc.net.au/news/science/2017-07-20/aboriginal-shelter-pushes-human-history-back-to-65,000-years/8719314>.
19 S Anna Florin, Andrew S Fairbairn, May Nango et al., 'The first Australian plant foods at Madjedbebe, 65,000–53,000 years ago', *Nature Communications*, no. 11, art. 924, 17 February 2020, <www.nature.com/articles/s41467-020-14723-0>.
20 *Aboriginal Land Rights (Northern Territory) Act 1976* (Cth), section 48H.
21 *Environment Protection and Biodiversity Act 1999* (Cth), section 310; Environment Protection Biodiversity Conservation Regulations 2000 (Cth), regulation 8A.06.

22 Paul Memmott, 'Bio-architectural technology and the Dreamtime knowledge of spinifex grass', paper presented at *CIB WBC13: 19th World Building Congress 2013*, Brisbane, 5–9 May 2013.
23 Terri Janke, 'From smokebush to spinifex: Towards recognition of Indigenous knowledge in the commercialisation of plants', *International Journal of Rural Law and Policy*, no. 1, 2018, 5713 [p. 18], <www.austlii.edu.au/au/journals/IntJlRuralLawP/2018/1.pdf>.
24 Northern Territory Government, *The Strehlow Research Centre*, Araluen Arts Centre, n.d., <https://araluenartscentre.nt.gov.au/strehlow-research-centre>.
25 Jason Gibson, Shaun Angeles and Joel Liddle, 'Deciphering Arrernte archives: The intermingling of textual and living knowledge' in Linda Barwick, Jennifer Green and Petronella Vaarzon-Morel (eds), *Archival Returns: Central Australia and Beyond*, Sydney University Press, Sydney, 2019, pp. 29–45.
26 Museum and Art Gallery Northern Territory (MAGNT), *The Strehlow Research Centre*, MAGNT, n.d., <www.magnt.net.au/strehlow-research-centre>.
27 Shaun Angeles Penangke, 'Indigenous leadership in the museum sector', *Arts Backbone*, vol. 17, no. 2, 2018, p. 4, <www.anka.org.au/archive/art-backbone/>.
28 Matthew Rimmer, 'The genographic project: Traditional knowledge and population genetics', *Australian Indigenous Law Report*, vol. 11, no. 2, 2007, pp. 33–54.
29 Mick Gooda, 'Chairman's report', *ANU National Centre for Indigenous Genomics 2017 Annual Report*, NCIG, Canberra, 2017, <https://ncig.anu.edu.au/files/NCIG-2017-Annual-Report.pdf>.
30 Emma Kowal, Simon Easteal and Mick Gooda, 'Indigenous genomics', *Australasian Science*, July/August 2016, <www.australasianscience.com.au/article/issue-julyaugust-2016/indigenous-genomics.html>.
31 NCIG, *ANU National Centre for Indigenous Genomics 2017 Annual Report*, p. 7.
32 Emma Kowal, Simon Easteal and Mick Gooda, 'Indigenous genomics'.
33 Dr Misty Jenkins, personal communication, 24 November 2020.
34 The Lowitja Institute, *Good Decisions Grow from Great Research*, Lowitja Instiutte, YouTube, 1 October 2013, <www.youtube.com/watch?v=-PqSEm15lSs>.
35 The Lowitja Institute, *About*, Lowitja Institute, 2020, <www.lowitja.org.au/page/about-us>.
36 Alison Laycock with Diane Walker, Nea Harrison and Jenny Brands, *Researching Indigenous Health: A Practical Guide for Researchers*.
37 Maiam nayri Wingara and Australian Indigenous Governance Institute, *Data for Governance: Governance of Data: Briefing Paper: 2018*, Maiam nayri Wingara, 2018, <www.maiamnayriwingara.org/s/Indigenous-Data-Sovereignty-Summit-June-2018-Briefing-Paper.pdf>.
38 CQ University, *Indigenous Elder to Present Paper at UN Forum*, CQ University, 16 April 2019, <www.cqu.edu.au/cquninews/stories/general-category/2019/cquniversity-indigenous-elder-to-present-paper-at-un-forum>.
39 CQ University, *Hectic Schedule Follows Top Honours for Innovative Indigenous Academic*, CQ University, 8 February 2018, <www.cqu.edu.au/cquninews/stories/general-category/2018/hectic-schedule-follows-top-honours-for-innovative-indigenous-academic>.
40 Terri Janke and Company, *Indigenous Knowledge: Issues for Protection and Management*, paper commissioned by IP Australia and the Department of Industry, Innovation and Science, IP Australia, Canberra, 2018, <www.ipaustralia.gov.au/sites/default/files/ipaust_ikdiscussionpaper_28march2018.pdf>.

12
ENABLING INDIGENOUS VOICES IN EDUCATION

I get a lot of emails from teachers and academics who want to know how to respectfully include Indigenous topics in their classes. They want to teach their students about Aboriginal history and culture, but they're scared they might get it wrong. They tell me of the absence of Indigenous content in their own education, or a story about that progressive teacher who would read Aboriginal creation stories to their class on a rare occasion. How do schools today address Indigenous topics in the classroom?

The Australian education system informs the way we understand our history, shaping our sense of personal and cultural identity. Teachers want to do the right thing but struggle with how to go about including the many Indigenous stories, histories and knowledges embedded in Australia's past and present. Just teaching out of textbooks might not be appropriate. Past curricula have either marginalised Indigenous viewpoints or left them out altogether.

Some of the emails I receive are long, and include questions like: Can we copy Aboriginal art styles in art class, or is that offensive? How can we put together a school play based on an Aboriginal Dreaming story? Can we all paint an Aboriginal mural in the school courtyard? If I record an Aboriginal elder's story, how do I do it respectfully? Do we need to pay Indigenous people who come into schools to teach and share their knowledge? How do we teach traditional language, and which one should we choose – a local language where the school is situated? Can non-Indigenous teachers teach Indigenous topics?

I don't always have the time to answer them all but I try my best to reply with something to encourage them, because I know they are trying to understand how to include Indigenous content. I know they are wanting to be respectful. I wish I'd had teachers who were half as enthusiastic as these ones.

I went to primary school in Cairns, in Far North Queensland. I started in 1972, only five years after the referendum to recognise Indigenous Australians in the Australian Constitution. 1972 was the year I learned about the history of Australia. I was taught that Australia was discovered by Captain Cook. I learned about Joseph Banks, Arthur Phillip and the First Fleet. I sketched men using blue and red pencils and drew brown people next to them. I remember drawing a gunyah, an Aboriginal shelter made of bark and twigs. Someone asked me if my house was like that. Another kid laughed. I couldn't answer. It was the start of that feeling of invisibility.

That same year, a 10-metre-tall statue of Captain Cook, with one arm aggressively stretched out, was erected on the highway in Cairns leading up to Cape York. This cast an even longer shadow across the growing town. I felt alienated from my classmates. They too were learning that we were different. My younger brother, John Paul, obviously felt it too. Reflecting on the lack of understanding about Aboriginal and Torres Strait Islander histories and cultures in school, he wrote: 'Textbooks told us that Captain Cook discovered Australia, Aboriginal people were nomadic hunter gatherers and the noble savages. There was no text talking about Aboriginal nations, of sovereignty, of achievements, of frontier conflict, of invasion, of theft of land and of massacres.'[1]

These were things we had to learn for ourselves: after school, at university, by listening to Aboriginal and Torres Strait Islander people who shared their stories and histories, and by reading a few remarkable non-Indigenous historians and academics, like Henry Reynolds, who wrote about the real history of Australia.

I watched my own children go through school in the 2000s. By then, things had changed a little bit. Teachers were grappling with introducing Indigenous topics into the classroom, and celebrating important

Indigenous events like NAIDOC Week, the anniversary of the 1967 referendum or National Reconciliation Week. In 2008, on the day then prime minister Kevin Rudd delivered the National Apology to the Stolen Generations, I visited the school to give an Aboriginal flag and a Torres Strait Islander flag to my children's school principal. She didn't know what to say to me. She took the flags and I never saw them again. She didn't seem interested in a dialogue about anything Indigenous.

There were a couple of younger teachers there trying to engage with the Aboriginal and Torres Strait Islander community, bringing together a group of Indigenous students and parents for Indigenous family meetings. It was a good start, and these two young women brought a lot of pride to my children, who felt honoured to have their cultures recognised and celebrated.

My own way to help make my children proud of their Indigenous heritage was to write books with them. When she was five, my daughter Tamina and I wrote *What Makes a Tree Smile?* (2003), a picture book about things that make a tree happy, like sun showers. Each page was beautifully illustrated by Indigenous artist Francine Ngardarb Riches, and the book was published with Magabala Books, based in Broome. After it was published, we gave copies to the school library, which made Tamina proud.

With my son Jaiki, the book was *Kin Island* (2011), a novel for young readers about visiting the Torres Strait Islands and connecting with our family. *Kin Island* was part of the Yarning Strong book series for Years 3–6 that gives Indigenous and non-Indigenous students a window into what it's like to be a young Aboriginal or Torres Strait Islander person in Australia. A teaching guide for schools, written by Indigenous educators Lisa Buxton and Leesa Watego, was also provided for the book. The series followed protocols and set a great example, with royalties going back to the Indigenous authors. Teachers can use these resources in the classroom to share authentic perspectives on Indigenous culture.

Indigenous trailblazers in education

When I was a kid there were no good books to read about Aboriginal and Torres Strait Islander people. The ones we did read were written by non-Indigenous authors. Today, there are many great Indigenous authors who have penned fiction and factual texts, poetry and illustrated picture books.

Wiradyuri author Professor Anita Heiss is the editor of the award-winning book *Growing Up Aboriginal in Australia* (2018). It's a book about changing the dialogue about Aboriginal people. As Anita says, 'Let's assist teachers in the classroom; let's give young Australians today a resource, a tool, to help them understand what it means to grow up Aboriginal in Australia over history and today.'[2]

Professor Marcia Langton wrote *Welcome to Country: A Travel Guide to Indigenous Australia* (2018) for a similar reason – to help young students understand Australia's First Nations when they are in school. Langton, speaking at the launch of the book in Sydney, spoke about the need for accessible resources for understanding Aboriginal culture.

At the launch of Marcia's book I spoke with Corey Tutt, a young man who started the Deadly Science initiative that donates thousands of books to schools in remote Aboriginal communities (see chapter 10, page 246). He is writing a book called *The First Scientists*, which aims to help young people learn more about First Nations science.

Gamilaroi man Luke Pearson is the founder of IndigenousX, a media and consultancy platform that amplifies Indigenous voices. Luke has a background in teaching and is a lover of history and a lover of story. He is passionate about truth telling, and wants us all to know more about Indigenous stories. 'There are stories about this country we should all know that I can't believe we didn't learn in school,' Luke says. 'We must tell the truths of the past so we can move forward together, Indigenous and non-Indigenous.' He talks about a need to give hope to Indigenous children, to make them proud of their heritage and their ancestors and place in this country.[3]

Luke believes the main issue is that schools are unsure how to teach Indigenous topics. He urges teachers to go to the experts – to bring Indigenous people in. The issue is that, so often, schools expect Indigenous knowledge to be freely given by people in the community. Schools expect community members to come in and work for free because it's for the children. They pay the maths consultant, but not the Aboriginal consultant. In 2020, IndigenousX partnered with the NSW Aboriginal Education Consultative Group (AECG) for Kooriculum, a program to teach Indigenous science in primary schools.

Indigenous culture in schools: Teaching and learning

So, while we still don't have enough Indigenous teachers, how can we appropriately and respectfully bring in Indigenous culture to schools?

Wiradjuri woman Dr Christine (Chris) Evans is an academic with a strong background in Aboriginal education and the arts. I have known Christine since the 1990s, when she worked at the Jumbunna Indigenous House of Learning at the University of Technology (UTS), now known as the Jumbunna Institute for Indigenous Education and Research. At the time, I was asked to be the subject coordinator and lecturer of the Social Research Ethics subject in a Master of Indigenous Social Policy. I was also lucky to attend an international conference Jumbunna held on Indigenous Cultural and Intellectual Property, which was attended by Indigenous academics Linda Tuhiwai Smith and James (Sa'ke'j) Youngblood Henderson.

Chris was a former teacher and, at the conference, we spoke a lot about the role of the education system. Chris was passionate about how the education system should include ICIP. Chris's doctoral research focused on improving Indigenous knowledge in teacher education curriculum through a process of cultural quality assurance. During her research, she asked Aboriginal community members what essential knowledge art teachers needed to have about Aboriginal Australia. Their responses apply to other teachers: 'They need to know whose country they're on. They need to know the local community of the school where they teach. They also need to know, beyond that, other groups. Are you teaching on Freshwater Country? Are you teaching on Saltwater Country?

And understanding the implications of that.' They also asked for teachers to know more about protocols.[4] Chris encourages collaboration between teachers and local Aboriginal community members to improve the quality of education.

Chris spent time working at the NSW Education Standards Authority (NESA). In 2017, NESA introduced a new model for the representation of Aboriginal and Torres Strait Islander histories and cultures in the NSW school curriculum, which recognises ICIP protocols. NESA's *Aboriginal and Torres Strait Islander Principles and Protocols* state that principles of cultural safety are founded on respectful behaviours and integrity. Among the principles for teaching Aboriginal and Torres Strait Islander histories and cultures, the document includes respect for and protection of the knowledge and cultural expressions of Aboriginal and Torres Strait Islander Peoples. For example, year 12 students in NSW who study Biology will investigate the application of Aboriginal protocols in the development of medicines and biological materials in Australia, to understand why the protection of ICIP is important.[5]

Teachers must therefore connect with the Aboriginal and Torres Strait Islander community. Professor Lester-Irabinna Rigney, introduced in chapter 11, is a Narungga, Kaurna and Ngarrindjeri man from South Australia with a long history of working in Aboriginal education. For more than 30 years he has been researching teachers' work, Aboriginal schooling, educational leadership and school reform. He has been studying the teaching approach called culturally responsive pedagogy, which identifies the particular cultural strengths of students. 'Findings from educators is that children are more likely to meaningfully engage in learning when their identities belong, and their socio-cultural context is invoked. Therefore, educators must cultivate authentic relationships that position students, parents and Elders as co-designers toward effective and culturally responsive learning,' he writes.[6] Lester's research demonstrates the importance of Aboriginal community involvement in education.

Another Indigenous educator, Professor Chris Matthews, a Quandamooka man from Queensland, has developed the Goompi Model that can be used to create innovative approaches to teaching by exploring the connection between mathematics and culture. An example of this is the 'Maths as Storytelling' (MAST) approach for teaching mathematics to Indigenous students. 'As people we all want to understand the world around us and we do that through our own cultural lens,' he explains.[7] When teaching algebra and arithmetic, Chris encourages Indigenous students to draw on their cultures to create stories relatable to mathematical expressions to understand the patterning and structure. These could be flying brolgas, kangaroos being hunted or rain falling from a cloud. He has also set up the Aboriginal & Torres Strait Islander Mathematics Alliance (ATSIMA) that aims to transform maths education for Aboriginal and Torres Strait Islander students. Like Lester-Irabinna Rigney, Chris is reforming education so that Indigenous cultures and contexts are part of how teaching occurs in Australia schools.

Indigenous community-controlled education organisations are also key to bringing Indigenous values into the education system. The NSW Aboriginal Education Consultative Group (AECG) was set up in the late 1970s to bring Indigenous studies to schools and promote Aboriginal participation in the decision-making process of education and training. The local AECG Network supports access and opportunities in education for Aboriginal people and their communities. The NSW AECG has done great work bringing Indigenous studies to schools, providing resources and training for teachers, bringing teachers and community members together, and enabling Indigenous communities to engage with the education system. Their fun, engaging resources for teachers are all linked to the Australian Curriculum; these materials contextualise Aboriginality and explain the connections between land, heritage and identity.

Community connections in schools

'More teachers need to connect with and understand Aboriginal and Torres Strait Islander students, parents and elders,' says Dr Kevin Lowe, a Gubbi Gubbi man and education researcher from south-east Queensland who now works at the University of New South Wales. Kevin runs a course for future teachers, educating them about how to work effectively with Indigenous peoples inside and outside the classroom. Kevin believes that teachers need to build trusting, respectful and mutually beneficial relationships with the Indigenous students and families in their schools. He calls these 'two-way learning relationships'.[8] Teachers should have open conversations with Aboriginal and Torres Strait Islander parents and community members. He tells teachers that this has 'the purpose of helping you to learn about this local community and to understand their fears and aspirations for their children'.[9] Kevin, like Lester-Irabinna Rigney, believes that teachers need to ask (and listen to) what local Indigenous families want for their children. The answer may be different to what most non-Indigenous parents want. Or it could be very similar. The important thing is to ask, and to open a space for ongoing conversation and engagement.

Non-Indigenous cultures and beliefs also have a big impact on Indigenous education in Australia. Kevin suggests that teachers can 'challenge their own and institutional practices that have for too long conditioned everyone to tacitly accept the level of student underachievement'.[10] He is referring to the commonly held yet unjustified belief that characterises Aboriginal students as less capable of learning than other students. Kevin argues that teachers can unlearn these negative assumptions through actively collaborating with Indigenous elders and community members; they will become 'professionally liberated' from these unconscious biases.[11] They can begin to see how negative stereotypes about Aboriginal people limit the performance of themselves as teachers, as well as the performance of their students.

ICIP protocols in education

In New South Wales, I worked with NESA to develop protocols and agreements for the use of NSW Aboriginal languages. Their vision is to teach Aboriginal languages in schools but to recognise the importance of protocols, such as the True Tracks protocols, and Indigenous peoples' ownership of their languages, cultures and knowledge.

The Victorian Department of Education and Training has also

developed protocols for teaching Aboriginal and Torres Strait Islander culture. There are three key guidelines:

- to consult with the traditional owners and custodians of the land where the school is situated before developing any activity or resource that makes use of Indigenous cultural expression
- to recognise that ICIP remains with the traditional owners and to attribute this ownership correctly in any published materials related to the teaching activity or resource
- to ensure that any school activities do not damage Indigenous cultural integrity.[12]

These guidelines embody the True Tracks principles of consent and consultation, attribution, cultural integrity and, overall, respect.

Jingili man Joe Sambono, introduced in chapter 10, is a curriculum specialist with ACARA. He has done amazing things to enable the teaching of Indigenous science in schools, offering practical examples of how teachers can put Indigenous ways of knowing into biology and chemistry classes, and into other science subjects. The ACARA science 'elaborations' that Joe helped to develop demonstrate that Indigenous knowledge is just as valuable as Western knowledge when it comes to teaching science. 'Science has moved beyond this process of dismissing and deriding Indigenous peoples and cultures and judging them by what they didn't have instead of what they did,' Joe says.[13] Educators, including science educators, need to move away from stereotypes of Indigenous deficit. They must understand the depth and value of Indigenous scientific knowledge and bring it into the classroom.

Terri Janke and Company worked with Joe and the South Australian Department of Education to develop protocols and consent forms covering the use of Indigenous knowledge in schools. The goal is to give life to Indigenous kids' lessons by involving members of the community in teaching. We worked with the Department and Indigenous consultants to develop an ICIP protocol for integrating South Australian Aboriginal perspectives into science teaching. We took the 95 science elaborations

SCIENCE IN SOUTH AUSTRALIA: TRUE TRACKS IN ACTION

Elizabeth's work with the SA Department of Education demonstrates some of the ways that the True Tracks principles can be put into practice. Elizabeth helped the SA Department of Education develop solutions to ICIP issues in teaching science.

1   Who is allowed to teach what?

Given the holistic nature of Indigenous cultures, scientific knowledge is wrapped up in culture. Australian teachers should be able to teach approved *applications* of Indigenous scientific knowledges, but not the cultures in which they are embedded. Getting this right depends on close relationships between the Indigenous knowledge holders and teachers. We devised consent forms to grant permission for the science to be taught in the sanctioned ways.

A code of conduct can also be useful here. In this case, it specifies that teachers are not allowed to use Indigenous scientific knowledge for any reason other than as agreed for the project. Without formal consent, teachers are not allowed to teach this knowledge in other schools, nor can they use the knowledge to create their own resources, such as books.

2   How can knowledge be protected once it is written down?

Once ICIP is recorded and made available for teachers, it can be difficult to control how others use it. One approach is to create very specific resources that discuss the applications of the science but not the details of the history, knowledge and cultures that inform the applications. This means that teachers must go back to traditional owners and custodians for more detail, encouraging ongoing partnerships and creating opportunities for elders, knowledge holders and custodians to work with schools. Additionally, teaching resources are only to be used for very limited purposes, and any additional uses require the consent of all of the partners.

3   How will the knowledge be stored?
This information needs long-term protection so that future generations and future teachers/schools can access the information.

4   How do you ensure the integrity and authenticity of teaching resources?
The resources must accurately reflect the perspectives of Indigenous knowledge holders from different communities. All resources had to be checked by each Indigenous group, who would then give approval or feedback for improvement.

5   How do you attribute Indigenous knowledge holders?
The individual knowledge holders who shared the knowledge should be attributed. Relevant communities should also be attributed (in this case, the Kaurna, Narungga and Ngarrindjeri peoples). They must be recognised as the source communities of the science knowledge.

....

set by ACARA and adapted them to reflect local knowledges and science. This model is one that could be taken up all over Australia – contextualising Indigenous ways of knowing within the local Indigenous lands upon which a school is situated. We also developed community clearance forms governing the use of Indigenous knowledge. The SA Department wanted to work with various Indigenous nations to contextualise their knowledges, technologies and processes to teach students Indigenous science concepts.

Elizabeth Mason, a solicitor at Terri Janke and Company, travelled to Adelaide with me to present to the SA Department and key stakeholders, including local Indigenous people. At the opening of the workshop, an elder presented a welcome to country and asked us to consider deeply the feathers and leaves and flowers from Kaurna country outside the window.

It was a first for a state education department to take on a project of this nature. In our office we had seen so many examples of information being taken and used without any consultation or thought. We were impressed by the South Australian approach. 'They cared about changing the way the education system works to make sure it achieves good outcomes for Aboriginal people and brings greater respect for Aboriginal cultures,' Elizabeth said. 'Staff at the department wanted a protocol so they could understand what process to follow and know what the key issues were – this is a theme that comes up again and again. Generally, people want to do the right thing but aren't sure what that is or where to start.'[14]

Bringing culture and people into the classroom

Instead of treating Indigenous people as a free resource or a traditional knowledge library that is there to be used and taken from at no cost, let's create employment opportunities for Indigenous knowledge holders to come into schools and deliver services and workshops, sharing their wisdom and expertise. Let's hire local Indigenous community experts to expand the minds of our next generation of educators, innovators and creators. And let's do it respectfully, following appropriate cultural protocols. Indigenous students and parents need teachers who feel confident engaging with Indigenous cultures, histories and perspectives. We can bring in Indigenous perspectives through bringing Indigenous people into the classrooms as guest speakers, and through the books, film and materials we give to children. The True Tracks principles can be a useful framework for doing so.

WHAT YOU CAN DO

- Review the resources by ACARA and state education agencies such as NESA (and other states), and the NSW AECG.
- Contact local Indigenous community members and allow for long time frames for consultation.
- Read books written by Indigenous authors.
- Talk openly and respectfully with the Indigenous families who have children in your schools.
- Engage with local Indigenous elders and invite them to your school. Pay them for any work that they do for you.
- Wherever possible, employ Indigenous artists, performers, storytellers and professionals to guide classroom activities involving Indigenous knowledge and perspectives.
- Encourage an understanding of Indigenous cultures as dynamic living cultures which, like all cultures, adjust to change and have a history.
- Ensure that any resources used are culturally sensitive and appropriate. If in doubt, consult with Indigenous people.
- Avoid aspects of Indigenous knowledge and culture containing sacred, secret or confidential information.
- Encourage an understanding that Indigenous people, cultures and knowledge are richly diverse and made up of many different communities. There is not one homogenous group. AIATSIS's *Map of Indigenous Australia* provides a good illustration of this.
- Acknowledge that Indigenous students may not necessarily be informed about all aspects of their cultural heritage.

Resources

Tyson Yunkaporta, *Sand Talk: How Indigenous Thinking Can Save the World* (Text Publishing, 2020)

First Languages, Law & Governance Guide (Terri Janke and Company, 2019): www.terrijanke.com.au/first-languages-law-governance-guid

Magabala Books – Education: www.magabala.com/pages/education

Map of Indigenous Australia (David R Horton and AIATSIS, 1996): https://aiatsis.gov.au/explore/map-indigenous-australia

Aboriginal Studies Association: www.aboriginalstudies.com.au

Indigenous Literacy Foundation (ILF): www.indigenousliteracyfoundation.org.au/

Stronger Smarter Institute: https://strongersmarter.com.au

Notes

1. John Paul Janke, keynote speech, *People, Power and Perspectives: History Teachers' Association of Australia Annual Conference*, Canberra, 2–4 October 2018.
2. Anita Heiss, in 'Speaking with: Author Anita Heiss on *Growing Up Aboriginal in Australia*' [podcast episode], *Speaking With*, 5 September 2018, <https://theconversation.com/speaking-with-author-anita-heiss-on-growing-up-aboriginal-in-australia-102644>.
3. Luke Pearson, *IndigenousX: Luke Pearson at TEDxCanberra*, TEDx Talks, YouTube, 3 October 2013, <www.youtube.com/watch?v=vvKlrvu7nws>.
4. Christine Evans, *Dr Christine Evans, NESA*, Kaldor Public Art Projects, YouTube, 29 January 2019, <www.youtube.com/watch?v=bIHt7_i7tqc>.
5. NSW Education Standards Authority (NESA), *Biology: Stage 6 Syllabus*, NESA, 2017, p. 55, <https://educationstandards.nsw.edu.au/wps/portal/nesa/11-12/stage-6-learning-areas/stage-6-science/biology-2017/>.
6. Lester-Irabinna Rigney, 'A time for change and "super diversity" in early childhood education', *The Spoke*, 20 September 2019, <http://thespoke.earlychildhoodaustralia.org.au/time-change-super-diversity-early-childhood-education/>.
7. Anna Salleh, 'Maths, story and dance: An Indigenous approach to teaching', *ABC Science*, 15 August 2016, <www.abc.net.au/news/science/2016-08-15/closing-the-maths-gap-with-story-and-dance/7700656>.
8. Kevin Lowe, 'Learning with connection: Shifting teachers' practice through authentic engagement with Aboriginal and Torres Strait Islander communities', in Deborah M Netolicky, Jon Andrews and Cameron Paterson (eds), *Flip the System Australia: What Matters in Education*, Routledge, London, 2018, p. 130.
9. Kevin Lowe, 'Learning with connection', p. 129.
10. Kevin Lowe, 'Learning with connection', p. 125.
11. Kevin Lowe, 'Learning with connection', p. 127.
12. State Government of Victoria, *Teaching Aboriginal and Torres Strait Islander Culture*, Victorian Department of Education and Traiting, 2019, <www.education.vic.gov.au/school/teachers/teachingresources/multicultural/Pages/koorieculture.aspx>.
13. Joe Sambono, 'Indigenous science goes far beyond boomerangs and spears', *IndigenousX*, 11 November 2018, <https://indigenousx.com.au/indigenous-science-goes-far-beyond-boomerangs-and-spears/>.
14. Elizabeth Mason, personal communication, 17 February 2021.

13
INDIGENOUS EXCELLENCE IN DIGITAL AND TECHNOLOGY

About ten years ago, I met the visionary tech entrepreneur Mikaela Jade, best known as the founder of Indigital, a trailblazing tech company that is bridging ancient Indigenous cultures and the digital economy.

Mikaela arrived at my office with Dr Ruth Mirams, her business partner at the time and fellow tech innovator. They were really excited to show me the Google Glass they had brought with them, essentially a little computer that you wear like spectacles. Mikaela let me try it out. The device produces a display screen in your field of vision. As you walk around, it can take photos, videos and sound recordings, and connect to the internet – like a hands-free smartphone. When I walked around I felt a little dizzy, but I got the point of Mikaela's enthusiasm.

'Wearing the Google Glass for the first time was a really emotional experience,' Mikaela told me. Mikaela is a Cabrogal woman of the Dharug nation, situated in Western Sydney. She is an environmental biologist by trade and in more recent years her work has involved emerging technologies. 'I worked in national parks for ten years. I can see the relevance of having this thing on your head while you're having a tourism experience, a digital tourism experience, [and] what that means. I can see what it means from a biological perspective when you can go out there and scan lands and do pest and weed incursion mapping and do climate change mapping ... It's an amazing tool for natural resource management.'[1]

It was ten years ago when Mikaela showed me Google Glass, and she was already thinking about what emerging technologies like Google Glass, drones and virtual reality mean for Indigenous peoples. What does it mean to take these devices onto country? In this digital or information age, technology is being invented and improved at an extremely rapid pace. Although the Google Glass didn't take off in the mainstream market, other new technologies with similar capabilities have broken through. Look at drones, for example: kids fly them in their backyards, travellers take them on their bushwalks and now people like Mikaela, and creatives such as Australian filmmaker Lynette Wallworth (see chapter 6), are harnessing their power to support the telling and preservation of Indigenous knowledge and story.

Mikaela is very enthusiastic about the digital technology industry. But she sees a need for constraints when these applications involve Indigenous knowledge and culture. 'I'm conscious, you know, of the dark side of it as well ... It's a catch 22. It's coming, and I'd rather be in the space where we can work together with developers ... and say "Okay, what do we want this thing to do?" And if we can dream it, we can do it. And there needs to be respect around cultural boundaries for this thing.'[2]

After we met, I felt inspired. I could see Mikaela's unique talents shine through, and her ability to understand how digital technologies can empower Indigenous peoples and support self-determination, and share and maintain Indigenous cultures. We later worked with her to develop protocols and agreements, and explained to her the copyright and IP implications. She was interested in the methodical and practical approach of True Tracks and has since become a big advocate for the use of protocols in the digital realm. Today, she says, 'I travel between the worlds of Indigenous belief systems, environmental science and information technologies helping to create platforms that capture the hearts and minds of our next generations.'[3]

Mikaela clearly sees the need for Indigenous peoples to be key players in the digital economy. One of her earlier projects was Indigital Storytelling, an augmented reality app that shared Indigenous story from Kakadu National Park in the Northern Territory. Kakadu is a UNESCO World Heritage site and the largest national park in Australia. Aboriginal people have lived in Kakadu for over 50,000 years. It is a rich cultural landscape with incredible scenery, rock art and archaeological sites.

The app allows you to use a smartphone camera to precisely spot and identify Indigenous places, artworks and objects. Once your camera 'sees' a place, artwork or object in your live environment, a traditional owner virtually shares their story with you. 'I use new technologies to stimulate the minds of our young ones,' Mikaela says. 'They see their stories being told with augmented and virtual realities, and that connects them to the world they live in but through their traditional narratives. It makes them proud and reinforces the relevance and truth of Country.'[4] The technology also allows elders to share their stories with the younger generation.

Mikaela carefully followed specific cultural protocols and consultation with senior traditional owners. Data ownership, intellectual property and copyright have been respected. Importantly, 50 per cent of all sales went to traditional owners.

New technology can bring to life culture and story in the arts too. A groundbreaking project is the Emmy Award–winning virtual-reality film *Collisions* (2016) by Lynette Wallworth, acclaimed Australian artist and director known for using emerging technologies to explore human cultures and nature. (See chapter 6, page 144, for more on this project.) Lynette uses emerging technologies such as virtual reality (VR), drones, immersive domes and interactive videos. For *Collisions*, Lynette closely collaborated with Martu elder Nyarri Morgan to share his story about a British atomic bomb test he witnessed in the 1950s at Maralinga, in the South Australian desert. The experience of *Collisions* is so unique: you wear a VR headset, which makes you feel like you are on country. To produce the film, Lynette carefully followed protocols. This is the power of the True Tracks protocols – they can be adapted for projects that are experimental and interdisciplinary, in this case, a project that merges new technology, filmmaking and storytelling.

The award-winning exhibition *Songlines: Tracking the Seven Sisters* (2017) is another groundbreaking art project that used new technologies. *Songlines* mapped the Seven Sisters Tjukurpa, significant Dreaming tracks that travel through Martu, Ngaanyatjarra, Pitjantjatjara and Yankunytjatjara lands and across the entire continent. For Indigenous people, the Dreaming is a world view that explains the creation of the cosmos, oceans, rivers, mountains, islands, land formations, plants and animals by ancestral beings who travelled the Earth – on, above and below it. These are the Dreaming tracks or songlines, recorded in story, song, dance and art, but it is through performance that the primary transmission of knowledge occurs. Passed down over millennia, songlines carry and transmit important knowledge for many Aboriginal nations and Torres Strait Islander language groups. They must continue to be passed on in various ways, so people can continue their cultural practices.

This is why there was a five-year heritage preservation project that preceded and fed into the *Songlines* exhibition. This arose from an urgent plea by Anangu elders from the Anangu Pitjantjatjara Yankunytjatjara (APY) lands in the early 2000s who feared that the knowledge of this Tjukurpa would die with them as the younger generation were more interested in the technological wonders of the 21st century. The elders feared that they may be gone by the time the younger generation was ready to receive the knowledge. They decided that if the younger generation was inhabiting the digital domain, they too would have to connect with them there. The cultural material that was revived and collected during the project was deposited into Ara Irititja, an Aboriginal-managed online archive.[5] Lead curator Margo Neale (Senior Curator, Adviser to the Director at the National Museum of Australia, and Head of the Centre for Indigenous Knowledges, of Irish, Kulin and Gumbayngirrr descent) formed a curatorium with the traditional owners, co-led by a senior law woman and custodian of the Seven Sisters, Inawinytji Williamson (see chapter 14, page 322). This functioned as a group of co-curators.

I attended the exhibition opening at the National Museum of Australia (NMA) in Canberra in 2017 with Tamina, my daughter, and Taryn Saunders, a colleague at the time. At the launch, the women from the desert performed. I was so pleased to run into my old friend and client, Rene Kulitja. Almost 20 years since we met, Rene was now an elder and lead the young dancers from the school onto the stage as they performed part of the Seven Sisters Dreaming story. Among the crowd were the Aboriginal women from across the three deserts, members of the host Aboriginal community and beyond, and people from participating art centres. Like the exhibition, the opening was Indigenous led. At the entrance were life-sized screens with images of the traditional custodians of the Seven Sisters songlines welcoming us into their space. Their virtual presence ensured we knew whose knowledge was within and invited us to learn about the country we all shared. Once inside, we saw epic paintings which were like portals to place, revealing the journey of the seven sisters and their knowledge of land, plants, people and stars. The paintings pulsated with the heat and radiance of the desert. Orange, yellow, red, pink and brown contrasted with purple, blue, black and white, suggestive of many other elements of the desert, including the coolness of the nights. There were 3D works and sculptures – ceramics, punu (woodcarving), bowls, spears and shields – and life-sized installations of the seven sisters, sitting on the earth and flying in the sky, woven with desert grasses, plant fibres, emu feathers and even human hair.

The centrepiece was the immersive state-of-the-art digital dome. The 7-metre dome offers a 360-degree viewing experience that draws on emerging technologies developed by Sarah Kenderdine and her then team at the University of New South Wales.[6] The footage in the form of photogrammetry projected in the dome was created in close consultation with the relevant communities. Lying on our backs looking up at the inside the dome, we were transported to the places through Country where the seven sisters encountered their shape-shifting pursuer Wati Nyiru or Yurla. Like gazing up at the night sky, or the rock art on the walls of a cave, we watched paintings come to life; it was captivating. The exhibition also included the Emmy Award–winning film *Collisions* by Lynette Wallworth and Curtis Taylor (see above).

It is exciting that Indigenous people are working in this space, innovating for the future. Mikaela is now working with Microsoft to develop holograms of Indigenous elders telling their stories their way, on country. Mikaela has always wanted to tell stories on country through augmented reality, she says, and it has taken a while for the technology to catch up with her vision. She's worked out the protocols to respect culture and recognise IP and moral rights, enabling Indigenous voices to shine through.

Artificial intelligence: Who owns the rights?

One day I received an email from Levi McKenzie-Kirkbright, a Gadigal, Yuin, Worimi, Biripi and Gamilaraay man, and software engineer with a background in biomedicine and clinical medicine. While studying engineering at the University of Melbourne, Levi was writing an article about artificial intelligence (AI) that can create artworks, and he was wondering what this technology means for Indigenous culture. AI is a fast-growing branch of computer science involving machines with the ability to do things typically requiring human intelligence.

In his article, Levi was considering the power of AI to recreate new artworks from pre-existing ones through technology known as neural style transfer. This brings up many questions. What if the image being used is an Indigenous painting or ceremonial design? Can a machine using algorithms misappropriate cultural works? And who owns the art created by the algorithm?

Through the lens of intellectual property, I thought about how this type of technology quickly brings into question traditional concepts of IP such as authorship and innovation. Does copyright apply? The World Intellectual Property Organization (WIPO) has said that copyright law currently does not allow for works generated by artificial intelligence.[7] This is because the law was written for human creators, not computers. One idea is to design a special sui generis system, meaning a standalone law, to address this.

Can a machine learn cultural protocols? There is a need for ethics and best practice protocols in the artificial intelligence industry. There is also a need for more Indigenous participation in the industry. 'The global digital economy is one of the greatest opportunities for Indigenous people to benefit from new forms of economic empowerment and cultural flourishing, Levi says. 'In order to have Indigenous perspectives participating in this 21st-century digital renaissance, we need more Aboriginal and Torres Strait Islander people entering and thriving in the technology industry, studying and working in diverse subdisciplines from data science to design.'[8]

Internationally, there has been discussion on how Indigenous protocols can inform AI. Old Ways, New – a cultural and technology consultancy – co-founded and funded the Indigenous Protocols and Artificial Intelligence (IP AI) working group in 2018. They released a paper on the topic, offering a starting point for people who want to create AI from an ethical position that centres Indigenous concerns.[9]

Indigenous data sovereignty

NAILSMA and I-Tracker

Some years ago, I had the immense pleasure of working with the North Australian Indigenous Land and Sea Management Alliance (NAILSMA), an Indigenous-led not-for-profit that operates across northern Australia. (See also chapter 10, page 242.) Established in 2001, NAILSMA supports the Indigenous communities of this region to manage their traditional estates. Compared to other areas of Australia, the Top End has a high proportion of Indigenous land estate – around 40 per cent, and growing.[10] It's a region that is incredibly rich in culture and biodiversity, where caring for country has been a central task for generations.

With the help of Rod Kennett, my firm assisted NAILSMA to manage the IP and ICIP rights involved in the I-Tracker project in 2010. I-Tracker, short for Indigenous-Tracker, is an application that provides mapping and data services for Indigenous rangers. Using the world-renowned CyberTracker data collection software, the app combines modern science and technology with traditional knowledge to care for animal species and habitats. It has been used for mapping and monitoring dugongs, seagrass and sea turtles, and to collect information on land management activities such as fire, weeds, feral animals, biodiversity, water health and visitor management.

We created a data-sharing protocol. Key to this was informed consent of traditional owners for data collection, and consultation with them on the appropriate use and sharing of collected data. This helps ensure that the I-Tracker apps meet the priorities of the communities using them, and that Indigenous people retain control of the knowledge that is recorded.

As explored in chapter 11, enormous amounts of data have been collected about Indigenous peoples and the environments, cultures, knowledges and resources they are connected to. This has often taken place without the consent of Indigenous peoples and used in ways outside of their control. Indigenous data sovereignty is the right of Indigenous people to determine what data is collected, how it is used and who owns it. Issues of data sovereignty arise when new technologies – such as drones, or devices like Google Glass – collect data on Indigenous lands or about Indigenous peoples.

Groups have started forming to advocate for these rights, including the Maiam nayri Wingara Indigenous Data Sovereignty Collective, established in 2017. They believe that when data is collected about Indigenous people, it should be done so according to the laws of the nation from which it is collected.[11] In New Zealand, data about Māori is considered to be *taonga*, meaning a cultural treasure. To protect this, the Māori Data Sovereignty Network, or Te Mana Raraunga, formed in 2015.[12]

Repatriation via digital technology

A good thing about digitisation and technology is that it allows for cultural materials and the archives to be more widely accessed, including on country. This allows Indigenous people to integrate living culture with the written records. You can see this with Mukurtu CMS, an online platform that stemmed from a project in 2007 involving researchers Kim Christen and Craig Dietrich, and the Warumungu community in the centre of the Northern Territory. The project created an online community archive that held stories, knowledge and cultural materials. It also allowed the community to use cultural data identifiers based on their own protocols to look after their cultural heritage on their own terms. (See also chapter 2, page 46.)

Mukurtu CMS is now a free, mobile and open-source platform that allows communities to store, manage and share their cultural heritage

THE KEEPING PLACE PROJECT

For more than 40 years, resource companies including BHP, Rio Tinto and Fortescue Metals Group have conducted significant surveys of the Pilbara region in north Western Australia. Recent developments include Rio Tinto blowing up the sacred site Juukan Gorge in Western Australia,[13] and mining companies are facing demands to stop interfering with Indigenous heritage.

To comply with heritage laws for the protection of Indigenous sites of significance, resource companies must undertake cultural heritage surveys of country prior to receiving government approval to undertake mining works. They engage anthropologists or archaeologists to carry out the surveys, and Aboriginal knowledge holders often share their cultural knowledge and information about the land with these researchers. This has resulted in a vast and valuable collection of cultural heritage information and data appearing in these heritage survey reports.

The Keeping Place Project was a collaborative repatriation project between traditional owner groups and resource companies in the Pilbara, and the Indigenous Land and Sea Corporation and the National Trust. The project has seen the development of a bespoke online platform to house heritage survey reports and records, and protect and manage cultural knowledge and cultural heritage. The Keeping Place is a secure, customisable online platform that enables traditional owners to regain data sovereignty, apply cultural protocols to knowledge and information, manage native title, map country, improve governance and contract management, and unlock social and economic opportunities for current and future generations.

Over a number of years, involving much consultation with the Indigenous Land and Sea Corporation and the local Yinhawangka and Nyiyaparli peoples, we helped the project develop the governance framework, best practice guidelines and associated contracts for The Keeping Place platform and the resulting legal entity.[14]

with community members and the wider public. While Creative Commons licences can be applied to third-party use of the material on a community's page, the community can also apply the Local Context Traditional Knowledge (TK) labelling system to ensure appropriate cultural protocols are also applied to the material. For example, TK labels that can be applied include TK Commercial, TK Non-Commercial, TK Men Restricted, TK Men General, TK Women Restricted and so on. (See chapter 14 for more about Mukurtu.)

In another project, Stephanie von Gavel from the CSIRO worked on the Indigenous digital parameters for the Atlas of Living Australia (ALA) project. The ALA is a collaborative national research infrastructure that brings together biodiversity data from multiple sources and makes it freely available online. The ALA, CSIRO and the Olkola peoples of the Cape York Peninsula undertook a two-way knowledge-sharing pilot phase, working on country and exploring how information management might build a bridge between Indigenous knowledge and Western science. Terri Janke and Company worked on the project to develop best practice protocols, agreements and cultural data identifiers, travelling to Cooktown to consult and collaborate with the Olkola people.

Indigenising new technologies

'Indigenous people have been developing tech from the very beginning of time,' says Angie Abdilla, a Palawa woman based on Gadigal land in Sydney.[15] Angie mentions the boomerang, the fish traps in Brewarrina, spinifex for thermoplastic resin, and sky mapping – the reading of not just the stars but space itself.[16] In 2016, Angie founded the cultural and technology consultancy business Old Ways, New. She has been a great advocate for integrating ICIP protocols within design and technology. She has spoken on tech panels across the globe and has worked with government and developers to promote the ethical integration of Indigenous concepts into creative and technical projects.

I visited Angie in her Redfern office, which she shared with a group of architects and designers. Over a cup of herbal tea, Angie explained how her technologies based on Indigenous knowledge systems can bring about solutions to problems, and creative outputs that generate new thinking. Often, technology is developed from human-centred or user-centred design; instead, Angie's approach is country-centred design. Angie explains, 'Country-centred design is a process that ensures that we're looking at the whole entire system.'[17] By country, Angie is referring to the wider concept of country by Indigenous people – a wholistic and interconnected world view of the land, water, people, plants and animals. An Indigenous perspective is different from one where humans are the centre of the world. Country is the centre, and we are in relationships with all things connected to it. This act of caring for country is about sustainability. It anchors Indigenous people. There are protocols to ensure that no resource is extracted without considering the impact, how it is used and how it relates to other things.[18]

This relationship and connection with country needs to be embedded into tech design. These principles should come through in all tech moving forward, including the quickly emerging area of AI, which is often the subject of ethical debates. Angie has been part of an international collective that has developed Indigenous AI protocols (mentioned above). Imagine if machine learning algorithms were informed by Indigenous knowledge and could use ICIP protocols within their decision making, to positively impact our futures?

There are some significant initiatives focusing on the positive impact that Indigenous perspectives can bring to the tech industry, including the Indigenous Digital Excellence (IDX) Initiative, co-founded by the National Centre of Indigenous Excellence (NCIE) and the Telstra Foundation. IDX is a platform for Indigenous people to connect and lead the way in digital technology: 'We are excited by what can happen when the ideas, perspectives and talent of Aboriginal and Torres Strait Islander peoples are channelled towards making and embracing new technology; from robotics and 3D printing; to using drones to capture imagery of country, coding and developing apps to preserve language and culture for future generations.'[19]

Another initiative is Indigitek, a community of Indigenous people in tech and a not-for-profit organisation founded in 2015 that aims to increase technology pathways for Indigenous people. Co-founder Liam Ridgeway, Gumbaynggirr and Wakka Wakka man, says that his dream is for Aboriginal and Torres Strait Islander people to be influencers, innovators and inventors of technology that reaches across the globe. His mission in life is to explore how his culture can be used to intersect and positively impact digital technologies in productive and sustainable ways, ultimately building the Indigenous digital economy and self-determination for his community.[20] Liam is also the co-founder of Ngakkan Nyaagu, a digital services agency.

Developing the digital and technology skills of young Indigenous people is also crucial. Mikaela Jade founded Indigital Schools, Australia's first Indigenous digital skills training program. The program teaches kids how to bring Indigenous knowledge and culture to life through augmented reality, Minecraft and Python coding, and working with Microsoft and Telstra Purple.[21]

Indigenous digital futures

Digital technology is a means of transferring knowledge and culture, and, in the future, its importance will continue to grow. My two children both chose careers as software engineers. They are at the forefront of technology, and even though I wished they might have become lawyers, I am proud they chose their own paths.

When I became an IP lawyer in the 1990s, I wanted to help Aboriginal and Torres Strait Islander people manage and control their arts and knowledge. This was for cultural practice reasons, but it was also an opportunity to build strong and economic foundations. In the future, so much of Indigenous arts and knowledge production and transmission will involve technogy and digital methods. In fact, we are already there. Databases, AI, VR, and collection management of films and sound recordings and data – all of these pose interesting issues for managing culture today. The generations of Indigenous people to come will draw virtual rock art walls, and they will travel digital songlines. As they do so, they will know they are linked within a long line of Indigenous innovative tradition.

WHAT YOU CAN DO ...

- Consider the context of using ICIP in a digital form. Does it shift the meaning of the cultural knowledge? If the knowledge is sacred or personal, think whether you should do it.
- Involve Indigenous communities in tech projects at the very early stages of concept design. Think about whether this project works for them and their needs.
- Give opportunities for Indigenous people to build their skills in tech, and support Indigenous software and computer engineers.
- Host forums that discuss the importance of Indigenous people keeping up with tech, but also highlighting the dangers, and develop plans to alleviate the problems.
- Discuss copyright and add ICIP clauses to development agreements. Discuss ownership in derivative works (works based on one or more pre-existing works), if allowable. Build a new system of contracts that include ICIP.
- Link with the Indigenous tech initiatives such as Indigenous Digital Excellence (IDX), Indigital, Indigitek and others.
- Think short-term benefits and long-term impact – does your project connect with Indigenous people, and how will it impact the future generations who want to connect with culture and the results of your project? How will it help them keep practising their culture?
- Consider storage and management for the long term and plan for changes of technology over time.

Resources

Telstra Foundation (ed), *Making the Connection: Essays on Indigenous Digital Excellence*, Vivid Publishing, Fremantle, 2014

Josh Harle, Angie Abdilla and Andrew Newman (eds), *Decolonising the Digital: Technology as Cultural Practice*, Tactical Space Lab, Sydney, 2018

Tahu Kukatai and John Taylor (eds), *Indigenous Data Sovereignty: Toward an Agenda*, CAEPR Research Monograph No. 38, ANU Press, Canberra, 2016

Indigenous Digital Excellence (IDX): https://ncie.org.au/idx/

Roadmap for Building Indigenous Digital Excellence: Looking to 2030 (IDX, 2018): https://ncie.org.au/wp-content/uploads/2018/02/Roadmap-for-Building-indigenous-Digital-Excellence-Looking-to-2030-Web.pdf

Indigital: https://indigital.net.au

Indigitek: www.indigitek.org.au

Mukurtu CMS: https://mukurtu.org

Atlas of Living Australia (ALA): www.ala.org.au

IndigenousX: https://indigenousx.com.au

Notes

1. Mikaela Jade, in *Meeting – Paramodic,* Alexander Hayes, YouTube, 12 June 2014, <www.youtube.com/watch?v=oCVDu8EBC0c>.
2. Mikaela Jade, *Meeting – Paramodic*.
3. Mikaela Jade, *Linear Artists: Mikeala Jade*, Museum of Applied Arts and Sciences, 15 November 2019, <https://maas.museum/linear-artists-mikaela-jade/>.
4. Mikaela Jade, *Linear Artists: Mikeala Jade*.
5. Margo Neale, personal communication, 18 January 2021.
6. Margo Neale (ed), *Songlines: Tracking the Seven Sisters*, National Museum of Australia Press, Canberra, 2017, p. 18.
7. World Intellectual Property Organization, *WIPO Conversation on Intellectual Property (IP) and Artificial Intelligence (AI): Summary of Conversation*, WIPO, Geneva, 27 September 2019, <https://www.wipo.int/edocs/mdocs/mdocs/en/wipo_ip_ai_ge_19/wipo_ip_ai_ge_19_inf_4.pdf>.
8. Levi McKenzie-Kirkbright, email correspondence, 28 January 2021.
9. Jason Edward Lewis (ed), *Indigenous Protocol and Artificial Intelligence Position Paper*, Initiative for Indigenous Futures/Canadian Institute for Advanced Research (CIFAR), Honolulu, 2020, <https://spectrum.library.concordia.ca/986506/>.
10. North Australian Indigenous Land and Sea Management Alliance (NAILSMA), 'Looking after country: The NAILSMA I-Tracker story', *CyberTracker*, 2014, <www.cybertracker.org/downloads/tracking/NAILSMA-2015-I-Tracker-Book.pdf>.
11. Maiam nayri Wingara, *History of Indigenous Data Sovereignty*, Maiam nayri Wingara, n.d., <www.maiamnayriwingara.org/projects-1>.
12. Te Mana Raraunga, *Our Charter: Tūtohinga*, Te Mana Raraunga, n.d., <www.temanararaunga.maori.nz/tutohinga/>.
13. See, for example, Calla Wallquist, 'Rio Tinto blasts 46,000-year-old Aboriginal site to expand iron ore mine', *The Guardian*, 26 May 2020, <www.theguardian.com/australia-news/2020/may/26/rio-tinto-blasts-46000-year-old-aboriginal-site-to-expand-iron-ore-mine>.

14 The Keeping Place, <https://thekeepingplace.com>.
15 Angie Abdilla, in Ann Deslandes, 'Indigenous design for the new world', *Matters*, 28 February 2018, <https://mattersjournal.com/stories/indigenousdesign>.
16 Angie Abdilla, in Ann Deslandes, 'Indigenous design for the new world'
17 Angie Abdilla, in *Technoethics – Shaping Our Future Through Ethical Tech Design, D61+ LIVE 2019*, CSIRO's Data61, YouTube, 28 May 2020, <https://algorithm.data61.csiro.au/indigenous-techno-ethics-shaping-the-future-through-ethical-tech-design/>.
18 ABC Radio National, 'Machines as kin or the new colonisers? Indigenous tech revolutionaries rethinking AI', Science Friction, 15 November 2020, <www.abc.net.au/radionational/programs/sciencefriction/12880998>.
19 National Centre of Indigenous Excellence (NCIE), *IDX*, NCIE, 2021, <https://ncie.org.au/idx/>.
20 Liam Ridgeway, email correspondence, 2 February 2021.
21 Indigital Schools, <https://indigitalschools.com>.

14
CREATING HARMONY IN GALLERIES, LIBRARIES, ARCHIVES AND MUSEUMS (GLAM)

When I was in London in 2012, I visited the British Museum in the hope of seeing the AC Haddon collection. Alfred Cort Haddon was a British anthropologist who went on an expedition to the Torres Strait Islands in the late 1890s, recording ceremony and song and collecting over 2000 cultural objects.[1] I had seen some of the film footage before and heard that it was the first ever recorded in Australia. These materials went back to England; some are still held by the Museum of Archaeology and Anthropology at Cambridge University, and some by the British Museum.

I remember the day clearly. There was a blue summer sky and the streets were packed with tourists and locals. We were on a family trip around Europe and my children were losing patience with me as I dragged them into all the museums and galleries.

In the British Museum, we walked up the big staircase wrapped around the middle of the foyer and looked at the artefacts from all over the world. Tamina and Jaiki were shocked to see the Egyptian mummies; we quickly turned away out of respect for the deceased and their spirit. I was eager to see the ceremonial masks from Mer (Murray Island), our own cultural heritage, thinking this would spark the kids' interest. We kept wandering through the passages and exhibits but it was not to be: the fire alarm rang, and everyone had to evacuate. I later found out that the masks from Mer that I was so excited to see were rarely on display. If you wanted to see them you had to make an official request for authorised purposes. We had come so close. Maybe they were stored in dark vaults somewhere underneath our feet.

A few years later, we finally saw some of the ancestral masks when they returned to Australia for the *Encounters* exhibition at the National Museum of Australia (NMA) in Canberra in 2015–16. *Encounters* featured Indigenous objects from the British Museum that had been taken or gifted during the first encounters. These objects were shown in relation to their cultural stories and presented alongside new works from the Indigenous communities in the show. The NMA included Indigenous voices and perspectives, engaging with Indigenous people and undertaking extensive consultation to enable the appropriate representation of the objects.

There were lots of people at the opening, walking through the fish trap–style tunnel that ran through the exhibition and cast crisscrossed shadows on the ground. I finally reached the Pop-le-op or turtle-shell mask. It had been collected from Mer around 1855. Made from turtle shell that looked like dark, smooth slate, the mask was regal, and it shone. It was carved with fine lines and intricate patterns that marked out the facial features. The eyes had dark pupils and the nose was long and pointed. Its expression gave nothing away. If you wore this mask you might feel 100 different emotions but from the outside appear unperplexed.

Seeing the turtle-shell mask was a special moment, stirring up strong feelings deep within me. I knew my grandmother Agnes was from Mer, but I had never been there. And then there was the fact that here it was, back in Australia again after so many years – behind glass, but still here. Around 300 more cultural objects were on show – baskets, spearheads, tools, jewellery and artworks – 151 of these from the British Museum's Indigenous Australian collection, which has around 6000 works in total.[2]

The centrepiece of the *Encounters* exhibition was the Gweagal Shield. Made of thick bark, it was oval and slightly pointed, the wood dark and aged with a small hole in the centre. The shield was suspended in a glass box beside two spears also belonging to the Aboriginal men who had confronted Captain Cook when he had first come ashore from the *Endeavour* at Botany Bay in 1770. They were shown beside a projection of the coastal site, Gweagal and Bidjigal country, where they were taken from.

Rodney Kelly is a descendant of the Gweagal warrior Cooman who was shot during that first contact in 1770. He has been calling for these artefacts to be repatriated or returned to their homeland. 'We are the living bloodline descendants of the Gweagal clan of the Dharawal tribe and are the rightful owners of our ancestral cultural artefacts,' Rodney said, 'The shield should return to where it was taken from, to show the truth, the history of this land.'[3] The shield went back to England after the exhibition. In May 2021, the British Museum announced it would repatriate three spears, but the call for the shield continues.

Memories and ancestral ties are connected to these cultural objects. Taken from their homelands by colonial powers, now they are held in galleries, libraries, archives and museums (GLAM) all over the world. Meanwhile, back in the countries of origin, children are growing up disconnected, and people are looking for their stolen pasts, eager to rebuild strong identities. A lot of what makes up Indigenous collections in these institutions was acquired during early colonisation, during a time when we had no voice and were viewed in a similar way to plants and animals. Generations of Indigenous peoples and those who have been touched by the brush of colonialism advocate for the return of this heritage, including art, ceremonial objects, human remains, natural history specimens, and intangible cultural heritage like sound recordings, films and photographs. Under customary laws, some materials are considered secret and sacred, connected with spirit, knowledge and beliefs, containing information that may only be made available to the initiated, or may only be seen by men or women or particular people in the community. Caring for these materials is particularly important.

Why should this important cultural heritage stay in European vaults and only be taken out for researchers to admire and write their PhDs about? Can they be back on country, to rest in their homelands? What power might that bring? The issue of repatriation should not be ignored and more should be done to facilitate returns back into communities, and to support communities to develop keeping places for everyone to learn from these objects and reignite cultural connections. Indigenous people call for the right to access their own heritage and maintain it for future generations. This is a difficult conversation, but we need to engage in difficult conversations.

Who owns Indigenous collections?

To Indigenous custodians, Indigenous collections and archives are not merely records belonging to the past. The books, artefacts, field notes, recordings, photographs and films are viewed as living culture, deeply connected to ancestors, the present and the future. They are links to culture and knowledge to be closely treasured. It makes sense that Indigenous people should be empowered to make decisions about the use, interpretation and ownership of these materials.

The complication with Indigenous collections is that the materials are often owned by the non-Indigenous researchers, ethnographers, filmmakers and photographers. As we have seen in earlier chapters, under Australian copyright law, the notebooks, photographs and film reels of ceremonial footage belong to the person who created them. As for the cultural objects we see in museum collections, these are often owned outright by the institution.

Luckily, there are many hard-working people who are championing Indigenous leadership in the GLAM sector.

The AIATSIS Collection

The Australian Institute of Aboriginal and Torres Strait Islander Studies (AIATSIS) was formed in 1964 and today it holds the world's biggest collection dedicated to Aboriginal and Torres Strait Islander cultures and histories.[4] Many of the materials were collected as a result of research, field work and film production, including approximately 40,000 hours of audio, 700,000 photographs, 6.8 million feet of film and 12,800 manuscripts, most of which are unpublished. AIATSIS's challenge is to manage access and use the materials in accordance with its obligation to not disclose information that 'would be inconsistent with the views or sensitivities of relevant Aboriginal persons or Torres Strait Islanders'. Under its establishing law – the *Australian Institute of Aboriginal Studies Act 1964*, now the *Australian Institute of Aboriginal and Torres Strait Islander Studies Act 1989* (Cth) – AIATSIS has the power to restrict access to sensitive, sacred or secret content held in the archives.[5] People wishing to access or use unpublished sensitive materials owned or controlled by AIATSIS, including orphan works (copyright works with unknown authors), must first obtain permission from the relevant Aboriginal or Torres Strait Islander community, or the relevant individual in the case of personal material.

AIATSIS's functions and obligations include the development, preservation and provision of a national collection of Aboriginal and Torres Strait Islander culture and heritage; the use of that national collection to strengthen and promote knowledge and understanding of Aboriginal and Torres Strait Islander culture and heritage; and to provide leadership in the fields of Aboriginal and Torres Strait Islander research, among other things. It is governed by the nine members of its Council, and today they are predominantly Indigenous Australian people.

Kirsten Thorpe and the Indigenous Archives Collective

Kirsten Thorpe is a Worimi woman and archivist who has done a lot of work leading the development of policies for Indigenous collections. In 2011, she established the Indigenous Archives Collective with Dr Shannon Faulkhead. This was a move to protect Indigenous cultural knowledge and champion Indigenous cultural heritage rights.[6] 'Indigenous people are very disenfranchised from collections. Archives must change from their colonial background of dispossession,' says Kirsten. 'Indigenous people have the right to know, the right of reply to the offensive records, and the ICIP rights to collected material. We must develop ways for libraries and archives to engage and involve Indigenous people.'[7]

Prior to her role as senior researcher, Jumbunna Research at UTS, Kirsten also worked with the State Library of NSW to develop library and archive systems. The Rediscovering Indigenous Languages project identified important Indigenous language material held in the Library's collection but, Kirsten observes, 'underlying the project there was no consideration of ICIP or ongoing rights for communities'. The project tried to 'give the voice of community' to sit alongside experimentation, but because many of the original materials had been collected without any attribution of the knowledge holders who had provided them, the records were flawed and possibly misrepresented those communities. Timing was also a problem, Kirsten reflects; there was a rush to get things online and full consultations were not carried out.[8] Recognising the complexity of these broken systems, we have to engage in a new framework. 'These new frameworks require us to embed protocols and principles of respect, reciprocity and mutual benefit. They require time to plan and adequately resource community engagement and involvement. These are considerations that are key to government libraries and archives establishing relationships with communities that incorporate and embed respect for ICIP rights,' says Kirsten.[9]

Collaborative collections

In 2013, my firm worked with the National Film and Sound Archive (NFSA) and the Australian National University (ANU) on a unique project called Deepening Histories of Place.[10] It was a digital history collaboration that explored histories of people and land related to three incredible areas in Australia – the Blue Mountains, Central Australia and Kakadu in the Northern Territory. Because the project involved collecting Indigenous people's stories and experiences, and filming on Indigenous lands and national parks, there was a need for protocols to handle the collection and use of this material. As well as protocols, we developed clearance forms to support the research relationships for the project, taking copyright and ICIP into account.

In 2007, Warumungu community members in the Northern Territory collaborated with researchers to produce the Mukurtu Wumpurrarni-kari Archive, a place where Warumungu people can share stories, knowledge, and cultural materials properly using their own protocols (see chapters 2 and 13). This grew into Mukurtu CMS, an open-source platform flexible enough to meet the needs of diverse communities who want to manage and share their digital cultural heritage in their own way, on their own terms.[11]

The State Library of NSW, in partnership with the Centre for Digital Scholarship and Curation at Washington State University and the Jumbunna Institute of Indigenous Education and Research at the University of Technology Sydney, has since launched the first Australian Mukurtu Hub, which builds capacity for communities to build their own keeping places. The State Library was introduced to the Mukurtu CMS as a way to disseminate Indigenous materials and digitally repatriate content back to communities. It is a platform that controls access based on protocols, and is specifically designed for use by Indigenous peoples, and will enable Indigenous communities to respond to items in the Library's Indigenous collection and apply their own cultural protocols for such items. Digital access to collections means that Indigenous people can get to know what is in the collection, and this in turn can be used to help with the revitalisation and protection of Indigenous languages.

Protocols in GLAM institutions

One way in which we perceive ourselves as individuals and nations is through our arts and cultural institutions. We hope to see our values and our dreams reflected in these spaces. In the past, as we have discussed throughout this book, it has been embarrassing and painful for Indigenous people to see how their cultural heritage has been referred to and dealt with, how their ancestral objects and ancestral body remains have been stolen and put in display cases without any names or provenance.

Marcus Hughes is the former Head of Indigenous Engagement and Strategy at the Museum of Applied Arts and Sciences (MAAS) in Sydney. With Marcus's help, Anika Valenti and Terri Janke and Company worked with MAAS to develop their ICIP protocol. 'For MAAS, the implementation of ICIP protocols represents a progressive step towards further respecting and protecting the rights of Indigenous Australians and their culture and heritage,' Marcus says. 'These processes and frameworks ensure that we are able to provide leadership within the sector by establishing initiatives with cultural integrity, authenticity and authority as we work towards building a post-reconciliation institution.'[12]

We also worked with the National Museum of Australia (NMA) in Canberra, which holds a lot of material from Aboriginal and Torres Strait Islander and other Pacific nations, including historical records, artworks, artefacts, images, film and sound recordings. We embedded the ten True Tracks principles in the museum's Indigenous engagement and ICIP policy. The museum also added an 11th principle of 'committing to a timely, transparent and respectful process for responding to feedback'.

Although this policy wasn't specifically developed for the *Encounters* exhibition (discussed above), it coincided with planning and programming across the NMA in the lead-up to the exhibition. With the involvement and experience of the museum's Indigenous Reference Group and all museum staff who contributed to *Encounters*, we saw how these principles could be applied in practical and meaningful ways.

I was thrilled to join the Council of the National Gallery of Australia in 2019. By the shores of Lake Burley Griffin in Canberra, the National Gallery holds the largest collection of Aboriginal and Torres Strait Islander art in the world, including a historically significant installation of 200 ceremonial hollow log coffins from Central Arnhem Land known as *The Aboriginal Memorial*.[13] Over its history, the National Gallery has put together trailblazing Indigenous exhibitions. As I write this, the exhibition *Defying Empire*, a showcase of artists speaking out against colonisation, has just finished its four-year national tour, and the national exhibition *Ceremony* and international *Ever Present* exhibition are soon to open.

The National Gallery has a Aboriginal and Torres Strait Islander Cultural Rights and Engagement Policy that recognises ICIP rights and protocols.[14] The Aboriginal and Torres Strait Islander Art team (Franchesca Cubillo, Tina Baum, Kelli Cole and Aidan Hartshorn),[15] in conjunction with Canberra-based Kaurna artist James Tylor, developed better documentation practices for Indigenous artists and works, which exemplifies a respectful and more culturally appropriate approach to

ICIP. When the NAIDOC 2017 theme was 'Our Languages Matter', the National Gallery started using traditional languages for locations, titles and mediums in exhibition labels, the collection database, and online and published content. Western-assigned terms like 'Unknown Artist' were renamed to more appropriate terminologies like 'Ancestor'. The first exhibition to incorporate these changes was the *Belonging* exhibition in 2019 on Indigenous and colonial experiences in Australia.[16] I really like this new system, which the National Gallery describes as a commitment to redress the imbalance of the Indigenous voice and representation at a national level.

On a recent visit to the gallery, I met Bruce Johnson McLean of the Wierdi and Birri Gubba peoples, who was hired as the Assistant Director of Indigenous Engagement in 2019. Bruce sees his role as being a conduit between the gallery and Indigenous communities. 'First Nations artists and communities are the heartbeat of the National Gallery's collection and programs,' Bruce says. 'Ensuring we build ongoing, less transactional, and more collaborative relationships with community is crucial to ensuring that our world-leading collection is displayed with authority and authenticity, and to ensuring that our artists and communities are *truly* seen and heard. Embedding First Nations voices and presences across all of our business is the only way forward.'[17] I think that's a pretty great way to be moving forward.

What about archives? Karen Manton, project officer at the CALL Collection of the Batchelor Institute of Indigenous Tertiary Education, says: 'We want to demystify [the] archive world going into the future, and have Indigenous people digitising their own materials, and managing materials ... The past and the future is present in collections and with people ... Really, the collection is about people and language, culture, country, and in particular identity and relationships.'[18] This is why protocols are so important.

ICIP protocols are also useful for libraries. The Aboriginal and Torres Strait Islander Library and Information Resource Network (ATSILIRN) is an association for professionals who work in Indigenous library, archive and information services. They created the ATSILIRN Protocols in 1995 because there were growing concerns about Indigenous exclusion from libraries, the offensive nature of materials about Indigenous people in archives, inappropriate and demeaning subject headings for Indigenous peoples and cultures, and access and service issues for Indigenous peoples and materials.[19] The protocols are intended to guide libraries, archives and information services to appropriately interact with Aboriginal and Torres Strait Islander people and their cultural materials.[20] The University of Sydney have also published some really great Aboriginal and Torres Strait Islander Cultural Protocols for their libraries in 2021.[21]

Repatriation: Returning cultural materials to country and community

In 2004, Gary Murray – Dja Dja Wurrung Ngurungaeta (elder) and Yung Balug clansman – along with others, reclaimed two Dja Dja Wurrung etched barks while they were on loan to Museum Victoria in Naarm (Melbourne). He claimed his right to do so on behalf of the Yung Balug clan of the Dja Dja Wurrung first nation using the federal *Aboriginal and Torres Strait Islander Heritage Protection Act 1984* (Cth). Court cases ensued, with Museum Victoria taking action so that the barks were eventually returned to the British Museum.[22] Shortly after, the Australian Government reviewed its cultural heritage laws and later passed the *Protection of Cultural Objects on Loan Act 2013*. If an object is normally in a foreign country but imported into Australia on loan for a temporary public exhibition under arrangements made by the museums and the minister, the Act limits the circumstances in which lenders, exhibition facilitators and exhibiting institutions can lose ownership or control of the object. Yung Balug are continuing negotiations in 2021 with the British Museum to return the sacred objects. A multipurpose Cultural Education Facility and Planetarium is also being scoped, along with a restructure of how Yung Balug do business on country with repatriations, treaty, native title and economic development.[23]

Aboriginal and Torres Strait Islander people dealing with the aftermath of colonisation know that the repatriation of their cultural materials from institutions around Australia and internationally can strengthen and revitalise culture. The connection we have with our cultural materials is complex. There are layers of emotion – pain, anger, grief, joy and hope. This is a story we share with other communities across the world, those communities whose national treasures have become collectables in the big museums of the so-called developed world. The Elgin Marbles, stripped from the Parthenon and their homeland by the British, raise the same sentiment for the Greeks. These objects hold ancestral power and a crucial link to a past that we wish to know more about. It hurts to feel that our treasures are owned and controlled, held in boxes far away in a land whose people enslaved us.

I am reminded of the final scene in the film *Raiders of the Lost Ark* where the men are sitting around a table discussing the enigmatic location of the ark. There is a sense of scepticism around the supposed safekeeping of the ark, a sense that it is hidden and that the whole truth is not being told – similar to the way museums hold onto Indigenous cultural materials. Or I think of the scene in the *Black Panther* film where the antagonist, Erik Killmonger from the fictional country Wakanda, prepares to steal back a looted artefact from the fictional 'Museum of Great Britain' in London. A museum official approaches him and attempts to tell the story of the original piece before Killmonger contradicts her by explaining the original purpose of the object. He offers to buy the work, but the museum official says it is not for sale. Killmonger then says, 'How do you think your ancestors got these? Do you think they paid a fair price? Or did they take it, like they took everything else?' The scene highlights a crucial issue for cultural objects: who gets to tell the story? How does it feel when an outsider is controlling this story?

Aboriginal and Torres Strait Islander collections are important to all Australians, but the living heritage and cultural wealth they hold is particularly significant for Indigenous peoples. Dr John Carty, head of humanities at the South Australian Museum, is passionate about reuniting communities with their cultural heritage materials. He says, 'Museums and galleries need to show courage and hand over control to Aboriginal storytellers and artists.'[24] The collections are meaningless without

Indigenous people engaging with them, with their voices and ownerships and family meanings and stories. It is time for people to consider the impact and time for Indigenous people to view the items alone, to honour and reflect.

There is no doubt that Indigenous collections also hold commercial value to researchers, filmmakers, artists and writers, and even commercial manufacturers of cosmetics and drugs. Tapping into and adding to traditional knowledge can be lucrative. GLAM institutions have a great role to play in safeguarding Indigenous cultural material. They also serve a role in appropriately making material and information available according to cultural or ICIP protocols. In this respect, their role becomes one of striking a balance. Above all, Indigenous custodians must be involved in the management and safeguarding of the Indigenous cultural record.

Ancestral remains

In the late 1960s, archaeologists came across the 40,000-year-old remains of a young woman whose body had been ceremonially prepared and cremated and deposited at Lake Mungo in south-west New South Wales. Mungo Lady was taken to the ANU for research and then held by the National Museum of Australia. After calls by Aboriginal people, she was returned to Lake Mungo – the traditional lands of the Mutti Mutti, Ngiyampaa and the Paakantyi people – and now rests in a decorated safe on the site. Both the Aboriginal and archaeological community have access to the safe.[25]

Sourced from graveyards, battlefields, massacre sites, and hospital morgues,[26] countless ancestral remains have been collected for their curiosity value and for scientific study, including comparative anatomy studies.

Under Indigenous belief systems, ancestors will not enjoy spiritual rest until they return to country and are given the last rites in accordance with traditional beliefs. The land also longs for the return of the ancestor. This is why Indigenous people feel a deep responsibility for the repatriation of their ancestors. Many people are distressed that they were stolen in the first place and now stored in other countries off their ancestral lands and without a connection to the descendants. It is also problematic when these are researched and displayed without consultation and consent.

Indigenous Australians are also concerned that national and international museums, universities and other collecting institutions fail to disclose information on the origin and identity of remains to the relevant communities. Instead, it is left to Indigenous people to investigate, locate and negotiate repatriation of their ancestors' remains. Their efforts in identifying ancestral remains are hampered because many collections were assembled without documenting names or information on the clan group or region.

Since the 1970s, communities have lobbied the government and museums for the return of ancestral remains. The Foundation for Aboriginal and Islander Research Action (FAIRA) was a significant organisation that played a role in this. These efforts have resulted in the repatriation of Aboriginal ancestors back to their country, such as the Kow Swamp fossils in 1990 and Mungo Lady in 1992.[27] The return of Mungo Man in 2018 highlights how coordination of museums, Indigenous people and government policy makers can achieve a respectful outcome.

What about ancestral remains returned from overseas but that have no clear provenance? This is an issue that comes up in the Australian Government's Indigenous Repatriation Program. To address this, the government's Advisory Committee for Indigenous Repatriation has called for a National Resting Place. This would be a place for the ancestors where spiritual connections can be made and contemplation can be undertaken, burial rites and associated ceremonies can be conducted, and a public space where reflection and prominence for the issue can be shared with all Australians. The committee have recommended that the National Resting Place be Indigenous controlled and run by Aboriginal and Torres Strait Islander peoples.[28] The development of such a place should be done in close consultation with community, and there should also be protocols for research and DNA testing, which should only be done with the free, prior and informed consent of Indigenous peoples. The approach of dynamic consent should be followed, such as that adopted by the ANU National Centre of Indigenous Genomics.[29] (See chapter 11, page 268.)

Truth-telling: Indigenous-led exhibitions

More and more, Indigenous cultures and voices are being placed at the centre of museums and galleries. National and state museums are supporting Indigenous artists and communities to design and lead unique projects and exhibitions. A standout is Tarnanthi, the Indigenous–led art festival in Adelaide that empowers artists and communities to take on new and exciting projects. Nici Cumpston, who is of Afghan, English, Irish and Barkindji Aboriginal heritage, is the artistic director. 'Tarnanthi is committed to delivering artist-led projects that empower artists and communities wanting to create new works and share cultural knowledge,' Nici says. 'We listen carefully to our artists so that their ambition and talent can shine on a national platform.'[30]

The 22nd Biennale of Sydney in 2020 was led by Brook Andrew, a Wiradjuri man and highly esteemed contemporary artist. The Biennale's title was *NIRIN*, a Wiradjuri word for 'edge'. Brook is the first Australian Indigenous person to be the Biennale's artistic director. 'It is important that communities have first say in the legacy, depiction and presentation of cultural materials,' Brook says. 'By working directly with communities, artists and creatives have the power to resolve, heal, dismember and imagine futures of transformation for re-setting the world. Sovereignty is at the centre of these actions. The community has control of how material, culture and histories are exhibited.'[31]

Wiradjuri man and librarian Nathan Sentance works at the Australian Museum in Sydney and is passionate about 'decolonising' the GLAM sector. On his blog *Archival Decolonist*, he shares his thoughts about what this means. Exhibitions and programs, Nathan says, 'should minimise white voices in regard to First Nations culture whenever possible', as this 'can centre a non-Indigenous person in a discussion of First Nations issues and take up space that a First Nations voice could fill'.[32]

When included in public spaces, Indigenous art and stories enrich our understanding of Australian history and what it means to be Australian. Melbourne-based Kamilaroi artist Reko Rennie created *Remember Me*, a monumental text and light installation outside Carriageworks in Redfern that glows red and speaks to the Indigenous history of the land. A similar effect comes with *Badu Gili*, the incredible light and sound installation on the sails of the Sydney Opera House that makes a lasting impression on tourists and locals. Curated by Rhoda Roberts, the Opera House's head of First Nations programming, it features the work of Indigenous artists from across Australia in an impressive seven-minute light and sound display.

Dr Gaye Sculthorpe is a Palawa woman, a descendant of the famous Fanny Smith (1834–1905), whose singing in a Tasmanian Aboriginal language was first recorded onto wax cylinder in 1899 – one of the earliest recorded traditional songs in Australia. Gaye is a highly experienced museum curator, having headed the Department of Indigenous Cultures at Museums Victoria for many years before moving on to the British Museum in London as the Curator and Head of the Oceania section within the Department of Africa, Oceania and the Americas. Recalling hearing Fanny Smith's songs playing when visiting the Tasmanian Museum and Art Gallery in Hobart during her childhood, she said, 'It's both an informative and formative experience, to visit a museum and view materials from your own culture and from cultures from across the world, especially when you are young.'[33]

When discussing the AMaGA Roadmap project (see page 323) with me, she said, 'It's so important for museums and galleries to involve Indigenous communities in the research, management and interpretation of their cultural materials in collections. While this is largely accepted as a principle in cultural institutions today, it does not automatically follow that sufficient resources are dedicated to do this core work, often relying on one-off special project funding such as when new buildings and exhibitions are constructed.' She also recommended that, 'Beyond their own institutional goals, museums should also be supporting projects and programs initiated by communities that meet the needs and cultural aspirations of those communities.'

An example of a good museum project like this is *kanalaritja: An Unbroken String*, a touring exhibition by the Tasmanian Museum and Art Gallery (TMAG), which was initiated by Pakana (Tasmanian Aboriginal) women elders who were worried that their traditional shell-making tradition would be lost if they didn't pass it on to the new generations. Lola Greeno, a Pakana elder and senior shell stringer who grew up on Cape Barren Island, says, 'With only a small number of women holding the knowledge of shell stringing, we were concerned about the continuation of the practice. It was my dream to enable other Aboriginal women from around Tasmania to learn and revive this important cultural practice within their families.'[34] Lola's shell necklaces are held by museums throughout the country and one was included in this exhibition alongside very old ancestral necklaces and ones made by the new wave of stringers, including young children. The exhibition was curated by Aboriginal curators Zoe Rimmer and Liz Tew, who each come from a long line of Tasmanian Aboriginal women.

THE NATIONAL MUSEUM OF AUSTRALIA AND INDIGENOUS ENGAGEMENT

The National Museum of Australia (NMA) has played an instrumental role in advancing Indigenous engagement in the GLAM sector. Within its establishing legislation, the NMA includes the charter to have an Indigenous Gallery – First Australians, a permanent exhibit inside the museum that occupies over one-third of the gallery spaces. The NMA gallery has had two Indigenous directors: Worimi man Bill Jonas (1996–99) and Tagalaka woman Dawn Casey (1999–2003). In 2016, the NMA developed the Indigenous Engagement and ICIP Protocols, which follow the True Tracks framework. The NMA added an 11th principle on feedback to enable Indigenous people to have a voice.

One of the National Museum of Australia's milestone exhibitions, *Songlines: Tracking the Seven Sisters*, ran for nearly six months from September 2017. *Songlines* was Indigenous led, with a curatorium of the traditional owners of the story from the Martu, Ngaanyatjarra, Pitjantjatjara and Yankunytjatjara people, co-led by senior lawwoman and custodian of the Seven Sisters, Inawinytji Williamson. Lead curator Margo Neale, who has worked at the NMA for 20 years – first as inaugural Director of the Gallery of First Australians and, later, as Senior Indigenous Curator and Adviser to the Director, and Head of the Centre for Indigenous Knowledges – explains how it came about:

> The museum responded to [the Anangu's] urgent plea that 'the Songlines are all broken up and we want you to help put them back together'. It took many years of travelling the songlines on Country across three deserts and listening to what they wanted saved of this knowledge system for both the archive and to gain public support through an exhibition . There was a lot of engagement by many key organisations including the NPY Women's Council, Anangku Arts and some 10 art centres ... [The curatorium was] not an advisory group or a reference group, they too were the curators along with us from the western institutional world. This enabled us to respect each other's knowledge and skills so that we all worked together as knowledge holders – the western expertise along with Aboriginal knowledge. The sharing of their knowledge was controlled by Anangu who wanted to teach all Australians that this was their story too. To share this history and continent we need to know the stories of its creation beyond the last 240 years.[35]

The exhibition was a magical universe, with intricate and bold paintings of country, exquisite hand-carved cultural objects, tjanpi (grass) sculpture and multimedia. The centrepiece was the state-of-the-art digital dome. Acclaimed as the world's first hi-res travelling dome, it visualises the story of the Seven Sisters Tjukurpa (see chapter 13, page 293). For its innovation and power, *Songlines* was awarded best exhibition in Australia at the Museums & Galleries National Awards in 2018. In 2020, it was the temporary opening exhibition for the Western Australian Museum, now called Boola Bardip, before going on tour to the UK, Europe, the USA, Canada and Asia, including the prestigious Humboldt Forum in Berlin, Musée du quai Branly in Paris and The Box in Plymouth, UK, taking the recognition of Australia's rich cultural knowledge onto a global stage.

The hard-hitting stories also need to be told – the dark parts of Australia's history. This has been done well by the Bunjilaka Aboriginal Cultural Centre at Melbourne Museum for the multimedia exhibition *Black Day, Sun Rises, Blood Runs*. The exhibition, narrated by traditional owners, shared significant stories about some of the conflicts and massacres that occurred in Victoria. The project was guided by the Yulendj Group, a reference group of Indigenous community members and elders from across Victoria, who work closely with Bunjilaka and their important permanent exhibition, *First Peoples*.

The Ten-Year Indigenous Roadmap

In 2017, Terri Janke and Company was commissioned by the Australian Museums and Galleries Association (AMaGA) to undertake a significant project on enhancing Indigenous engagement in the museums and galleries sector. AMaGA is the peak body that represents and advocates for museums and art galleries across Australia. They wanted to update their Indigenous engagement policy and create a new ten-year plan – a Roadmap – for the sector. It was clear from the beginning that this was going to require an in-depth approach. We needed to hear what Indigenous artists, curators, elders, museum and gallery professionals, museum and gallery visitors, academics and archivists had to say. Alex Marsden, the National Director of AMaGA at the time, brought great enthusiasm and support to the project, as did Mathew Trinca and the Indigenous Advisory Committee. My colleagues and I travelled around the country to hold workshops to talk about the issues, including some Indigenous-only workshops to create a safe space for discussion.

Community members presented their views to evoke discussion. As we sat around and talked about the issues, creating mindmaps and taking notes, we soon learned that while some of the conversations were happy and hopeful, some were harder to have, bringing up pain and grief. People wanted to reconnect with their cultural and ancestral materials and revive the story and knowledge held in collections. We talked about the need for increased Indigenous employment and leadership in museums and galleries, the care of collections involving cultural heritage materials, and the management of sacred and secret material.

We wanted to make sure that a multitude of Indigenous voices informed the directives of the Roadmap; it needed to align with their needs and aspirations. Alongside the Roadmap, we prepared an extensive research report on all our findings. All of this built on AMaGA's previous policy documents. The Roadmap features five key elements for change: reimagining representation; embedding Indigenous values into museum and gallery business; increasing Indigenous opportunity; two-way caretaking of cultural material; and connecting with Indigenous communities.[36]

The repeated theme was: 'Nothing about us without us.'

Indigenous people want greater access and information to collections, and they want to ensure that their cultural material is respected and safeguarded. Indigenous people want closer engagement with museums and galleries. When we went out and spoke with communities for the Roadmap project, it was still really apparent to me that they didn't know what was in the institutions; they didn't feel confident walking into the institutions, if they ever visited; they felt like they couldn't engage with the cultural objects; and they were worried about how their intellectual property and knowledge was being used. Yet they realised the importance of that content for their continuing cultural practice. And that's important historically because of the treatment of Indigenous people: the dispossession, the eradication of languages, the massacres – all of it. It's even more important for us to be able to connect with the collections held by these cultural institutions, the records, objects and content that connect us to our ancestors.

In our research, we found that 85 per cent of institutions were 'super keen or interested' in having a closer connection with Indigenous people, yet 59 per cent of institutions did not have any Indigenous employees. Only one-fifth of organisations had an Indigenous curator, and just 21 per cent had a Reconciliation Action Plan.

Reconciliation Action Plans, or RAPs, guide organisations to support the national reconciliation movement. 'RAPs have been successful in bringing together Indigenous and non-Indigenous people through setting goals such as increasing Indigenous employment, setting procurement targets, increasing staff cultural awareness, and celebrating and honouring Indigenous events,' says Bundjalung woman Karen Mundine, Reconciliation Australia CEO. [37] They are used by schools, universities, businesses, corporates, government and community organisations, and also in museum and galleries.

RAPs help to move museum and gallery values away from their Eurocentric foundations. They encourage everyone in the organisation to shift their thinking of Indigenous people and get excited about Indigenous engagement. Other shifts towards encouraging Indigenous values need to occur in policy updates, interpretation guidelines and including Indigenous programming in budgeting. Additionally, there need to be Indigenous voices on boards, and cultural competency training. This will help make Indigenous Australians and Indigenous staff feel safe in museums and galleries.

Even when Indigenous people were employed in institutions, there were discussions about the lack of cultural safety and systemic support. Indigenous people working in these institutions aren't given pathways to progress to higher levels, and often feel like they're in a bit of a bind – stuck between two worlds. Wiradjuri woman Tasha James, who has worked in archives and museums for many years, joked that she felt like 'a black Google', which I thought was funny. I come from one country and can't speak for all Indigenous people.

A really good thing we found out during these consultations was that lots of non-Indigenous people understood the need for institutions to better engage, and wanted to see and support this change, but they had a fear of doing the wrong thing, of not being culturally aware – afraid that someone would call them out and embarrass them. Implementing protocols can help eradicate this sort of fear.

The Roadmap is really about changing the way these organisations connect with Indigenous peoples and deal with the Indigenous content that they carry. This is about internal change but also about Indigenous leadership: we should have Indigenous people as directors of museums and CEOs. We should also have a national museum. What might it be like to see a national institution that shines as an example, that tells truths about our past but addresses the possibilities of our shared identity? This would be a place for all our children, for the next ten generations and beyond.

It was refreshing to be able to set a new pathway, but it is up to all of us to make it work. During the project, I was chatting with an Aunty who had done lots of voluntary museum work throughout her life. I was saying that it was a ten-year Roadmap, and she said, 'Add some more zeros – a 10,000-year roadmap is what we need!' The message is clear: we cannot let this go. Although, for now, it's a ten-year Roadmap, we must keep it up long beyond that timeframe.

The way ahead

Galleries, libraries, archives and museums are important places for all Australians. They play a very important role in maintaining records and reporting on the progress of knowledge, but they also enable the development of new knowledge. So, for Indigenous people, the way that these institutions deal with Indigenous knowledge can have a profound impact. There are many different issues to do with ICIP, including cultural ownership, managing what is sensitive or sacred, display and collection, public access, digitisation and interpretation of the record, and the focus of future collections. If every institution in the country was to set up systems for ethically managing ICIP, we would see a situation that not only supports the self-determination of Indigenous people, but benefits every Australian in understanding the cultural heritage of the land on which they live.

> **WHAT YOU CAN DO ...**
>
> - Reconnect Indigenous custodians to cultural materials and information in collections.
> - Ensure Indigenous management of those resources.
> - Repatriate materials and ancestral remains to the cultural owners, and hold these materials in places that the living descendants can access.
> - Empower Indigenous curation and Indigenous-led exhibitions.
> - Make digital collections more accessible – open them up to Indigenous people.

Resources

First Peoples and Australian Museums and Galleries: A Report on the Engagement of Indigenous Australians in the Museums and Galleries Sector (Terri Janke and Company, 2018): www.amaga-indigenous.org.au

First Peoples: A Roadmap for Enhancing Indigenous Engagement in Museums and Galleries (Terri Janke and Company/AMaGA): www.amaga-indigenous.org.au

Aboriginal and Torres Strait Islander Library, Information and Resource Network (ATSILIRN): https://atsilirn.aiatsis.gov.au

Indigenous Archives Collective: https://indigenousarchives.net

Mukurtu CMS: https://mukurtu.org

Local Contexts: https://localcontexts.org/

Notes

1. Art Gallery of New South Wales, *Art of the Torres Strait Islands*, AGNSW, n.d., <https://m.artgallery.nsw.gov.au/artsets/hav5uo>.
2. Gaye Sculthorpe, 'Same objects, different stories: Exhibiting "Indigenous Australia"', *Journal of Museum Ethnography*, no. 30, 2017, pp. 79–103.
3. 'Calls for British Museum to surrender Indigenous Gweagal shield', *ABC News*, 29 March 2016, <www.abc.net.au/news/2016-03-29/calls-for-british-museum-to-surrender-gweagal-shield/7280532?nw=0>.
4. AIATSIS, *AIATSIS Collection*, AIATSIS, n.d., <https://collection.aiatsis.gov.au/>.
5. AIATSIS, *Access and Use Policy: AIATSIS Collection*, AIATSIS, 2018, <https://aiatsis.gov.au/sites/default/files/2020-09/aiatsis-access-and-use-policy-2018.pdf>.
6. Indigenous Archives Collective, *About*, Indigenous Archives Collective, n.d., <https://indigenousarchives.net/about/>.
7. Kirsten Thorpe, personal communication, 8 February 2021.
8. Kirsten Thorpe, *ICIP in Practice – Kirsten Thorpe, Jumbunna Institute for Indigenous Education & Research*, presentation at Blurring Lines – the Australian Digital Alliance

Copyright Forum 2020, Australian Digital Alliance, YouTube, 6 March 2020, <www.youtube.com/watch?v=Z1r6TtK1YWA>.
9   Kirsten Thorpe, personal communication, 8 February 2021.
10 ANU, *Deepening Histories of Place*, <www.deepeninghistories.anu.edu.au>.
11 Mukurtu CMS, *About*, Mukurtu, n.d., <https://mukurtu.org/about/>.
12 Terri Janke and Adam Broughton, 'Why cultural institutions need an ICIP protocol' [blog post], Terri Janke and Company, 17 April 2019, <www.terrijanke.com.au/post/2019/04/17/why-cultural-institutions-need-an-icip-protocol>.
13 National Gallery of Australia (NGA), *The Aboriginal Memorial: Introduction*, NGA, 2021, <https://nga.gov.au/aboriginalmemorial/home.cfm>.
14 NGA, *Aboriginal and Torres Strait Islander Cultural Rights and Engagement Policy*, NGA, 2017, <https://nga.gov.au/collection/pdfs/atsiculturalrights_policy.pdf>; *Protocols for Indigenous Arts and Culture*, NGA, n.d., <https://nga.gov.au/exhibitions/pdf/protocols.pdf>.
15 Franchesca Cubillo, Larrakia/Wardaman/Yanuwa/Bardi peoples, Senior Curator; Tina Baum, Larrakia/Wardaman/Karajarri peoples, Curator; Kelli Cole, Warumungu/Luritja peoples, Curator Special Projects; Aidan Hartshorn, Walgalu/Wiradjuri peoples, Wesfarmers Assistant Curator.
16 NGA, *Belonging: Stories of Australian Art*, NGA, 2021, <https://nga.gov.au/belonging/>.
17 Bruce Johnson McLean, personal communication, 3 March 2021.
18 Karen Manton, *ICIP in Practice – Karen Manton, Batchelor Institute of Indigenous Tertiary Education*, presentation at Blurring Lines – the Australian Digital Alliance Copyright Forum 2020, Australian Digital Alliance, YouTube, 18 March 2020, <www.youtube.com/watch?v=6DamRytnNPM>.
19 Martin Nakata and Marcia Langton (eds), *Australian Indigenous Knowledge and Libraries*, Australian Academic & Research Libraries, Canberra, 2005, p. 195.
20 ATSILIRN, *Aboriginal and Torres Strait Islander Protocols for Libraries, Archives and Information Services*, ATSILIRN, 2012, <https://atsilirn.aiatsis.gov.au/protocols.php>.
21 University of Sydney Library, Aboriginal and Torres Strait Islander Cultural Protocols (2021) <https://ses.library.usyd.edu.au/bitstream/handle/2123/24602/University%20of%20Sydney%20Library%20Cultural%20Protocols%202021.pdf?sequence=2&isAllowed=y>.
22 Paul Daley, 'Enduring controversy: BP sponsorship ignites new row over British Museum's Indigenous exhibition', *The Guardian*, 21 July 2015, <www.theguardian.com/australia-news/postcolonial-blog/2015/jul/21/enduring-controversy-bp-sponsorship-ignites-new-row-over-british-museums-indigenous-exhibition>.
23 Gary Murray, personal communication, 1 March 2021.
24 John Carty, in Terri Janke and Company, *First Peoples and Australian Museums and Galleries: A Report on the Engagement of Indigenous Australians in the Museums and Galleries Sector*, report commissioned by Australian Museums and Galleries Association (AMAGA), AMaGA, Canberra, 2018, p. 50, <www.amaga-indigenous.org.au>.
25 Sharon Sullivan, 'Repatriation', *The Getty Conservation Institute Newsletter*, vol. 14, no. 3, 1999, pp. 18–21, <www.getty.edu/conservation/publications/newsletters/14_3/feature1_6.html>.
26 United Kingdom House of Commons Select Committee on Culture, Media and Sport, *Session 1999–2000: Seventh Report*, vol. I, section 158, 18 July 2000, <https://publications.parliament.uk/pa/cm199900/cmselect/cmcumeds/371/37107.htm#a17>.

27 Cressida Fforde and Lyndon Ormond-Parker, 'Repatriation developments in the UK', *Indigenous Law Bulletin*, vol 5, no. 6, p. 9, <www5.austlii.edu.au/au/journals/IndigLawB/2001/10.html>.
28 Advisory Committee for Indigenous Repatriation, *National Resting Place Consultation Report 2014*, Attorney-General's Department, 2015, <www.arts.gov.au/documents/national-resting-place-consultation-report-2014>.
29 Terri Janke and Company, *First Peoples: A Roadmap for Enhancing Indigenous Engagement in Museums and Galleries*, report commissioned by Australian Museums and Galleries Association (AMaGA), AMaGA, Canberra, 2018, p. 35, <www.amaga-indigenous.org.au>.
30 Nici Cumpston, email correspondence, 26 October 2020.
31 Biennale of Sydney, *Biennale of Sydney and Australian institute of Aboriginal and Torres Strait Islander Studies: Working Together with Local Indigenous Communities for Cultural Renewal and Pride* [media release], Biennale of Sydney, 2020, <www.biennaleofsydney.art/media/media-releases/biennale-sydney-and-australian-institute-aboriginal-and-torres-strait-islander-studies-working-together-local-indigenous-communities-cultural-renewal-and-pride/>.
32 Nathan Sentance, 'Maker unknown and the decentring [of] First Nations People', *Archival Decolonist*, 21 July 2017, <https://archivaldecolonist.com/2017/07/21/>.
33 Gaye Sculthorpe, email correspondence, December 2020.
34 Australian National Maritime Museum (ANMM), *Celebrating the Unique Practice of Tasmanian Aboriginal Shell Stringing*, ANMM, 2019, <www.sea.museum/whats-on/exhibitions/kanalaritja>.
35 Margo Neale, in Terri Janke and Company, *First Peoples and Australian Museums and Galleries: A Report*, p. 15.
36 Terri Janke and Company, *First Peoples*.
37 Karen Mundine, personal communication, 18 January 2021.

15
REIMAGINING INDIGENOUS TOURISM

Australia is a unique continent with an old soul. The landscapes, faces, stories and songs of country are the things that visitors want to see and hear. It is more than just shrimp on the barbie at Bondi Beach in the summer. As the home of the oldest continuing cultures on Earth, there is an opportunity for tourism that is about cultural immersion and enabling Indigenous stories to be told authentically by Indigenous people. Tourists are looking for that genuine experience, to learn and experience the culture and stories of the first Australians. When you move through country, you can open your mind and your heart.

In the year 2000, I travelled to Kakadu National Park in the Northern Territory. Kakadu is a UNESCO World Heritage site covering almost 20,000 square kilometres. Here, there are more than 5000 ancient rock art sites, depicting motifs and stories of creation ancestors, ceremony, trade and biodiversity. The Bininj/Mungguy have called this place home for some 65,000 years.[1]

In 2000, the Olympic Games to be held in Australia were just around the corner, so there were plenty of travellers visiting Kakadu. My husband Andrew Pitt and I went up there with our two small babies to meet up with our friend Mandy Muir, who was working at the National Park at the time. Mandy grew up in the area, with ancestral connections to the place as a descendant of the Murumburr clan (central Kakadu) through her mother and the Wardaman clan through her father's side. She showed us around her family's place. There was a beautiful waterhole, full of waterlilies; stories of country, so old; magpie geese, purple and white waterlilies, and crystal-clear water. Not a place that crocodiles would like, but I kept a watchful eye on our surroundings.

The next day, I met Mandy at Nourlangie Rock, an area she is strongly connected to. It is rich with rock art galleries and ancestral stories. We walked the path barefoot. I was trying to be tough, but my feet did hurt. As we came to the rock art sites, we turned a corner and were surprised by a king brown snake, one of the deadliest snakes in Australia. Half coiled up, its scales were glistening in the sunlight as it moved. Mandy reached for me, pulling me behind her. It was a powerful snake and I felt honoured to see it there.

Once we had safely passed it, Mandy told me, 'Nearby is the King Brown Dreaming on Mirarr clan country, where the Ranger mine site is.' Her voice calmed me in an instant.

Years later I caught up with Mandy in Melbourne and we reminisced about that day. 'I'm still trying to work out what that meant,' she said, laughing about the snake. 'It is a very powerful animal and our old people used to eat them. I think it appeared because you are a very powerful woman, Terri Janke. Some of us stand out from the rest.'

What is so inspirational about Mandy is her deep understanding of the crucial role Indigenous tourism plays in maintaining culture and keeping traditional knowledge alive. 'While working in the local tourism industry as a trainee in my earlier days, I began to notice that people were looking for a genuine Aboriginal cultural experience,' Mandy says. 'I decided to start my own tourism business.' She is now leading the way in using tourism to keep traditional knowledge strong for future generations. She is the director of Kakadu Billabong Safari Camp, a family business for safari-style accommodation on the famous Jim Jim Creek in the region her ancestors are from.

Indigenous people have consistently called for greater opportunities in tourism, especially in how their cultural heritage is commercialised in the industry. Not only in Australia but in tourism all over the world, indigenous peoples complain that their knowledge of country, places and cultural practices is used by tourism operators without their involvement or consent. This might involve cultural stories or knowledge about the properties and uses of plants.

For example, an Indigenous tourism operator I worked with had knowledge of a substance that was good for skin remedies. She showed it to tourists but was always concerned someone might take that knowledge and exploit it. It is probably a good thing she was concerned, as she is not protected by the law if someone decides to commercialise the knowledge for a new medicine or food, as has been done in the past (see chapter 9).

The other issue is that people may hear the stories, traditional stories, told by rangers or Indigenous tour guides, then write them up and publish them without consent. These stories are often copied incorrectly and their sources not credited.

Supporting Indigenous-led tourism

In 2012, communities from all over the globe gathered on Larrakia country in Darwin for the Pacific Asia Indigenous Tourism Conference, the first of its kind. I was pleased to be the MC for the proceedings. There were around 200 people from 16 countries. Many of the presenters spoke about the issues around protecting their knowledge and arts in the industry. After much discussion, we arrived at the Larrakia Declaration, a statement outlining the principles the industry should follow when working with Indigenous communities.[2] Informed by the UNDRIP, the Larrakia Declaration is about respecting Indigenous intellectual property rights, cultures and traditional practices, and having this at the forefront of decision-making processes in the industry.

It is time to move beyond an industry where Indigenous people are left empty-handed despite the industry investing in their culture. The old approach was to increase Indigenous employment in the tourism industry; however, that led to an imbalance where communities were sharing their valuable and sacred cultural knowledge but did not receive the full economic benefits they deserved.[3] The focus on Indigenous employment loses sight of the very real potential for Indigenous business ownership that supports self-determination and empowers families and communities.

The cultural connections stay true when Indigenous custodians, such as Mandy Muir, are the tour guides and business owners, as they are in control of what and how knowledge is shared with domestic and international visitors. There is power and authenticity in this, opening the way to deeply move and connect tourists to people and culture as they travel on country.

Around the time of the Larrakia Declaration, I was on the board of Tourism Australia. I saw that there was a need to not only support First Nations in their tourism businesses, but to encourage international guests to engage in the authentic Indigenous cultures that have survived despite colonial and other pressures. In 2017, Tourism Australia estimated that around one million tourists participated in an Indigenous tourism activity during their visit to Australia. This may sound like a lot, but it's only 12 per cent of those who visited Australia that year.[4] We must try to improve on this percentage.

Indigenous communities face many challenges in the tourism industry, yet there are many businesses working to protect the cultural heritage rights of Indigenous communities that should be celebrated. By respecting these rights, the tourism industry can empower Indigenous communities and support the strengthening of culture, increasing pride and leading to socioeconomic benefits.

Respecting cultural sites and traditional knowledge

Traditional owners often fear that the sheer number of tourists who flock to popular destinations each day can harm the cultural sites and biodiversity. When I was in Ulladulla on the south coast of New South Wales, I spoke with Noel Butler, a local Budawang elder of the Yuin Nation. Noel works as a cultural educator, hosting workshops and programs for locals and visitors to the area. 'I've always been careful about showing people too many important cultural sites to prevent damage and vandalism. The industry needs to be sustainable and show respect for the sites and the knowledge being shared,' he told me.[5]

This is a concern shared by Indigenous groups around Australia, such as in Gariwerd, or the Grampians, a special place in Victoria for the Djab Wurrung and the Jardwadjali people. The impact of recreational activities such as rock climbing, abseiling and mountain biking has created problems in this region. In many places the ground has been compacted and cleared, plants and rocks damaged and parts of the ecosystem lost.[6] There is also the risk of damaging the precious rock art and natural rock formations themselves. There have unfortunately been instances where this has happened due to vandalism.[7]

There have been many more cases of people desecrating cultural sites and stealing items of significance, causing great devastation. In 2011, ancient rock art of the Burrup Peninsula in Western Australia's Pilbara region was vandalised, with rock art expert and Greens politician Robin Chapple saying, 'Acts of this nature inflict cultural trauma on the Indigenous custodians of the Burrup. It's the equivalent of vandalising Stonehenge or the Pyramids.'[8] The Indigenous art of this land is even older than these structures.

Budj Bim Cultural Landscape: Joint management

The Budj Bim Cultural Landscape on Gunditjmara country in south-eastern Australia is one of the world's largest and oldest aquaculture systems. The Budj Bim lava flows provide the basis for the complex system of channels, weirs and dams developed by the Gunditjmara in order to trap, store and harvest kooyang (short-finned eel – *Anguilla australis*). The highly productive aquaculture system provided an economic and social base for Gunditjmara society for generations. The Budj Bim Cultural Landscape is the result of a creational process narrated by the Gunditjmara as a deep time story, referring to the idea that they have always lived there. From an archaeological perspective, deep time represents a period of at least 32,000 years. The ongoing dynamic relationship of Gunditjmara and their land is nowadays carried by knowledge systems retained through oral transmission and continuity of cultural practice.

The park is co-managed by Parks Victoria and the Gunditj Mirring Traditional Owner Aboriginal Corporation, who represent the rights and interests of the Gunditjmara community and have developed ICIP protocols and branding guidelines to ensure that their knowledge and arts are not exploited.[9]

Photography and Uluru

Uluru is central to the culture and law of the A̲nangu people. Uluru-Kata Tjuta National Park has been jointly managed since 1985, and the Park's Board aims to protect cultural rights by increasing employment, cultural experiences and support of Aboriginal culture.[10] The nearby Yulara (Ayers Rock) Resort is owned by Voyages Indigenous Tourism, a company owned by the Indigenous Land and Sea Corporation. There are also tourism and arts producers such as Maruku Arts. Local Indigenous tourism guides take people around the base of Uluru.

The Park attracts millions of tourists who visit the area and many would, until 2019, climb the rock. It is against A̲nangu law to climb the site and it also causes ecological damage to the site, but for decades, visitors had been climbing it anyway. In 2019, it was at the centre of discussions on Indigenous tourism due to the decision to officially close the climb for good. Now, if you climb it, there are penalties in place that are enforced under Australian environmental law by the *Environment Protection and Biodiversity Conservation Act 1999* (Cth). The site is also further safeguarded under the *Northern Territory Aboriginal Sacred Sites Act 1989* (NT).

But there are also issues with the sites around the area. Under traditional law they are sensitive or sacred sites and therefore are not to be desecrated. The National Park has published film and photography guidelines that are published on websites and indicated on signage at those locations.[11] There are also guidelines for commercial photography and for using captured images from the Park for commercial purposes.

What about permission to use the image of Uluru? The site is not protected by Australian copyright legislation. While permission can be granted for the use of Uluru's image for commercial purposes, the A<u>n</u>angu people do not legally have copyright protections unless they themselves have taken the footage or image and thus are owners of copyright for that material. Permission to use an image of Uluru is granted by the Uluru-Kata Tjuta National Park, not the community itself. There are guidelines also about artistic reproductions. Commercial film crews, still photographers, artists and sound recordists will need a permit to carry out commercial activities in the park. A commercial permit is also required to use an existing image of the Park for a commercial purpose.[12]

It is also necessary to respect Uluru, and not remove rocks from the Park as souvenirs. I worked with the Park in the early 2000s to review ICIP policies and approaches, and found it useful to see the issues that local A<u>n</u>angu dealt with. Staff in the media and communications office showed me the many returned packages they had received; every day, packages arrive containing rocks taken, then returned, by guilty tourists from as far away as Germany, France, the UK and the US. The Park staff call them 'Sorry Rocks'. Often the packages include notes of apology. Some even talk about bad luck the people have experienced. The returned rocks pose a problem, as the rangers often don't know where they were taken from and how to return them. Now all the rocks are catalogued so that they can be managed.[13] Removing rocks and sand from the park is disrespectful to A<u>n</u>angu and their culture. It is also illegal and can result in fines of up to $8500.

Rip-offs and fake Indigenous tourism

While there are opportunities for Indigenous tourism, there are also negative impacts. Watch out for the bogus and unscrupulous tours and products that aren't Indigenous-led or engaged with Indigenous people. These tourism experiences reference Indigenous knowledge, may use Indigenous names and talk about the Indigenous stories and culture connected to land. But when this doesn't come from Indigenous voices, it may be misinformed, misrepresenting culture, history and place.

Indigenous tourism that doesn't involve Indigenous people also runs the risk of commodifying Indigenous culture, as Indigenous peoples and their cultural practices are packaged up into tourism products. There is a risk that audiences then exoticise or stereotype the people and culture. The problem of inauthenticity arises here. The Tourism Tropical North Queensland Cultural Protocols offer good guidance on engaging with Aboriginal and Torres Strait Islander communities.[14]

Fake tourism products also include the fake art industry that preys on ignorant tourists who may not know any better when purchasing a piece of what they might think is authentic Indigenous art. In 2018, a company called Birubi Art was found guilty of misleading and deceptive conduct for selling Aboriginal souvenirs like mini boomerangs as if they were authentic artworks made by Aboriginal people in Australia. Birubi had misled consumers via false information about the origins of the items when they had in fact been made in Indonesia. The court fined Birubi $2.3 million as a deterrent for companies that might in the future exploit Indigenous art with false labelling. I speak about this case in more detail in chapter 3.

Sharing stories in tourism: Beware big ears

Here's a scenario that offers a snapshot of the issues that can arise when knowledge is shared in the tourism sector. An Indigenous community decides to operate a bus tour of its local area. Members of this community know a lot of information about the local area, including the whereabouts of specific sites and their associated stories, and the types of plants that can be eaten. The tour involves taking tourists to various sites where a respected Indigenous community member shares stories and other cultural knowledge with the group. This information does not have an identifiable author as it has been handed down through the generations. It belongs to the practices and traditions of the community. One of the tourists writes detailed notes on some of the cultural information shared in the tour. He then goes on to interpret and publish this information in a guidebook.

Does copyright law protect the interests of the community? Does it protect their information and the integrity of its interpretation? Generally, no. Copyright protects the material form, and not the oral expression or underlying idea. The copyright in the guidebook would be vested in the non-Indigenous writer who put the idea into material form.

Let's say another tourist has taken a photograph of a rock art site on the tour and goes on to reproduce the photo on postcards to sell. Can the Indigenous community invoke copyright law to stop the sale of the postcards? Again, no. Copyright law assumes some forms of Indigenous arts and cultural expression are in the public domain, where they are free for all to use and exploit. Copyright in an artistic work lasts for 70 years after the death of the artist. Rock art is often so old that copyright laws do not apply. The photographer, as the maker of the photograph, will own copyright in the photograph and, under copyright laws, is generally free to exploit that photograph commercially.

My firm worked with the Festival of Pacific Arts and Culture to develop a guide for Indigenous participants who were sharing their cultures (see chapter 8 for more details). Participants were worried about how tourists might copy and use their images and their knowledge. Working for WIPO, I wrote a guide for protecting IP at festivals. The guide asked that festival-goers 'respect the rights of the performers, artists and creators by recognising their IP' and advised that it was 'wrong to photograph, record, film, copy or use the performances and exhibitions in an offensive way. By respecting creators' rights you respect their creative endeavours and livelihoods, and can support cultural industries in the Pacific.'[15]

To make the most of the goodwill of the festival's attendees, the guide recommended a traditional knowledge notice that event organisers could put on programs, and participants could have at their stalls, so that people would respect their rights to their knowledge:

Traditional knowledge notice

The Festival displays a range of materials, including art, body painting, tattoos, dance, music, ceremonies, plays, films, sound recordings, traditional knowledge, lifestyles, food preparation, traditional healing and technical skills.

These materials may be protected by IP laws and customary laws of Pacific people. Some expressions of culture may be sacred and/or culturally sensitive.

Cultural protocols for respecting traditional knowledge and expressions of culture should be followed. Shared cultural expressions should be respectfully used.

Dealing with part or whole of the performances and displays, for any unauthorised purpose, may be a serious breach of customary laws.[16]

The growth of Indigenous cultural festivals around Australia is also an important part of Indigenous tourism, such as the Laura Dance Festival in Cape York, the Garma Festival of Traditional Cultures in north-east Arnhem Land, Barunga Festival in the Katherine region and Quandamooka Festival on Minjerribah (North Stradbroke Island). There are also the important art fairs like the Cairns Indigenous Art Fair, Darwin Aboriginal Art Fair and Tarnanthi in Adelaide, which give tourists and locals the opportunity to purchase authentic art and craft products, and to meet the artists.

Using Indigenous knowledge in tourism

For Indigenous communities to enjoy the benefits of sharing their cultures, it is important that Indigenous people are involved in the telling of their own histories – whether through employment opportunities, economic compensation or extensive consultation with traditional custodians. To have a healthy and vibrant Indigenous tourism industry

THE RESPECTING OUR CULTURE (ROC) CERTIFICATION

The Respecting Our Culture program is a certification system that allows tourism operators to be acknowledged for their role in protecting the cultural heritage rights of Aboriginal and Torres Strait Islander communities. Most importantly, it provides tourists who want to support the protection of cultural knowledge to choose experiences with companies that respect Indigenous culture.[18]

The program is managed by Ecotourism Australia, but was initiated by Aboriginal Tourism Australia as a result of continuous consultation with Aboriginal and Torres Strait Islander elders and those involved in the tourism industry.

The criteria for companies to use the certification logo are based on ICIP protocols: first, respect for Indigenous culture and the land; and, second, consultation with traditional communities before projects for tourism experiences are constructed.

The protocols of interpretation, integrity and benefit sharing are also important. Tourism operators must:

- enable traditional owners to interpret cultural knowledge
- ensure that all experiences and cultural items are not fakes
- ensure that Indigenous communities who share culture receive economic and cultural benefits.

in Australia, cultural heritage rights issues must be addressed to protect Indigenous artists and communities. It is difficult for tourists to pick up on whether a tourism company or business is exploiting Indigenous communities for economic gain. Many visitors are unaware if an artist or performer, for example, is being ethically and financially compensated for sharing Indigenous cultural knowledge, especially if a business appears to be legitimate.

Where effective consultation does not occur between the tourism industry and Indigenous people, the cultural integrity of the cultural knowledge is not maintained. An example is the use of the didgeridoo, which has become so embedded in the tourism industry that it has become an identifier of Aboriginal culture – even though didgeridoos did not traditionally originate from all Aboriginal communities. Yet these practices are performed to live up to false, preconceived ideas of the Aboriginal identity.[17]

In 2018, academic Marcia Langton released her Indigenous travel guide *Welcome to Country*, a beautiful hardcover book featuring hundreds of Indigenous tourism attractions across Australia. A year after it was published, I went to the launch of the youth edition of the book. Rather than being a tourist guidebook, this edition focuses on learning about Indigenous history, arts and sciences, designed for young readers but interesting for all. The message of both books is clear – if we understand the Indigenous cultures of Australia, we can better relate to each other, heal and come together as a country.

Collaborating for cultural competency in tourism

There are also opportunities for tourism companies to engage with Indigenous tourism operators for the purpose of increasing cultural competency. BlackCard is a 100 per cent Indigenous owned and operated company founded by Dr Lilla Watson, a respected Aboriginal elder, artist and educator, and Indigenous professional Mundanara Bayles. They offer cultural competency training and programs for companies and individuals, as well as cultural tours in Brisbane for people to learn about the Aboriginal history of the region.

Similar tours and education training experiences occur in other cities, like Aunty Margret Campbell's The Rocks Aboriginal Dreaming Tour through Dreamtime SouthernX.

Digital tourism apps

The land holds old stories, and the voices of Indigenous people can open our eyes to these. Digital technology is one way that Indigenous people and their collaborators are telling these stories, celebrating them and keeping them alive. Digital pioneer Mikaela Jade created Digital Custodians, an augmented reality Indigenous cultural app that teaches you traditional stories at key tourism sites around Australia. The app recognises Indigenous peoples' voices, and the singing of country can be heard by people visiting sites; royalties go back to the elders involved. See chapter 13 for more about Mikaela Jade.

Knowing country: The future direction of Indigenous tourism

In 2020, all around the world, economies collapsed due to the COVID-19 pandemic. With travel bans and restrictions, airports became ghost towns and the global tourism industry came to a standstill. In Australia, summertime tourism operators were just coming out of peak season, but the operators in the central and northern parts of Australia who rely on the high visitor numbers from the south during winter months were left without access to their usual income.

This affected all tourism operators, Indigenous and non-Indigenous. For the many Indigenous families like Mandy Muir's in Kakadu, and communities in the Kimberley and Mparntwe (Alice Springs) who rely on the influx of tourists each peak season as a major source of revenue, the economic crash had a catastrophic effect on business. 'Because of the effects of the coronavirus our business was deregistered,' Mandy says. 'We lost all our business for the season, which was over ten groups adding up to 500 students across Australia. We were also affected earlier in the year as well because of the fires.' The good news is that Mandy's family business, Kakadu Billabong Safari Camp, was able to be registered again. 'I am very pleased and proud to get up on our feet again and my mother and I, the owners of the business, are looking forward to a great season in 2021,'[19] she says.

The Queensland Government had even named 2020 as the Year of Indigenous Tourism, without knowing the pandemic was just around the corner. Unfortunately, all of this was put on hold. But this still indicated a strong intention to support Aboriginal and Torres Strait Islander people in Queensland and beyond to economically prosper in the industry.[19]

Reimagining tourism in Australia to include Indigenous culture and support self-determination is primarily about enabling Indigenous people to be the ones who are presenting their culture to the world. The number of Indigenous tourism experiences is increasing and, if we support them, they will continue to grow and strengthen. Many research papers have outlined pathways for the sustainability of Indigenous tourism, and there needs to be further investment by government to assist. However, for now, we can do positive things in the short term by just engaging and seeking out legitimate and authentic Indigenous tourism businesses.

For all tourism businesses, the True Tracks principles offer a useful framework for moving forward. Governments around the globe bear the responsibility to ensure that the tourism industry respects these protocols. More needs to be done to legislate and regulate the companies who work in the tourism industry and ensure that they respect Aboriginal cultures, and allow Indigenous people to have self-determination to decide how knowledge is shared.

Jason Eades is the CEO of Welcome to Country, an organisation set up to promote Aboriginal and Torres Strait Islander Experiences. They do this through the Welcome to Country website (www.welcometocountry.com), a portal for Indigenous tourism experiences. The site links you to experiences from visiting rock art sites, to cultural tours on stand-up paddleboards. It is like a marketplace for Indigenous-owned, -operated or -delivered experiences. Indigenous culture makes tourism a richer experience – to have the opportunity to walk country with custodians, to hear stories, to see art and dance, and to listen to knowledge.

WHAT YOU CAN DO ...

As a tourism operator:
- Consider how you can work with Indigenous people to enable an Indigenous experience on the land and sea on which you conduct your tours.
- Do not use Indigenous knowledge, artistic and cultural expression without consent of the performer and knowledge holder. If you want to develop a commercial opportunity, speak to the Indigenous person and share benefits after getting consent.
- Do not allow tourists to take samples of plants, rocks and other natural resources away from country unless permission is given.

As a tourist:
- Understand that Indigenous cultures are diverse across the country. Leave stereotypes at home and recognise living cultures.
- Support Indigenous tourism operators, especially in local and regional areas. The Welcome to Country website (www.welcometocountry.com) is a good starting point.
- Travel sustainably. Listen to the land and the ancestors, and be responsible on country so that future generations can enjoy it.
- Respect privacy. Ask permission before photographing and filming people, and respect their wishes if they say no.
- Do not take samples of plants, rocks and other natural resources away from country.
- Buy authentic, locally and regionally made art products.
- Do not barter with Indigenous artists.
- Beware of fake art and souvenirs! Ask about the products, the artists and the cultural source. (There's more on this in chapter 3.)
- When you go home, advocate for the Indigenous experience to your friends and family, and share this on social media.

Resources

Marcia Langton, *Welcome to Country: A Travel Guide to Indigenous Australia*, Hardie Grant, Melbourne, 2018
Bruce Pascoe and Vicky Shukuroglou, *Loving Country: A Guide to Sacred Australia*, Hardie Grant, Melbourne, 2020
Welcome to Country: www.welcometocountry.com
Discover Aboriginal Australia (Tourism Australia): www.tourism.australia.com/en/about/our-programs/signature-experiences-of-australia/discover-aboriginal-experiences.html
Cultural Protocols: Engaging with Aboriginal and Torres Strait Island Communities (Tourism Tropical North Queensland): https://tourism.tropicalnorthqueensland.org.au/wp-content/uploads/2019/04/Cultural-Protocols_V1.pdf
Western Australian Indigenous Tourism Operators Council (WAITOC): www.waitoc.com

Notes

1. Tourism Northern Territory, *Kakadu National Park*, <https://northernterritory.com/kakadu-and-surrounds/destinations/kakadu-national-park>.
2. 'The Larrakia Declaration on the Development of Indigenous Tourism', *Adventure Travel News*, 11 May 2012, <www.adventuretravelnews.com/the-larrakia-declarationon-the-development-of-indigenous-tourism>.
3. Michelle Whitford and Lisa Ruhanen, 'Indigenous tourism businesses: An exploratory study of business owners' perception of drivers and inhibitors', *Tourism Recreation Research*, vol. 39, no. 2, 2014, pp. 149–68.
4. Australian Government Department of Foreign Affairs and Trade (DFAT), *Indigenous Tourism Surge*, DFAT, 2019, <www.dfat.gov.au/about-us/publications/trade-investment/business-envoy/Pages/january-2019/indigenous-tourism-surge>.
5. Noel Butler, personal communication, 24 February 2021.
6. Parks Victoria, *Rock Climbing in the Grampians National Park*, Parks Victoria, n.d., <www.parks.vic.gov.au/projects/rock-climbing-in-the-grampians-national-park>. In November 2020, Parks Victoria and Gariwerd traditional owners released a Rock Climbing Decision Framework with rules about where and how rock climbing can occur in the Gariwerd landscape.
7. Luke Waters, 'Traditional owner condemns vandals of ancient rock art', *SBS News*, 5 February 2017, <www.sbs.com.au/news/traditional-owner-condemns-vandals-of-ancient-rock-art>.
8. Robin Chapple, *Vandalism of Burrup Rock Art a preventable tragedy*, Hon. Robin Chapple MLC, n.d., <www.robinchapple.com/vandalism-burrup-rock-art-preventable-tragedy>.
9. UNESCO World Heritage Centre, *Budj Bim Cultural landscape*, <https://whc.unesco.org/en/list/1577/>.
10. Director of National Parks and Uluṟu-Kata Tjuṯa Board of Management, *Uluṟu-Kata Tjuṯa National Park Management Plan 2010–2020*, Director of National Parks, Canberra, 2010, <www.environment.gov.au/resource/management-plan-2010-2020-uluru-kata-tjuta-national-park>.
11. Parks Australia, 'Photography', *Uluru-Kata Tjuta National Park*, n.d., <https://parksaustralia.gov.au/uluru/do/photography/>.

12. Australian Department of Agriculture, Water and the Environment (DAWE), *Permits, Licences and Leases: For Media and Artists*, DAWE, n.d., <www.environment.gov.au/resource/media-and-artists-0>.
13. Parks Australia, *Sorry Rocks*, Parks Australia, 2015, <https://parksaustralia.gov.au/uluru/pub/fs-sorryrocks.pdf>.
14. Tourism Tropical North Queensland (TTNQ), *Cultural Protocols: Engaging with Aboriginal and Torres Strait Island Communities*, TTNQ, n.d., <https://tourism.tropicalnorthqueensland.org.au/wp-content/uploads/2019/04/Cultural-Protocols_V1.pdf>.
15. Terri Janke, *Intellectual Property and the 11th Festival of Pacific Arts, Solomon Islands, 2012*, World Intellectual Property Organization, Geneva, 2012, p. 2, <www.wipo.int/edocs/pubdocs/en/tk/tk_fpa/tk_fpa_2012.pdf>.
16. Terri Janke, *Intellectual Property and the 11th Festival of Pacific Arts*, p. 18.
17. Dennis Foley, *Australian Aboriginal Tourism an Opportunity but Keep the Culture Intact*, research paper, Faculty Education & Arts, University of Newcastle, March 2014, <https://essaydocs.org/australian-aboriginal-tourism-still-an-opportunity-but-keep-th.html>.
18. Ecotourism Australia, *Respecting Our Culture (ROC) Certification*, Ecotourism Australia, n.d., <www.ecotourism.org.au/our-certification-programs/eco-certification-4/>.
19. Mandy Muir, email correspondence, 4 May 2020.
20. Queensland Department of Tourism, Innovation and Sport (DTIS), *Year of Indigenous Tourism*, DTIS, 2020, <www.ditid.qld.gov.au/our-work/year-of-indigenous-tourism>.

16

TAKING CARE OF BUSINESS – THE ICIP WAY

In the summer of 2000, I did a lot of reflecting on how to bring about changes to stop the theft of Indigenous knowledge, arts and culture in Australia. This was not long after the release of *Our Culture: Our Future*, the landmark report on Indigenous cultural heritage rights that I'd written at the law firm Michael Frankel and Company (see chapter 1). Bringing about those changes would take a shift in mindset, and in the way business and government worked. It would mean Indigenous people would need to stand up. That got me thinking about what it would mean to own and run my own business.

Our Culture: Our Future had called for Australian governments to bring in new laws. But the government did not respond with new laws and I began to feel that three years of work on the report might have been for nothing, and that the 380-page report was just going to be used by government officers to adjust the height of their computer monitors. I felt like I was waiting for something to be done, until I thought, 'Maybe there are things I can do now – if only I take the opportunity.'

I never thought I would own my own business. My husband Andrew was good at business. His family were businesspeople; they worked hard and had done well. So a conversation began – in my head, and with Andrew. 'If I really want to change the way people value Indigenous intellectual property and knowledge,' I said, 'I should set up my own legal practice.'

I was scared, but there was something about being a new mother that gave me a direction and a new energy; Jaiki, my son, was only four months old, and Tamina, my daughter, was still a toddler. Looking back now, perhaps it was postnatal euphoria. I did not want to feel the waiting and helplessness that I had felt in the past, looking at the government reports and the international intellectual property (IP) scene, with its big meetings and conferences seemingly going nowhere. Perhaps there *was* a space for me to stand up and make a difference.

I wanted to provide access to the law for Indigenous clients. I was committed to bringing IP law to Indigenous people and bringing Indigenous values to IP. I thought about how this would contribute to the bigger picture of Indigenous rights and economic empowerment. Indigenous peoples come from a 65,000-year-old knowledge base. If we use this respectfully, we can build a strong economic base and bring positive change into the world. I knew that by working independently, I could choose to do work that would positively impact Indigenous people and change lives.

At the end of that summer, I announced my intention to set up my own law firm. Andrew told me that he would back me and help me set it up; he really believed in me. I stepped out of the safety of my job with Michael Frankel, leaving behind the role of employee to set up my own firm. I only had $3000 in savings, but that was enough to pay a bond and buy a computer, a printer and stationery.

By April 2000 I had officially established Terri Janke and Company. I set up in Redfern, behind an architect's office; the building was old and rundown, with two small offices, but I liked it. I had to bring in lamps because there were no lights in the ceiling, which was lucky because it meant I did not work too late into the night.

That first year was not easy, especially with two small kids. In the morning, I would take them to the childcare centre, one holding my hand, the other in the baby capsule and my briefcase slung over my shoulder. The laptops were heavier in those days!

Initially, I took on a job for the World Intellectual Property Organization (WIPO), writing case studies on how Indigenous Australian artists have used copyright laws to protect their cultural expressions. The project took me around the country, which was a good thing: I got to meet a lot of people and connect. This work led to the publication *Minding Culture: Case Studies on Intellectual Property and Traditional Cultural Expressions*.[1]

The hardest thing was getting my first clients. I didn't make any money those first few months. I still had enormous passion for the nature of the work, but I had a lot to learn about the economic side of being in business.

The day Aunty Lorraine Peeters, Gamilaroi and Wailwan woman, walked into my office helped me to believe in myself. She was my first client after WIPO and I was so lucky to be approached by this strong woman, strong in life and in business. I still remember the day she visited my little office with her daughter Shaan and said, 'I heard that there was an Indigenous lawyer with a firm of their own here.' I was amazed she had found me as I didn't have much publicity going back then.

Aunty Lorraine is very passionate and devoted to supporting the healing process of Indigenous people healing from the trauma of being forcibly removed from their families. Based on her own healing journey in this, she created a healing model now known as the Marumali Program® for her business, Winangali Marumali. Her work has been very well received and made huge positive impact within Indigenous communities. She came to me wanting to protect her intellectual property in this business model. Working with her has been a strong connection, helping me to understand how my work can support Indigenous businesses making a difference to the community.

What all businesses can do

Worldwide, businesses have a responsibility to respect human rights, including the rights of indigenous peoples. Human rights standards are reflected in Australian and international law. Internationally, the rights of people to be treated as equals and not be subjected to racism were enshrined in the United Nations International Convention for the Elimination of Racial Discrimination of 1969. Then, Australia enacted the *Racial Discrimination Act 1975* (Cth), a law that prohibits discrimination

BUSINESS AND THE UNDRIP

Businesses can look to the UNDRIP principles to improve their engagement with indigenous peoples. The United Nations Global Compact, an international leadership platform that encourages ethical practice in business policy and practice, published *The Business Reference Guide to the UN Declaration on the Rights of Indigenous Peoples* (2013), which states: 'All businesses, regardless of size, sector, operational context, ownership or structure, have a responsibility to respect indigenous peoples' rights.'[3]

The guide suggests practical actions that relate to specific Articles in the UNDRIP, including Article 31 regarding cultural heritage and traditional knowledge. It advocates for free, prior and informed consent (FPIC) for the use of cultural heritage in any business: 'Obtain consent before using any cultural or intellectual property of indigenous peoples. Do not apply for patents or assert copyright based on indigenous heritage materials without such consent.'[4] Other principles it advocates for includes benefit sharing and respect for indigenous cultural heritage.

It also notes the positive benefits for businesses of engaging with indigenous communities:

> Businesses are also reporting that positive engagement with indigenous peoples can bring a range of benefits – stronger relationships with communities and other stakeholders resulting in fewer conflicts and disputes, stronger government relationships, reputational benefits, employee engagement, boost in employee morale, recognition by investors, and the ability to partner with and learn from indigenous peoples' unique knowledge (with consent and respect for such indigenous peoples' intellectual property).[5]

based on race, colour, descent or national/ethnic origin, and, in some circumstances, immigrant status. It covers discrimination in all areas of public life including employment, provision of goods and services, the right to join trade unions, access to places and facilities, land, housing and other accommodation, and advertisements.[2]

Although indigenous rights were not expressly stated in the original international human rights framework, indigenous peoples have gained a place within the UN rights machinery and continue to gain momentum. The United Nations Declaration on the Rights of Indigenous Peoples (UNDRIP) was passed by the UN General Assembly in 2007. It had been a long time coming; 'a long road' is how it is often referred to by the many indigenous advocates who had worked since 1993 to reach the final text.

There are many practical actions that businesses can take to engage with Indigenous communities. One step businesses can take towards engagement is having an acknowledgment of country on their websites and at the entrance of business locations, offices and meeting rooms. The framework for these acknowledgments can be found on the Australian Government's Indigenous portal (indigenous.gov.au).[6] Delivering an acknowledgement of country at the start of meetings is also a sign of respect. Anyone can give an acknowledgement of country, as long as they open their hearts when they do it. A welcome to country can be delivered before bigger events and conferences; these are special ceremonies led by Aboriginal or Torres Strait Islander peoples who have the authority to welcome people onto their traditional lands. These ceremonies show respect for the traditional custodians of the land and acknowledge the continuing connection that Indigenous people have to country.

Businesses can also observe and support Aboriginal and Torres Strait Islander events throughout the year, such as National Close the Gap Day, National Sorry Day, Survival Day, Mabo Day, NAIDOC Week and National Reconciliation Week. They can also donate to Indigenous initiatives, charities and organisations.

Employment opportunities and joint ventures

More substantial steps include increasing Indigenous employment opportunities. For example, businesses can employ more Indigenous people and create clearer career pathways from entry-level to senior roles.

In 2015, the government introduced the Indigenous Procurement Policy (IPP) to increase Indigenous employment and participation in the Australian economy. It has seen Indigenous businesses team up with mainstream corporates in joint ventures to market to specific sectors and set up new income streams. Joint ventures are particularly useful when the parties have similar goals and value systems but different resources, skills and strengths. For example, a 'money partner with no time' might link up with a 'skilled partner with no money' to create a viable joint venture; when they combine, there can be a clear sense of purpose and stronger resources.

However, with the IPP comes the risk of 'black cladding'. Black cladding is a term that is now being used in Australia to refer to businesses that pretend to be black – that is, Indigenous – to win government contracts under the procurement policy. This happens when a non-Indigenous business enters into superficial arrangements with an Indigenous party in order to qualify as 'Indigenous', but it is not clear what role the Indigenous partner has or if they have any real say or control over the business. Examples that I have seen in practice in Australia include when a 51 per cent shareholding is given to an Indigenous director who is not involved in the day-to-day running of the company. I have also seen instances where the shareholder's deed sets up different voting rights that hinder the control of the Indigenous shareholder, or situations where there is no shareholder deed at all. Indigenous business partners need to have a genuine role in the business, not just a 51 per cent shareholding.

Beyond creating job and partnership opportunities, knowledge and culture must be respected in business transactions. The Indigenous employment and participation targets for companies who go for procurement contracts under the IPP often see them working with Indigenous people and businesses who bring substantial ICIP. For instance, Indigenous consultants may hold cultural knowledge, artists share designs from their heritage and Indigenous caterers prepare bushfoods. Cultural protocols are a vital business pathway for incorporating this knowledge into work projects.

Supply Nation: Choosing Indigenous suppliers

Businesses can support supplier diversity by choosing Indigenous suppliers. My firm chooses Indigenous businesses when buying stationery, some kitchen supplies, and catering for our workshops and events.

Supply Nation is a not-for-profit membership body that connects Australian businesses and government bodies with Indigenous-owned, -controlled and -managed suppliers. Since 2009, Supply Nation has provided registration for Indigenous businesses that verifies a business as 'Indigenous Owned'.[7] Supply Nation also manages an online database of registered Indigenous businesses for corporate, government and not-for-profit members, called Indigenous Business Direct.

Laura Berry, CEO, says that in the last five years, the Indigenous business sector has grown at a rate of 13 per cent each year – far outpacing the broader economy. There are more Indigenous entrepreneurs now than at any time in our history. With policies and targets at federal and state government levels, as well as a continued strong commitment from the private sector, there has never been a better time for Indigenous entrepreneurs to run their own business and take control of their financial destiny.[8]

The Indigenous Business Direct database is a one-stop shop for anyone looking to buy from an Indigenous business, and is mandated by the Australian Government as the first reference point for government buyers when fulfilling their targets under the IPP. Supply Nation uses a five-step verification process to ensure that the businesses on the database are Indigenous owned, and conducts regular audits of the businesses over time. To become a registered business on Indigenous Business Direct, the business must:

- be at least 50 per cent owned by Indigenous people
- be located in Australia
- make the majority of its revenue through providing a product or service, not through grants and donations.

Once a business is registered, they are able to use the Supply Nation Registered Supplier logo on marketing materials, websites and tender documentation (subject to certain terms and conditions).[9] Supply Nation–registered businesses are only permitted to use the logo during the period of their registration.

In addition, if a business is majority owned, controlled and managed by Aboriginal and/or Torres Strait Islander people, it may be eligible to become a Supply Nation Certified Supplier. Certification is the gold standard of verification that many of Supply Nation's members require when looking to engage Aboriginal and Torres Strait Islander businesses.[10]

If Supply Nation finds that a business should not be registered, the business will be immediately de-registered. In cases where there may have been fraudulent activity leading to registration, legal proceedings or referrals to the police in relation to suspected criminal offences may also be considered.

Businesses should keep in mind that Supply Nation registration and certification is voluntary, so not all legitimate Indigenous businesses will appear in the database.

Cultural safety and competency training

Is a business's workplace culturally safe? Cultural safety and cultural competency training helps non-Indigenous employees understand many of the issues that Indigenous people face when working or entering these spaces. Non-Indigenous employees can be more empathetic when working with Indigenous people or Indigenous cultural material. Businesses can also ensure culturally safe workplaces through cultural training for staff. There are programs like AIATSIS's Core Cultural Training, a ten-module course run in partnership with the Department of the Prime Minister and Cabinet and the Department of Social Services.[11]

Reconciliation Action Plans: Tools for change

Reconciliation Action Plans (RAPs) are strategic plans that help organisations work towards reconciliation. The RAP program started in 2006 and is headed by Reconciliation Australia, the lead body for reconciliation in Australia. 'At the heart, reconciliation is about creating better relationships,' says Bundjalung woman Karen Mundine, Reconciliation Australia CEO. 'RAPs set out practical targets and commitments to embed Indigenous values in the business planning process. They bring together Indigenous and non-Indigenous people and importantly, they can address truth telling.'[12] Today, more than 1100 corporate, government, big-business and not-for-profit organisations in Australia have RAPs, including Google, Lendlease, Fred Hollows Foundation and the National Australia Bank (NAB), to name just a few.

NAB, one of the biggest banks in Australia, developed their first RAP in 2008 because they wanted to better support Indigenous people in Australia. At the time, I was on the bank's Indigenous Advisory Committee with several other Indigenous people, working with board members like Danny Gilbert, a director of the board and co-founder of the law firm Gilbert + Tobin. Their objectives include increasing the number of Aboriginal and Torres Strait Islander people employed in their branches and business banking centres. NAB was the first bank to have an 'Elevate' RAP, a level that reflected its experience in building relationships with Indigenous communities and its desire to raise the bar through economic participation, employment and career development. Other major banks also have RAPs that have increased the employment of Indigenous people in banks; improved access to programs such as school-based training; offered not-for-profit microfinance products in Indigenous communities; and provided financial mentors for Indigenous community members.

Karen Mundine explains: 'To develop a RAP, your organisation must be a workplace with a certain degree of autonomy and the capacity to turn good intentions into action. If a RAP is not right for your organisation, you can still support national campaigns for Aboriginal and Torres Strait Islander social justice by engaging with [Reconciliation Australia's] resources and programs.'[13]

Indigenous businesses and ICIP

At Terri Janke and Company, we also work with many Indigenous organisations or businesses who want to ensure that their ICIP is protected when they are consulting or working on projects with their clients. We have done this for clients including language centres and health organisations, and consultants.

I am often approached by Indigenous people who want to start a business and make commercial use of their cultural heritage or ICIP. Indigenous language words, traditional knowledge of bush tucker and medicines, information about cultural sites, and traditional cultural expressions such as art, design and song are some examples of ICIP that may be used in business.

Indigenous business owners want to identify their products and services as being 'Indigenous', and may also have knowledge and skills handed down to them which they wish to promote in return for economic benefits. Indigenous Cultural and Intellectual Property belongs to the group of Aboriginal and Torres Strait Islander people that have culturally inherited this heritage, and Indigenous businesses should follow ICIP protocols and consult with the custodians of any knowledge they wish to commercialise.

Another issue Indigenous people face in business is when they go to work for an organisation and bring their knowledge and personal culture to the workplace. Usually, an employer will own any IP that their employees create in the course of their work. But what if an Indigenous person is bringing their ICIP to the business? Does the employer have the right to use that ICIP after the employee leaves? Indigenous cultural protocols would probably say no, and it is best that these issues are discussed at the outset, when a person is employed.

Commercialising Indigenous knowledge

A common question that businesses have is whether permission is needed to commercially use the cultural assets of Indigenous people – our knowledge, stories, languages, arts, bush medicines and traditional foods. How can businesses ethically engage with Indigenous people, land and knowledge – whether in bush products businesses, pharmaceutical companies, architecture and construction projects, technology companies, or any other industry?

Chapter by chapter throughout this book, we have looked closely at those issues. The short answer is that current Australian intellectual property laws do not legally require consent to be obtained from Indigenous groups to use and commercially exploit Indigenous cultural heritage. However, ICIP is a continuing cultural asset that belongs to an Indigenous clan, community or family, and there is a cultural obligation to consider the impact on the group and to seek consent from people who can speak for the collective.

Some points to consider are:

1. **Are you a member of the cultural group that owns this knowledge?**
   If you are not, consider whether you should use this knowledge at all. If you still want to go ahead, consult with and get consent from relevant Indigenous people and/or organisations. Check if your business idea is acceptable to elders, traditional knowledge holders or relevant community organisations. Even if you are culturally linked to the ICIP, you should get consent from your family, clan or community. It is best practice to get this in writing.

2. **Is the proposed commercial use derogatory, and will it affect the cultural integrity of the ICIP or the group?**
   For example, the Navajo people in the US objected to the use of their cultural designs on underwear and on alcohol flasks.

3. **Have you addressed benefit sharing with the community?**
   If you are making money from the group's cultural assets, you should consider ways of sharing this with the group.

It's great to see big businesses in Australia licensing artworks, such as clothing company Gorman licensing designs from Mangkaja Arts in the Kimberley, and Qantas licensing the artwork of famous artists Paddy Bedford (Gija), Emily Kame Kngwarreye (Anmatyerre) and Rene Kulitja (Pitjantjatjara) for designs on plane fuselages, in conjunction with Balarinji, an Indigenous design team (see chapter 3). Large companies are licensing the works with Indigenous artists and negotiating the terms of the agreement.

ICIP protocols that are based on the True Tracks principles can help guide ICIP management and protection in business. As noted in chapter 1, Lendlease, a multinational construction company, developed their document *Place and Protocols: Indigenous Art, Languages and Cultures* by working with our firm, and we have presented workshops around Australia to their team.

The bottom line is: Don't take knowledge without permission from traditional custodians. Consult with and seek consent from cultural custodians.

Indigenous language words in business names

What about Indigenous languages? Can businesses use Indigenous language words for their business names, products, trade marks, domain names, brands, services or programs? The answer is: don't just do it flippantly because you think it is trendy, but think about it deeply. Consider the impact of the word or term. Do you have a connection to that culture? Why are you doing it? Then ask:

- Is it appropriate for the word to be used in the proposed context?
- Will it be misleading or deceptive? Will people think it is associated with an Indigenous clan or community?

- Has the proposed use been discussed with relevant traditional owners?
- Has consent been obtained to use the Indigenous language word? You will need to obtain free, prior and informed consent from the relevant owners for its use.
- What recognition and attribution will be given to the traditional owners?
- If the context is extremely wide and the use is commercial, consider how benefits can be shared with the traditional language owners' group, and enter into a benefit sharing agreement.

There have been cases of Indigenous languages being used without permission in advertising, and trade marked by businesses for marketing their products. Advertising agencies also need to consider cultural protocols when they are acting for their clients, not only in language but in art forms like visual arts, music and dance (see chapters 3, 5 and 8).

Borobi, the surfing koala

In 2018, the Commonwealth Games were held on the Gold Coast, the traditional lands of the Yugambeh people. The mascot for these games was a blue koala named Borobi, the Yugambeh word for koala. A couple of years prior, the Gold Coast 2018 Commonwealth Games organising committee filed two trade marks – one for the word 'Borobi' and another for a blue koala image.[14] This was opposed by Jabree, the registered cultural heritage body for the Yugambeh people, which argued that the committee had failed to appropriately consult with and follow the decision-making processes of the group, and therefore failed to comply with the *Aboriginal Cultural Heritage Act 2003* (Qld) under which the organisation was established. Jabree felt that this use of the language word and totem was offensive and exploitative, despite other members of the group agreeing to it. The opposition was refused, with the delegate not accepting the arguments that the use of the trade mark was likely to offend or scandalise in a way contemplated by the Trade Marks Act.[15]

The Borobi case highlights issues for those seeking to file trade marks with Indigenous content. The consultation process should be wide and in line with cultural protocols, and you should consider integrity and interpretation, and the impact on the cultural dynamic.

Another interesting case in respect of offensiveness is the football team Washington Redskins, its name a derogatory slur referring to Native Americans. This trade mark was removed after years of lobbying from Native Americans. While the law has not changed, the case highlighted the impact that offensive marks can have.

Telstra and muru-d

In 2013, Telstra carefully included Indigenous language in the name of their start-up accelerator program based in Sydney. Telstra wanted to choose an Aboriginal language word from the local area to acknowledge that the business operates on Aboriginal land belonging to the Eora nation. To do this, Telstra engaged Shane Phillips, Bundjalung, Wonnarua and Bidjigal, and a respected leader in the Sydney Aboriginal community, who acted as an ambassador and cultural consultant. The name chosen for the start-up was muru-D: muru means 'pathway' in the Eora language, and the D stands for 'digital', as the organisation is a digital business incubator hub.

Shane is currently the CEO of Tribal Warrior Aboriginal Corporation, an Indigenous mentoring and cultural tourism company. He is also a founding member and Director of the Australian Indigenous Chamber of Commerce that supports Aboriginal people in business. Shane says, 'Sharing culture leads to strong business partnerships, we work together on a common future.'[16]

Shane provided cultural consent for use of the word muru by consulting with the Aboriginal community. He spoke with key Aboriginal stakeholder organisations in the area, including the Metropolitan Local Aboriginal Land Council. It was essential that the idea received the full support of these organisations. Shane also consulted with local community elders and language experts to make sure the use was culturally appropriate and respectful. We included an ICIP clause in the contract that recognises the cultural ownership of the Aboriginal language word and the associated cultural knowledge.

A logo was developed for the business by Telstra in consultation with Shane. At the launch of the business, he presented a welcome to country ceremony. James Simon, a local Indigenous artist, produced an artwork for the office space. Telstra continues to keep links with Shane by consulting him on their use of the brand name. It also made a community grant to the Clean Slate language and cultural project in Redfern, and re-consulted with Shane on future uses, including its use in new offices in Singapore.

Big business and Indigenous cultural heritage

Running my own business made me think deeply about the impact of business activities on Indigenous peoples. Indigenous communities are often vulnerable to the impacts of business and commercial development. 'Many of the world's indigenous people have suffered abuse, discrimination and marginalization, including at the hands of business,' the United Nations Global Compact says.[17] There are countless stories of multinational oil, mining and gas companies extracting resources from indigenous land, or big pharmaceutical and biotechnology companies accessing plants and using indigenous knowledge for new inventions.

The case of Rio Tinto

Too often we have seen the extraction of natural resources from traditional lands at the expense of Indigenous cultural heritage. The mining giant Rio Tinto attracted media attention after destroying a sacred site on the land of the Puutu Kunti Kurrama and Pinikura peoples (PKKP) in May 2020. To expand an iron ore mine, the company blew up 46,000-year-old caves in Juukan Gorge, in the Hamersley Range of the Pilbara in Western Australia. The company's investors raised the alarm and questioned the ethics of the act.

Unsurprisingly, Rio Tinto faced widespread criticism for its actions. The PKKP peoples lost Dreamings and songlines in the caves' destruction. This was deeply devastating, leaving traditional owners to grieve the loss of connection to their ancestors and their land.[18] The apology says Reconciliation Australia revoked its endorsement of Rio Tinto's Reconciliation Action Plan (RAP) and suspended the company from their RAP program.[19] The lack of consultation and regard for ancient cultural heritage has raised ethical questions, and Rio Tinto's action was widely condemned.

At the time, Rio Tinto had had an established relationship with the PKKP people for almost a decade.[20] Professor Marcia Langton has researched the relations between Indigenous communities and mining companies. Her 2015 research paper for the Minerals Council of Australia, *From Conflict to Cooperation*, looked closely at the way the Australian minerals industry engages with Indigenous peoples.[21] Professor Langton called the loss 'heart-breaking', and said it was 'insulting that such a gross act of vandalism was timed to occur at the commencement of Reconciliation Week. This represents for Indigenous Australians a sharp turning point in relations with this company.'[22]

In the wake of the blast, Rio Tinto launched an inquiry and publicly apologised, and the company's CEO and two other key executives were forced to step down. Many mining agreements with traditional owners contain 'gag' clauses that restrict traditional owners from raising concerns about the destruction of cultural heritage; the company has said it will 'modernise those agreements' and will not enforce any gag clauses. 'We are absolutely committed to listening, learning and changing,' Rio Tinto's apology statement said. 'The destruction of the rock shelters should not have happened.'[23]

In 2021, the Senate conducted an inquiry into the incident. Aboriginal people call for an overhaul of the heritage laws so that they have a say in caring for their sites, heritage and associated knowledge. Unfortunately, the law does not properly protect Indigenous cultural sites, and Rio Tinto's action was legal under the Western Australian Aboriginal Heritage Act 1972. This shows the limitation of these laws, and that the legal focus is not on protecting heritage but enabling development. There is a need for changes to these laws.

Business is an opportunity

When I decided to set up my law firm, I felt I had to do something that would shine a light and open opportunities for my children and our future descendants. I wanted to let them know that they could imagine, create and innovate, and that their ideas could contribute to the Australian economy. I wanted them to see a world where Indigenous peoples are empowered to prosper in their creative and business endeavours. Being in business opened my mind to the impacts that the commercial world has on society and culture. Businesspeople are movers and shakers. Business is a space for opportunity.

When businesses act on human rights, they also influence the choices of consumers and investors. The responses to the killing of George Floyd and the Black Lives Matter movement in the US in 2020, at the height of the COVID-19 pandemic, showed this clearly. It prompted businesses around the world to declare their support and solidarity. Statements of support from huge multinational corporations and small businesses were released. Donations were pledged. Danish toy company Lego called for marketing of their police-related products to be removed, and pledged $4 million in donations. In the United States, McDonald's pledged $1 million to the National Association for the Advancement of Colored People (NAACP), a small slice of its approximately $21 billion in revenue in 2019.[24]

But the type of systemic racism spotlighted by Black Lives Matter had been happening for years. In Australia, Indigenous people have had fewer employment and education opportunities, workplaces have been exploitative and have limited the opportunities for Indigenous people, and the statistics on Indigenous deaths in custody are shocking. It is now widely known that more than 450 Indigenous people have died in police custody since the 1991 Royal Commission into Aboriginal Deaths in Custody.[25] In Australia, people protested in the streets of major cities and towns, from Melbourne to Brisbane, from Perth to Byron Bay, from Adelaide to Innisfail in Far North Queensland. Black Lives Matter has pushed Australians to think about how our corporations and organisations include diverse cultural backgrounds, where the blind spots are, and how we can come together to bridge the divide.

Three weeks after the death of George Floyd, I sat in the home of my niece, Turia Pitt, a mining engineer, athlete, positive businesswomen, motivational speaker and author. She had set up the Spend With Them initiative in early 2020 after the devastating bushfires on the NSW south coast, inspired to make a difference and connect customers with small businesses in her home region. Turia had always asked me about Indigenous culture, but that day she wanted to know how she could do something.

Turia has an Australian father and a Tahitian mother, and she wanted to know more about the Indigenous peoples of the land on which she lived – the Yuin people. As a first step, she added an acknowledgment of country to her book *Happy*, published in late 2020. 'I grew up on the south coast of Australia but only learned the names of the local Aboriginal people in the past two years,' Turia told me. 'I want to know more about Indigenous culture. I want to learn more by reading books, reaching out to the people in the community. I want to make the change.'

We spoke about all the shifts and changes we could make if businesspeople were mobilised to work together to make a difference. There is a need for businesses to consider the UNDRIP principles of free, prior informed consent, especially where cultural heritage is impacted. This heritage is as valuable as the Pyramids, and the knowledge associated with it is part of the oldest living cultures in the world. Businesses can develop and follow protocols based on the True Tracks principles, including these in RAPs to assist in Indigenous engagement and to respect Indigenous cultural and intellectual property. Whether you are an employer, employee, customer, supplier, consumer or community member, you have a positive role to play in respecting Indigenous culture in the world of business.

WHAT YOU CAN DO ...

- Consider how you business practices might be open opportunities for Indigenous businesses, and support and promote the rights of Indigenous peoples. Refer to the *Australian Business Guide to Implementing the UN Declaration on the Rights of Indigenous Peoples*, listed in the Resources below.
- Do not appropriate Indigenous culture and knowledge in your business. Undertake consultations and get consent for use of Indigenous knowledge and cultural heritage material (e.g. Indigenous languages, plant and medicinal knowledge, etc.).
- Get permission before filming on Indigenous lands or using any images of Indigenous people for business or advertising purposes.
- Engage in genuine collaborations with communities and Indigenous-led organisations that empower Indigenous people.
- Develop a Reconciliation Action Plan (RAP) for your business.
- Develop ICIP protocols for your business.
- Choose Indigenous suppliers – become a member of Supply Nation.
- Employ Indigenous people and create meaningful career pathways for them.
- Ensure a culturally safe and culturally diverse workplace. Train staff in cultural competency.
- If your business is a retail outlet, make sure you only sell authentic Indigenous products.
- Be a conscious consumer. Before you buy, ask: 'Does this business and its products respect Indigenous peoples and cultures?'

Resources

The Australian Business Guide to Implementing the UN Declaration on the Rights of Indigenous Peoples (Global Compact Network Australia, KPMG and UTS, 2020): https://unglobalcompact.org.au/wp-content/uploads/2020/11/Australian-Business-Guide-to-Implementing-the-UN-Declaration-on-the-Rights-of-Indigenous-People_FINAL.pdf
Indigenous Business Australia (IBA): www.iba.gov.au
Reconciliation Australia: www.reconciliation.org.au
RAP Development Process: www.reconciliation.org.au/wp-content/uploads/2018/05/rap-development-process-1.pdf
Supply Nation: https://supplynation.org.au
Indigenous Procurement Policy (IPP): www.niaa.gov.au/indigenous-affairs/economic-development/indigenous-procurement-policy-ipp
Welcome to Country or Acknowledgement of Country: www.indigenous.gov.au/contact-us/welcome_acknowledgement-country
Australasian Centre for Corporate Responsibility (ACCR): www.accr.org.au
Corporate Social Responsibility & Human Rights (Australian Human Rights Commission, 2008): https://humanrights.gov.au/our-work/corporate-social-responsibility-human-rights
The Business Reference Guide to the UN Declaration on the Rights of Indigenous Peoples (UN Global Compact, 2013): www.unglobalcompact.org/library/541
Indigenous Peoples' Rights and the Role of Free, Prior and Informed Consent (UN Global Compact, 2014): www.unglobalcompact.org/library/931
Indigenous Joint Ventures (Terri Janke and Company/Indigenous Business Australia, 2018): https://www.iba.gov.au/wp-content/uploads/Indigenous_JV_InfoGuide.pdf
Law Way: Indigenous Business and the Law (Terri Janke and Company, 2013): www.terrijanke.com.au/law-way-publication
Terri Janke, Keynote Presentation at the IBA Strong Women Strong Business Conference, 2018: www.strongwomenstrongbusiness.com/conferences/conference-2018/swsb-conference-keynotes

Notes

1. Terri Janke, *Minding Culture: Case Studies on Intellectual Property and Traditional Cultural Expressions*, World Intellectual Property Organization, Geneva, 2003, <www.wipo.int/edocs/pubdocs/en/tk/781/wipo_pub_781.pdf>.
2. Australian Human Rights Commission, *A Quick Guide to Australian Discimination Laws*, AHRC, 2014, <https://humanrights.gov.au/sites/default/files/GPGB_quick_guide_to_discrimination_laws_0.pdf>.
3. United Nations Global Compact, *The Business Reference Guide to the UN Declaration on the Rights of Indigenous Peoples*, UN Global Compact, New York, 2013, p. 11, <https://www.unglobalcompact.org/library/541>.
4. United Nations Global Compact, *The Business Reference Guide to the UN Declaration on the Rights of Indigenous Peoples*, p. 74.
5. United Nations Global Compact, *The Business Reference Guide to the UN Declaration on the Rights of Indigenous Peoples*, p. 7.
6. Australian Government, *Welcome to Country or Acknowledgement of Country*, indigenous.

gov.au, 2020, <www.indigenous.gov.au/contact-us/welcome_acknowledgement-country>.
7   Supply Nation, *How We Verify Aboriginal and Torres Strait Islander Businesses*, Supply Nation, 2020, <https://supplynation.org.au/benefits/indigenous-business/>.
8   Laura Berry, personal communication, 22 March 2021.
9   Supply Nation, *Supply Nation Registered and Certified Suppliers Terms and Conditions*, Supply Nation, 2020, <https://supplynation.org.au/terms-and-conditions/suppliers/>.
10 Supply Nation, *Supply Nation Registered and Certified Suppliers Terms and Conditions*.
11 AIATSIS, *Core Cultural Learning*, AIATSIS,. n.d., <https://aiatsis.gov.au/about/what-we-do/core-cultural-learning>.
12 Karen Mundine, email correspondence, 16 January 2021.
13 Karen Mundine, email correspondence, 16 January 2021.
14 IP Australia, *Trade Mark 1762487* <https://search.ipaustralia.gov.au/trademarks/search/view/1762487>; IP Australia, *Trade Mark 1762488* <https://search.ipaustralia.gov.au/trademarks/search/view/1762488>.
15 *Jabree Ltd v Gold Coast Commonwealth Games Corporation* [2017] ATMO 156.
16 Shane Phillips, personal communication, 19 March 2021.
17 United Nations Global Compact, *Indigenous Peoples*, UN Global Compact, n.d., <www.unglobalcompact.org/what-is-gc/our-work/social/indigenous-people>.
18 Matthew Hall, 'Anthropologists slam Rio Tinto for destroying ancient Aboriginal site', *Mining Technology*, 3 June 2020, <www.mining-technology.com/features/anthropologists-rio-tinto-aboriginal-site/>.
19 Reconciliation Australia, *Statement on Rio Tinto*, Reconciliation Australia, 9 June 2020, <www.reconciliation.org.au/statement-on-rio-tinto/>.
20 Rio Tinto, *Statement on Juukan Gorge*, Rio Tinto, 31 May 2020, <www.riotinto.com/en/news/releases/2020/Statement-on-Juukan-Gorge->.
21 Marcia Langton, *From Conflict to Cooperation: Transformations and Challenges in the Engagement Between the Australian Minerals Industry and Australian Indigenous Peoples*, research paper produced for the Minerals Council of Australia, Minerals Council of Australia, Canberra, February 2015, <https://minerals.org.au/news/conflict-cooperation-prof-marcia-langton>.
22 Matthew Hall, 'Anthropologists slam Rio Tinto ....'.
23 Rio Tinto, in Barbara Smith and Associated Press, 'Rio Tinto says executives will lose their bonuses after blowing up 46,000-year-old rock shelters – but some say that's not enough', *Business Insider*, 25 August 2020, <www.businessinsider.com/rio-tinto-ceo-loses-35m-over-destroyed-indigenous-sites-2020-8>.
24 Elly Duncan, 'Brands are speaking up on Black Lives Matter. But are they taking action behind the scenes?', *The Drum (ABC News)*, 13 June 2020, <www.abc.net.au/news/2020-06-13/brands-on-black-lives-matter/12344476>.
25 Australian Institute of Criminology, *New Deaths in Custody Report Released* [media release], Australian Institute of Criminology, 16 December 2020, <www.aic.gov.au/media-centre/news/new-deaths-custody-report-released>.

17
APPRECIATE, DON'T APPROPRIATE: IT'S FASHIONABLE TO BE CULTURALLY RESPECTFUL

Each year, the Indigenous fashion show 'From Country to Couture' is held on Larrakia country at the Darwin Aboriginal Art Fair. It began in 2015, to foster community relationships and collaborations, and to bring together Aboriginal and Torres Strait Islander fine art and high-end fashion. The runway showcases bright-coloured prints and designs on silks and cottons, hand-dyed and hand-printed fabrics and handwoven bags.[1] Cairns Indigenous Art Fair has also had a fashion show, focusing on Queensland art and fashion creators, as part of its cultural program. I attended the event in 2018 at the Tanks Arts Centre in Cairns. It was a fashion performance with several designers showcased. The vibrant colours of the artworks by Mornington Islander artists were reproduced on clothing, and Indigenous models showed off the outfits, stealing the show. Music, dance and performance were entwined; it was better than Paris, New York or Milan because it was original, fresh and Indigenous.

Australia's fashion industry generates $25 billion every year,[2] but Indigenous fashion has not been celebrated as part of mainstream Australian fashion. Yatu Widders Hunt, an Indigenous social media commentator and advocate, has been frustrated at this: 'Indigenous fashion is a thriving industry,' she says. 'We just need to shine the spotlight on it, and give opportunities to Aboriginal and Torres Strait Islander designers.'[3]

Yatu is on the board of First Nations Fashion + Design (FNFD), launched by Torres Strait Islander designer Grace Lillian Lee in 2018 to support the growth and voice of the Indigenous fashion industry and strengthen its place in the Australian fashion narrative. 'I wanted to enable and create opportunities for [Indigenous] people like myself to be able to connect with their lineage through the act of creating textiles and being a part of fashion performances,'[4] Grace says. 'It's powerful to have your voice heard in the fashion space, it's also beautiful and a lot of fun.'[5] The launch of this organisation was the catalyst for the first National Indigenous Fashion Awards that took place in 2020, celebrating many of our Indigenous designers. The First Nations Fashion Council (FNFC) was also launched in 2020 to provide mentorship and links to industry bodies, including the Australian Fashion Council.

Indigenous fashion is expanding throughout the world, too. Vancouver Indigenous Fashion Week (VIFW) in Canada was first held in 2018 to showcase indigenous fashion designers and artisans. In Aotearoa (New Zealand), Miromoda, the Indigenous Māori Fashion Apparel Board, was established to advance the quality status of Māori fashion design and to raise its artistic and professional standards. Miromoda nurtures Māori designs; they had their first show at NZ Fashion Week in 2009 and are heading there again in 2021.

The rise of Indigenous fashion designers

Recently there has been a rise in Australian Indigenous-owned and -led fashion houses and designers appearing at Indigenous art fairs, and on the national and international runways. But many have worked in this space in the past, including Bronwyn Bancroft, who set up Designer Aboriginals in the 1980s, and Lenore Dembski Paperbark Woman, a model turned fashion designer whose celebrated work was included in fashion shows of the 1990s.

Kirrikin, a 100 per cent Aboriginal-owned business printing artwork onto luxury clothing and accessories, is owned by Wonnarua woman Amanda Healy who lives in Perth, Western Australia. Kirrikin (or kirikin) translates to 'Sunday's best clothes' in the Wonnarua language, says Amanda.[6] Kirrikin designs are seen at NAIDOC Balls and corporate events. Earthy orange designs and the colours of the sea feature in their jumpsuits and kaftans; there is also a swimwear range. Kirrikin licenses art from Aboriginal artists including Emma Kerslake, Palawa artist, and has also licensed art designs to other fashion manufacturers, such as cycling wear made by Babici.

Artist and designer Shannon Brett (Wakka Wakka, Butchulla and Gurang Gurang) has a long history of working in Indigenous communities and a background working with textiles and fashion. Currently, Shannon is designing fabrics, garments and accessories using a colourful palette for her internationally exhibited fashion label LORE.[7] Debra Beale is a NSW artist who makes beautiful designs that she markets under the label Deboriginal, currently being registered as a trade mark. Clothing The Gaps is a Melbourne-based Aboriginal-owned and -led social enterprise driven by Gunditjmara woman Laura Thompson and co-founded with ongoing business and impact partner, non-Indigenous woman Sarah Sheridan. As a social enterprise they commit to an ethical, sustainable and responsible business model while donating at least 51 per cent of the profits from sales to the Clothing The Gaps Foundation. The Clothing The Gaps Foundation is committed to adding years to Aboriginal peoples' lives across the country.

Have you seen the intricately woven necklaces and body pieces by Grace Lillian Lee? Grace is a descendant of the Meriam people of Mer (Murray Island). Her fashion pieces reflect the cultural practice of 'grasshopper weaving', which she learned from renowned artist and mentor, Uncle Ken Thaiday from Erub (Darnley) Island.[8] Grasshopper weaving traditionally uses palm leaves to make toys and baskets.

I first met Grace when we were both sharing the Cairns TED Talk stage in 2016. Her clothing and accessories have been showcased in Cairns, Darwin, Sydney and Melbourne, and internationally in San Francisco and New Zealand, and are held in collections such as the Museum of Applied Arts and Sciences. Grace has worked with lots of Indigenous artists, including the community on Mornington Island and at remote art centres using techniques like weaving, silkscreen, batik, natural dyeing and embroidery.

There are also Indigenous businesses making textiles used for fashion. Others, such as Bima Wear, have been operating independently for decades. Bima Wear was established by Tiwi women in 1969 on Bathurst Island, one of the Tiwi Islands off the coast of Darwin, and their fabrics feature cultural prints from the Tiwi Islands. Across the Top End of the Northern Territory, there are also businesses like Bábbarra Designs, a social enterprise for women in Maningrida and the surrounding homelands. The artists here screen-print their beautiful designs and stories onto textiles. Not too far from Maningrida, in the town of Ramingining, is Bula'bula Arts, which has a similar business.

While Indigenous designers, artists and community groups weave their magic in the fashion industry and their designs start new trends, the risk of cultural appropriation increases. There have been instances where designers, fashion labels and manufacturers have used Indigenous cultural elements without following proper procedures.

Inspiration or stealing?
Cultural appropriation in the fashion industry

What is cultural appropriation? Brigitte Vézina, an intellectual property lawyer and specialist in cultural appropriation, defines cultural appropriation as 'the act by a member of a relatively dominant culture of taking a traditional cultural expression and repurposing it in a different context, without authorization, acknowledgement and/or compensation, in a way that causes harm to the traditional cultural expression holder(s)'.[9]

The fashion industry has a controversial track record when it comes to appropriating Indigenous cultural expressions. Over the years, traditional designs and cultural symbols have been misappropriated by top fashion labels including Gucci, Dior, Valentino, Carolina Herrera, Chanel and more.[10] A Victoria's Secret model walked the catwalk in 2012 wearing a Native American headdress and a bikini; the model later apologised. The company then made the same mistake again in 2017.[11] Urban Outfitters released a line of products that deeply offended people of the Navajo nation, illegally using the Navajo name and their cultural designs on underwear, flasks and other products. This led to a trademark infringement lawsuit that was eventually settled, involving a supply and licence agreement to collaborate on a line of jewellery. An arrangement like this is a good solution to the misuse of Indigenous culture in the fashion industry.

In 2013, Nike produced a range of women's exercise clothing based on the Samoan Pe'a tattoo. This traditional tattoo design of dense patterns covering the thighs, buttocks and lower waist is restricted to Samoan men as a culturally significant coming-of-age ritual. Nike printed a very similar pattern onto its 'Pro Tattoo Tech Gear', including women's leggings, sports bras, jumpsuits and singlets. Many found this to be highly insensitive and inappropriate, and Nike removed them from sale.[12]

And in 2017, French high-fashion brand Chanel released a 'designer boomerang' priced at A$1930. It was made of wood and black resin with the Chanel logo stuck in the middle. That incident triggered a backlash, deeply offending Indigenous people in Australia, who were angered that the Chanel product had no context or connection to its Indigenous origins. Boomerangs are works of artistic craftmanship and are important identifiers of Indigenous culture. Many Indigenous communities, such as the artists at Maruku Arts in Central Australia, carve and hand-craft boomerangs. Chanel did not identify with any Indigenous clans or communities, and it was unclear as to whether any Indigenous people were consulted or involved in producing the product.

Nayuka Gorrie, a Kurnai/Gunai, Gunditjmara, Wiradjuri and Yorta Yorta writer and performer, was critical of the product, joking on twitter, 'Have decided to save for the next three years so I can connect with my culture via @CHANEL.'[13]

The interesting thing about the Chanel boomerang is that Chanel potentially could have worked with an Aboriginal artist on a collaboration. Where did the Chanel designer find the information to develop the item? They might have gone to research publications, or to anthropological and ethnographic texts. They might have searched the internet and found Aboriginal craft. Intellectual property law does not recognise that the concept or idea of the boomerang belongs to the Australian Aboriginal people. But items of cultural expression like the boomerang are an important part of the living culture of Indigenous groups today. There is a need for more education for designers, and better recognition of Indigenous cultural content in the law.

'It's fairly common for fashion designers to take stylistic inspiration from a variety of sources,' writes Brigitte Vézina. 'Could you imagine living in a world where designers had to stay inside the lines of their own culture? What a lacklustre world that would be. Cross-cultural influences are nothing new and they enrich our world, but there's a boundary of respectfulness that needs to be set.'[14]

That boundary can be defined through protocols and consent agreements that ensure the source culture is respected and involved in the new creations. The fashion industry needs to adopt protocols for how they develop and use Indigenous design, and to give opportunities to Indigenous artists and fashion designers. Copying from Indigenous cultures is appropriating someone else's story. We want to keep those connections to the living culture and people strong to avoid economic and cultural harm. This means truly collaborating with Indigenous artists and designers to bring their visions to life, whether that's in new clothing lines, in fashion photo shoots or on catwalks.[15]

Intellectual property and Indigenous fashion design

It is clear that Indigenous peoples see the appropriation of their art and culture by fashion designers as cultural appropriation. However, the law doesn't protect them because if the appropriation is general – if it has the look of traditional dress, for example – and does not substantially copy from an existing designer's work, it is not usually an infringement of copyright. This 'look' or reference to traditional dress is not protected, as it does not meet the originality requirements of copyright law. Copyright protects the designs of clothing, hats, jewellery and shoes that are 'original' as 'artistic works', but traditional designs are in the public domain according to the law. So, it becomes a question of ethics and protocols.

These were issues we discussed at a roundtable at WIPO's Intergovernmental Committee on Intellectual Property and Genetic Resources, Traditional Knowledge and Folklore (IGC) session in Geneva in 2016. The rest of the world has issues with designers copying indigenous fashion too. Some countries do have laws that protect traditional designs, however. In Mexico and Panama, you can register traditional costume and design styles to protect them. In 2015, the news that French designer Isabel Marant had copied a design belonging to the indigenous community of Santa Maria Tlahuitoltepec (the Mixe community) in the state of Oaxaca, Mexico, caused great controversy. According to the media, Isabel Marant copied the designs of the blouses and was trying to obtain protection over those designs to prevent the Mexican community from 'manufacturing and commercialising' the blouses with those designs. Then Marant clarified that the designs had come from the Mixe community, and denied that she was trying to obtain protection over them.[16] The label was in the media again for a similar issue in 2020.

I travelled to Mexico in 2019, where my best friend Veronica Dounis, a South American-Australian, organised a special trip to visit indigenous Oaxacan artisans who made traditional dresses in colourful fabrics with embroidery, including huipils, as well as hand-woven rugs and bags. I was interested to learn how these local indigenous artisans set up their arts businesses. On this visit, the women in business that we met worked in small family businesses, and were supported by micro-loans through the help of a not-for-profit organisation. It was good to see how they labelled their products to note the authenticity of the items. Some artisans were suspicious of tourists filming, worried that their designs would be stolen. As in Australia, Mexican indigenous people have called for copyright protection for traditional cultural expressions.[17] In 2020, the Mexican Federal Copyright Law was amended to include a section on popular cultures and traditional cultural expressions. Companies must get written consent from the indigenous community for use of their cultural expression. The difficulty is enforcing this right internationally.

Cultural appropriation remains a problem. In 2021, Australian designer Zimmermann was called out on social media for appropriating the designs of traditional dresses of the Mazatec people of Oaxaca. Zimmermann is reported to have contacted the Instituto Oaxaqueño de las Artesanías, the government body that represents the artisans of the Oaxaca region, offering a formal apology for the offence caused.[18] The dresses were removed from sale.

Trade mark law

Trade marks can help to protect brand names, especially Indigenous words, but not many Indigenous fashion labels register trade marks, and when they do, they may not register them in all countries where they expect to market their products.

TRADE MARKS AND FASHION BRANDS

In the fashion industry, a company's name or logo is generally its most valuable asset. However, to profit from your fashion brand via sales or licensing, you must first register your brand as a trade mark.

A fashion brand may consist of a combination of different features – a business name, a trade mark, particular shapes, distinctive colour schemes and labelling used to market products or services. Brands are used to distinguish and differentiate goods and services of traders in the market. Famous fashion brands in Australia include sass & bide and Alex Perry.

A trade mark is a word or logo that: (1) identifies one seller's goods and distinguishes them from goods sold by others; (2) signifies that all goods bearing the trade mark come from a single source; (3) signifies that all goods bearing the trade mark are of an equal level of quality; and (4) facilitates in the advertising and selling of goods. A trade mark will generally not be registrable if it is merely descriptive of the goods and services in question, meaning words that describe the qualities, features or functions of the product in a straightforward way that does not allow for differentiation.

Unfortunately, many emerging fashion companies fail to trade mark their name or logo. Then, after substantial money has been invested in promotions and public relations – such as business cards, invoices and signage – the company learns an expensive lesson: their 'brand name' has already been registered as a trade mark by another company and they are unable to register that particular brand name.

For example, the COWICHAN clothing trade mark in Canada is registered by the Cowichan Band Council of Cowichan Tribes, a First Nations organisation on Vancouver Island, as a certification trade mark to certify that their clothing has been hand-knitted in one piece in accordance with traditional tribal methods, by members of the Coast Salish Nation (the Cowichan are one group of the Coast Salish peoples), using raw, unprocessed, undyed, hand-spun wool made using traditional tribal methods. This trade mark appears to be in continuing use as part of the commercial activities of the Cowichan Band Council.

Designs law

Designs law too, does not help, as it protects only registered designs that are novel, and Indigenous traditional dress styles are deemed to be in the 'public domain'. The *Designs Act 2003* protects the overall appearance of a product resulting from one or more visual features of the product that are registered with IP Australia. Once examined and registered, a designer will own rights to the design of the item but there are some big issues with registered designs being enforced. Indigenous designers do not often use this law to protect their designs or any traditional Indigenous designs, motifs and symbols they use in their fashion. However, it has been used by some including Rene Kulitja, Jennifer Taylor and Pamela Taylor from Walkatjara Art in Uluru, who registered a design for a U-shaped bench in 2006.

Ethical collaborations in fashion

There are some great ethical collaborations between Indigenous and non-Indigenous designers, artists and organisations that have begun paving the way for a positive future in the fashion industry.

Mangkaja x Gorman

Lisa Gorman, founder of the Australian fashion label Gorman, teamed up with artists from Mangkaja Arts in Fitzroy Crossing, a small town in the Kimberley region of Western Australia, to create the 'Mangkaja x Gorman' collection in 2019. She worked closely with my friend Ngarralja Tommy May, a talented Wangkajunga and Walmajarri artist, one of the founders of the Karrayili Adult Education Centre that later became the Mangkaja arts centre.

Ngarralja Tommy May was one of the key people who initiated the project. Ngarralja says, 'We talked about this, we worked on this for a long time before anything happened. We did this the right way. The way things happened was all alright, nothing was stolen. This was my idea and I want it to run for a long time, I want it to have an impact.'[19]

Specially made artworks by Mangkaja artists were featured in the collection; the artists include Ngarralja Tommy May, Sonia Kurarra, Daisy Japulija, Nada Tigila Rawlins and Lisa Uhl. Their vibrant artworks were incorporated into dresses, skirts, shirts, raincoats, trousers and jackets. Indigenous models were featured in the campaign.

The project was a first for Lisa Gorman. 'I love the work of Indigenous artists and have always wanted to do a collaboration like this but wasn't sure how to go about it,' Lisa said. 'I wanted to make sure I followed a respectful and ethical approach.'[20] A key part of ensuring respect was allowing long time frames, and using written agreements or licences to protect the rights of the artists.

The licences were facilitated by the Copyright Agency, Australia's national copyright licensing organisation for the publishing, media, surveying and visual arts industries. CEO Adam Suckling noted that the Copyright Agency worked with Mangkaja and Gorman to negotiate 'fair and reasonable' licensing fees: 'We made sure terms, conditions, attributions and acknowledgment of the artists were negotiated to protect the artist and the reproduction of the artwork. And crucially, we ensured the artists had approval throughout the whole process, from concept to instore delivery, and the approach to promotion via online platforms and social media.'[21]

The clothing line was launched in 2019 at the Museum of Contemporary Art in Sydney's Circular Quay. It was a proud moment for the artists. Ngarralja delivered a speech in traditional language. The project sets a benchmark for future collaborations of its kind, showing us that fashion collaborations like this are possible when you follow cultural protocols and allow for long time frames.

Frillneck Australia

This approach also works for smaller projects. Terri Janke and Company drafted art licence agreements for Frillneck Australia, a 100 per cent Indigenous-owned business from Darwin, owned by Steven Ludwig. Frillneck wanted to develop a range of micromesh throws and hats that incorporated the artistic designs of four Aboriginal and Torres Strait Islander artists – Jennifer (Lulu) Coombes, Les Huddleston, Norma Chidanpee Benger and Eddie Janama Kitching. The licence protects the interests and rights of both parties, setting out the terms and conditions for the reproduction of the artwork on Frillneck products.[22]

Buluuy Mirrii

It was an exciting opportunity when Colleen Tighe Johnson, Gomeroi woman and fashion designer, contacted Terri Janke and Company wanting help to protect her works being showcased at the PLITZS New York City Fashion Week in 2017. Her award-winning label is called Buluuy Mirrii, meaning 'black star' in the Gomeroi language of south-east Australia.

The designs on Colleen's fashion garments are created by Gomeroi artists whose works are licensed to Colleen for use on the garments. Each garment is unique, depicting ancestral stories, symbols and traditional cultural expressions – that is, the ICIP – of the Gomeroi nation. Colleen is also passionate about environmental sustainability and thinks carefully about the materials she uses and the link to Mother Earth.[23]

Buluuy Mirrii proceeds are shared with the community. Colleen owns copyright to the Buluuy Mirrii designs and has a duty to safeguard the ICIP of the Indigenous peoples and communities who have shared and expressed their stories with her. She has developed a strong brand to protect the intellectual property rights in her fashion garments. It was great to be part of the project.

Reviving clothing traditions: Possum skin cloaks

What about the fashion that existed in Australia before invasion? You may be familiar with the possum skin cloak and the booka (kangaroo skin) cloak. These cloaks are now being created by Aboriginal artisans and are worn by Aboriginal people at special ceremonies. For example, Victorian Greens senator Lidia Thorpe wore a possum skin cloak when she was being sworn into parliament, as federal MP Ken Wyatt did with a kangaroo skin cloak. Indigenous university students and academics also wear them to academic ceremonies. (See chapter 4, page 106 for more on the revival of possum skin cloaks.)

Flags and fashion

The bright yellow circle against the red and black that is the Aboriginal flag is an unforgettable symbol of Aboriginal Australia. It became an official flag of Australia in 1995 under the law known as the *Flags Act 1953* (Cth). It has been used for protest and as a unifying symbol for Aboriginal people in Australia. It is not only used as a flag, but on clothing, bags, socks, stickers and magnets; it has been painted on murals, and even tattooed on skin (as is the case for Linda Burney, Wiradjuri woman and federal MP).

Many Aboriginal businesses have used it in some way, making it part of their logo or embedding it into their products.

As discussed in chapter 4, over the past couple of years, the copyright status of the Aboriginal flag has been in the spotlight. Is there copyright in the flag and who owns it? In 2019, the issue exploded in the media.

Harold Thomas, a Luritja artist, is the copyright owner of the flag. He has granted licensing rights for use of the flag to three companies: WAM Clothing, Flagworld and Gifts Mate. To reproduce the flag on clothing, in part or whole, you must get permission. But the flag is an item that many people want to wear proudly. This has caused enormous debate about whether Indigenous fashion producers, and football codes making jumpers, should have to pay the fees. It should be noted that under copyright law, it is perfectly legal for Harold Thomas, the copyright owner of the flag, and his exclusive licensee WAM Clothing, to seek licence fees. Thomas also has the right to be attributed as the creator of the design, and he also has the moral right of integrity, which means the work should not be altered in a way that changes it to be derogatory of his reputation. The love of the flag remains constant and the role of copyright in managing who can reproduce it has been called into question. Many Indigenous people have called for the Australian Government to compulsorily acquire the flag. Given that it is a nationally recognised flag, they argue, it should be able to be used freely like the other flags.

But compulsory acquiring of the flag for commercial purposes seems like taking away the rights to copyright that Indigenous artists have tried to get for so long. To take the rights away from Harold Thomas seems unjust. It could also set a dangerous precedent. In 2021, as I write this book, the Australian government is in negotiations with Harold Thomas to acquire the rights. Let's hope a deal is struck so that Indigenous people can use the flag to call for rights and celebrate culture. In the meantime, any reproductions of the flag will need to deal with Thomas's copyright, and moral rights.

The Torres Strait Islander flag – the green, blue and green stripes behind a white dhari (headdress) and star – was also legally recognised as an official flag of Australia under the Flags Act.[24] It was designed by

Bernard Namok Snr from Thursday Island in 1992, and was the winning entry in a design competition.[25] The five points of the star represents the five major island groups in the Torres Strait, and the star itself represents an unspecified navigational star.[26] The copyright owner is the Torres Strait Island Regional Council (TSIRC) and their 15 communities. To reproduce it, you must request permission from the TSIRC.

The Australian national flag is in the public domain, and anyone can use or reproduce it for commercial purposes without formal permission, as long as this is in line with government guidelines.[27]

Setting a trend of respect

My mum, Joanna Janke, makes clothes. In the mid-1990s, she bought some Aboriginal material – white, black and ochre brown, with lines, birds and round circles – from a fabric shop to make a shirt for me. It turned out that the fabric was the same one that infringed copyright in the second Johnny Bulun Bulun case, *Bulun Bulun v R & T Textiles* (1998). (See chapter 3, page 78.) We felt devastated that we might have been disrespecting culture by making clothes with these sacred country images, especially without consent or an acknowledgment of connection. Obviously I never wore the shirt, and make sure to always check the source of material. The case put an end to the sale of the fabric, but it left suspicion and harm for Mr Bulun Bulun and his community, and for us as well. I'm sure a lot of people feel like this.

The fashion industry has seen many cultural appropriation controversies. It's time to appreciate and not appropriate. Indigenous cultural expression is part of a living, vibrant, contemporary culture. Fashion designers may think that they can seek inspiration from a number of sources, and this leads them to dip into the Indigenous cultural bag. However, care must be taken not to appropriate culture: this can be seen as insensitive, uninformed and offensive.

In many of the controversial cases, the issue could have been avoided if there was communication with source communities, or if the fashion house had engaged with Indigenous artists and designers to collaborate. It's good to see that others *do* collaborate. There is a need to establish genuine, positive collaborations through licensing and consent agreements, as well as ICIP protocols. These agreements could cover issues such as licensed rights, attribution, payment and benefit sharing, as well as recognition for the source communities and marketing.

Further, we must support the development of an Indigenous fashion design industry that brings understanding of cultural traditions and that has connections with the Indigenous community. The stereotypes in the industry must also be addressed so that the environment is culturally safe. Fashion can be a way to express culture and share culture, and if we empower Indigenous people to be creators and collaborators, we can set a trend of respect.

WHAT YOU CAN DO ...

- Support Indigenous fashion designers, brands and respectful collaborations.
- Support Indigenous models to showcase Australian fashion. Do not buy clothes and fashion items that appropriate Indigenous cultures.
- Follow the True Tracks principles and protocols in your fashion projects.
- Engage in genuine collaborations that empower Indigenous people.
- Use art licensing agreements to license Aboriginal and Torres Strait Islander artwork for fashion garments.

Resources

National Indigenous Fashion Awards (NIFA): https://nifa.com.au
Aboriginal Bush Traders: Fashion: https://aboriginalbushtraders.com/pages/fashion
First Nations Fashion + Design: https://firstnationsfashiondesign.com/
Curbing Cultural Appropriation in the Fashion Industry (Brigitte Vézina, 2019): www.cigionline.org/sites/default/files/documents/paper%20no.213.pdf
Think Before You Appropriate: Things to Know and Questions to Ask in Order to Avoid Misappropriating Indigenous Cultural Heritage (Intellectual Property Issues in Cultural

Heritage Project, 2015): www.sfu.ca/ipinch/resources/teaching-resources/think-before-you-appropriate/
'Promoting ethical manufacture of Indigenous art products with art licensing agreements' (Terri Janke and Adam Broughton, 2019): www.terrijanke.com.au/post/2019/10/29/promoting-ethical-manufacture-of-indigenous-art-products-with-art-licensing-agreements
'Beware of bogus boomerangs: Should we protect traditional cultural expression that is deemed to be in the public domain?' (Terri Janke with Tamina Pitt, 2017): www.terrijanke.com.au/post/2017/08/31/beware-of-bogus-boomerangs-should-tce-laws-only-protect-those-things-that-are-not-already

Notes

1. Michael McHugh, 'From country to couture', *MiNDFOOD*, 10 August 2017, <www.mindfood.com/article/from-country-to-couture/>.
2. Australian Fashion Council (AFC), *Indigenous Fashion Update*, AFC, 3 September 2019, <https://ausfashioncouncil.com/council-of-textile-fashion-blog/2019/9/3/afc-indigenous-fashion-update>.
3. Yatu Widders Hunt, personal communication, 4 February 2021.
4. Grace Lillian Lee, *Culture to Catwalk: Grace Lillian Lee*, TEDx JCU Cairns, TEDx Talks, YouTube, 20 December 2016, <www.youtube.com/watch?v=vTqVWdZHhC8>.
5. Grace Lillian Lee, personal communication, 3 March 2021.
6. Kirrikin, *About Kirrikin*, Kirrikin, 2020, <https://kirrikin.com/pages/about-kirrikin>.
7. Shannon Brett, LORE, Shannon Brett, n.d., <www.shannonbrett.com/lore/4594958400>.
8. Post Office Gallery, *Grace Lillian Lee*, Federation University Australia, 2020, <https://federation.edu.au/pogallery/guirguis-new-art-prize-gnap/2019/grace-lillian-lee-qld>.
9. Brigitte Vézina, 'Curbing cultural appropriation in the fashion industry with intellectual property', *WIPO Magazine*, August 2019, <www.wipo.int/wipo_magazine/en/2019/04/article_0002.html>.
10. Brigitte Vézina, 'Cultural appropriation keeps happening because clear laws simply don't exist', *Centre for International Governance Innovation*, 24 December 2019, <www.cigionline.org/articles/cultural-appropriation-keeps-happening-because-clear-laws-simply-dont-exist>.
11. 'Victoria's Secret is being accused of cultural appropriation yet again', *Harpers Bazaar*, 23 November 2017, <www.harpersbazaar.com/uk/fashion/fashion-news/a13880726/victorias-secret-cultural-appropriation-native-american/>.
12. 'Nike offends Pasifika community with tattoo prints', *Otago Daily Times*, 14 August 2013, <www.odt.co.nz/sport/other-sport/nike-offends-pasifika-community-tattoo-prints>.
13. Nayuka Gorrie, 'Have decided to save ...' [tweet], Nayuka Gorrie, 15 May 2017, <https://twitter.com/NayukaGorrie/status/863972903552929792>.
14. Brigitte Vézina, 'Cultural appropriation keeps happening'.
15. For an overview of cultural appropriation in the fashion industry, see Brigitte Vézina, 'Curbing cultural appropriation in the fashion industry', *Centre for International Governance Innovation*, 3 April 2019, <www.cigionline.org/publications/curbing-cultural-appropriation-fashion-industry>.

16. Naomi Larsson, 'Inspiration or plagiarism? Mexicans seek reparations for French designer's look-alike blouse', *The Guardian*, 17 June 2015, <www.theguardian.com/global-development-professionals-network/2015/jun/17/mexican-mixe-blouse-isabel-marant>.
17. Gobierno de México, Secretaría de Cultura, *Pueblos y comunidades serán los titulares del derecho para el uso y aprovechamiento de sus elementos culturales*, 18 May 2019, <www.gob.mx/cultura/prensa/pueblos-y-comunidades-seran-los-titulares-del-derecho-para-el-uso-y-aprovechamiento-de-sus-elementos-culturales?idiom=es>.
18. Bianca O'Neill, 'With Zimmermann under fire for cultural appropriation, it's time to ask: Why does this keep happening in fashion?', *Fashion Journal*, 21 January 2021,<https://fashionjournal.com.au/fashion/zimmerman-cultural-appropriation/>.
19. Copyright Agency, *Mangkaja and Gorman Create an Indigenous Collection Setting a Benchmark in Collaboration*, Copyright Agency, July 2019, <www.copyright.com.au/2019/07/mangkaja-and-gorman-create-an-indigenous-collection-setting-a-benchmark-in-collaboration/>.
20. Lisa Gorman, personal communication, 6 February 2021.
21. Copyright Agency, *Mangkaja and Gorman Create an Indigenous Collection*.
22. Terri Janke and Adam Broughton, 'Promoting ethical manufacture of Indigenous art products with art licensing agreements' [blog post], Terri Janke and Company, 29 October 2019, <www.terrijanke.com.au/post/2019/10/29/promoting-ethical-manufacture-of-indigenous-art-products-with-art-licensing-agreements>.
23. Colleen Tighe Johnson, personal communication, 18 March 2021.
24. AIATSIS, *Torres Strait Islander Flag*, AIATSIS, n.d., <https://aiatsis.gov.au/explore/torres-strait-islander-flag>.
25. AIATSIS, *Bernard Namok: Designer of the Torres Strait Islander Flag*, AIATSIS, n.d., <https://aiatsis.gov.au/bernard-namok>.
26. Duane W Hamacher, Alo Tapim, Segar Passi and John Barsa, '"Dancing with the Stars": Astronomy and music in the Torres Strait', in Nicholas Campion and Chris Impey (eds), *Dreams of Other Worlds: Papers from the Ninth Conference on the Inspiration of Astronomical Phenomena*, Sophia Centre Press, Lampeter, UK, 2017, pp. 1–12, <https://arxiv.org/pdf/1605.08507.pdf>.
27. Department of the Prime Minister and Cabinet (DPMC), *Commercial Use of the Australian National Flag*, DPMC, n.d., <www.pmc.gov.au/government/australian-national-flag/commercial-use-australian-national-flag>.

LIST OF ACRONYMS

AIATSIS	Australian Institute of Aboriginal and Torres Strait Islander Studies
CBD	Convention on Biological Diversity
FPIC	Free, prior and informed consent
GLAM	Galleries, libraries, archives and museums
ICIP	Indigenous Cultural and Intellectual Property
IGC	World Intellectual Property Organization Intergovernmental Committee on Intellectual Property and Genetic Resources, Traditional Knowledge and Folklore
IP	Intellectual property
TK	Traditional knowledge
UNDRIP	United Nations Declaration on the Rights of Indigenous Peoples
WIPO	World Intellectual Property Organization

GLOSSARY

Access and benefit sharing (ABS) is about making sure, through agree-ments and protocols, that benefits flow back to individuals and communities when their biological resources and traditional knowledge are accessed for commercial use and research projects. To gain access, users must first get permission, known as free, prior and informed consent (FPIC). Benefits can be monetary (e.g. royalties) and/or non-monetary (e.g. the development of research skills and knowledge).[1]

Biological resources are 'genetic resources, organisms or parts thereof, populations, or any other biotic component of ecosystems with actual or potential use or value for humanity'.[2]

Biopiracy refers to the 'appropriation of the knowledge and genetic resources of farming and Indigenous communities by individuals or institutions who seek exclusive monopoly control (patents or intellectual property) over these resources and knowledge'.[3]

Bioprospecting is 'corporate drug development based on medicinal plants, traditional knowledge, and microbes culled from the "biodiversity-rich" regions of the globe – most of which reside in the so-called developing nations'.[4]

Biotechnology refers to 'any technological application that uses biological systems, living organisms, or derivatives thereof, to make or modify products or processes for specific use'.[5]

Data sovereignty, as it relates to Indigenous peoples, is the right to govern the collection, ownership and application of data about Indigenous communities, peoples, lands and resources.

Dynamic consent is a new way of approaching consent in research that allows people to choose more granular, or detailed, consent options regarding their research participation over time.[6]

Folklore is defined as traditions, observances, customs and beliefs as expressed in music, dance, craft, sculpture, theatre, painting and literature. Folklore covers both material objects and more abstract concepts, such as idioms and themes. The use of 'folklore' has been out of favour with Indigenous Australians since the 1990s;[7] however, the term is referenced in the *Copyright Act 1968* with respect to provisions adopted in the 1990s to do with performers' protection.[8] The term is currently used by the World Intellectual Property Organization's IGC (see 'WIPO', below) and is still commonly used in African countries.

Free, prior and informed consent (FPIC) is a process in which accurate information is provided to Indigenous people on all the proposed uses of their cultural heritage, and on the future implications of consent.[9]

Indigenous refers to the Aboriginal and Torres Strait Islander people, the original inhabitants of the land and seas in Australia. An Indigenous person is a someone who is of Aboriginal or Torres Strait Islander descent, who identifies as Aboriginal or Torres Strait Islander, and is accepted as Aboriginal and Torres Strait Islander by the Indigenous community.

Indigenous Cultural and Intellectual Property (ICIP) refers to the tangible and intangible aspects of Indigenous cultural heritage, including artistic works, literature, performance, traditional and scientific knowledge, documentation, cultural property and objects, human remains and documentation. The scope of ICIP is constantly evolving and it belongs to a living heritage. The term has become widely used in Australia since the report *Our Culture: Our Future* was launched in 1999.[10] The report followed the terminology used in the draft of the United Nations Declaration on the Rights of Indigenous Peoples (UNDRIP) in the mid-1990s, and in the pivotal international study conducted by Erica-Irene Daes in the early 1990s.[11]

Indigenous customary law or **Indigenous law** in Australia is the body of rules, values and traditions which are accepted by the members of an Indigenous community as establishing standards or procedures to be upheld in that community. Indigenous customary law is observed and practised by many Indigenous Australians and varies from community to community.

Indigenous ecological knowledge (IEK) comes from Indigenous people. This knowledge is in a continual state of change 'as it acquires deeper and more extensive understandings of the local environment and adapts to environmental changes and intercultural interaction.'[12] IEK has been predominantly used in land management and in the natural resource management sector.[13]

Indigenous knowledge is knowledge handed down by Indigenous people from generation to generation, belonging to a particular community, clan or family. Indigenous knowledge includes traditional and contemporary knowledge in recorded form; artistic, oral, creative, and written knowledge; cultural practices and beliefs; stories and oral histories; geographic and genealogical information; and information about plants and animals.

Public domain is a legal term that generally refers to creative material that is not protected by intellectual property laws and does not have any legal restriction upon its copying by the public. A public domain work can be used without the need for permission.

Repatriation is the return of Aboriginal and Torres Strait Islander materials (ancestral remains, secret sacred objects, cultural artefacts, data and information) to their communities of origin.

Secret sacred refers to objects, places and information that, under customary laws, are secret or sacred. Such information may only be made available to the initiated, or may only be seen by men or women or particular people in the community. Much of the secret and sacred is associated with burial or items created for ceremony. The information may be knowledge and beliefs, and it may be oral in form, or recorded in film and photographs.

Traditional ecological knowledge means a 'cumulative body of knowledge, practice and belief, evolving by adaptive processes and handed down through generations by cultural transmission, about the relationship of living beings (including humans) with one another and with their environment'.[14]

Wandjinas are the sacred beings and spirit ancestors of the Worrorra, Ngarinyin and Wunambal Gaambera people of the Kimberley in Western Australia. Believed to be the creators of the land, Wandjinas are depicted on rock forms in this region and continue to be represented by custodians today.[15]

WIPO refers to the World Intellectual Property Organization, the United Nations organisation created in 1967 to encourage creative activity by promoting the protection of intellectual property internationally. Since 2000, WIPO has convened an Intergovernmental Committee on Intellectual Property and Genetic Resources, Traditional Knowledge and Folklore ('IGC') to discuss issues relating to access to genetic resources and benefit sharing; the protection of traditional knowledge, innovations and creativity; and the protection of expressions of folklore.

Notes

1   Secretariat of the Convention on Biological Diversity (CBD), *Access and Benefit-Sharing*, Secretariat of the CBD, 2011, <www.cbd.int/abs/infokit/revised/web/factsheet-abs-en.pdf>.
2   Convention on Biological Diversity (Rio de Janeiro, 6 May 1992) [1993] ATS 32, article 2.
3   ETC Group, *Biopiracy*, ETC Group, n.d., <www.etcgroup.org/content/biopiracy>.
4   Cori Hayden, *When Nature Goes Public: The Making and Unmaking of Bioprospecting in Mexico*, Princeton University Press, Princeton, 2003, p. 1.
5   Convention on Biological Diversity, article 2.
6   Australian Genomics Health Alliance (AGHA), *Dynamic Consent*, AGHA, March 2020, <www.australiangenomics.org.au/wp-content/uploads/2020/04/1.-Evidence-Summary_CTRL_March-2020-1.pdf>.
7   Terri Janke, *Our Culture: Our Future – Report on Australian Indigenous Cultural and Intellectual Property Rights*, report commissioned by the Australian Institute of Aboriginal and Torres Strait Islander Studies (AIATSIS) and Aboriginal and Torres Strait Islander Commission (ATSIC), Michael Frankel & Company, 1998, <www.terrijanke.com.au/our-culture-our-future>.

8 *Copyright Act 1968* (Cth), subsection 84(f). The definition of 'live performance' includes 'a performance of an expression of folklore'.
9 Food and Agriculture Organization of the United Nations (FAO), *Free, Prior and Informed Consent: An Indigenous Peoples' Right and a Good Practice for Local Communities*, FAO, 2016, <www.un.org/development/desa/indigenouspeoples/publications/2016/10/>.
10 Terri Janke, *Our Culture: Our Future*.
11 Erica-Irene Daes, *Study on the Protection of the Cultural and Intellectual Property of Indigenous Peoples*, United Nations Commission on Human Rights, UN Document E/CN.4/Sub.2/1993/28, 28 July 1993.
12 Adrian Fordman, William Fogarty, Ben Corey et al., *Knowledge Foundations for the Development of Sustainable Wildlife Enterprises in Remote Indigenous Communities of Australia*, CAEPR Working Paper No. 62, Centre for Aboriginal Economic Policy Research, 2010, p. 5, <https://caepr.cass.anu.edu.au/research/publications/knowledge-foundations-development-sustainable-wildlife-enterprises-remote>.
13 Terri Janke, *Indigenous Ecological Knowledge and Natural Resources in the Northern Territory: Report on the Current Status of Indigenous Intellectual Property*, report commissioned by the Natural Resource Management Board (NT), April 2009.
14 Fikret Berkes, Johan Colding and Carl Folke, 'Rediscovery of Traditional Ecological Knowledge as adaptive management', *Ecological Applications*, vol. 10, no. 5, 2000, p. 1252.
15 Mowanjum Aboriginal Art & Culture Centre, *About*, Mowanjum, n.d., <https://mowanjumarts.com/about>.

ACKNOWLEDGMENTS

This book arose following the completion of my thesis in 2019, *True Tracks: Indigenous Cultural and Intellectual Property Principles for putting Self-Determination into practice* (2019), which gave me the chance to take part in the deeper debates and visionary thinking for protecting Indigenous knowledge and culture. Now I am grateful for the opportunity provided by NewSouth Publishing to share this book to make further impact in broader society.

I have always been fascinated by Indigenous arts and culture. It connected me to my culture. As a law student, I found the topic of Indigenous intellectual property compelling. I worked at the Aboriginal Arts Board in the 1990s and learned about copyright as Indigenous artists were taking cases to court for copyright protection. I was further encouraged to focus on this area when I was working at the National Indigenous Arts Advocacy Association in the mid-1990s. My thanks go to Colin Golvan QC, Bronwyn Bancroft, Michael McMahon and Banduk Marika, who were all involved in the fight for greater recognition of Indigenous artists' rights. Indigenous cultural and intellectual property was what I chose to focus on as a lawyer.

I acknowledge fellow Indigenous lawyer and friend Robynne Quiggin, who has co-authored key papers with me. It was great to have someone to bounce ideas off and to give guidance and feedback.

I also acknowledge my many clients who gave us work to set my deep thinking into practice. Thanks must also go to the team who I work with at Terri Janke and Company. Thank you to my professional mentor Pamela Pearce who has guided me to bring more organisation into my business so I can spend more time writing.

To my supervisors at the National Centre for Indigenous Studies at Australian National University (ANU): Diane Smith and Cressida Fforde (and previous supervisors Mick Dodson, Peter Veth and Matthew Rimmer). It took me a while but I got the PhD finished. I express my sincere gratitude. And thank you to the markers of the PhD for the great feedback and encouragement.

Turning this work into a book was a big job, and one I could not have done without help. Thank you to Gabriela Dounis for assisting me to bring this book together. It took an enormous effort – bringing notes and ideas together, helping with research, and contacting people for clarifications and permission. Thanks for your great coordination; it has been wonderful to share this journey with you.

Thanks also to the rest of the team at Terri Janke and Company who have worked on many matters described in this book – Anika Valenti, Elizabeth Mason, Laura Curtis, Patrick Goulding, Charisma Cubillo, Clara Klemski, Andrew Pitt, Kevin Anderson, Sam McNeil, Juanita Kelly-Mundine and Adam Broughton. It was hard to write this book while running a growing law firm, so I am grateful for Andrew and Anika, who are a strong leadership team. I also acknowledge the great support of my business mentor, Pamela Pearce. Thanks also to Emily Reid, my niece, for transcribing my voice recordings. Dr David Coombs should also be mentioned and thanked for drafting assistance, and also Juanita for help in the final stage.

A big thank you to publisher Elspeth Menzies for your enthusiasm and support, especially at the beginning stages, helping guide the purpose and tone of the book. Thank you to editor Emma Driver for your rigour and skill, assisting us to bring it all together. Thank you also to project editor Sophia Oravecz and the team at NewSouth Publishing.

A special thank you to artist and friend Bibi Barba, for letting me feature your beautiful painting on the front cover of the book. Thank you also to Debra Billson for the bold cover design.

A warm thank you to Anita Heiss, Tyson Yunkaporta, Tara June Winch, Marcia Langton and Turia Pitt for your heartfelt endorsements, and their continuing inspiration.

Acknowledgments

Thank you to all the people in Australia and around the world who allowed me to share your precious stories, voices and work in the book, including your cultural expressions and knowledge. Your contributions are deeply treasured and make this book what it is. Thank you also to everyone who provided input and feedback for the information in the book.

Thanks so much – Marcus Hughes, Victor Steffensen, Amy Hammond, Ryan Griffen, Falen Doug Passi, Annie Reynolds, Tasmanian Aboriginal Centre, Jacinta Tobin, Isabella Manfredi, Lynette Ackland, Melissa Kirby, Faith Baisden, Theresa Sainty, Jill Vaughan, Kirsten Thorpe, Damien Webb, Jacqui Allen, Jack Buckskin, Cris Edmonds-Wathen, Rob Amery, Len Collard, Kylie Bracknell, Clint Bracknell, Magdalen Kelantumama, Karen Manton, Banduk Marika, Lavinia Ketchell, Laurie Nona, Colin Golvan, Mikaela Jade, Tara June Winch, Bibi Barba, Gabrielle Sullivan, Stephanie Parkin, Judy Grady, Bronwyn Taylor, Laurie Nona, Lydia Miller, Patricia Adjei, Shane Hamilton, Robyn Ayres, Paul Sweeney, Albert Namatjira Family, Sophia Marinos, Rene Kulitja, Erub Arts, Mick Harding, Rodney Dillon, Terry Yumbulul, Elena Wangurra, Annie Tenant, Brenda L Croft, Hetti Perkins, Jefa Greenaway, Dillon Kombumerri, Karilyn Brown, Paul Memmott, Rueben Berg, Esme Timbery, Jonathan Jones, Bruce Pascoe, Vicki Couzens, Lee Darroch, Louis Anderson Mokak, Lena Nyadbi, Wes Morris, Donny Woolagoodja, Eleanor Dixon, Yirrmal, Donna Woods, Miiesha, Stephen Collins, Matt Harding, Bernie Heard, Paul Jarman, Leah Flanagan, Shellie Morris, Jessie Lloyd, John Morseu, Rhoda Roberts, Aaron Corn, Will Stubbs, Lewis Burns, Rob Collins, Warwick Thornton, Rachel Perkins, Sally Riley, Marcia Langton, Darlene Johnson, Curtis Taylor, Lynette Wallworth, Darren Dale, Jane Anderson, Tasha James, Rawiri Taonui, Lydia Campbell, Ellen van Neerven, Jared Thomas, Anna Moulton, Rachel Bin Salleh, Phillip Gwynne, Estelle Castro-Koshy, John Dallwitz, Sasha Wilmoth, Kate Grenville, Deborah Cheetham, Anita Heiss, Lucy Treloar, Rachael Maza, Elma Kris, Kim Walker, Stephen Page, Laura Hough, Margo Neale, Colin Saltmere, Shaun Angeles, Misty Jenkins, Larissa Behrendt, Kim Walker, Bev Manton, Christine Anu, Aroha Mead, Liza-Mare Syron, Lily Shearer, Ali Murphy-Oates, Gerry

Turpin, Lee Doherty, Mark Olive, Noel Butler, Clayton Donovan, Kieron Anderson, Pat Torres, Rayleen Brown, Henrietta Marrie, Peter Cooley, Sharon Winsor, Robert Dann, Tracy Hardy, Tom Suchanandan, Corey Tutt, Joe Sambono, , Paul Marshall, Sonia Cooper, Bradley Moggridge, Chels Marshall, Ray Lovett, Mark Wenitong, Kelvin Kong, Karlie Noon, Karen L Martin, Jane Anderson, Lester-Irabinna Rigney, Payi Linda Ford, Reuben Bolt, Susan O'Sullivan, Margot Livsey, Penangke, Martin Nakata, John Paul Janke, Luke Pearson, Christine Evans, Chris Matthews, Kevin Lowe, Margo Neale, Levi McKenzie-Kirkbright, Angie Abdilla, Rod Kennett, Stephanie von Gavel, Liam Ridgeway, Rodney Kelly, John Carty, Nathan Sentance, Nici Cumpston, Bruce Johnson McLean, Gary Murray, Advisory Committee for Indigenous Repatriation, Lola Greeno, Shannon Faulkhead, Gaye Sculthorpe, Zoe Rimmer, Liz Tew, Brook Andrew, Mandy Muir, Damein Bell, Robin Chapple, Shane Phillips, Wesley Aird, Sam Davidson, Lorraine Peeters, Shaan Peeters, Laura Berry, Karen Mundine, Annie Tennant, Turia Pitt, Yatu Widders Hunt, Grace Lillian Lee, Brigitte Vézina, Nayuka Gorrie, Ngarralja Tommy May, Adam Suckling, Lisa Gorman, Colleen Tighe Johnson.

My family must have a big acknowledgment for the years of encouragement. Thanks Mum for always being optimistic. Thanks Dad for your love of books, which lead to me wanting to study law. Thanks Toni for being the one to lead the way through law school. Thanks John Paul for the many ideas and yarns. And thanks to Veronica my bestie, who gave me that backpack to go back to uni, and a lot of support throughout my life.

The most precious thanks must go to my husband and kids. Andrew Pitt, thanks for giving me so much love and support to build my business. You believed in me and backed my vision. And to my children, Tamina and Jaiki Pitt, you continue to inspire me and I just love you so much. Thank you to Andrew, Tamina and Jaiki for continuously being the sun, the moon and the stars – you are my universe.

INDEX

ABC
   Wild Kitchen 216
Abdilla, Angie 300–301
Aboriginal and Torres Strait Islander Commission (ATSIC) 10, 11, 83
Aboriginal and Torres Strait Islander flags 107–109
   copyright 107–109, 380
   fashion and 379–81
Aboriginal and Torres Strait Islander Heritage Protection Act 1984 (Cth) 315
Aboriginal and Torres Strait Islander Library and Information Resources Network (ATSILIRN) 314–15
   ATSILIRN Protocols 314–15
Aboriginal and Torres Strait Islander Mathematics Alliance (ATSIMA) 283
Aboriginal Art Centre Hub Western Australia (AACHWA) 60, 72
Aboriginal Arts Co-operative 89
Aboriginal Cultural Heritage Act 2003 (Qld) 359
Aboriginal Enterprise Novelties 71
Aboriginal Land Rights (Northern Territory) Act 1976 (NT) 65, 263
Aboriginal Languages Act 2017 (NSW) 48
Aboriginal Languages Trust (NSW) 48–49
Aboriginal Nations 141
Aboriginal Studies Press 178
Aboriginal Tent Embassy 59
Aboriginal Tourism Australia 340
access and benefit sharing (ABS) 103, 102, 222, 226, 235, 261, 264, 386 *see also* benefit sharing
Ackland, Lynette 36
acknowledgement of country 17, 130, 351
acronyms 385
Adjei, Patricia 67, 82, 86
Afunakwa 117–18
Anangu Ngangkari Tjutaku Aboriginal

Corporation (ANTAC) 244
Anderson, Dr Jane 153
Anderson, Geoff 42
Anderson, Kieron 216
Anderson, Poul 156
Andrew, Brook 319
Andrews, Gordon 74
Anno, Kitchell 2
Anu, Christine 121, 129–30, 188
   'Baba Waiar' 129–30
   'Kulba Yaday' ('Old Talk') 130
   'My Island Home' 121
APRA AMCOS 125, 129, 132–33
APY Art Centre Collective 60, 66, 72
Ara Irititja 294
Aratjara: Art of the First Australians 62
Archival Decolonist 319
archives *see* GLAM (galleries, libraries, archives and museums) sector
Armstrong, Driller Jet 105
Arnhem Land bark paintings 59–60, 104
Arnhem, Northern and Kimberley Artists (ANKA) 60, 66, 72
Arnold Bloch Leibler 82, 199
artificial intelligence, ownership rights 296–97
Artists in the Black (AITB) 67–68
Artists of Ampilatwatja 60
Arts Law Centre of Australia 67, 68, 196
   Artwork Licensing Intellectual Property Toolkit 72
Ashby, Rhonda 45
Ashley, Djardie 80–81
Atlas of Living Australia (ALA) project 300
attribution 9, 16, 25–26, 38–39, 43, 89, 118, 144, 147, 168–69, 176, 180, 182, 190, 191, 259, 264, 272, 273, 285, 311, 359, 378, 382
Australia Council for the Arts 65, 67, 95, 165, 198

Aboriginal and Torres Strait Islander Arts
   Board 58–59, 61–63, 65
First Nations Arts Strategy Panel 62
Protocols for Producing Indigenous
   Australian Performing Arts 186–87
Protocols for Producing Indigenous
   Australian Visual Arts 85, 89
Protocols for Using First Nations Cultural
   and Intellectual Property in the Arts 21,
   27, 122, 124–25, 177, 180
Australian Business Guide to Implementing the
UN Declaration on the Rights of Indigenous
Peoples 365
Australian Competition and Consumer
   Commission (ACCC) 69
Australian Copyright Council 62
Australian Curriculum, Assessment and
   Reporting Authority (ACARA) 246, 285,
   287
Australian Fashion Council 369
Australian Film Commission 139
Australian Government's Indigenous
   Repatriation Program 318
Australian Indigenous Design Charter
   (AIDC) 100
Australian Indigenous Doctors' Association
   (AIDA) 243
Australian Institute of Aboriginal and Torres
   Strait Islander Studies (AIATSIS) 8, 10,
   83, 257
   access to materials 310
   Audiovisual Archives Access and Use
      Policy 154
   AUSTLANG database 51
   Code of Ethics for Aboriginal and Torres
      Strait Islander Research 21, 236, 249,
      254–55
   Core Cultural Training 354–55
   functions and obligations 310
   Indigenous collection 309–310
   Map of Indigenous Australia 289
   Return of Cultural Heritage project 267
Australian Institute of Aboriginal and Torres
Strait Islander Studies Act 1989 (Cth)
   310
Australian Institute of Architects
   First Nations Advisory Working Group
      and Cultural Reference Panel 100
Australian Mukurtu Hub 312

Australian Museum 319
Australian Museums and Galleries
   Association (AMaGA)
   Indigenous Roadmap 19, 320, 323–26
Australian National Maritime Museum 67
Australian National University (ANU) 244,
   311
   National Centre of Indigenous Genomics
      (NCIG) 268–70, 319
Australian Rules 141, 170
Australian Senate's Select Committee on the
   Aboriginal Flag 108
Australian Society of Authors 178
Avery, Eric 115
Ayres, Robyn 67

Bábbarra Designs 371
Babici 370
Badu Art Centre 61
Baisden, Faith 36, 41
Baker Boy 115
   'Marryuna' 115
Balarinji 86, 358
Bancroft, Bronwyn 46, 76, 369
Bangarra Dance Theatre 129, 185–87, 188
Banks, Kirsten 245
Barangaroo's *Shell Wall* 96–98
Barba, Bibi 68, 84–85
Barclay, Barry 142
   Mana Tuturu 142
Barker, Carolyn 36
Barkly Regional Arts 129
Barton, William 120
Barunga Festival 339
Batchelor Institute (NT) 47, 178
   CALL Collection 314
Baum, Tina 313
Bayles, Mundanara 341
BBC *Hidden Treasures of...* 151
Beale, Debra 370
Bedford, Paddy 94, 358
   Thoowoonggoonarrin 94
Behrendt, Professor Larissa 163, 166
Bell, Jon 146
Bell, Tyrone 45
benefit sharing 9, 16, 26, 39, 43, 52, 54, 155,
   176, 210, 217, 223, 235, 264, 272, 340,
   350, 358, 359, 382
Benger, Norma Chidanpee 378

Index

Bennelong and Yamroweny
    'Barrabu-la' 114
Berg, Rueben 99–100
Berne Convention for the Protection of Literary and Artistic Works 13
Berry, Laura 353
BHP 299
Bibi Barba case 12
Biennale of Sydney 319
Big hART 82, 199
Bima Wear 371
Bindam Mie 220
Bin Salleh, Rachel 177–78
biological resources 386
biopiracy 205–207, 208–10, 386
bioprospecting 386
biotechnology 386
Biri Biri Catering 216
Birubi Art 69, 108, 337
Blackadder, Jesse 171
    Paruku: The Desert Brumby 171
BlackCard 341
'black cladding' 352
Blackfella Films 138, 152
Black Lives Matter movement 363–64
Black Olive Catering 215
Blacktown Arts 198
Blacktown City Council 198
Blair, Wayne 136–37, 146, 197
BlakDance 188
Blakeney, Professor Michael 208–209
Blak Markets 71
Blanco, Victor 2
Blight, Rosemary 146
Boehme, Jacob 188
Bolt, Professor Reuben 260
Boola Bardip (Western Australian Museum) 323
Boomalli Aboriginal Artists Co-operative 61, 72, 141
Borroloola Songwomen 128–29
    Ngambala Wiji li-Wunungu (Together We Are Strong) 128–29
Bostock, Lester 143
Brackenreg, John 81–82
Bracknell, Kylie (Kaarljilba Kaardn) 34–35
Bradshaw, Caroline 45
Brandl, Eric 257
Brando, Marlon 154

Brett, Shannon 370
Briscoe, Deline 115
British Museum 151, 306–307, 315, 320
Brown, Karilyn 95
Brown, Rayleen 218–19
Buckskin, Jack 35
Budj Bim Cultural Landscape 334–35
Bula'bula Arts 371
Bulun Bulun, Johnny 77, 78–79, 381
    Magpie Geese and Water Lilies at the Waterhole 80–81
Bulun Bulun v Nejlam Investments Pty Ltd (1989) 66, 78–79
Bulun Bulun v R & T Textiles 7, 80–81, 381
Buluuy Mirrii 378–79
Burarrwanga, George 121
Burney, Linda 379
Burns, Lewis 121
bush foods and traditional medicine 203
    access and benefit sharing 222
    biopiracy 205–207, 208–10
    bush foods and products 214–17
    collective knowledge 222
    commercialisation 203–205, 211, 214, 226
    connection to country 203–204
    cultural heritage rights 203–205
    Gumby Gumby plants 210–11
    Indigenous chefs 215–16
    Indigenous growers and harvesters 217–20
    Indigenous health and wellbeing businesses 221
    Indigenous knowledge, integration of 216–17
    Indigenous leadership 224–25
    Indigenous wholesalers, businesses and buyers 220–21
    kava (*Piper methysticum*) 209–10
    Neem plant (*Azadirachta indica*) 209
    patents 207–211
    resources 226
    restaurants 216
    rooibos tea case study 222–24
    scientific research 221–22
    smokebush (*Conospermum*) 208–209
    what you can do 226
Bush Medijina 219
Bushfoods with Benefits 211

businesses
    Aboriginal and Torres Strait Islander events, support for 351
    big business and Indigenous cultural heritage 361–63
    'black cladding' 352
    Business Reference Guide to the UN Declaration on the Rights of Indigenous Peoples 350
    cultural safety and competency training 354–55
    employment opportunities 352–53
    engagement with Indigenous communities 351
    Indigenous businesses and ICIP 356–58
    Indigenous language words in business names 358–59
    Indigenous suppliers, choosing 353–54
    joint ventures 352–53
    opportunities from 363–64
    Reconciliation Action Plans (RAPs) 325, 355–56, 365
    resources 366
    respect for human rights 349, 351
    UNDRIP 350
    what you can do 365
Butler, Noel 215–16, 333–34
Buxton, Lisa 279

CAAMA Music 131
Cairns Indigenous Arts Fair 71, 72, 339, 368
Cameron, James 155–56
    Avatar 155–56
Campbell, Aunty Margret's The Rocks Aboriginal Dreaming Tour 341
Carmen, Leon 164
Carmody, Kev 115, 126
    'From Little Things Big Things Grow' 126
'carpets case' 6–7, 76–78
Carr, Chryss 127
Carty, Dr John 316
Casey, Dawn 321
The Cat Empire 122
Centre for Australian Languages and Linguistics (CALL) 47
Chanel boomerang 372–73
The Chant of Jimmie Blacksmith 140
Chapple, Robin 334

Cheetham, Deborah 115, 172
Chi, Jimmy 200
    Bran Nue Dae 200
Chirac, Jacques 93
Christen, Kim 298
City of Sydney 27–28
Clayton-Dixon, Callum 45
Clean Slate project 361
Clothing The Gaps 370
    Foundation 370
Cole, Kelli 313
Collins, Rob 136–37, 146
colonisation, impact of 4, 7, 18, 22, 30, 32, 155, 156, 169, 308, 315
Commonwealth Games 2018 359–60
consent and consultation 15, 20–22, 42–43, 110, 141, 181–82, 201, 272, 344
    dynamic consent 146–47, 268, 318–19, 387
    free, prior and informed consent (FPIC) 20, 261, 297, 318, 350, 364, 387
Convention on Biological Diversity 103, 210, 235
    Nagoya Protocol 103, 210, 218, 223, 235, 249
Cook, Captain James 165, 278, 307
Cooley, Peter 219, 224
Cooman 308
Coombes, Jennifer (Lulu) 378
Coombs, HC 'Nugget' 75
Cooper, Sonia 239–40
copyright
    Aboriginal flag 107–109, 380
    authorship 49, 167–69, 176
    controlling ownership 52–53
    dance 191
    fashion design 373
    film 147, 153
    first Aboriginal copyright case 75–76
    Indigenous artworks 62–63, 65, 66, 73–74
    Indigenous languages 36, 48–53
    'joint ownership' 196
    legislation 49
    licensing in visual arts 85–86
    music 117–20, 125, 129
    native title claims evidence 5
    old film recordings 193–94
    oral-based cultures and 168

Index

original works requirement 49
ownership 50, 52–53, 107–109, 167–68, 255–57
sacred imagery reproduction 256–57
Torres Strait Islander flag 108–109, 381
traditional dance and 195
Copyright Act 1968 (Cth) 14, 49, 73, 169, 198, 387
Copyright Agency 68, 70, 72, 86, 89, 377–78
Couzens, Dr Vicki 107
COVID-19 342, 363
COWICHAN clothing trade mark 376
Cox, Professor Brian 246
Cracknell & Lonergan Architects 93
Crane, Richard 76
Create NSW 68, 198
Creative Commons licences 300
Crocodile Dundee 136
Croft, Brenda L. 61, 94, 95
Crown Resorts Foundation 198
CSIRO 241, 300
   Indigenous STEM Awards 245
   Indigenous STEM Education Project 247
   Our Knowledge, Our Way 237
Cubillo, Franchesca 313
cultural appropriation 89, 100, 169–70, 382
   fashion industry, in 371–73, 374–75, 381
cultural heritage, meaning 9
cultural integrity 9, 15, 23–24, 32, 43, 71, 81, 95, 105, 132, 147, 149, 169, 176, 187, 189, 225, 267, 272, 285, 287, 313, 340–41, 357, 360, 380
Cumpston, Nici 319
Curtis, Laura 35–36

Daes, Erica-Irene 10, 387
Daiyi, Ngulilkang Nancy 259
Dale, Darren 138, 152
dance *see* Indigenous performing arts
Dance Rites 200
Dann, Robert 220
Darroch, Lee 107
Darwin Aboriginal Art Fair 71, 72, 339, 368
Davis, Jack 197
   No Sugar 197
Davis, Megan 20
Dawes, William 45–46
Deadly Awards 123

Deadly Science 231, 246
Deboriginal 370
Deep Forest 117–18
de Heer, Rolf 147–50, 156
Delaney, Ian 11
Dembski, Lenore (Lenore Dembski Paperbark Woman) 369
De Napoli, Krystal 245
Department of Education and Training
   Indigenous Knowledge in the Built Environment: A Guide for Tertiary Educators 101
Desart 66, 69–70, 72, 89
   SAM Database 70
design *see* Indigenous architecture and design
Designer Aboriginals 369
Designs Act 2003 (Cth) 376
Dickinson, Kristy 71
didgeridoo (yidaki) popularity 120–21, 340–41
Dietrich, Craig 298
Digital Custodians 342
Dillon, Rodney 83–84
discrimination 349, 351
   systemic racism 363
Dixon, Charles 'Chicka' 59
Dixon, Eleanor 115
Dixon, Janey 'Namija' 115
Djerrkura, Gatjil 11
Djigirr, Peter 147
Dodson, Mick 11
Doherty, Lee 211
Donovan, Clayton 216
Dounis, Veronica 374
drama *see* Indigenous performing arts
Dreamtime SouthernX 341
Dugalunji Aboriginal Corporation 265
Dungay, Robbie 198
Durack, Mary 162
   Kings in Grass Castles 162

Eades, Jason 343
Easteal, Dr Simon 268
Eckermann, Ali Cobby 163
Ecotourism Australia 340
Edmunds, Dr Mary 10
education 277–79
   community connections in schools 283–84

culturally responsive pedagogy 282
employment opportunities for
    Indigenous experts 288
Goompi Model 282–83
ICIP protocols in 284–88
Indigenous culture in schools 281–83
Indigenous histories, lack of 278
Indigenous trailblazers 280–81
'Maths as Storytelling' (MAST) 283
non-Indigenous cultures and beliefs,
    impact 284
principles and protocols 282
resources 279, 280, 290
respectful inclusion of Indigenous topics
    277–78
what you can do 289
Ellis, Aaron 42
Enoch, Wesley 197, 199–200
environmental management and Indigenous
    knowledge 236
    fire management 237–39
    Indigenous rangers and ranger programs
        242–43
    Indigenous seasonal management
        241–42
    water management 239–41
*Environmental Protection and Biodiversity
    Conservation Act 1999* (Cth) (EPBC Act)
    235, 240, 264, 335
Erub Arts 60–61
    ghost net artworks 61
Evans, Dr Christine 281–82
Evans, Penny 46

Far West Languages Centre (FWLC) 36, 38
Faulkhead, Dr Shannon 310
Federation of Victorian Traditional Owner
    Corporations (FVTOC) 225
Festival of Pacific Arts and Culture 191–92,
    338
Festival of the Dreaming 131, 121, 200
*Finding a Space for First Peoples' Science: A
    Vision for a National First Peoples Science
    Centre* 247
Firesticks Alliance 238
First Australians 138, 152
First Hand Solutions 224
First Languages Australia (FLA) 36–37, 41
First Nations Blockchain 70

First Nations Bushfood & Botanical Alliance
    Australia 225
First Nations Fashion Council (FNFC) 369
First Nations Fashion + Design (FNFD)
    368–69
Flags Act 1953 (Cth) 379, 380
Flagworld 107, 380
Flanagan, Leah 115, 133
Floyd, George 363, 364
Fogarty, Lesley 62
Foley, Dennis 123
Foley, Fiona 61
Foley, Professor Gary 58
folklore 387
Ford, Dr Payi Linda 259–60
    *Aboriginal Knowledge Narratives and
        Country: Marri kunkimba putj
        marrideyan* 259
    *Narratives and Landscapes: Their Capacity
        to Serve Indigenous Knowledge Interests*
        259
Fortescue Metals Group 299
Foundation for Aboriginal and Islander
    Research Action (FAIRA) 318
Frankel, Michael 10, 139
free, prior and informed consent (FPIC) 20,
    261, 297, 318, 350, 364, 387
    dynamic consent approach 146–47, 268,
        318–19, 387
French, Alison 82
French National Centre for Scientific
    Research 117
Frillneck Australia 378

Gab Titui Cultural Centre 61
Gale, Uncle Colin 171
galleries *see* GLAM (galleries, libraries,
    archives and museums) sector
Garimara, Doris Pilkington 163
    Follow the Rabbit-Proof Fence 163
Garma Festival of Traditional Cultures 131,
    192, 339
geographical indicators (GIs) 219–20
George, Dr Tommy 238
Gervais, Ricky 84
Gifford, Brenda 198
Gifts Mate 108, 380
Gilbert, Danny 355
Gilbert, Kevin 163, 197

Index

The Cherry Pickers 163, 197
Gilbert + Tolbin 355
Gillawarra Arts 71
Ginibi, Ruby Langford 46, 163
   Don't Take Your Love to Town 163
Girrawaa Creative Work Centre 99
GLAM (galleries, libraries, archives and museums) sector 19, 326
   AMaGA Indigenous Roadmap 19, 320, 323–26
   ancestral remains 317–19
   collaborative collections 311–12
   cultural materials held by 306–309
   'decolonising' 319
   Deepening Histories of Place 311
   Indigenous collections, ownership of 309–12
   Indigenous languages collections 45–47
   Indigenous languages, protocols 40–41
   Indigenous-led exhibitions 319–23
   National Resting Place, calls for 318–19
   protocols in 312–15
   Reconciliation Action Plans (RAPs) 325
   repatriation of cultural objects 266–67, 308, 315–17
   resources 327
   truth-telling 319–23
   what you can do 327
glossary 386–89
Glynn, Erica 142
Goanna 122
   'Solid Rock' 122
Golvan, Colin 6–7, 76–77
Gondwana Choirs 121–22
Gondwana Indigenous Choir 122
Gooda, Mick 268–69
Google Glass 291–92
Goorie, Nayuka 372
Gordon, Vicki 127
Gorman 358, 377
Gorman, Lisa 377–78
Governor, Jimmy 140
Grant Snr, Dr Uncle Stan 42–43, 49
Greenaway, Jefa 99, 101
Greeno, Lola 321
Grenville, Kate 171
   The Secret River 171
Griffen, Ryan 146–47, 176
   Cleverman 136, 146–47, 176

Griffith University 234–35
Groves, Aroha 198
Gulpilil, David 136, 148, 149, 156–57
Gumbula, Djawa 153
Gumbula, Dr Joe 153
Gunditj Mirring Traditional Owner Aboriginal Corporation 335
Gundjeihmi Aboriginal Corporation (GAC) 262–63
Gunn, Jeannie 162
   We of the Never Never 162
Gurruwiwi, Djalu 120
Gurugirr, Jesse 220
Gweagal Shield 307–308
Gwynne, Phillip 141, 170
   Deadly, Unna? 141, 170

Haddon, Alfred Cort 152, 306
Hagan, WT 253
Hale, Horatio 46
Hamacher, Duane 245
Hamilton, Shane 70
Hamm, Dr Treahna 107
Hammond, Ruby 58
Hanson-Young, Sarah 69
Harding, Matt ('Dancing Matt') 117–18
Harding, Mick 71
Hardy, Tracy 221
Harris, Rolf 122
   'Tie Me Kangaroo Down, Sport' 122
Harrison, Jane 197
Hartshorn, Aidan 313
Haus of Dizzy 71
Healy, Amanda 369
Heard, Bernie 122
Heiss, Professor Anita 161–62, 175–76, 177, 280
   Bila Yarrudhanggalangdhuray (River of Dreams) 177
   Growing Up Aboriginal in Australia 280
   Yirra and Her Deadly Dog, Demon 175–76
Henderson, James (Sa'ke'j) Youngblood 10, 281
Herbert, Xavier 162
   Capricornia 162
Herzich, Paul 99
Herzog, Werner 139
   Where the Green Ants Dream 139–40

Huddleston, Les 378
Huggins, Jackie 163
   Auntie Rita 163
Hughes, Marcus 232, 312–13
human rights 349, 351
Hunt, Yatu Widders 368
Hunter, Ruby 115
Hurst, Krystal 71

IAD Press 178
Ilbijerri Theatre Company 195–96, 197
Iltja Ntjarra Many Hands Art Centre 83
Impact of Inauthentic Art and Craft in the Style of First Nations Peoples inquiry 78
Indigenous architecture and design 98–100
   Aboriginal and Torres Strait Islander flags 107–109
   Barangaroo's *Shell Wall* 96–98
   case studies on Indigenous traditional design 105–107
   Indigenous designs beyond country 109
   Musée du quai Branly (MQB) Australian Indigenous art commission 93–96
   patents, inventions and Indigenous knowledge 101–104
   possum skin cloaks 106–107
   protocols in 100–101
   resources 110
   traditional designs 104
   Wandjina sculpture 105–106
   what you can do 110
Indigenous Architecture and Design Victoria (IADV) 99
Indigenous Archives Collective 310
Indigenous art 58–59
   Aboriginal and Torres Strait Islander art centres 59–61, 66
   advocates for 61–63, 71
   art fairs 71, 73
   artists' moral rights 89, 95–96
   authentication 67, 70
   blockchain technology 70
   cases 74–83
   copyright 62–63, 65, 66, 73–74, 89
   ethical buying 70–74
   exploitation of 83–85
   fake/appropriation 63–65, 66, 68–70, 344
   'Fake Art Harms Culture' campaign 68–69
   Indigenous Art Code (IartC) 68
   labelling and certification 87–88
   licensing agreements 89
   Musée du quai Branly 93–96
   overseas exhibitions 62
   popularity 66
   protocols and licensing 85–86
   QR code technology 70
   rarrk 60, 69, 71, 95, 104
   resale royalty scheme 68
   resources 90
   royalties 96
   selling by Indigenous artists 71
   styles and traditions 59–60
   what you can do 89
Indigenous Art Centre Alliance (IACA) 60, 72
Indigenous Art Code (IartC) 68, 72, 89
Indigenous Arts and Craft Alliance (IACA) 89
Indigenous astronomy 244–45
Indigenous authors 162–63 *see also* Indigenous writing
   copyright 167–69
   exploitation of Indigenous themes and stories 165–67
   false claims 164–65
   identity and 164–65
   literary theft 168
Indigenous Business Direct 353–54
Indigenous businesses and ICIP 356
   commercialising Indigenous knowledge 357–58
Indigenous Cultural and Intellectual Property (ICIP) 8–10
   cultural heritage, protection of 9
   Darug 44–45
   meaning 9, 387
   native title claims and 5
   origin of term 10
   protocols 27–28
   rights 9
   Social Justice Package 4
   True Tracks framework 13–14
   True Tracks principles 15–27, 42–43
   UNDRIP 13
Indigenous cultural sensitivity readers,

Index

engaging 174
Indigenous cultures and knowledge
   big business and cultural heritage 361–63
   colonisation, impact of 7
   commercialisation and ICIP 357–58
   commodification in tourism 337
   copyright law and 6–7
   diversity 8
   intellectual property reforms in Australia 213–14
   meaning 7, 9, 388
   native title claims 5
   respecting Indigenous stories 180–81
   sacred or secret information 5
   storytelling 161–62
   traditional medicine *see* bush foods and traditional medicine
   understanding and protecting 7–8
   Western science and *see* science and ancient knowledge
Indigenous cultures, maintaining 16, 26, 43, 182
Indigenous customary law 388
Indigenous data sovereignty 270–71, 297–98, 386
Indigenous Digital Excellence (IDX) Initiative 301, 303
Indigenous ecological knowledge (IEK) 236, 388
Indigenous fashion industry 368–69
   cultural appropriation 371–73
   designs law 376
   ethical collaborations in 377–79
   flags 379–81
   Indigenous fashion designers 369–71
   intellectual property and 373–76, 382
   possum skin cloaks, reviving 106–107, 379
   resources 382–83
   respect 381–82
   trade marks 375–76
   what you can do 382
Indigenous film and television
   archival films 152–54
   BBC protocols in Torres Strait Islander filming 151
   consultation, importance of 141
   copyright 147, 153

developing protocols 141–44
   Indigenous presence 136–38
   Indigenous themes in Hollywood movies 154–56
   industry protocols 139–41
   misappropriation 139–40
   misrepresentation 139–40
   pre-protocol films 152
   protocols 140, 141, 144–45, 151
   release forms 142–44
   resources 157–58
   sacred Wandjinas 150–51
   stereotypical representations 139–40
   storytelling 137
   what you can do 157
Indigenous genomics research 267–70
Indigenous health and wellbeing 243–44
   research 267–70
Indigenous Land and Sea Corporation 4, 299, 335
Indigenous languages
   business names, in 358–59
   collections, caring for 45–47
   copyright 36, 48–50, 52–53
   cultural heritage and identity 33
   diversity 33
   endangered 34
   First Languages, Law & Governance Guide 35–37, 54
   Kaurna 35, 39
   legal protection, lack of 36–37
   music and 115
   naming project, event or program 51–52
   Noongar 34–35
   place names 52
   protocols and ethical guidelines 37–39
   publication without consent 31–32
   Queensland Indigenous Languages Project 40–41
   resource or project, using in 50–51
   resources 55
   revitalisation 33, 34–35, 37
   songwriting 44–45
   Tasmanian (palawa kani), reviving 30–32
   what you can do 54
   Wiradjuri language in *The Yield* 41–43, 176–77

Indigenous Literacy Foundation 162
Indigenous, meaning of 387
Indigenous medical doctors 243–44
Indigenous music 114–16
   archives and collections 119
   communal ownership 119
   contemporary songs 121–24
   copyright 117–20, 125, 126, 129
   digeridoo popularity 120–21
   ethical collaborations 125–28
   festivals, concerts and events 130–31
   Indigenous record labels 131
   moral rights 132
   National Indigenous Music Office 132–33
   ownership of traditional songs 119–20
   performances, recordings of 121
   protocols 122, 124–25, 127, 133
   recording and publishing agreements 131–32
   resources 134
   respect for ritual 116
   royalties 125, 129
   songs of power and reclamation 128–30
   songwriting collaborations with groups 126
   traditional Aboriginal and Torres Strait Islander song and music 116
   what you can do 133–34
Indigenous performing arts 185
   copyright law 191, 193–94, 196–97
   cultural appropriation 189–91
   dance companies 185–88
   drama and theatre 195–96
   empowerment and collaborations 200–201
   festivals 191–93
   illegal filming/photography 192–93
   Indigenous playwrights and theatre companies 197–200
   Indigenous theatre and copyright 196
   old film recordings 193–94
   performance dance and the law 189
   Protocols for Producing Indigenous Australian Performing Arts 186–87
   resources 201
   theatre collaborations 197, 199
   traditional dance and copyright 195
   what you can do 201

Indigenous person, definition 164–65
Indigenous Procurement Policy (IPP) 352
Indigenous publishing 177–78 *see also* Indigenous writing; Indigenous authors
Indigenous research 253–54
   access to land and resources 263–64
   AIATSIS Code of Ethics 254–55
   appropriate use of 261–62
   'archival captives' 253–54
   best practice approach 259–61
   consent 261–62
   copyright, sacred knowledge and uses of 256–57
   exploitation 254
   guidance and standards, recommendations 271–72
   history of 254–55
   Indigenous data sovereignty 270–71
   Indigenous genomics 267–70
   Indigenous knowledge and higher education institutions 260
   Indigenous-led research 264–65
   Indigenous researchers, need for 258
   Lowitja Institute guidelines 269
   Madjedbebe research project 262–63
   ownership issues 255–56
   protocols 272
   repatriation of sacred objects 266–67
   research partnerships 262–64
   resources 274
   spinifex partnership 265–66
   Strehlow Research Centre 266–67
   university policies 261–62
   what you can do 273
   working together 271–72
Indigenous science *see* science and ancient knowledge
Indigenous tourism 330–32
   Budj Bim Cultural Landscape 334–35
   collaborating for cultural competency in 341
   copyright protection 336, 338
   COVID-19 impact 342
   cultural sites and traditional knowledge, respecting 333–34
   digital tourism apps 341–42
   fake 336–37
   future direction of 342–43
   Indigenous knowledge, using 339–41

Index

Indigenous-led, supporting 332–33
   joint management 334–35
   Larrakia Declaration 332–33
   photography and Uluru 335–36
   recreational activities, impact 334
   resources 345
   Respecting Our Culture (ROC) certification 340
   rip-offs 336–37
   sharing stories in, issues 337–38
   Tourism Tropical North Queensland Cultural Protocols 337
   traditional knowledge notice 339
   what you can do 344
Indigenous writing *see also* Indigenous authors
   copyright 167–69, 176
   exploitation of Indigenous themes and stories 165–67
   Indigenous authorship and identity 164–65
   Indigenous writers and protocols 175–77
   international appropriations of story 169–70
   non-Indigenous writers 165–67, 169–73
   protocols and non-Indigenous writers 170–73, 180–81
   protocols for sensitivity readers 174–75
   resources 183
   respecting Indigenous stories 180–81
   rise of 162–64
   secret and sacred information 173
   True Tracks principles 180–81
   what you can do 181–82
IndigenousX 280–81
Indigiearth 220
IndigiGrow 219
Indigital 38, 291–92, 303
   Digital Custodians Project 38
   Indigital Storytelling 292–93
Indigital Schools 302
Indigitek 301–302, 303
Ingrey, Raymond 45
Intellectual Property Act 2011 (Samoa) 210
International Decade of Indigenous Languages 37, 130
International Indigenous Design Charter 100–101

interpretation 15, 22–23, 43, 71, 110, 172, 176, 182, 309, 320, 325, 326, 338, 340, 360
inventions and Indigenous knowledge 101–104
IP Australia 103, 213–14

Jaaning Tree restaurant 216
Jabree 359
Jackson, Kayla 115
Jade, Mikaela 38, 291–93, 295, 302, 342
James, Andrea 197, 198
James, Beau 67
Jamieson, Trevor 199
Janke, Joanna 179, 381
Janke, Terri *see also* Terri Janke and Company
   Butterfly Song 178–80
   children 10, 11, 179, 267, 279, 294, 306, 347–48
   grandmothers 2, 307
   great-great-grandmother Annie 2
   writing family stories 178–80, 279
Japulija, Daisy 377
Jarlmadangah Burru Aboriginal Corporation 234–35
Jarman, Paul 123
   'Pemulwuy' 123
Jarrett, Michael 45
Jenkins Dr Misty 270
Johnson, Colleen Tighe 378–79
Johnson, Darlene 143
Johnson, Dr Vivien 76–77, 256
Johnson, Eva 197
Jonas, Bill 321
Jones, Jonathan 12, 97
Joseph Medcalf Funeral Services 198
Joseph, Samantha 67
Junyirri: A Framework for Planning Community Language Projects 54
Juukan Gorge 299, 361–62

Ka Mate haka 190–91
Kakadu Billabong Safari Camp 331, 342
Kakadu National Park 330
Kakadu plum (*Terminalia ferdinandiana*) 214, 217–18, 219, 221, 222
Kardajala Kirridarra ('Sandhill Women') 115
Karul Projects 188
Katter, the Hon. Bob 69
Kaurna Warra Karrpanthi (KWK) 39

Kaurna Warra Pintyanthi (KWP) 39
Keeping Place Project 299
Kelly, Paul 123, 126
   'From Little Things Big Things Grow' 126
   'Special Treatment' 123
Kelly, Rodney 308
Kelly, Thomas ES 188
Keneally, Thomas 140, 162
   The Chant of Jimmie Blacksmith 140, 162
Kenderdine, Sarah 295
Kennett, Rod 297
Kerslake, Emma 370
Ketchell, Lavinia 61
Kimberley Aboriginal Law and Cultural Centre (KALACC) 106
Kirby, Melissa 34
Kirrikin 369–70
Kitching, Eddie Janama 378
Kngwarreye, Emily Kame 86, 358
   Yam Dreaming 86
Kombumerri, Dillon 99
Kong, Dr Kelvin 243
Kooemba Jdarra Indigenous Performing Arts Company 197
'Kookaburra' song 125
Kooriculum 281
Koorie Heritage Trust Melbourne 72
   BLAK Design Matters 99
Kow Swamp fossils 318
Kris, Elma 186, 188
Kruszelnicki, Dr Karl 246
Ku Arts 60, 66, 72
Kulitja, Rene 12, 73, 85–86, 294, 358, 376
   Ancient Tracks and Waterholes 73
   Yananyi Dreaming 85–86
Kungkas Can Cook 218
Kupka, Karel 74
Kurarra, Sonia 377

La Perouse Public School 176
Laguna Bay Publishing 180
Lajamanu Teenage Band 131
Lake, Blanch 67
Lake Condah Possum Skin Cloak 106–107
Langton, Marcia 139, 143, 280, 341, 362
   From Conflict to Cooperation 362
   Welcome to Country: A Travel Guide to Indigenous Australia 280, 341

Laughton, Kenny 163
   Not Quite Men, No Longer Boys 163
Laura Dance Festival 121, 339
Law Council of Australia
   John Koowarta Reconciliation Law Scholarship 6
Lee, Grace Lillian 368–69, 370
Legend Press 81–82, 199
Leibler, Mark 199
Lendlease 27, 97, 358
   Place and Protocols: Indigenous Art, Languages and Cultures 28, 98, 358
Leslie, Katie 198
Letterstick Band 131
Levi, Miseron 129
   'Baba Waiar' 129–30
Lewis, Beatrice 'Nalyirri' 115
Leyah, Azzie 2
libraries *see* GLAM (galleries, libraries, archives and museums) sector
Lingard, Dr Kylie 204
Littlefeather, Sacheen 154
Little, Jimmy 114
   'Royal Telephone' 114
Living Archive of Aboriginal Languages 51
Lloyd, Jessie 129, 172
Loban, Dr Heron 204
Local Context Traditional Knowledge (TK) labelling
LORE 370
LORE Australia 220
Lovett, Ray 244, 270
Lowe, Dr Kevin 283–84
Lowitja Institute 244
   Researching Indigenous Health: A Practical Guide for Researchers 269
Lucashenko, Melissa 163, 171
Ludwig, Steven 378
Luhrmann, Baz 143
   Australia 143
Lui, Nakkiah 199
   Black is the New White 199

Mabo Day 351
Mabo decision 3–5, 6, 17, 230
Mabo, Eddie Koiki 6, 59, 245
Madjedbebe research project 262–63
Magabala Books 177–78
   My Own Sweet Time 164

Index

Maiam nayri Wingara Indigenous Data Sovereignty Collective 270, 298
Mailman, Deborah 146
Malangi, Dr David 62
　appropriation of artwork 74–75
　Mortuary Feast of Gurrmirringu, the Great Ancestral Hunter 75
Manfredi, Isabella 44, 124
Mangkaja Arts 60, 358, 377–78
Mangkaja x Gorman fashion collection 377–78
Maningrida Arts & Culture centre 59–60
Manton, Bev 189–90
Manton, Karen 47, 314
Marant, Isabel 374
Mardiroosian, Zaven 199
Marika, Banduk 77, 78
Marika, Wandjuk 58, 64–65, 77, 139
　Wandjuk Marika: Life Story 65
Marliya 122
Marrie, Henrietta 208, 253, 271
Marsden, Alex 323
Marshall, Chels 241
Marshall, Paul 234
Martin, Karen (Booran Mirraboopa) 254
Martumili Artists 70, 72
Maruku Arts 60, 73
Marumali Program 349
Mason, Elizabeth 286, 287–88
Matthews, Professor Chris 282–83
Mauboy, Jessica 115
Mawurndjul, John 59–60, 94–95
　Mardayin at Milmilngkan 94
Mayi Harvests 218
Mayi Kuwayu 243–44
Maynard, John 171
May, Ngarralja Tommy 377, 378
Mayor, Modesta (Maudie) 2
Maza, Rachael 195–96
McCallum, Kerry 169
McKellar, Hazel 169
　Woman From No Where 169
McKenzie-Kirkbright, Levi 296
McLean, Bruce Johnson 314
McMahon, Michael 76
McNaboe, Diane 45
McNeill, Pearlie 178–79
Mead, Aroha 213
Meeanjin Markets 71

Melbourne Museum 106, 107, 323
　Black Day, Sun Rises, Blood Runs 323
　Bunjilaka Aboriginal Cultural Centre 323
　First Peoples 323
Mellor, Doreen 85
Memmott, Paul 98, 265
　Gunyah, Goondie and Wurley: The Aboriginal Architecture of Australia 98
Men at Work 125
Mer Gedkem Le (Torres Strait Islanders) Corporation 230
Michael Frankel and Company 10–11, 139, 347, 348
Mickey of Ulladulla 46
Microsoft 38, 295
Midnight Oil 122–23
　'Beds Are Burning' 122–23
Miiesha 116
　Nyaaringu 116
Milirrpum v Nabalco Pty Ltd land rights case 139
Miller, Lydia 88
Miller, Marilyn 188
Milroy, David 197
Minding Culture: Case studies on Intellectual Property and Traditional Cultural Expressions 349
Minerals Council of Australia 362
Mirams, Dr Ruth 291
Miriuwung Gajerrong case (*Western Australia v Ward*) 4
Miromaa Aboriginal Language and Technology Centre 36
Miromoda (Indigenous Māori Fashion Apparel Board) 369
Mission Songs Project 129, 172
Moa Arts 61
ModroGorje Wellness and Art Centre 105
Moffatt, Tracey 137
　Bedevil 137
Moggridge, Bradley 240
Mokak, Louis Anderson 100
Moody, Gillian 142
Moogahlin Performing Arts 197–98
　Broken Glass 198
Morgan, Marlo 166
　Mutant Message Down Under 166
Morgan, Nyarri 144–45, 293

Morgan, Sally 62, 163
   My Place 62, 163
Morrison, Joe 242
Morrison, Kyle J 34
Morris, Shellie 128–29
   Ngambala Wiji li-Wunungu (Together We Are Strong) 128–29
Morris, Wes 106
Morseu, John 129
Moulton, Anna 178
Mountford, Charles 173, 257
   Nomads of the Australian Desert 173, 257
Mouquet, Éric 117–18
Muir, Mandy 256, 330–32, 333, 342
Mukurtu Wumpurrarni-kari Archive 311–12
   Rediscovering Indigenous Languages project 310–11
Mundine, Karen 325, 355–56
Mungo Lady 317, 318
Mungo Man 318
Murdi Paaki Languages Hub 51
Murray, Gary 315
Musée du quai Branly (MQB) 93, 109
   Australian Indigenous art commission 93–96
Museum of Applied Arts and Sciences (MAAS) 28, 232, 248, 312–13
Museum of Contemporary Art Australia 378
   John Mawurndjul: I am the Old and the New 60
Museums Victoria 315, 320
museums *see* GLAM (galleries, libraries, archives and museums) sector
Musgrave, Dr George 238
Musicological Society of Australia 116
Myuma Group 265

NAIDOC Awards 156
NAIDOC Week 279, 351
NAISDA Dance College 129, 187–88, 190
Nakata, Professor Martin 271
   Disciplining the Savages: Savaging the Disciplines 271
Nannup, Derek 215
Namatjira 197, 199
Namatjira, Albert 81–83, 199
Namatjira Legacy Trust 82–83, 199
Namatjira Project 199
Namatjira, Vincent 83

Namok Snr, Bernard 108, 381
Napurrula, Ningura 94
   Untitled (Wirrulnga) 94
Nash, Jacob 146
National Aboriginal and Torres Strait Islander Indigenous Music Office (NATSIMO) 132–33
National Apology to the Stolen Generations 279
National Association for the Visual Arts (NAVA) 85
National Australia Bank (NAB) 355
National Bushfood Symposium 224
National Centre of Indigenous Excellence (NCIE) 301
National Close the Gap Day 351
National Film and Sound Archive (NFSA) 119, 153–54, 311
National Gallery of Australia (NGA) 313
   Aboriginal and Torres Strait Islander Cultural Rights and Engagement Policy 313–14
   Indigenous exhibitions 313–14
National Indigenous Art Fair 2019 71–72
National Indigenous Arts Advocacy Association (NIAAA) 6, 66–67, 76–77, 87
National Indigenous Arts & Cultural Authority (NIACA) 88–89
National Indigenous Bushfood Statement 224–25
National Indigenous Dance Forum (NIDF) 188
National Indigenous Fashion Awards 369
National Indigenous Science Education Program (NISEP) 247
National Indigenous Television (NITV) 51, 67
National Museum of Australia (NMA) 28, 107, 294, 307, 313, 317, 321–22
   Encounters exhibition 307, 313
   Indigenous engagement 321
   True Tracks principles 313, 321
National Reconciliation Week 279, 351
National Recording Project for Indigenous Performance in Australia (NRPIPA) 116, 118
National Seed Science Forum 204
National Sorry Day 351
National Trust 299

Index

native title 3–4
   rights to cultural knowledge 4
Native Title Act 1993 (Cth) 4
native title claims, evidence 5
Neale, Margo 294, 322
A New Wiradjuri Dictionary 43, 49
Ngakkan Nyaagu 302
Ngarga Warendj – Dancing Wombat 71
Ngurrara Canvas II 5
Nike 372
Ninti One 204
Nona, Laurie 64
NoongarPedia 51
Noonuccal, Oodgeroo (Kath Walker) 163
North Australian Aboriginal Justice Agency 76
North Australian Indigenous Land and Sea Management Alliance (NAILSMA) 242, 297–98
Northern Australia Aboriginal Kakadu Plum Alliance (NAAKPA) 217–18
Northern Territory Aboriginal Sacred Sites Act 1989 (NT) 335
North Queensland Regional Aboriginal Corporate Language Centre (NQRACLC) 41
Nouvel, Jean 93–94
Noyce, Phillip 163
NSW Aboriginal Education Consultative Group (AECG) 141, 281, 283
NSW Aboriginal Land Council 189–90
NSW Department of Public Works and Services
   Merrima Aboriginal Design Unit 99
NSW Education Standards Authority (NESA) 282, 284
   Aboriginal and Torres Strait Islander Principles and Protocols 282
NSW Geographical Names Board 52
Nyadbi, Lena 95
   Dayiwul Lirlmim 95, 109
   Jimbirla and Gemerre (Spearheads and Cicatrice) 95

O'Brien, Kevin 98, 99
Old Ways, New 300
   Indigenous Protocols and Artificial Intelligence working group 297
Olive, Mark ('The Black Olive') 215

On The Street 132
Onus, Bill 71
Onus, Lin 59, 70, 77
   Fruit Bats 70–71
Our Culture: Our Future report 10–12, 88, 347, 387
Oxfam Australia 28

Pacific Asia Indigenous Tourism Conference 332
Page, Alison 98–99
Page-Lochard, Hunter 146
Page, Stephen 186, 188
Papunya Tjupi Arts 59
Papunya Tula art movement 59, 84
Parkin, Stephanie 68, 84
Parks Victoria 335
Pascoe, Bruce 98, 152, 214, 232, 233
   Dark Emu 98, 152, 232
Passi, Falen D 230–31, 233
patents
   Australia, in 103
   bush foods 207–211
   definition 207
   inventions and Indigenous knowledge 101–104
   Māori knowledge and 208
   smokebush (*Conospermum*) 208–209
   spinifex partnership 265
   what can be patented 207
Patents Act 1990 (Cth) 207, 233
Patyegarang 45–46
Pearson, Luke 280–81
Peeters, Aunty Lorraine 349
Pemulwuy 123
Penangke, Shaun Angeles 266
Perkins, Hetti 94, 95
Perkins, Rachel 137, 138, 140, 152
   First Australians 138, 152
   Jasper Jones 138
   Redfern Now 138
Phillips, Shane 360–61
Pilot, Jenny 62
Pitjantjatjara Council 173
Pitt, Andrew 330, 347, 348
Pitt, Turia 364
   Happy 364
PLITZS New York City Fashion Week 378–79

Plum, Thelma 115
Pope, Annalee 36
possum skin cloaks 106–107, 379
Prichard, Katharine Susannah 162
    Coonardoo 162
proppaNOW arts collective 61, 72
Protection of Cultural Objects on Loan Act 2013 (Cth) 315
public domain 388
published works 25
    Indigenous languages and consent 31–32
    Traditional Custodian notices 25–26
PULiiMA Indigenous Languages & Technology Conference 30
Purcell, Leah 136, 146
Puri, Professor Kamal 209
Puutu Kunti Kurrama and Pinikura peoples (PKKP) 361–62

Qantas 85–86, 215, 358
Quandamooka Festival 339
Queensland Indigenous Languages Project 40–41
Queensland Indigenous Languages Advisory Committee 41
Quinn, Professor Ron 234

Rabbit-Proof Fence 136, 163
Racial Discrimination Act 1975 (Cth) 349–50
Ramingining 147–50
Randall, Bob 114–15
    'Brown Skin Baby' 114–15
Rankin, Scott 197
Raven, Dr Margaret 211
Rawlins, Nada Tigila 377
recognition and protection 16, 27, 43
Reconciliation Action Plans (RAPs) 325, 355–56, 362, 365
Reconciliation Australia 325, 355–56, 362
recording and publishing agreements 131–32
repatriation 266–67, 308, 315–17, 327, 388
    digital technology, via 298–300
Reed, Alexander Wyclif 167
    Aboriginal Legends: Animal Tales 167
Rennie, Reko 320
    Remember Me 320

respect 15, 17–18, 33, 38, 42, 51–52, 54, 116, 182, 381–82
    cultural sites and traditional knowledge 333–34
    human rights 349, 351
    Indigenous stories 180–81
Respecting Our Culture (ROC) certification 340
Returning Photos: Australian Aboriginal Photographs from European Collections project 194
Rhys Jones, Griff 151
Ridgeway, Aden 82
Ridgeway, Liam 302
Riebl, Felix 122
Rigney, Professor Lester-Irabinna 258, 282, 283, 284
Riley, Michael 61, 94
    cloud series 94
Riley, Sally 142
Rimmer, Zoe 321
Rings, Frances 188
Rio Tinto 299, 361–62
    Reconciliation Action Plan (RAP) 362
Riptide Churinga 256
Ritchie, Eamon 5
Roach, Archie 115, 126, 200
Roberts, Rhoda 131, 150, 199, 200, 320
Robinson, Professor Daniel 206, 211
rooibos tea case study 222–24
'Rorogwela' 117, 119
Rose, Lionel 114
    I Thank You 114
    Jackson's Track 114
Ross, Steven 247
Roughsey, Dick 58, 163
Royal Commission into Aboriginal Deaths in Custody 363
Rudd, Kevin 88, 279
Rudder, Dr John 43, 49

Sainty, Theresa 30–31
Sakkal, Gabriel 199
Saltmere, Professor Colin 265
Sambono, Joe 232, 233, 246, 285
Samuel, Professor Graeme 235, 240
Samuels, Jeffrey 141
Sanchez, Michel 117–18
Sansbury, Taree 188

Index

SBS: *On Country Kitchen* 215–16
schools *see* education
Schultz, Clinton 221
science and ancient knowledge 230–33
    Barringtonia acutangula potential 234
    biodiscovery laws 235–36
    ethics guidelines 235, 236
    First Peoples Science Centre, vision for 247–48
    Indigenous astronomy 244–45
    Indigenous environmental management 236–37
    Indigenous fire management 237–39
    Indigenous medical doctors 243–44
    Indigenous rangers and ranger programs 242–43, 297–98
    Indigenous science education 246–47
    Indigenous seasonal knowledge 241–42
    Indigenous and Western science, integration of 233–36, 248
    patents 233, 234–35
    protocols 237
    research partnerships 234
    resources 249–50
    water, working with 239–41
    what you can do 249
Scott, Belinda 147
Scott, Kim 162, 163
    Benang: From the Heart 162
Screen Australia 27, 142
    Pathways & Protocols: A Filmmaker's Guide to Working with Indigenous People, Culture and Concepts 141, 142–43, 170
Sculthorpe, Dr Gaye 320
secrecy and privacy 16, 24–25, 43, 173, 344
secret/sacred, meaning 388
Seidel, Peter 199
self-determination 14, 15, 18–20, 42, 44, 54, 89, 100, 224, 255, 264, 272, 292, 302, 326, 332–33, 343
Sen, Ivan 137
    Beneath Clouds 137
Sentance, Nathan 319
Shared Path Aboriginal and Torres Strait Islander Corporation 38
Shearer, Lisa 198
Sheridan, Sarah 370
Sherriff, Kyas 67

Sherry, Christine 155–56
Shiva, Vandana 206
Short Black Opera 172
Simon, James 361
Simon, Paul 118–19
    Graceland 118–19
Simpson, Nardi 172
Skye, Alice 131
Slockee, Clarence 204
Smith, Dick 82
Smith, Fanny 320
Smith, Professor Linda Tuhiwai 254, 258, 281
Smith, William Ramsay 168
    Legendary Tales of the Australian Aborigines 168
Songlines: Tracking the Seven Sisters exhibition 293–95, 322–23
songwriting with Indigenous language 127, 130 *see also* music
    'Yanada' by The Preatures 44–45, 123–24
South Australian Department of Education science and True Tracks principles 286–88
South Australian Museum 120, 316
Spend With Them 364
State Library of NSW 46, 310–11, 312
    Indigenous language collection 46–47
    Living Language: Country, Culture, Community 45–46
    Mukurtu CMS 46–47, 298, 300
State Library of Queensland (SLQ) 40–41
Steadman, Brad 45
Steffensen, Victor 238–39
    Fire Country 238–39
Stevens, Nicole 142
Stevens, William (Willy) 245
Stewart, Sonja 248
Stiff Gins 172
Storm Boy 136
Strehlow, Professor TGH 266
Strehlow Research Centre 266–67
Strehlow Research Centre Act 2005 (NT) 266
Suckling, Adam 378
Sullivan, Gabrielle 68
Sulter, Maureen 45
Supply Nation 353–54
    Certified Suppliers 354

database 220–21, 353
  Registered Supplier logo 354
Survival Day 121, 351
'Sweet Lullaby' controversy 117–18
Sydney Festival 198, 199–200
Sydney Olympics 121, 150–51
Sydney Opera House
  Badu Gili 200
  First Nations programming 131, 200
Sydney Theatre Company 199
Syron, Liza-Mare 198
Szydzik, Sarah 248

Talbot, Alicia 247
Taonui, Dr Rawiri 155
Tarnanthi 319, 339
Tasmanian Aboriginal Centre (TAC) 31–32
  palawa kani Language Program 30
Tasmanian Museum and Art Gallery 320
  kanalaritja: An Unbroken String 321
Taylor, Curtis 145, 295
Taylor, Jennifer 376
Taylor, Pamela 376
Taylor, Russ 10
Te Mana Raraunga Māori Data Sovereignty Network 270–71, 298
Te Rauparaha 190
technology 291–95
  artificial intelligence, ownership rights 296–97
  digital tourism apps 341–42
  drones 292
  Indigenising new technologies 300–302
  Indigenous data sovereignty 297–98
  Indigenous digital futures 302–303
  Keeping Place Project 299
  NAILSMA and I-Tracker 297–98
  repatriation via digital technology 298–300
  resources 304
  Songlines: Tracking the Seven Sisters exhibition 293–95
  virtual reality 292–93
  what you can do 303
television see Indigenous film and television
Telstra and muru-D 360–61
Telstra Foundation 301
Ten Canoes 147–50
Tench, Watkin 165

Tennant, Annie 97–98
Tenodi, Vesna 105
terra nullius 3, 6, 59
Terri Janke and Company 12–13, 35–36, 52, 145, 187, 219, 222, 261, 268, 271–72, 285–86, 287–88, 300, 312, 323–34, 347–49, 356, 363, 378–79
Tew, Liz 321
Thaiday, Uncle Ken 370
theatre see Indigenous performing arts
Therapeutic Goods Act 1989 (Cth) 219
Thiele, Colin
  Storm Boy 162
Thomas, Dr Jared 175
  Calypso Summer 175
  Songs That Sound Like Blood 175
Thomas, Harold 107–108, 380
Thompson, Laura 370
Thomson, Donald 148–49
Thornton, Warwick 136, 137
  The Beach 137
  Samson and Delilah 137
  Sweet Country 137
  We Don't Need a Map 137
Thorpe, Kirsten 47, 310–11
Thorpe, Lidia 379
Timbery, Aunty Esme 96–97
Tjapaltjarri, Billy Stockman 59
Tjapaltjarri, Clifford Possum 59
Tjapaltjarri, Warlimpirrnga 84
T'oa, Juliane 142
Tobin, Jacinta 44, 124
Torres, Pat (Mamanyjun) 218
Torres Strait Island Regional Council (TSIRC) 108, 381
tourism see Indigenous tourism
Tourism Australia 333
Towney, Tysan 146
The Tracker 136
trade marks 106, 212
  'Borobi' the blue koala 359
  Indigenous culture and 212–13, 359–60
  Indigenous fashion 375–76
  Māori 213
Trade Marks Act 1995 (Cth) 212, 359
Trade Marks Act 2002 (NZ) 213
Traditional Custodian notices 25–26, 38
traditional ecological knowledge 389
traditional knowledge notice 339

Index

traditional medicine *see* bush foods and traditional medicine
Traditions Knowledge Digital Library (TKDL) 102
Tranby Indigenous College 47
Treloar, Lucy 181
 Salt Creek 181
Tribal Warrior Aboriginal Corporation 360
Trinca, Mat 323
Tropical Ethnobotany Centre (TIEC) 203–204
Troy, Jakelin 45
True Tracks
 best practice framework 15
 development of 13–14
 principles 15–27, 42–43, 285
 South Australian Department of Education 286–88
Turpin, Gerry 204
Tutt, Corey 231, 232, 233, 246, 280
 The First Scientists 281
2020 Close the Gap report
 We Nurture Our Culture for Out Future and Our Culture Nurtures Us 244
2020 Summit
 National Indigenous Cultural Authority recommendation 88
Tylor, James 313

Uhl, Lisa 377
Uluru-Kata Tjuta National Park 335–36
 photography and Uluru 335–36
Unaipon, David 46, 101, 163, 168
United Nations Declaration on the Rights of Indigenous Peoples (UNDRIP) 12–13, 32, 218, 235, 332, 350, 351, 387
 business guide to 350
 Draft Declaration on the Rights of Indigenous Peoples 10, 13
United Nations Expert Mechanism on the Rights of Indigenous Peoples 20
United Nations Global Compact 350, 361
United Nations International Convention for the Elimination of Racial Discrimination 349
United Nations Permanent Forum on Indigenous Issues (UNPFII) 155
United Nations Working Group on Indigenous Populations 10

University of Queensland 265
University of Sydney
 Aboriginal and Torres Strait Islander Cultural Protocols 315
 Wingara Mura design principles 101
University of Technology Sydney (UTS)
 Jumbunna Institute for Indigenous Education and Research 47, 281, 310, 312
Urban, Keith 121
 'Tumbleweed' 121
Urban Outfitters 371–72

Valenti, Anika 219
Vancouver Indigenous Fashion Week (VIFW) 369
Van Hout, Vicki 188
van Neerven, Ellen 163–64
 Comfort Food 163–64
 Throat 163–64
Van-Oploo, Aunty Beryl 216
Vézina, Brigitte 371, 373
Victorian Aboriginal Corporation for Languages (VACL) 36
Victorian Department of Education and Training 284–85
von Doussa, Justice 80
von Gavel, Stephanie 300
Voyages Indigenous Tourism 335

Waight, John 68
Walkatjara Art 376
Walker, Clinton 171–72
 Buried Country: The Story of Aboriginal Country Music 172
 Deadly Woman Blues: Black Women & Australian Music 171–73
Walker, Kim 188, 190
Wallworth, Lynette 144–46, 292, 293, 295
 Awavena 145–46
 Collisions 144–46, 293, 295
Walt Disney Company
 Frozen 154–55
WAM Clothing 107–108, 380
Wandjinas 150, 389
 Wandjina Watchers in the Whispering Stone sculpture 105–106
Wangka Maya Pilbara Aboriginal Language Centre 36

Warlukurlangu Artists 72
Warmun Art Centre 60
Warndu Mai 214
Warumpi Band 121, 126, 131
Washington State University Centre for Digital Scholarship and Curation 312
Watego, Leesa 279
Watson, Auntie Edna 171
Watson, Dr Lilla 341
Watson, John 234
Watson, Judy 62, 94
    museum piece 94
    two halves with bailer shell 94
Watson, Tommy 94
    Wipu Rockhole 94
Webb, Damien 46
welcome to country ceremony 17, 127, 130, 133, 201, 287, 351, 361
Welcome to Country organisation 343, 344
Wenitong, Dr Mark 243
Western Australian Aboriginal Heritage Act 1972 362
Western Desert art movement 59
White, Sharna 68
Wikimedia 31–32, 51
Wikipedia 31–32
Wilcannia Health Service project 99
Williams, Lyn 122
Williamson, Inawinytji 294, 322
Willmot, Eric
    Pemulwuy: The Rainbow Warrior 123
Winangali Marumali 349
Winch, Tara June 41–43, 162, 176–77
    Wiradjuri language in *The Yield* 41–43, 162, 176–77
Winsor, Sharon 220, 221
Winter Olympic Games 'Aboriginal Dance' 189–90
Wiradjuri Council of Elders 42
Wiradjuri Study Centre 42
Woods, Greg 234
Woolagoodja, Donny 105
Working Party on the Protection of Aboriginal Folklore 66

World Intellectual Property Organization (WIPO) 348–49, 389
    Intergovernmental Committee on Intellectual Property and Genetic Resources, Traditional Knowledge and Folklore (IGC) 103, 168, 374, 387
Wright, Alexis 162
    Carpentaria 162
The Wrong Girl 136
Wunungmurra, Yanggarrny 75–76, 79
    Long-necked Freshwater Tortoises by the Fish Trap at Gaanan 75–76
Wyatt, Ken 379

Yalabin Dining 216
Yangarriny Wunungmurra v Peter Stripes Fabrics (1983) 66, 75–76
Yarning Strong 180, 279
Yei-Nie Institute 271
Yidaki 120
The Yield 41–43
    True Tracks principles in 42–43
Yinarr Maramali 25–26
Yirra Yaakin Theatre Company 197
Yirrmal 115
    'Marryuna' 115
Yorta Yorta Nation Aboriginal Corporation 239
Yothu Yindi 115, 120, 132
    'Treaty' 120, 132
    Tribal Voice 120
Yothu Yindi Foundation 116, 192–93
Yulendj Group 323
Yumbulul, Terry
    Morning Star Pole case 79–80
Yunupingu, Gulumbu 94
    Garak, the Universe 94
Yunupingu, Mandawuy 120

Zemp, Hugo 117–18, 119
Zimmermann 374–75

www.ingramcontent.com/pod-product-compliance
Lightning Source LLC
Chambersburg PA
CBHW051241300426
44114CB00011B/846